ANDRÉ CHÉNIER

Oxford University Press, Amen House, London E.C.4

GLASGOW NEW YORK TORONTO MELBOURNE WELLINGTON
BOMBAY CALCUTTA MADRAS KARACHI LAHORE DACCA
CAPE TOWN SALISBURY NAIROBI IBADAN ACCRA
KUALA LUMPUR HONG KONG

ANDRÉ CHÉNIER
Bronze medallion by David d'Angers
Musée de Carcassonne

ANDRÉ CHÉNIER

HIS LIFE AND WORK

1762–1794

FRANCIS SCARFE

*Director of the British Institute
in Paris*

OXFORD
AT THE CLARENDON PRESS
1965

© *Oxford University Press 1965*

PRINTED IN GREAT BRITAIN

FOR
C. M. GIRDLESTONE
WITH AFFECTION
AND RESPECT

CONTENTS

LIST OF PLATES

ABBREVIATIONS

References (D1, F1, G1, &c.) are to the items so numbered in the Bibliography.

A. C.	André Chénier
M.-J. C.	Marie-Joseph Chénier
BN	Bibliothèque Nationale
BN, NAF	Bibliothèque Nationale, Nouvelles Acquisitions Françaises (manuscripts)
BMC	Bibliothèque Municipale de Carcassonne, Fonds Chénier
BN, FF	Bibliothèque Nationale, Fonds Français
BMN	Bibliothèque Municipale de Nancy
CAIEF	*Cahiers de l'Association Internationale des Études Françaises*
ENF	Éditions de la Nouvelle France
LR	*Langues Romanes*
MF	*Mercure de France*
MLR	*Modern Language Review*
PIFMLL	*Proceedings of the International Federation for Modern Languages and Literatures*
RDM	*Revue des Deux Mondes*
REH	*Revue d'Études Historiques*
RF	*Revue Française*
RG	*Revue de Gascogne*
RHLF	*Revue d'Histoire Littéraire de la France*
RI	*Revue Indépendante*
TM	*Les Temps Modernes*

INTRODUCTION

It is not easy to justify writing a book, and even less so for a modernist to defend his intrusion into the eighteenth century, and for one with no bent for biography to explore the tantalizing life of a poet whose origins, movements, and motives are so wrapped in mystery. To reply that there was, previously, no book in English on André Chénier would be a poor excuse; for that is not the reason why this book was written. Chénier forced himself on my attention seven years ago when I was collecting material for a revaluation or 'panorama' of early nineteenth-century poetry. As his work only appeared in 1819, twenty-five years after his death, I proposed to write four or five pages about him. The five pages became ten, and the ten, fifteen: I was in his clutches as I had been in Valéry's some years before, and for much the same reasons. Other activities were cast aside in order to read what had been written about him; to look at the numerous editions and pore over his manu-scripts. Meanwhile, I edited a selection of his poems in order to make them more accessible to English readers. Both that book and this are the outcome of an obsession which brought many hours of happiness and anxiety, often frustrated by administrative tasks. The desire to enter more deeply into Chénier's work became complicated by an urge to grasp the elements of his biography, and, if possible, to add to them. Here, much disappointment was in store, for at every turn much of the evidence which is normally required in a biography has long since disappeared.

While relying heavily on the excellent studies by Sainte-Beuve (the first French critic to be obsessed by Chénier, whom he wished to estab-lish as the master of the so-called Romantics, or else of a 'school' of his own); Becq de Fouquières (equally obsessed, on reading Chénier he gave up his commission as a colonel in the army and taught himself Latin and Greek in order to edit his works); the painstaking Moland and Abel Lefranc; P. Dimoff (whose two volumes of biography and three volumes of the works are indispensable), as well as G. Walter, J. Fabre, and G. Venzac—anyone who sets out to present Chénier to the English-speaking world is faced with rather different problems from theirs. Dimoff was able to end his study at 1789, believing that what happened to Chénier thereafter was of no importance for literature. G. Walter, as an historian, was able to ignore the work and approach the poet mainly as one of a social and ideological group. The abbé Venzac confined himself to adding some details to what was known of the poet's youth. In his short but useful survey, Professor Fabre was able to take the details for granted and thus avoid controversy.

Little can be taken for granted, however, in an English study of this kind. It was necessary to make a synthesis of existing knowledge and opinion on the subject, together with many minor adjustments in points of detail. The life and work had to be described in a way acceptable to those who are not specialists in eighteenth-century literature, or historians of the French Revolution, while avoiding contradiction, as far as possible, from those who are both. A great deal of reading of memoirs, histories, and pamphlets of the period has borne very little fruit, except to enable me to state with less uncertainty than otherwise what part the poet played in contemporary events. Meanwhile, just as this book was finished and the bicentenary of the poet's birth was being (very quietly) celebrated, Mlle S. Balayé produced the fine exhibition devoted to Chénier at the Bibliothèque Nationale, together with its catalogue. Though I was already familiar with most of the material, this contribution has enabled me to amend certain notes, while also confirming several points of interpretation. It is particularly pleasing to see that further manuscripts or documents have come to light at Angers, Nantes, and Zurich: the day may come, perhaps, when some German library will restore the items which were removed by German troops from the Latouche collection at the Vallée-aux-Loups in 1871.

As little is known of the order in which Chénier wrote his works, the biographer cannot discuss them, as he would like to do, *pari passu* with the account of his life down to 1789. It is only after that date that something like a chronological method may be used. The reader who is looking for a 'straight' biography of Chénier will not find one anywhere; but he might be tempted, if not encouraged, to pass directly • from the first to the third part of this book. He will find that, although the evidence is everywhere meagre enough, everything possible has been done towards reducing the Chénier legend to its true dimensions; yet he emerges a more heroic figure than before. The third part contains a closer account of the last phase than has so far been attempted. On the other hand, the reader who is more concerned with Chénier's poetry and prose will have to share the bafflement of all his editors and critics in the face of many irritating problems. I have not tried to simplify the student's task by imposing an arbitrary order on the *Bucoliques*, as others have done, but have described the manuscripts in the disorder in which the poet left them.

Chénier has never been a 'popular' poet, and never will be; but he deserves to be read more widely than he is. It may be that those scholars who, in the nineteenth-century manner, overstressed his considerable learning, or attached too much importance to the fact that he became the idol of the Parnassians, did not perform for him the kind of service that he now requires. Most of his *Bucoliques* may be enjoyed without delving into his sources or classical allusions, and the days are gone when such diversions were a substitute for criticism or appreciation. Apart from that group, he wrote many other excellent poems which demand no such apparatus of scholarship. But if he has never been 'popular', and if for too many people he is only a legendary figure to whom conventional praise or blame is given, it is interesting to observe that in the period since his death there has been an average of one new edition of his work in every three years. He has had, at least, that modest but devoted following that he deserves. Perhaps other conclusions may be drawn from the renewed attention that was given to him during and immediately after the recent war. It suggests that there may be something else which in his life and work responds to certain needs in the modern mind: whether it be his commitment or his heroism, or perhaps something profoundly French in his work which no critic can manage to define, or perhaps something larger and more permanent, such as the fine example he gives of the variety and nobility of the European tradition.

My thanks are here expressed to the Leverhulme Trust for assistance in the early stages of research, which enabled me to see the family papers at Carcassonne.

F. S.

Paris
December 1962

PART I

THE LIFE, DOWN TO THE REVOLUTION

I

BEGINNINGS

ANDRÉ-MARIE CHÉNIER was born in Le Han Saint-Pierre, Galata, Constantinople, on or about the 30th of October 1762, which is the date of his baptismal certificate. He was to die on the scaffold on 7 Thermidor, An II, that is to say the 25th of July 1794. His martyrdom at the age of thirty-one has naturally resulted in his becoming a symbolic figure, a representative of the romantic ideal of 'the poet as hero' —to use Carlyle's term—which he was one of the first of the modern poets to embody. His legend and the heroic image created of him by his first biographers had, perhaps, more influence on the following generation than his poetry. Published twenty-five years after his death, his poetry has always had a small but firm circle of admirers; but it was the legend more than the poetry that impelled Lamartine, Hugo, and others to believe that a poet must also be a man of action. In any study of Chénier it is necessary to reduce his legend to its proper proportions and try to set his work—which today is rather neglected in France—in its real perspective. Then it may be seen that Chénier achieved heroism almost by accident, and that in the last days of his life it lay not so much in going to the guillotine for his opinions as in overcoming an intense egotism and identifying himself with all those who were oppressed. In a sense this truth is more impressive than the legend; but it remains necessary to show that Chénier's status as a poet depends on the work that he actually created before he died, and not on sentimental speculations as to what he might have become.

There were few signs, in the poet's early life, of that heroic and rebellious spirit which was to reveal itself during the Revolution and result in his premature death. On his father's side he came of an undistinguished bourgeois family, traceable back to Poitou in the sixteenth century, but which was long connected with Carcassonne and Limoux, in Bas-Languedoc. His great-grandfather served in the navy of Louis XIV before marrying a draper's daughter and settling in Carcassonne as an attorney, where he flourished to the extent of being appointed as a 'secrétaire du Roi' or civil servant.[1] He was the first of the family to call himself 'de Chénier', but he died in 1702 before receiving titles of nobility, though he had already devised his coat of arms, which featured an oak.[2] The poet's grandfather, Guillaume, born in 1685, did not follow the Law. After various commercial ventures he found himself in reduced circumstances after taking over a foundry at Montfort, near Limoux. The poet's father, Louis, born in 1722, was educated at Limoux. His whole life offers a model of probity and intelligence, while showing how hard it was in the eighteenth century for a good man to prosper without having an unusual capacity for intrigue. But it was especially to his favourite and most gifted son, André, that he passed his love of literature and scholarship, his gentle melancholy and passionate honesty, and the kind of generous nature that is frustrated by poverty. When he left school, Louis was helped by his uncle, Pierre Vallon, who was not only in the blanket trade but was inspector for the whole Carcassonne region. Vallon initiated the boy into the export trade and sent him out to Constantinople as representative of a prosperous firm. Madame Vallon later left sums of five hundred *livres* to her brother Guillaume, and a thousand to her niece Marie, who later took the poet, André, into her charge.

Louis Chénier set out for Constantinople in August 1742, at the age of twenty. Normally, he ought to have made his fortune quickly, but business was poor owing to a state of war with England. Finding himself in the doldrums, he took the opportunity of completing his education, writing to his uncle, 'Je fais des réflexions, et j'en écris aussi.' Far from having any hopes of a succession from his father, we find him in 1747 trying to find employment for him. In the same year his own employers returned to France, leaving him in Constantinople as a partner and director of the firm. Within two years he was elected as deputy or official representative of the French community in the city. Taken into the confidence of the French ambassador, M. des Alleurs,

[1] Inspector of Mines for Languedoc.
[2] 'Argent au chêne de sinople, fruité de trois glands d'or, planté sur une terrasse de sinople, et accosté de deux rochers à trois coupeaux de sable issants de la terrasse.'

he soon assumed the functions and status of consul and commercial attaché, a title which the Ambassador allowed him before dying in 1755. Unfortunately, des Alleurs had been living beyond his means, and Saint-Priest tells us that he left debts of over 100,000 *écus*, of which the king paid 30 per cent. to his creditors.[1] For a time the gap was filled by a 'Sieur Pérote' until the arrival of Charles Gravier, comte de Vergennes, in May 1755. Recalled in 1768, Vergennes was then appointed to Sweden, after which he had a very powerful influence on affairs in France. He went to the guillotine the day before André Chénier, after being imprisoned with him in Saint-Lazare.

Vergennes, called on to account for his predecessor's extravagance, could hardly approve of his management of affairs, and must have looked with a jaundiced eye on Louis Chénier who had been his counsellor. Louis Chénier was thus left in a somewhat ambiguous position until he returned to France in 1765, shortly after which he was appointed to the thankless office, as it proved to be, of Consul-General and chargé d'affaires in Morocco. In the meantime he had married, in 1754, Elisabeth Lomaca (or Santi-Lhomaca), the daughter of a goldsmith who, for some reason, enjoyed a privileged position at the Turkish court: his children are said to have played with those of the royal family. There has been much controversy, into which we do not propose to enter, about the poet's mother. She claimed to be of Greek origin, and also to be descended from the great royal house of Cyprus, the Lusignans. The Lomacas are said to have come from Chios, an island with such a mixed population that they were not necessarily Greek: some biographers neatly dismiss the problem by describing them as 'Levantine'. It has recently been proved beyond reasonable doubt that on the female side Madame Chénier came of the Petri family, emigrants from the island of Mykonos or Myconi, in the Cyclades.[2] Though she was married as a Catholic, she died in the Greek Orthodox faith. She knew Greek to the extent of singing in that language and giving exhibitions, in her salon, of Greek folk-dances, while she also wrote two long essays or letters on Greek customs which

---

[1] Saint-Priest: *Mémoires de l'Ambassade de France en Turquie*, 1877, pp. 265 et seq. See H1, p. 2, which gives the following appreciation of Louis Chénier by the Ambassador, des Alleurs: 'Élu député de la nation, Louis Chénier se rend indispensable à l'ambassadeur: "Je ne puis assez me louer de la dextérité, de l'intelligence et des attentions du Sr. Chénier. . . . L'expérience que j'ai fait[e] de ses talents et de son discernement, me le fait regarder comme le négociant le plus consommé de cette Échelle. Il est plus au fait qu'aucun que j'aie vu ici des lois et des usages turcs."'

[2] F97; F96, Introduction and pp. 23-58.

were published in 1776. Her manuscripts show that she could hardly write French (in one of them she wrote 'Ma tres chere belle fille, votre beau frere de l'institu es venu peu apres que vous est parti, et a ete fache de navoir eu l'honeur de vous voire') and it is likely that her friend Guys took down her articles from dictation.

Chénier's eminent biographer, P. Dimoff, believed that his mother was the offspring of a second marriage on the part of Antoine Lomaca, but no evidence has been produced for this.[1] Dimoff's thesis has since been contested by G. Walter, J. Fabre, and G. Venzac. It is certainly curious that, while claiming to be Greek in religion, Madame Chénier was married as a Catholic; but she might well have been married in the vestry. This might explain another odd circumstance, which was that there were no representatives of the European community present, and that the bride's father was not there, either. There is a mystery about her origins as well as her marriage; but it does not help to invent a new grandmother for the poet. It is better to accept the mystery as it stands: all that is really known is that Elisabeth claimed to be of Greek descent, and that she was married to Louis Chénier.

Madame Chénier was known to her contemporaries in Paris as 'la belle Grecque' and all her family accepted this without question. André himself had no doubt about it, and was proud of his Greek ancestry, even if he were also part French and part Turk:

> Galata, que mes yeux désiraient dès longtemps . . .
> Car c'est là qu'une Grecque, en son jeune printemps,
> Belle, au lit d'un époux nourrisson de la France,
> Me fit naître Français dans le sein de Byzance.

His conviction that he was of Greek origin was one of the main impulses in his development as a poet. It gave him an emotional attachment to hellenism which had been lacking in the French writers of the neo-classical tradition, and helped him to become one of the finest classical scholars that France had known since the Renaissance. While his contemporaries wrote second-hand, hackneyed imitations of the classics, he was able to believe that he was continuing, though in French, the ancient tradition that was his birthright. He had the same kind of emotional regard for Greece as Yeats had for Ireland. It is hardly exaggerating to say that the impartiality which Chénier claimed to be his, when judging the events of the Revolution, was only possible because he did not feel himself to be solely or entirely French. In

[1] F34, t. i, pp. 23–26. See also BMC 11783/415/314 and 11794/416.

1791 he was actually called on to prove his French citizenship before having the right to vote. While at school he won a prize, but was described in the Sorbonne honours list as 'Chénier constantinopolitanus'. At the height of the Terror he wrote a satirical Ode to Byzantium, in which he compared French barbarity with the state of enlightenment in Turkey:

> Liberté qui nous fuis, tu ne fuis pas Byzance;
> Tu planes sur ses minarets.

Chénier was not even a characteristically French type: Lacretelle was not the only one to notice his 'teint basané' or swarthy complexion which set him apart from other people. Many poets tend to create a kind of myth around themselves in order to feel different from other men; but in Chénier's case the strangeness, the otherness, was already there.

His parents produced an unusual family, as did his aunt, Marie Amic (*née* Lomaca), who became the grandmother of the great statesman Thiers, who was thus the poet's nephew 'à la mode de Bretagne'. The only daughter, Hélène-Christine (b. 1758), married an impoverished aristocrat, already in his sixties, the comte Latour de Saint-Ygest. The snobbish Madame Chénier no doubt imagined this to be a successful marriage; but it did little for her daughter's happiness or for the family fortunes: in 1788 we find André having to pay some of his brother-in-law's debts, which he had left behind in London. The eldest son, Constantin (b. 1757), studied Law and became his father's secretary in Morocco. He held various consular posts during the Revolution and the Empire, and lived to a ripe old age. However, he took to drink, and discredited himself towards the end of his life, when he was found selling some of André's books in order to make ends meet. The second son, Louis-Sauveur (b. 1761), had a chequered career in the army. At the outbreak of the Revolution he incited his troops to revolt. He gradually modified his opinions, to the point of denouncing the Jacobin commissar, Dumont, with the result that he was thrown into prison in 1794. He became a General in the Ordnance, under Napoleon. André Chénier was the third son. The youngest was Marie-Joseph (1764–1811), who was destined to become a famous Jacobin, the official dramatist of the Revolution, and later a founder of the Institut and a member of the French Academy, of which thirty-nine members were his enemies. His play, *Charles IX*, was a mediocre but powerfully topical work which helped to start the Revolution. It is no exaggeration to say that his struggle against the censorship, at the outset of his career, was for a time a symbol of liberty against oppression. Marie-Joseph had neither wisdom nor constancy, for under the Directory he was responsible for tightening the censorship and banishing his enemies to islands from which there was no return. The portrait of Marie-Joseph, by Louis David, which hangs in one of the halls in Versailles, shows a handsome but foolish young man with his eyes cast up to the heavens, and his mouth wide open, as if waiting, like some giant fish, to catch the bait of inspiration. It only came to him once, when in 1794 he wrote *Le Chant du Départ*, which was set to music by Méhul. But, whatever his faults, Marie-Joseph had in 1794 the courage to call for 'Des lois, et non du sang', and more than once he saved people who were not his friends.

André Chénier was only in his third year when his family moved from Constantinople to Paris, so that it is unlikely that he had any memory of the country of his birth. His mother went to live in Paris with her youngest and favourite son, Marie-Joseph, while the father set off alone on his precarious mission to Morocco, where he was to spend seventeen years in solitude, underpaid by his government and unsupported by his wife. As he had no private fortune and could not offer the Sultan the extravagant gifts that were expected of a man of his status, he was thrown on his own resources. He spent his time in laying the foundation of his sons' careers, and on patient historical research which resulted in an important but neglected book, his *Recherches historiques sur les Maures* which he published in 1787.

It is generally assumed that André Chénier was at once given into the care of his godfather, André Béraud, a prosperous draper in Carcassonne. He is said to have married Louis's sister, Marie, and yet Gabriel de Chénier, the poet's nephew, asserted that Marie remained a spinster.[1] It seems a little surprising that André should have been practically abandoned by his mother at the age of three: indeed the same nephew, Gabriel, also stated that it was at the age of eight that the poet went to Carcassonne.[2] However, to tell the story as it is usually told, André stayed with his uncle and aunt in the Traverse Malcousinat (4, and now 8, rue Pinel), a high, dark, and forbidding house in a narrow street, but obviously the property of a thriving bourgeois. This was in the old city, not yet restored by Viollet-Le-Duc

[1] D7, t. i, p. vi, 'Marie de Chénier, *morte célibataire* ...'.

[2] Ibid., p. 5: 'Venu à Paris avec toute sa famille, il reçut d'abord, comme ses frères, les premiers éléments d'instruction dans la maison paternelle. *Vers huit ans*, il alla passer quelques mois dans le bas Languedoc, auprès d'une sœur de son père.' Gabriel de Chénier's reputation for unreliability does not mean that he was wrong on all occasions.

but still embraced by its massive walls, with the great turrets falling into decay yet still inhabited, and with the heavy drawbridge and colossal gate that was closed every night at dusk, turning the town into a ghostly fortress, glinting white in the moonlight. Though far from his parents, the boy seems to have been happy enough. He spent part of his time in the picturesque old city, and part in the little country town of Limoux, not far away, where his father had gone to school before him. He was also familiar with the equally picturesque 'low town' outside the walls, where he must often have seen the grand Gothic house of his grand-uncle, Louis Vallon, and gone to mass in the old church of Saint-Vincent. In this church one of the great bells was inscribed 'Dédiée à M. André Béraud at à dame Marie Chénier, sous l'invocation de Saint-André'. This bell was dedicated in November 1773, at a ceremony at which the boy was probably present: he would then be eleven years of age. This bell explains some interesting things about the poet. Its making underlies the magnificent metaphor in his *Épître sur ses Ouvrages* in which he compared his manner of composing with the craft of a bell-founder:

> . . . Vous avez vu sous la main d'un fondeur
> Ensemble se former, diverses en grandeur,
> Trente cloches d'airain, rivales du tonnerre?
> Il achève leur moule enseveli sous terre;
> Puis, par un long canal en rameaux divisé,
> Y fait couler les flots de l'airain embrasé;
> Si bien qu'au même instant, cloches, petite et grande,
> Sont prêtes, et chacune attend et ne demande
> Qu'à sonner quelque mort, et du haut d'une tour
> Réveiller la paroisse à la pointe du jour.

> Moi, je suis ce fondeur: de mes écrits en foule
> Je prépare longtemps et la forme et le moule,
> Puis sur tous à la fois, je fais couler l'airain:
> Rien n'est fait aujourd'hui; tout sera fait demain.

Such a description could hardly be written by a person who had not been impressed by seeing that complex operation. In interpreting it, we have to recall that he had probably seen the bell made at Limoux, and that his own grandfather had tried his fortune as a master founder. The second point is that the bell was dedicated to his uncle and aunt under the patronage of Saint Andrew. It was perhaps in honour of his uncle that, a few years later, Chénier affected the title 'Chénier de Saint-André' or 'chevalier de Saint-André'. One of the poet's first actions on reaching London in 1787 was to spend his salary on a fine watch, which he sent to his uncle and which is now to be seen in the library at Carcassonne.

If it is true that Chénier spent so much of his childhood there, then he would have gone to school in the old walled city, at first, before being sent down to the College in the lower town, which his brother Constantin is known to have attended. This school had recently passed out of the hands of the Jesuits into those of the Doctrinaires, who had a very liberal attitude towards education. At the age of nine he signed his name in the parish register as 'Mr. André Chénier', being a witness when his aunt became the godmother of another child. Thus we can be sure that he was present in the south at the age of nine, at least.

Apart from mentioning the Aude region several times in his poems, Chénier noted down two of his early memories there, both of which have some religious significance. The first of these was set in a satirical context in which he was mocking self-important politicians, but it contains a charming evocation of his childhood:

Quand j'étais bien enfant, je faisais de belles chapelles . . . beaucoup de bougies . . . Je furetais partout pour m'emparer de quelques petits morceaux de satin, rouges, bleus, pour en faire une belle chasuble galonnée de papier doré. Je chantais la messe, je prêchais, on m'écoutait, on se signait; et quand, le soir, au salut, à la lueur de cent petites bougies, après bien des génuflexions et des antiennes, j'élevais un petit Saint-Sacrement de plomb, mon vieux père nourricier ôtait son chapeau, et ma tante Juliette, et ses amis se mettaient à genoux.

The 'aunt Juliette' and 'foster-father' must have been a peasant family to which he was sent for a time, possibly at Limoux. His second reminiscence describes a pilgrimage which they all made from Limoux to a chapel on a hill-top, known as Notre-Dame de Marceille. This pilgrimage was made every year on the 8th of September:

En me rappelant les beaux pays, les eaux, les fontaines, les sources de toute espèce que j'ai vus dans l'âge où je ne savais guère voir, il m'est revenu un souvenir de mon enfance que je ne veux pas perdre. Je ne pouvais guère avoir que huit ans, ainsi il y a quinze ans (comme je suis devenu vieux!) qu'un jour de fête on me mena monter une montagne. Il y avait beaucoup de peuple en dévotion. Dans la montagne, à côté du chemin à droite, il y avait une fontaine dans une espèce de voûte creusée dans le roc; l'eau en était superbe et fraîche, et il y avait sous la petite voûte une ou deux madones. Autant que je puis croire, c'était près d'une petite ville nommée Limoux, au bas-Languedoc. Après avoir marché longtemps, nous arrivâmes à une église bien fraîche, et dans laquelle je me souviens bien qu'il y avait un grand puits. Je ne m'informerai à personne de ce lieu-là, car j'aurai un grand plaisir à le retrouver lorsque mes voyages me ramèneront dans ce pays. Si jamais j'ai, dans un pays qui me plaise, un asile à ma fantaisie, je veux y arranger, s'il est possible, une fontaine de la même manière, avec une statue aux nymphes, et imiter ces inscriptions antiques: *D[icatum] fontibus sacris* etc.

It is amusing to see that Chénier already saw himself as an old man when he was only twenty-three. The passage not only shows that he must have been only eight years old, or less, when he went to Limoux, but the reference to his travels helps to situate his journey to Italy in 1785 or later. Both of these passages show much more than his sharp observation, delicate sensibility, and liveliness of style. The tone in which they are written shows an unspoilt nature, still full of respect for the simple things of life.

Chénier was eleven years old when he finally came to Paris. His father had leave from Morocco in 1773, and no doubt took the boy with him across France, in his coach. His mother was comfortably installed with the other children at 8 rue Couture Sainte-Catherine (now the rue Sévigné), where the family remained until the outbreak of the Revolution. That quarter, the Marais, was then one of the most fashionable parts of Paris.

Without leading the life of a 'mondaine', Madame de Chénier, as she called herself, had cleverly created her own special place in society. She held open house for artists and men of letters and, more particularly, classical scholars. Even if it is easy to regard her as a scatter-brained person (for her son André once referred to her as 'no more than a child'), there can be no doubt about her social achievement, even if she took it further than her circumstances warranted. She had her carriage, two lackeys in uniform, and four serving-women whom she is said to have brought with her from Constantinople.

A large portrait of the whole family, painted by the rather mediocre artist Cazes (fils) in 1774, shows them all standing in a row near the Seine, near what is now the Samaritaine, with the Pont-Neuf and the Institut behind them. They are dressed in fine style, in accordance with Louis de Chénier's rank, but not his purse. Madame strikes a dramatic pose with one arm outstretched and the other gracefully held aloft, as though about to execute one of her Greek dances. Someone must have made a joke against her, for she protested against certain Parisians who had 'répandu du ridicule sur les personnes qui,

passé trente ans, oseraient encore danser'. Her pose is both supple and
dignified. She is clad in long, loose robes, not unlike those which were
to be affected by Isadora Duncan, but with what looks rather like
a turban on her head. Being a smallish woman, she is set well in the
foreground so that she looks taller than everyone else. The rest of the
family, in a dismal row, looking as though they had stood thus for
weeks while being painted, are spread out in no particular pattern, as
though they were there almost by accident. The excellent Consul-
General, looking startled by all this fuss and expense, stands tall and
dignified, somewhat melancholy, wearing his official uniform and
sword, with his hand thrust into his waistcoat, anticipating Napoleon.
André, aged about twelve, stands close behind his mother, looking
the most serene of them all, as though enjoying the occasion; but in
general all the male bodies look wooden. The servants are arranged in
appropriate places, the womenfolk at one side and the two lackeys at
the other, their expressions hesitating between boredom and amusement. Behind them stands the family carriage and, on the bridge, the
statue of Henri IV on his horse. This family group was commissioned
as a gift for André Béraud, the poet's uncle and godfather, who duly
hung it on his wall in Carcassonne.

Madame Chénier's salon escapes ridicule because it certainly served
a useful social purpose, in keeping with the best traditions of the
century. It was also appropriate to her husband's status, his cultured
tastes, and the needs of her intelligent sons. Among her regular guests
were the painter, Cazes, son of the late director of the Académie
royale, whom Madame Chénier perhaps commissioned to paint some
panels of scenes from the *Iliad*, though it is also said that she painted
them herself. It has often been stated that André Chénier took drawing-
lessons from him, though there is no evidence for this. Then there was
the scholar Pierre-Augustin Guys, father of the artist Constantin Guys,
whom the Chéniers had first met in Constantinople. In 1771 he published a *Voyage littéraire en Grèce*, and he was now preparing a second
edition which appeared in 1776. This new edition contained two letters
on Greece by Madame Chénier herself: a *Lettre sur les danses grecques*
and a *Lettre sur les enterrements*. Another firm friend was the famous
poet Écouchard Le Brun—so famous that he was known as Pindare
Le Brun: it was partly under his guidance that André Chénier served
his apprenticeship to poetry. The circle was completed by such
scholars as Palissot; perhaps the learned Brunck, famous for his edition
of the Greek Anthology, and certainly Villoison. Villoison brought

to the salon such distinguished guests as Oberlin from Strasbourg, and the Duke of Saxe-Weimar. However, we cannot believe, as some of Chénier's biographers appear to do, that every scholar in Europe passed through the salon in the rue Couture Sainte-Catherine.[1]

Madame Chénier seems to have been well qualified for the part she was playing. She was listed among the 'persons of condition', in the *Almanach de Paris*, and though not over-intelligent she was lively and entertaining. At times she would deck herself in long flowing robes and shawls, and sing to her own accompaniment on the guitar, or perform her Greek dances with the help of a tambourine, or show her paintings of Theseus, Ariadne and the Minotaur. She certainly knew something about folk-lore and loved the arts. Though she appears to have failed in affection towards some of her family—perhaps all the family except the spoilt Marie-Joseph—she did much to fire her son André's imagination, for some of his poems are based on her songs and dances. G. Venzac has recently shown that the story of Ariadne is portrayed in 'la Candiote', one of Madame Chénier's favourite dances, while the theme of his well-known poem *Le Jeune Malade* comes from a popular folk-song from the Cyclades, which she used to sing.[2]

It was the same Cazes who painted the fine portrait of André Chénier in 1773, at about the age of eleven. It shows the boy in a beautiful costume of yellow velvet embroidered with little white flowers. He wears a black ribbon in his hair, lace cuffs, and a lace jabot. The curved hand, rising towards the jabot, is sensitive though not well drawn. The face is animated, full of humour, with a broad domed brow, wide intelligent blue eyes, and long sensitive lips.

This portrait must, then, have been painted not long after André Chénier left Carcassonne, when he was still full of rustic health and impressed by the elegant surroundings in which he found himself. We can imagine him listening to Le Brun reciting his Odes, or watching Cazes at work on his canvases, or standing in awe beside his mother when she received the great Duke of Saxe-Weimar. It must have been an event for them all, later, when Villoison read aloud the letter which he had written for the Duke, and which accompanied a presentation copy of the *Voyage en Grèce*:

Madame Chénier, cette si aimable Grecque, chez laquelle j'ai eu l'honneur de vous accompagner est son amie [i.e. the friend of Guys], et lui a adressé pour la seconde édition de cet ouvrage, une lettre fort curieuse et supérieurement écrite sur les danses grecques, qu'elle a longtemps dansées elle-même

[1] F34, t. i, pp. 75–80.   [2] F96, pp. 32–35.

et que vous avez pu voir chez elle peintes de sa main. J'ai cru que cette lettre, qui ne sera publique de plus un an, pourrait vous intéresser; et, en conséquence, j'ai pris la liberté de vous l'envoyer ci-jointe. Vous y retrouverez les regrets d'Ariane abandonnée par Thésée, qu'elle a eu l'honneur de chanter en votre présence, avec ce ton triste que Son Altesse, Monseigneur votre frère, a si bien défini, lorsqu'il dit qu'elle faisait passer dans l'âme l'impression délicieuse d'une douce mélancolie et d'un sentiment profond.[1]

Louis de Chénier had already sent his two eldest sons, in spite of the expense, to the famous Collège de Navarre, and in 1774 it was André's turn to become a pupil there, where he remained for at least five years. Though Gabriel de Chénier maintained that when André was twelve years of age his father tried to have him admitted to the École royale de Marine, there is no evidence for this, while it is a fact that he was enrolled at the Collège de Navarre.[2] This college was founded in 1304 by Jeanne de Navarre, and has been described as 'le berceau de la noblesse française' and 'l'honneur de l'Université de Paris'. In 1805 Napoleon converted it into the École Polytechnique. Among its most outstanding pupils had been Henri IV, Bossuet, and, more recently, the philosopher Condorcet for whom Chénier had so much admiration. At that time it was the most advanced and most select school in Paris, comparable with Eton. The number of pupils was strictly limited and there were only about 150 when Chénier was there. Far from being orthodox in its teaching, as much stress was laid on mathematics, modern history, and the natural sciences, as on the classics.

Although one of his schoolfellows, sixty years later, described Chénier as being, at school, 'd'un caractère froid et sérieux',[3] and his younger brother Marie-Joseph as, on the contrary, 'très vif, taquin et espiègle', there is no doubt that André Chénier had the gift of making and keeping friends, just as Marie-Joseph had the gift of making enemies. At Navarre he formed friendships which never wavered, in spite of long separations and those political differences which so often turned friends into foes: indeed it has to be admitted that his affections

---

[1] F34, t. i, p. 77.

[2] A letter from Louis Chénier to the Ministre de la Marine is in BMC 11801. Venzac (F96) relates it to his son Louis-Sauveur.

[3] See BMC 11798, Cailhé de Geine, letter to Constantin Chénier in 1836: 'J'étais plus particulièrement lié avec le plus jeune des Messrs Chénier, que nous appelions *Marocain*. L'aîné en 1778 venait de finir sa Rhétorique et remporta le prix d'honneur à l'université. Le puîné [André] était en seconde ou en troisième et le cadet [Marie-Joseph] en cinquième ou sixième. Les deux aînés étaient d'un caractère froid et sérieux, tandis que le cadet était très vif, taquin, et espiègle, ce qui souvent établissait entre lui et moi un échange de coups de poings.'

led him further to the Right in politics than he would naturally have gone of his own accord. First of these was Abel de Malartic de Fondat (1760–1804), who shortly before the Revolution retired to his estates in the south of France to become president of the Conseil de Roussillon.[1] Chénier dedicated two of his elegies to him, one of which contains memories of their sitting together on the school benches and being caned:

> Abel, mon jeune Abel, et Trudaine et son frère,
> Ces vieilles amitiés de l'enfance première,
> Quand tous quatre, muets, sous un maître inhumain,
> Jadis au châtiment nous présentions la main.

The other two friends mentioned here are Louis Trudaine de Montigny (b. 1764) and Charles-Michel Trudaine de la Sablière (b. 1766). The Trudaines were an old and wealthy family, descended from one of Louis XIV's greatest ministers. Their father, who was Intendant des Finances, was the only member of the government to encourage Louis de Chénier in his uphill struggle in Morocco, and this, together with the fact that the Trudaines had long lived in the rue Couture Sainte-Catherine, might explain the beginning of the close relationship between the boys. The two Trudaines died on the scaffold the day after Chénier.

The other close friends were the brothers Louis and François de Pange, sons of the millionaire, the marquis de Pange, who was one of the most important landowners in France. It was François de Pange who was at school at Navarre with Chénier, though it was apparently the elder brother Louis (b. 1763) who for a long time gave the poet his financial support.[2] François de Pange was perhaps Chénier's closest friend. He had an encyclopaedic mind, and though his writings (later collected by Becq de Fouquières) are mainly political pamphlets, he was an ardent Greek scholar and also left behind him an important documentation for his unfinished history of the province of Champagne.

These young men were typical of all that was best in the French aristocracy of that time. We have heard quite enough of the evils of the aristocracy of the *ancien régime*, but if a proper history of their achievement in the eighteenth century were written, such names as

---

[1] It is Malartic and not the young Abel de Pange who is referred to in A. C.'s elegies and epistles. That he remained in contact with Paris is shown by his name being given as a member of the Club de Valois in 1789.

[2] For the de Pange family see F6 and F76.

Trudaine and de Pange would hold an honourable place. In spite of
their fortunes and privileges, which might well have encouraged them
to idleness, they were cultured and scholarly. They thought and wrote
seriously, they were dedicated to the public service, they held their
minds open to the new ideas of the *Encyclopédie*; they were in sympathy with the great wave of liberalism which passed through Europe
from England and America. Like Chénier, they were bound to come
to the forefront of whatever society they lived in, because of their
intelligence and probity. They were bound to welcome a Revolution
that swept away their own privileges, because they were completely
honest and disinterested. Their genuine respect for literature led them
to cherish and respect André Chénier in spite of his poverty and his
inferior station, and to encourage him in everything he did, because
they believed in his genius.

Little is known about Chénier's schooldays at the Collège de
Navarre. He probably spent his holidays at the Château de Montigny
with the Trudaines in 1775, when he was about fourteen: it is unlikely
that this could be in the following year, as the Trudaines then went to
Gex. Some idea of the civilized atmosphere at Montigny may be gained
from a letter from Suard to Mlle de Lespinasse which may be consulted in the Bibliothèque Nationale:

> Je ne vous peindrai donc pas ce beau grand château, ni ces grands bois dont
> il est entouré, ni cet air de solitude imposante qui me plaît assez quoi qu'on
> m'accuse d'être fou amoureux de dissipation et de variété. Je trouve ici
> beaucoup de liberté, de commodité, une conversation raisonnable, un peu
> de musique.[1]

Chénier later recorded a charming anecdote about what happened
when he was there, which shows that he was at once precocious and
rather naïve. He had been reading Montesquieu's *Lettres Persanes* and
was struck by a remark on the subject of friendship. Full of his enthusiasm for this discovery, he passed it on to a priest who must have
been rather overcome by this effusion:

> Je me souviens qu'étant à Montigny à l'âge de quatorze ou de quinze ans,
> la veille de notre départ, je trouvai sous ma main les *Lettres Persanes*. Je me
> mis à les lire. A la fin de la première lettre, arrivant à cette phrase: 'Sois sûr
> qu'en quelque lieu du monde où je sois, tu as un ami fidèle', j'en fus ému
> et frappé fortement, et j'aurais donné tout au monde pour avoir un ami Rus-
> tan dont il fallût me séparer, afin de la lui répéter. Il y avait là un bon et

[1] BN, NAF 23647.42.

honnête curé qui me voulait beaucoup de bien, mais qui sûrement n'avait jamais trouvé sous la main les *Lettres Persanes*; au moment où je montais en voiture, il arrive pour m'embrasser et me souhaiter bon voyage. Je me retourne, je l'embrasse, et, lui serrant la main, je lui récite d'un ton sublime et pathétique, la phrase de Montesquieu, et je pars.[1]

This passage has, however, another significance than the devotion to the idea of friendship which permeates all his work. The writers and thinkers of Chénier's generation are often divided into those who followed Montesquieu and those who followed Rousseau. Chénier was influenced by both of them. His early enthusiasm for the author of *L'Esprit des Lois* was the basis for his future political stand, while his ambitious *Essai sur la Décadence des Lettres et des Arts* was an obvious development of Montesquieu's *Grandeur et Décadence des Romains*. Though Chénier ended by rejecting Rousseau's theory of equality, the kind of sensibility expressed in the *Élégies* and *Odes* has much in common with Rousseau, even if it sprang from his own experience rather than from literary sources. Chénier's formation as a revolutionary (before 1791) owed very much to Rousseau, while his constitutional position (1791–2) owed more to Montesquieu.

As the Trudaines' parents died in 1776 and 1777 (the death of the elder Trudaine being, no doubt, a blow to Louis de Chénier's ambitions) it is not likely that Chénier visited Montigny or any of their other estates for a while. It was now that he was invited to the estates at Mareuil and Songy by François de Pange. These visits were only the prelude to many more of the same kind over the next ten years. They left an indelible impression on the poet, who wrote nostalgically in his fine elegy, 'O jours de mon printemps . . .':

> Et là nous souvenir, au milieu de nos fêtes,
> Combien chez eux longtemps, dans leurs belles retraites,
> Soit sur ces bords heureux, opulents avec choix
> Où Montigny s'enfonce en ses antiques bois,
> Soit où la Marne lente, en un long cercle d'îles,
> Ombrage de bosquets l'herbe et les prés fertiles,
> J'ai su, pauvre et content, savourer à longs traits
> Les Muses, les plaisirs, et l'étude et la paix.

So far as his studies were concerned, he was a satisfactory pupil. In the *concours général* of 1778 he won two prizes. This open competition was created in 1740, and the colleges all over France entered their best

---

[1] D22, p. 685.

pupils for it. Unfortunately the records of the Collège de Navarre were destroyed during the Revolution. By now Chénier had finished his 'rhetoric' or classical studies. He presented himself for examination in the same year as Camille Desmoulins and Baudelaire's father. He came first in the competition for what was called 'amplification française', that is to say an impromptu speech on a set theme. The award reads:

Primum orationis gallice scriptae proemium, inter recentiores meritus et consecutus est Andraeas Maria de Chénier, constantinopolitanus, e Regia Navarra.

His other success was an *accessit* or distinction in translation from Latin into French. The formal prize-giving was held in the Sorbonne on 5 August 1788.[1]

Chénier's biographers assert, without justification, that he probably left Navarre in 1778, though the family tradition had it that he remained there until 1781.[2] There seems to be no valid reason for doubting the family tradition in this case. Chénier had now begun writing verse. The earliest specimens that have survived are dated October and December 1778. One of these is an adaptation from Homer, and the other an imitation of Virgil's eighth Eclogue, and though they show some originality it is most likely that they were school exercises. It is possible that he stayed on at Navarre while being exempt from the full time-table and discipline that was imposed on the other boys: in other words, after passing the 'concours général' he would have the status of a Scholar.

The first of these compositions is as follows:

XANTHUS

Le beau Xanthus succombe, et rend avec effort
Son âme en flots de sang sur la terre épandue.
Du mont Ida jadis au Xanthe descendue,
Sa mère mit au jour ce tendre nourrisson;
Le Xanthe le vit naître, et lui donna son nom.
Il expire loin d'elle, et sa reconnaissance
Ne paiera pas les soins que coûta son enfance;
Faible, à peine allumé, le flambeau de ses jours
S'éteint: dompté d'Ajax, le guerrier sans secours
Tombe, un sommeil de fer accable sa paupière,
Et son corps palpitant roule sur la poussière.

This short passage already shows two characteristics of the poet's *Bucoliques*. The first is a tendency to modify his classical sources as he

---

[1] F96, pp. 254–9.   [2] D7, t. i, pp. xii–xiii.

PLATE I

a. André Chénier, aged 11, by Cazes (*fils*)
Musée de Carcassonne

b. André Chénier's mother in 'Greek' costume, by Cazes (*fils*)
Musée de Carcassonne

c. Mme Françoise (Fanny) Lecouteux de la Noraye. After the portrait by Louis David

wished. Here, the *Simoïsis* of Homer is transposed into Xanthus, and *Simoïs* into Xanthe. Further, Chénier's passage, which concerns Ajax, has little or nothing to do with the Homeric source. We see, then, already at the age of sixteen his tendency to write not translations but rather variations on a given theme. The second characteristic is his startlingly bold use of enjambment, in three cases here, of which the most striking are:

> ... le flambeau de ses jours
> S'éteint ...

and

> ... le guerrier sans secours
> Tombe ...

The result is that not only three, but six of the lines out of eleven are dislocated. This brutal use of enjambment is very effective here: in the first instance it gives what we can only call 'a dying fall', while the second conveys a sensation of violence. Chénier was later to make a brilliant use of this device, which is so much condemned in France, in the passage in *L'Aveugle* in which he described the battle of the Lapiths and Centaurs. In many respects Chénier's versification remained conventional, but in his often excessive use of enjambment we see, not so much an affront to the rules laid down by Malherbe and Boileau, as a personal obsession.

We do not propose, at this stage, to analyse the second poem which he wrote at sixteen (*Médée*) beyond saying that at moments he captures, as he was so frequently to do in the *Bucoliques*, the tragic tone and majestic movement of Racine, in such lines as

> Tu raillais ma pâleur et ma langue glacée,
> Mes cheveux négligés et ma barbe hérissée;
> Et moi, faible, crédule, impuissant de mes feux,
> Tu m'étais chère encore et possédais mes vœux.

And here, in addition, we see a further general characteristic of his *Bucoliques*, which is his preference for writing in the first person. He almost always allows his characters to speak for themselves, with the result that his book is a collection of dramatic lyrics or dramatic monologues which is unique in the French language. Chénier added a little note to *Médée*: 'J'avais 16 ans. Il y a quelques bons vers.' He was quite right in saying so: few schoolboys have ever entered into the spirit of the classics, and at the same time contributed something of their own, as brilliantly as he did.

Meanwhile, it is also possible that Chénier had already experienced the pangs of disappointed love, and this explains much of the amorous frustration of his later years. It is said that, while staying at the Château de Songy (sometimes spelt Songis) with François de Pange, he had fallen in love with his friend's cousin, Anne-Marie-Louise de Domangeville. This girl was a year younger than himself, but was already engaged to a man of fortune, de Pange's other cousin, Antoine Mégret de Sérilly. After Sérilly's death on the scaffold in 1794 she married François de Pange, who by then was in failing health and died in the following year. There could be no future for Chénier's affections in the heart of a young heiress destined for such a marriage, but they remained good friends. This adolescent experience perhaps explains the repeated vows of solitude and 'sagesse' which he expressed in his elegies. It helps to explain, also, why he never married. It was not because he was incapable of love, or because he had experienced an early disappointment, but he must have realized, at an impressionable age, that in the rich and noble circles in which he was moving he was really a *déclassé*. Unable to marry into his own social sphere, he had none the less an ardent and affectionate nature. The result was that he drifted into the libertine way of life that was so common at the end of the eighteenth century, and which a corrupt society hardly thought of condemning. At times his sensitive nature rebelled against this, and for that reason there is much anguish and shame expressed in his elegiac poems; though to seek his sensibility in all its refinement we must turn to the laments of the *Bucoliques*, in which love and sensuality are conveyed in all their purity.

In the eighteenth century poets commonly pretended to be more than usually precocious. In the Age of Reason poetry was regarded as a natural but irrational gift. A man was either a poet in his childhood or not at all: in Pope's words, 'He lisped in Numbers, for the Numbers came'. The truth of the matter is that although musicians and mathematicians often give early signs of their bent, this is rarely the case with poets, who in few cases discover their vocation before adolescence.

André Chénier was explicit and honest about himself in this matter, and made it plain that it was towards the age of sixteen that he found he was a poet. In his epistle to de Brazais he wrote:

> Dans le bel art des vers je n'ai point eu de maître:
> Il n'en est point, ami. Les poètes vantés
> Sans cesse avec transport lus, relus, médités,

Les dieux, l'homme, le ciel, la nature sacrée
Sans cesse étudiée, admirée, adorée,
Voilà nos maîtres saints, nos guides éclatants.

A peine avais-je vu luire seize printemps,
Aimant déjà la paix d'un studieux asile,
Ne connaissant personne, inconnu, seul, tranquille,
Ma voix humble à l'écart essayait des concerts;
Ma jeune lyre osait balbutier des vers.

Though Le Brun is generally considered to be Chénier's first 'master'
it is clear that Chénier was insisting that he had begun writing spontaneously, though inspired by the classics, at the age of sixteen. If he
owed anything to Le Brun, that came later. He stressed his love of
nature, solitude, books, above society. The truth of this may be measured by reading a commentary which he began writing on Malherbe
when he was only eighteen or nineteen.

In a note dated 1781 and written in the book, Chénier relates how he
lent his handsome copy of Malherbe to someone who returned it all
blotted with ink:

J'ai prêté il y a quelques mois, ce livre à un homme qui l'avait vu sur ma
table et me l'avait demandé instamment. Il vient de me le rendre en me
faisant mille excuses. Je suis certain qu'il ne l'a pas lu. Le seul usage qu'il en
ait fait a été d'y renverser son écritoire, peut-être pour me montrer que lui
aussi il sait *commenter* et couvrir les marges d'encre. Que le bon Dieu lui
pardonne, et lui ôte à jamais l'envie de me demander des livres.

After this incident Chénier never wrote in his books again, but made
a habit of writing his notes on little slips of paper which he inserted
between the leaves. Perhaps this also affected his method of composing
his poems, for he made jottings for them also on similar short slips
of paper, which he presumably carried about with him. However, the
same copy of Malherbe was to cause a scandal about fifty years later,
when his brother Constantin, perhaps no longer in full possession of
his faculties and living in reduced circumstances, was found selling it.
The book was found by Tenant de Latour, who in 1842 published an
edition of Malherbe with Chénier's notes serving as a preface.

These notes help us to form some idea of Chénier's mind, his
knowledge and enthusiasm, at an early age.[1] He corrected and praised
Malherbe by comparing him with the poets he most admired, and these
were Horace, Martial, Pindar, Virgil, Tibullus, and Ovid. Among the

[1] See D22, pp. 805–31.

moderns he referred most frequently and enthusiastically to Racine
and Corneille, La Fontaine, J.-B. Rousseau (whom he called 'le grand
Rousseau' as though Jean-Jacques were less important), Boileau, and,
surprisingly, Petrarch, whom he quoted in the original.

It is not Chénier's erudition which makes his notes interesting, but
his point of view. He did not hesitate to condemn one of the Odes as
'un peu froide et *vide de choses*, comme tout ce qu'a fait Malherbe, car
il faut avouer que le poète n'est guère recommandable que pour le
style'. At the same time he was prepared to forgive what he called 'the
detestable subject-matter' of *Les Larmes de Saint-Pierre* because 'la
versification est étonnante' and for 'cette musique de ses vers qu'aucun
de nos poètes n'a surpassée'. He condemned mixed metaphors (which,
later, he was to find so 'barbarous' in Shakespeare) as well as forced
wit, putting his finger unerringly on one of the most obvious devices
of Malherbe and his school: 'Il est plaisant de voir Malherbe, comme
son modèle, travailler à finir chaque strophe par un trait d'esprit
presque toujours ridicule, du moins par la place qu'il occupe.'

From the kind of things Chénier admired, we can gain some idea of
his conception of poetry. He wrote, for instance, 'Cette ode est belle,
elle est *courte* et pleine de chaleur.' The emphasis on brevity and
precision occurs over and over again, and this already points to that
remarkable effort of concentration which he was to make himself in
his *Bucoliques*. He praised an image as being 'moderne, riche et belle'
—he was not content with ordinary poetic currency. Just as he praised
what was 'modern' so he welcomed the invention of new words,
praising Malherbe for using the word 'cavaient' instead of 'creusaient'.
In spite of his constant praise of Malherbe's 'music' he showed no
dislike of didactic writing, praising what he called a 'strophe philosophique' in the *Ode sur la prise de Marseille*. But he found Malherbe
wanting in 'la véritable ivresse poétique'. What he was looking for was
poetry 'pleine de tableaux' or 'remplie de tableaux tendres', or, as he
put it more simply, 'pleine de choses'. This constant stress on imagery,
incident and detail marks him off from the poets of his own century.
According to him the essence of poetry could be resumed in two
words: warmth and enthusiasm. He liked images which were 'new,
striking, bold'. With a penetration far beyond his years or his time
he dared to condemn Malherbe for a lack of spontaneous feeling, and
underneath that coldness detected a lack of human experience: 'Mais
ces vers-là prouvent qu'il n'a jamais aimé. Ce sont de froides et galantes
fadaises, qui n'ont aucun *poison*, et le jeune et amoureux peut les lire

sans danger.' This remark is astonishing for a person of his age: the word *poison*, so worthy of Stendhal or Baudelaire, shows that he was well aware that poetry is not made only of fine sentiments. Indeed this commentary astonishes the reader at every turn: he speaks of a passage in a poem being a 'magnifique tableau plein de chaleur et de mouvement', looking at poetry with the same eye as he brought to the plastic arts. He must have been the first modern critic ever to have thought of the critical value of manuscripts, writing, 'Il serait quelquefois à désirer que nous eussions les brouillons des grands poètes, pour voir par combien d'échelons ils ont passé.'

What is most striking about this youth is his complete independence of judgement. At a time when it was a heresy to lift a finger against Malherbe (and, indeed, in France it still is a heresy), he showed no mercy for the courtier-poet's lack of integrity, 'd'insulter à la juste disgrâce d'un homme qu'on avait loué dans la prospérité'. He dared to say of one of the epigrams 'Il n'y a rien au monde de plus bête que cette épigramme'. Nobody but Chénier—for even the Romantics did not do so—would have dared to have called any of Malherbe's work 'fade et plat'.

There is one aspect of the Commentary which stands out from the rest. After quoting a phrase of Malherbe's,

> De ceux qui . . .
> Virent de leur matin leur beau jour accourci,

he then noted another, 'Le soir fut avancé de leurs belles journées'. Then he remarked:

Le même vers que j'ai noté p. 12. Peut-être à cette source nous devons le vers divin de La Fontaine:
> Rien ne trouble sa fin, c'est le soir d'un beau jour.
Pétrarque a dit un vers délicieux, par la bouche de Laure:
> Et compi mia giornata innanzi sera.
Et moi, dans une de mes élégies:
> Je meurs: avant le soir j'ai fini ma journée.

These comparisons, ending with a line of his own which is in no way inferior to those of his great predecessors, show more than the scholarly bent of his mind. They show that, like Valéry (and like Ronsard and Du Bellay, for that matter), he had the art of making lines by analogy, confirming Valéry's distinction between 'vers donnés' and 'vers imités'. This process of intellectual creation shows exactly what he meant, in his long poem on that subject, by 'Invention'. More

important, however, is the fact that this note, in which he brings four
lines together, shows his desire to understand and cling to the European
tradition—indeed to a tradition which, by his time, was almost lost.
Further, it shows that he had, like all great artists, a mind that tended
naturally towards synthesis. His relationship to the past makes him the
only bridge between the nineteenth-century Romantics and the great
poets of the sixteenth and seventeenth centuries.

2

'GALLUS'

CHÉNIER was not a handsome man according to the standards of his time. In order to be considered such, a man had to have a tall, slim figure and an aquiline nose: faces were painted longer, and eyes larger, than they really were, and it was a crime to have a broad face, a wide mouth, or a powerful chin. The standards of male portraiture were on the whole effeminate. The portrait of Chénier as a young man which is now in the Carnavalet Museum in Paris is usually disowned because it does not conform to the accepted notions of what a gentleman had to look like in those days.[1] However, this portrait is obviously in the style of David, and would form a perfect pendant to the portrait of Marie-Joseph Chénier, by David, which is to be seen at Versailles. It shows a young man in his early twenties, with a massive head set on broad shoulders. His eyes have the same penetrating gaze as that of André Chénier's portrait at the age of eleven: there is the same powerful nose, the same dimple in the same heavy chin, the same combination of dignity, sensuality, and intellectual power. When we compare it with another portrait, to be seen at Carcassonne, the hair has by now receded and shows a wide, domed brow, but except that the eyes are more slanting and smaller in proportion to the face as a whole, the same essential features, the same general appearance of inward power and confidence, are to be seen.[2]

Chénier was rather short and thick-set, and the countess Hocquart de Turtot, sister of his friend Fanny Lecoulteux (also spelt Lecouteulx) described him as 'rempli de charme et fort laid, avec de gros traits et une tête énorme'.[3] Later, his friend Charles de Lacretelle, describing him as he was at the age of twenty-nine, wrote: 'Ses traits fortement prononcés, sa taille athlétique, sans être haute, son teint basané, ses yeux ardents, fortifiaient, illuminaient sa parole.'[4] Other

---

[1] On this anonymous portrait see Sarraute in F97, p. 319.

[2] Ibid., p. 320: 'Non signé. Vêtu de brun rougâtre, col ouvert, jabot. Une main apparaît. La physionomie est d'un homme plus âgé qu'André Chénier, les yeux plus allongés, le nez moins fin, la bouche plus grande.' Reproduced in F101.

[3] D6, p. xxi.   [4] See full text on p. 245, below.

witnesses have stressed his more refined physical and social qualities. The youngest of the de Pange brothers (later marquis de Pange) wrote long afterwards, in 1837, referring to Chénier's voice when he read aloud:

> Dans ces réunions, monsieur votre oncle faisait souvent des lectures de poésies ou d'articles destinés à être insérés dans les journaux. L'aménité de son caractère, la douceur de son organe et de sa physionomie contrastaient d'une manière qui me frappait beaucoup, avec l'énergie qu'il mettait dans son indignation, quand il venait d'avoir lieu quelques préludes dans l'anarchie féroce dont on était menacé et qu'il avait si à cœur de combattre dans ses discours et dans ses écrits.[1]

Chénier's friend Boissy d'Anglas stressed his melancholy disposition as well as his gentleness: 'Il était naturellement mélancolique et accablé, si je peux parler ainsi, sous le poids d'une sensibilité dominatrice; il n'était pas né pour être heureux . . . il était le plus doux, le plus posé et le plus modeste des hommes.'[2]

Perhaps melancholy, reserve, and modesty, together with the thought that he was not as handsome as a poet is expected to be, were not quite the qualities which would help a penniless young man to find happiness in the amorous adventures into which he now flung himself. To make matters worse he was never for long in good health, suffering from gall-stones and digestive troubles. Yet Chénier's first 'art poétique' shows his belief that poetry must arise from experience, and both in his elegies and his epistles he made it plain that Venus is the first of the Muses. The poet must have not only an open heart, but an erotic temperament:

> L'homme insensible et froid en vain s'attache à peindre
> Ces sentiments du cœur que l'esprit ne peut feindre . . .
>
> Aimer, sentir, c'est là cette ivresse vantée
> Qu'aux célestes foyers déroba Prométhée.
> Calliope jamais daigna-t-elle enflammer
> Un cœur inaccessible à la douceur d'aimer?
> Non; l'amour, l'amitié, la sublime harmonie,
> Tous ces dons précieux n'ont qu'un même génie:
> Même souffle anima le poète charmant,
> L'ami religieux, et le parfait amant.
>
> *Épître à de Brazais*

In his late 'teens and early twenties Chénier spent as much time on writing personal, intimate elegies about love and friendship as he

---

[1] D7, t. i, p. xxvii.　　　　　[2] See Appendix A, below.

spent on his *Bucoliques*; yet we cannot always be sure that the experiences he related in the elegies were really his own. His first love-poems were a close account of his frustrated passion for an actress, or perhaps one of the young dancers of the Opéra, whom he called 'Lycoris'. This name had already been used by other poets such as Le Brun and Gentil-Bernard—never mind the Alexandrian poets—to celebrate their amours. There are half a dozen poems in which her name, or the pseudonym 'Gallus', which he affected at this time, occurs frequently. It was only in this cycle of poems that he called himself Gallus, or 'Gallus de Byzance', and he dropped the name when this affair came to an end. The original Gallus was the Cornelius Gallus mentioned by Virgil in his sixth Eclogue. Gallus, a man of humble birth, became a viceroy under Augustus, and was one of Virgil's patrons. He loved an actress called Cytheris, but he wrote elegies for her (which have since been lost) in which he addressed her as Lycoris and complained of her unfaithfulness. Thus, if Chénier called himself Gallus, it was because he, also, was writing elegies for his unfaithful Lycoris.

Although the theme of jealousy was common in poetry in the eighteenth century—indeed it was a form of compliment, in those days, to pretend to be jealous—the warm tones in which Chénier handled it suggests that he was genuinely thwarted in love. Only one of the elegies for Lycoris seems to have sprung from a mood of complete happiness. This is the beautiful poem which he wrote very quickly on the evening of 23 April 1782, 'avant l'Opéra où je vais à l'instant même', and on which he left a very lively commentary of his own. In his notes on the poem he spoke of having composed ninety lines. There are ninety, but unfortunately it is almost impossible to fit them together, as there are gaps here and there which no editor's ingenuity has yet been able to fill.[1] The poem begins with an *allegro* movement:

> Animé par l'amour, le vrai Dieu des poètes,
> Du Pinde en mon printemps j'ai connu les retraites,
> Aux danses des neuf sœurs entremêlé mes pas,
> Et de leurs jeux charmants su goûter les appas.
> Je veux, tant que mon sang bouillonne dans mes veines,
> Ne chanter que l'amour, ses douceurs et ses peines,
> De convives chéris toujours environné,
> A la joie avec eux sans cesse abandonné . . .

---

[1] See my attempted reconstruction in D25.

Fumant dans le crystal, que Bacchus à longs flots
Partout aille à la ronde éveiller les bons mots.
Reine de mes banquets, que Lycoris y vienne;
Que des fleurs de sa tête elle pare la mienne.
Pour enivrer mes sens, que le feu de ses yeux
S'unisse à la vapeur des vins délicieux.
Amis, que ce bonheur soit notre unique étude.
Nous en perdrons si vite la charmante habitude!
Hâtons-nous. L'heure fuit. Hâtons-nous de saisir
L'instant, le seul instant donné pour le plaisir.

The poet then goes on to describe the pleasures that will be left for him
in his old age—the study of science, the classics, and agriculture, before
ending the poem with the same youthful vigour with which it began:

Cependant jouissons; l'âge nous y convie.
Avant de la quitter, il faut user la vie:
Le moment d'être sage est voisin du tombeau.
Allons, jeune homme, allons, marche; prends ce flambeau:
Marche, allons. Mène-moi chez ma belle maîtresse.
J'ai pour elle aujourd'hui mille fois plus d'ivresse.
Je veux que des baisers plus doux, plus dévorants,
N'aient jamais vers le ciel tourné ses yeux mourants.

Chénier's nephew Gabriel was scandalized that anyone should imagine that his uncle had enjoyed himself when he was young, saying,
'De ce que, dans ses élégies, on trouve la trace de ces exceptions à ses
habitudes studieuses et tranquilles, il ne faut pas en conclure que sa vie
fut dissipée et livrée à des plaisirs échevelés, comme on parle aujour-
d'hui.'[1] It was stated by the chronicler Rétif de la Bretonne (in his half-
true and half-fanciful *Nuits de Paris*) that Chénier was seen with his
friends the Trudaines, Fontanes, Joubert at the wild banquets given
by the dandy Grimod de la Reynière.[2] This wealthy young aristocrat
was for a time locked up by his father to keep him out of harm's way.
At his banquets there were fountains of red and white wine, champagne
and coffee, and all kinds of extraordinary dishes, for he was the author
of the *Almanach des Gourmands*—a richer and more practical Oscar
Wilde. Gabriel de Chénier's explanation of all this was that the
eccentric Grimod was a friend of the Trudaines, as well as being a
nephew of the minister Malesherbes, and a cousin of the M. de La
Luzerne who took Chénier with him to London when he became
Ambassador to the Court of Saint James.

[1] D7, p. xxi.   [2] *Monsieur Nicolas*, t. vi, p. 11.

However, there is no reason for doubting that, for a while, Chénier set out to enjoy himself thoroughly in the company of the Trudaines. However delicately he did it, he also described in his elegies what he himself called 'amoureuses orgies', and there is no reason for painting this stage of his life in pastel shades. What does offset the picture painted by Rétif, however, is the fact that Chénier was not a libertine but a sensitive person who at once developed a sentimental attachment to the women with whom he came into contact. This caused him an emotional suffering which seems to have astonished him: he found that his enjoyment was only skin-deep, while the humiliation of not being taken seriously remained. His own commentary on the elegy we have just quoted shows at once a very erotic temperament and a lively wit. It is useless for Gabriel de Chénier to remind us that much of it was imitated from Propertius: the particular genius of André Chénier enabled him to make an extraordinary synthesis of literary reminiscence and personal experience, so that we can never tell where the exercise ends and personal experience begins: this is the same kind of problem that faces us in reading Donne. In his prose commentary, which is as entertaining as the poem itself, he admitted that the idea of describing the banquet came from Propertius: 'but I have not set out to copy him. I have enlarged upon him; I have often left him in order to work in, according to my habit, pieces from Virgil and Horace and Ovid, and whatever came to hand; and often, also, to follow nobody but myself.' The prose commentary shows a licence and indiscretion which are not present in the poem. Whereas the poem contains the charming, inoffensive lines:

> Que Laïs sans réserve abandonne à nos yeux
> De ses charmes secrets les contours gracieux,

he comments wittily, 'You, whom I have not named, will see, if ever you read me, that it is your beautiful bottom which made me write these pretty verses. Why do I not dare to write your name instead of that of Laïs? I should not need to change the rhythm of the line. Unfortunately for me, too many people would have recognized that I was telling the truth, and that you have the loveliest bottom in the world.' But what is admirable about Chénier's poetry, even at its most erotic, is that it has always a delicacy and discretion which are lacking in his prose comment. This is because he had a proper respect for poetry. At the end of his life he was able to write, truthfully: 'Je me livrai aux égarements d'une jeunesse fougueuse, mais, toujours dominé par l'amour de la poésie, des lettres et de l'étude, souvent chagrin et découragé par la fortune ou par moi-même, toujours soutenu par mes amis, je sentais au moins dans moi que mes vers et ma prose, goûtés ou non, seraient mis au rang du petit nombre d'ouvrages qu'aucune bassesse n'a flétris.'[1]

Although the elegies for Lycoris are written in a lively manner, it is quite evident that there was little happiness for Chénier in such a relationship. Though it is never quite clear when he was writing from experience or from convention, the beauty of his style helps us to forget what was conventional and, indeed, somewhat effeminate in them. Unlike his contemporaries he distilled in these early poems a wealth of imagery and suavity of music which recalls the *bel canto* of the sixteenth century, as well as often rejoining the baroque tradition. For instance, in the fine poem addressed to his Muses, he developed the colourful conceit of the liberated soul taking one form after another, as far as it could be carried, before even mentioning Lycoris:

> Ainsi, bruyante abeille, au retour du matin
> Je vais changer en miel les délices du thym.
> Rose, un sein palpitant est ma tombe divine.
> Frêle atome d'oiseau, de leur molle étamine
> Je vais sous d'autres cieux dépouiller d'autres fleurs.
> Le papillon plus grand offre moins de couleurs,
> Et l'Orénoque impur, la Floride fertile
> Admirent qu'un oiseau si tendre, si débile,
> Mêle tant d'or, de pourpre, en ses riches habits,
> Et pensent dans les airs voir nager des rubis.
> Sur un fleuve souvent l'éclat de mon plumage
> Fait à quelque Léda souhaiter mon hommage.
> Souvent, fleuve moi-même, en mes humides bras
> Je presse mollement des membres délicats,
> Mille fraîches beautés que partout j'environne;
> Je les tiens, les soulève, et murmure et bouillonne.

At first sight the poems for Lycoris are the poetry of play; there is much playing at love, at jealousy and melancholy, and especially at being 'the poet in love'. But it is brilliantly done, and at moments we feel that the tradition of Petrarch and Ronsard is being maintained:

> Vois ta brillante image à vivre destinée,
> D'une immortelle fleur dans mes vers couronnée.

[1] D22, p. 624.

> L'étranger, dans mes vers contemplant tes attraits
> S'informera de toi, de ton nom, de tes traits,
> Et quelle fut enfin celle qui, dans la France
> Était la Lycoris de Gallus de Byzance . . .

But behind all this play there is a strong sense of mortality, constantly showing through the surface, whether in such echoes of Catullus as

> Nous n'avons qu'un seul jour, et ce jour précieux
> S'éteint dans une nuit qui n'aura point d'aurore,

or the anguished cry, in an elegy dominated by the threat of suicide,

> Pourtant, ô Lycoris, ô trop funeste amante,
> Si tu l'avais voulu, Gallus, plein de sa foi,
> Avec toi voulait vivre et mourir avec toi.

This and other poems of the Lycoris cycle show that already Chénier's friends were trying to restrain him, as they were to do again later in his unhappy passion for Camille. One of Le Brun's odes (II, xv), addressed 'A un jeune Ami', was obviously intended for Chénier and contains the following lines:

> A ta volage Cythéride,
> Ami, c'est trop donner de Regrets et de Pleurs:
> Abjure une plainte timide;
> Dédaigne une Amante perfide
> Dont la Pitié superbe insulte à tes douleurs.

This poem can refer only to Lycoris, for, as we have already seen, the mistress of Cornelius Gallus was called Cytheris and Le Brun speaks of Cythéride. Le Brun continued:

> *Souviens-toi* des mœurs de Byzance!
> Digne de ton berceau, maîtrise la Beauté:
> Ou du moins implorant l'absence,
> Arme-toi contre la puissance
> De ces yeux où périt ta douce liberté.

This poem of Le Brun's is one of the few proofs that we have that Chénier's passion for this girl came before his experience of life in the army: it ends in a way that suggests that the young poet was about to don uniform:

> Entends-tu le cri de la Gloire?
> Cours défendre ces bords où pâlit le Croissant:

De Vénus éteins la mémoire;
Ceins le glaive de la victoire,
Et fais payer tes pleurs au Scythe frémissant.

During the same period as Chénier was writing about Lycoris he had begun an *Art d'aimer* of which about fifty fragments survive. A number of these pieces were written on paper which bears the watermark 1780. This is very much a work of immaturity containing silly advice to lovers, yet a note concerning a book in the Bentley Collection suggests that he was still adding to it when he was in London, some years later. The fragments of the *Art d'aimer* show a conventional and irritatingly superior attitude to the other sex, with the usual emphasis on the tricks by which the two sexes may captivate each other. At this stage of his life he affected to have no use for intelligent or educated women, and mocked the 'femme savante' or blue-stocking:

Belles, le ciel a fait pour les mâles cerveaux
L'infatigable étude et les doctes travaux.
Vous avez les talents aimables et faciles.
O, le sinistre emploi pour les grâces badines
De poursuivre une sphère en ses cercles nombreux,
Ou du sec A plus B les sentiers ténébreux . . .

Although he exclaimed on one occasion 'Les beaux garçons sont souvent si bêtes', the sentiment was no doubt to be expressed by a 'belle' rather than representing his own point of view. His immature idea of women was characteristic of his century's attitude of unquestioned male superiority, which, save in the case of one or two enlightened men like Voltaire, doomed women to subjection. There was much talk of the 'rights of man' during the Revolution, but the women never received the right to vote, and Olympe de Gouges was guillotined for demanding it. So, for Chénier, women were only playthings and ornaments, in this stage of his unhappy career:

Une femme est toujours inconstante et futile,
Et qui pense fixer leur caprice mobile,
Il pense avec sa main retenir l'aquilon,
Ou gravir sur les flots un durable sillon.

At the same time, he added in one of his notes: 'Ce n'est pas que je veuille condamner les femmes à ne songer qu'aux affaires du ménage. J'aime fort qu'une belle main, habile à manier la plume et l'aiguille, cultive à la fois l'une et l'autre Minerve.' He also admitted that 'Un homme doit se conformer au goût des femmes. Il doit quelquefois coudre, broder, faire de la tapisserie. Mais il ne faut pas qu'il s'y montre trop adroit: au contraire, il vaut mieux qu'il affecte de s'y prendre mal. Hercule auprès d'Omphale; sa maladresse qui amusait cette dame.'[1] But it is clear enough that, for the young poet, eroticism was a shallow game beneath which he hid his finer feelings, which only emerged in spite of himself. One of the erotic passages in the *Art d'aimer* sets us thinking, not only about the pastoral quality of his eroticism but about the possible identity of one of his mistresses. The movement has a certain sadistic side to it, though it is mild enough, for the poet chastises her with a flower; but it ends beautifully:

> Fontenay! lieu que l'Amour fit naître avec la rose,
> J'irai (sur cet espoir mon âme se repose)
> J'irai te voir, et Flore et le ciel qui te luit.
> Là je contemple enfin (ma déesse m'y suit)
> Sur un lit que je cueille en tes riants asiles
> Ses appas, sa pudeur, et ses fuites agiles,
> Et dans la rose en feu l'albâtre confondu,
> Comme un ruisseau de lait sur la pourpre étendu.

The Fontenay in question was Fontenay-aux-Roses, not far out of Paris, where it so happened that the writer and publicist Suard lived. Suard was a friend not only of Le Brun but of the Trudaines (whom he visited at Montigny), and indeed of the whole social set with whom Chénier was to have such close relations in the years to come— Madame de Bonneuil as well as Fanny Lecoulteux. Is it possible that he met Madame de Bonneuil at Fontenay? Or did he love Fanny Lecoulteux before her marriage? All that we know is that if Chénier went to Fontenay it was not only to visit the learned, refined, and indolent Suard.

Chénier's nephew Gabriel relates how at the age of twelve the poet thought of entering the navy. According to him, his father got in touch with the Admiralty in order to have him admitted to the École Royale de Marine, but was not able to produce the proofs of nobility that were necessary to satisfy d'Hozier, who was then responsible for examining such claims.[2] Needless to say, this was contested by Becq de Fouquières, who hated Gabriel de Chénier for not allowing him to consult the poet's manuscripts. Whether it is true or not, or whether it concerned one of Chénier's elder brothers, the incident is important, because it shows that already in 1774 or thereabouts Louis de Chénier

[1] D13, t. ii, pp. 187, 175.   [2] See p. 12, above.

was struggling against the old régime and doing his best to set his sons on the aristocratic ladder to success, as it then was.

By 1781, Louis de Chénier, as we shall call this fine gentleman who, after all, was carrying out the work of an aristocrat by directing French affairs in Morocco, had managed to place both Louis-Sauveur and Marie-Joseph in regiments. The future General, Louis-Sauveur, was attached in 1780 to the Bassigny regiment, while Marie-Joseph, two years younger than André, enlisted, thanks to the help of the Malartic family, in the Lescure Dragoons in 1781. Either André Chénier was still continuing his studies, or else (as his poems suggest) he was already in ill health, suffering from nephritis: there seems to be no other explanation why his younger brother Marie-Joseph entered the army before him. André Chénier was never lucky in anything he did. In May 1781, by which time Marie-Joseph was accepted for the army, a new law was passed obliging gentlemen cadets to furnish evidence of their noble birth. Underneath all the so-called liberalism of Louis XV and Louis XVI, there lurked this kind of stupid restriction which merely served to embitter the younger generation. Anyhow, this new law probably explains why André Chénier was not accepted into the army until 1782. On the male side of the family, Louis de Chénier was able to establish that his grandfather had held a gentleman's office (as 'conseiller du roi') under Louis XIV. On the mother's side Madame de Chénier, who always claimed descent from the great Lusignans of Cyprus, obtained a certificate from the Chevalier de Lusignan attesting André Chénier's gentle birth, though not specifically stating that he was of Lusignan blood. In any case this intervention by the Chevalier de Lusignan suggests that there must have been some grounds, which have not yet been discovered, for Madame de Chénier's seemingly extravagant claim.[1] The Chevalier de Lusignan's certificate reads as follows:

Je soussigné, Vincent de Lusignan, chevalier commandeur de l'ordre de Saint-Lazare, certifie que messire André Marie de Chénier est noble, d'ancienne extraction, que ses ancêtres ont servi dans les troupes de Sa Majesté en qualité de Capitaines et qu'il se trouve dans le cas des ordonnances du Roi pout être admis dans les troupes du Roi en qualité d'officier. En foi de quoi j'ai signé le présent certificat à Versailles, le 11 juin 1781, auquel j'ai apposé le sceau de mes armes.[2]

[1] See D34, t. i, pp. 26 and 585–6.
[2] BMC 11800. The official 'certificat de noblesse' (in Archives nat. ét. cxiii. 524) was signed by Lusignan; le comte de Violaine; le chevalier Pelletier de Villement; le marquis

So, in the summer of 1782, André Chénier set out, with his new military outfit and sword, for the garrison at Strasbourg to join the Angoumois regiment, which was commanded by the Marquis de Bonnac d'Usson. Here again we witness the astuteness and devotion of Louis de Chénier; for d'Usson was not only, like himself, of Languedoc birth, but his father had been ambassador to Turkey from 1716 to 1725.

Although Chénier's biographers have speculated freely about his social contacts at Strasbourg—with the hellenists Schweigheuser and Oberlin, and Ramond de Carbonnières—there is no direct evidence that he met any of them there, or that he attended lectures at the University. The life of a supernumerary cadet, as he then was, could have left him but little leisure, while it was almost obligatory for young men of his status to spend what spare time they had, in dissipation. The young cadets lived four to a room—a room in which they had to sleep, eat, read, and write, and in which the orderly both cooked and served their meals. Such surroundings could only have driven Chénier out to the coffee-house or library, or, when the weather was fine, for walks down the Rhine. When he was not too tired after rising early and an endless series of fatigues—drills, parades, lessons on tactics, constant guards which fell to his lot because so many of the officers were absentees—he might set out with his comrades in search of a cheap flirtation. In any case, if he had any bent for military life it was quickly disappointed, and after about nine months he quitted his regiment, just as Marie-Joseph had done. Here the typical bad faith of the *ancien régime* is apparent. A decree of 22 May 1781 had laid down that 'gentlemen cadets cannot hold third-lieutenancies, which are exclusively reserved for sub-lieutenants in their regiments, and for new enlistments'. Chénier was one of the recent recruits under the new scheme, and should have been promoted to third-lieutenant after about six months' service. However, in March 1783 the commission he was waiting for was given to a certain Monsieur de Warin, a gentleman cadet from the Military College in Paris, who had never served with a regiment. Maybe in some respects this was the best solution for Chénier, who was not in good health and who must have been keenly aware of his poverty in a regiment where men younger than himself could, thanks to their private income or nobility, receive rapid

de Lacagnes de Beaufort: it is dated 25 juin 1781. (See H1, p. 9.) H1 has also recently produced a new document (item 46, p. 10) which shows that Chénier's claim to a lieutenancy was foiled because he did not produce a certificate of nobility from Chérin.

promotion and live on the fat of the land while engaging others to perform their duties. His friend the comte de Moriolles was made a captain of cavalry at the age of seventeen, without any previous training.[1] François de Pange, who was a Chevalier of the Order of Malta at the age of four, became a gentleman cadet in 1778, and was a lieutenant at the age of seventeen and a captain by 1785, when he was only twenty-one.

This short spell of military life did have some influence on Chénier, though it left but little mark on his work. It strengthened his feeling of revolt against privilege and helped to determine his political position at the outbreak of the Revolution. So far as his early poetry is concerned, it contributed much to that dark melancholy which pervades the elegies. At the same time it explains the obstinacy with which in 1792 he attacked the organizers of the ceremony in honour of the mutineers of the Châteauvieux regiment (see Chapter 11). He had at least absorbed the notion of order and discipline, and faith to the military oath.

Yet there had been certain consolations for him during that unhappy phase in his life: in particular the development of his friendship with Le Brun and the marquis de Brazais. Alexandre Ferdinand du Hamel, marquis de Brazais, was born in 1743 and lived until 1817. In about 1765 he began a long poem (L'Année) on the seasons, and did not finish it until 1814.[2] He was both a catholic and a monarchist and joined the emigrant army in 1791. In 1787 he began a long erotic poem, Psyché, which he later destroyed before beginning one on a religious theme, Le Messie. When Chénier was stationed at Strasbourg, de Brazais was a captain in the same regiment. He was, usually, an absentee officer, but now he came to spend a month or two in Strasbourg. At the same time Chénier received an extraordinary honour in the shape of an Epistle, one of the best written by Le Brun, who was thirty-three years his senior.[3] In this poem, Le Brun celebrated not only Chénier's departure for the army but his genius as a poet, in the most flattering terms:

> Oui, l'astre du génie éclaira ton berceau;
> La Gloire a sur ton front secoué son flambeau;
> Les abeilles du Pinde ont nourri ton enfance.

[1] F73, pp. vi–vii.   [2] For de Brazais, see G6, pp. 83–97.
[3] Le Brun, Œuvres, t. ii, p. 131. The Epistle was printed ten years later in L'Almanach des Muses (1792) with the note: 'A M. de Chénier l'aîné, frère de l'auteur tragique. Ce jeune officier qui avait de grandes dispositions pour la poésie allait rejoindre son régiment.'

Phœbus vit à la fois naître aux murs de Byzance,
Chez un peuple farouche et des arts ennemi,
A la Gloire un Amant, à mon Cœur un Ami . . .

After saluting the 'naissante audace' of Chénier's writings, he went on
to praise his integrity:

Non, non; j'en ai reçu ta fidèle promesse:
Tu ne trahiras point les Nymphes du Permesse.
Non, tu n'iras jamais, oubliant leurs Amours,
Adorer la Fortune, et ramper dans les Cours.
Ton front ne ceindra point la mitre et le scandale;
Tu n'iras point, des Loix embrouillant le dédale,
Consumer tes beaux jours à dormir sur nos Lys,
Et vendre, à ton réveil, les arrêts de Thémis.

This, of course, was only another way of saying that Chénier had
abandoned all the easiest roads to success by taking the uniform. It was
fitting, then, that he should, as a hero himself, write heroic poetry: he
exhorted Chénier to write an epic and thus fill the place to which Voltaire had aspired and failed; or to continue writing Propertian elegies
or Pindaric odes, or, most ambitious of all, some didactic work:

Ou soit que de Lucrèce effaçant le grand nom,
Assise au char ailé de l'immortel Newton,
Ta Minerve se plonge au sein de la Nature,
Et nous peigne des Cieux la mouvante structure —

a reference, surely, to the astronomical passage in the Lycoris elegy
(from which we have quoted on p. 26), as well as a hint of Chénier's
intention, which perhaps he had already formulated, to write his
Hermès?

Chénier's reply to this epistle, in which Le Brun had set all the
emphasis on glory and the importance of being 'inscribed in the
Temple of Memory', is an effort worthy of his master, for it is written
in equally arrogant but flattering terms which make it almost a parody
of Le Brun's style. He announced that he preferred love and friendship
to posthumous glory:

Qu'un autre soit jaloux d'illustrer sa mémoire.
Moi, j'ai besoin d'aimer, qu'ai-je besoin de gloire?

The main message of this epistle was that he intended to continue
his amorous adventures, and writing elegies about them: he left it to
Le Brun (who for years had been announcing a poem on *La Nature*,
inspired by Buffon, which was never finished) to tread in the wake of

Lucretius, if he wanted to, and to write a work 'digne de la Nature et digne de Buffon'. After an inflated tribute to Le Brun's poetic powers he dared to suggest that Le Brun himself obtained more satisfaction from the admiration of the fair sex than from the other glories of Parnassus. Chénier's epistle is a perfect example of the *vers de société* of that time, with its extravagant compliments, classical allusions, and refined wit.

There is a companion piece, addressed to Le Brun and de Brazais, written when de Brazais was leaving Strasbourg at the beginning of the winter: it is a fine tribute to friendship. However, this, the best of the Epistles written from Strasbourg, must have been written during the winter, when Chénier was alone and unhappy: it starts with a lively description of Paris, where Le Brun occupied one of the little rooms in the Louvre, but ends on a very personal, poignant note which shows how little the poet was enjoying the military life:

> Que toujours à m'écrire il est lent à mon gré;
> Que, de mon cher Brazais pour un temps séparé
> Les ruisseaux et les bois et Vénus et l'étude
> Adoucissent un peu ma triste solitude.
> Oui, les cieux avec joie ont embelli ces champs
> Mais, Le Brun, dans l'effroi que respirent les camps,
> Où les foudres guerriers étonnent mon oreille,
> Où loin avant Phœbus Bellone me réveille,
> Puis-je adorer encore et Vertumne et Palès?
> Il faut un cœur paisible à ces Dieux de la paix.

The epistle shows no enthusiasm for the military life and gives a painful picture of the poet killing time. De Brazais did not return to Strasbourg, and one of the few interesting distractions during the winter was the demonstration of magnetism given by the quack, Cagliostro, whom Chénier later caricatured in his play *Les Charlatans*. It was in connexion with this event that Ramond de Carbonnières, a scholar and seeker after the picturesque, visited Strasbourg.[1] Ramond later became a Deputy and a Feuillant, and if they did not meet now, it is likely that they did later, during the Revolution.

Towards the spring things went from bad to worse. So far, Chénier had been housed in the Finckmatt barracks near the centre of the town, but in May the regiment moved to the Citadelle which was half an hour's walk away. In the meantime, he had heard in March that he had lost the commission for which he was waiting. His disappointment

---

[1] F34, t. ii, p. 121.

must have been the greater as four of his companions at Strasbourg did receive promotion in the proper way. Hartmann[1] has suggested that the reason for this is that Chénier was not in good health, and there might be some grounds for this interpretation. It is not known exactly at what date Chénier left his regiment, never to return; but as his sister Hélène was married in Paris on the 26th of June 1783, it is highly probable that he was present at the wedding, and, after some discussion with his father, decided to remain in Paris.[2]

Whatever the reasons for the setback in Chénier's military career, it has to be remembered that the same fate was reserved for his brothers. Marie-Joseph remained only a few months with his regiment before deciding to withdraw and pursue a literary career. André was at Strasbourg for under a year. Louis-Sauveur, the most military-minded of them all, left his regiment in despair after four years of service, and, undaunted but gifted for mathematics, began his studies as a military engineer which later resulted in his becoming a General in the Ordnance. Their unfortunate experience in the army turned all three brothers against the *ancien régime* and laid the basis for their later revolt. The blow fell heaviest on the most sensitive of them all, André, whom it certainly embittered; he wrote later: 'Pour moi, ouvrant les yeux autour de moi au sortir de la jeunesse, je vis que l'argent et l'intrigue étaient presque la seule voie pour aller à tout.'[3] In spite of his frequent references in his poems to the blessings of poverty, the theme of the fickleness of fortune, and his lack of security in the society in which he lived, was to become one of the main currents in his Elegies.

Chénier's passionate nature made him vary between extremes of sensuality and disgust, enthusiasm and depression. After leaving the army he went to live with his father, and at first resigned himself to poverty and study, with a wonderful feeling of liberty that he had not hitherto known: the opening passage of *La République des lettres*, which inspired Baudelaire's *Paysage*, sums up all that is best in the period after his army service, when Chénier, despite many social distractions, gave himself to study and poetry:

> Il n'est que d'être roi pour être heureux au monde.
> Bénis soient tes décrets, ô sagesse profonde,

[1] F50, p. 8.
[2] The marriage-contract, dated 11 June 1783 (in the Archives nationales), was signed by André and all the rest of the family except Constantin. See H1.
[3] D22, p. 624.

Qui me voulus heureux, et, prodigue envers moi,
M'as fait dans mon asile et mon maître et mon roi.
Mon Louvre est sous le toit. Sur ma tête il s'abaisse.
De ses premiers regards l'orient le caresse.
Lits, sièges, table y sont portant de toutes parts
Livres, dessins, crayons, confusément épars.
Là je dors, chante, lis, pleure, étudie et pense.
Là dans un calme pur je médite en silence
Ce qu'un jour je veux être, et seul à m'applaudir,
Je sème la moisson que je veux recueillir.

Here, then, in a room all his own, with the cheerful disorder of
a poet's den, in his attic into which the sun came to peep at dawn,
he was able to elaborate his future works while leading an intense
emotional life and meditating on his destiny. However, this period
of independence started badly, for it was probably at this time that he
had a very serious attack of nephritis which laid him low for a while.
Allowing for a certain exaggeration which is typical of all Chénier's
verse about himself, he was and remained haunted by his physical
weakness, and the theme of suicide was not, in his case, borrowed from
Gilbert and Chatterton. One of the unfinished elegies suggests that
the first attack came in 1782, when he was only twenty, and this would
confirm Hartmann's opinion:

De maux prématurés la foule qui m'assiège
Méconnaît de mes ans le faible privilège,
Et je vivrais, aux pleurs, aux tourments condamné,
Esclave volontaire à la vie enchaîné,
Pour maudire mon sort, mes douleurs, ma faiblesse,
Pour traîner à vingt ans une infirme vieillesse,
Dans mes reins agités quand des sables brûlants
S'ouvrent un dur passage et déchirent mes flancs.

However, he was not so ill that he could not make capital out of it
for his poetry, for he added, 'Finir par quelques pensées mélancoliques
et un peu sombres, et enfin par ce mot ancien: que le premier bonheur
est de ne pas naître, et le second, etc.' At the same time he wrote a long
elegy addressed to his friends, beginning:

Aujourd'hui qu'au tombeau je suis prêt à descendre,
Mes amis, dans vos mains je dépose ma cendre.

The fact that he asked to have a burial unattended by priests and somewhere 'près d'une eau pure, au coin d'un bois tranquille' has impressed
those who believed him to be an atheist; but in actual fact these lines

are a close translation of Propertius. It was probably, also, at this time
that Chénier wrote one of the longer *Bucoliques*: *Le Malade*. It now appears a trifle effeminate, though the beginning (as Becq de Fouquières
pointed out) shows Chénier already assuming the powerful accents of
Racine for the first movement of the monologue:

> Apollon, dieu sauveur, dieu des savants mystères,
> Dieu de la vie, et dieu des plantes salutaires,
> Dieu vainqueur du Python, dieu jeune et triomphant,
> Prends pitié de mon fils, de mon unique enfant.
> Prends pitié de sa mère aux larmes condamnée,
> Qui ne vit que pour lui, qui meurt abandonnée . . .

This poem, which certainly contains some fine lines, was much
admired by the Romantics, though its sentimental theme—the languish-
ing of a young man, who is saved from death by the love of the girl
for whom he was pining—is not one which recommends it to modern
taste. It suffers from that moral weakness which spoils some of
Keats's poems, and lacks virility. *Le Malade* is interesting for other
reasons: though it is one of the *Bucoliques* it shows Chénier grafting
the old on to the new, for the traditional theme is handled in a way
which shows the influence of the eighteenth-century romance—we
might even say the eighteenth-century romance at its worst. That is to
say, the cynicism of the Age of Reason, in matters of love, sought its
compensation in an idealized, sentimental view of love which is just
as unreal and psychologically unsound as the cynicism to which it
was opposed. *Le Malade* has the weaknesses of Keats's *Isabella*, though,
in the same way, it has some moments of genuine poetry. Without
going so far as to argue that a poem's subject is of the first importance,
yet when a poem sets out to tell a story and the story is feeble, a poet's
utmost genius would be necessary to triumph over that initial weakness.

More important than the composing of this poem at that time, is the
fact that Chénier's illness and intimation of death were to permeate the
whole of the *Bucoliques*, most of which are lamentations. Whatever
part or parts of the *Bucoliques* Chénier had written before 1783, it is
certain that his genius crystallized after the setback to his army career,
followed by illness. The characteristic tragic tone and the choice of
themes for the *Bucoliques* were imposed on him from within.

A typical and sometimes dangerous reaction on the part of energetic
young people who have been stricken by sickness is to throw themselves even more ardently than before into the pursuit of pleasure. Thus
in the period that followed (late 1783 to 1787) Chénier's life shows the

two sides of a medal: the one giving us the impression of a grave and saturnine character, determinedly forming himself into a great scholar, and the other showing a reckless young man dominated by an intense lust for life. His friend François de Pange, who normally had a stabilizing influence on him, did not return from his regiment until 1784. The Trudaines, who were rich and strong enough to combine pleasure of every kind with their functions as legal counsellors to the Paris *Parlement*, initiated Chénier into the society of the capital at every level. De Brazais had returned to his estates in a huff, after being told by Le Brun that he was not so much of a poet as he had hoped. We have only two records of Chénier's activities in 1783. The first of these was a visit to the prison in the bois de Vincennes, which left an indelible impression on his mind and strengthened his hatred of man's inhumanity to man: though he did not see any prisoners he was horrified at the sight of underground cells and the story of how an enormous dog was used to overpower one of those who had lost his reason.[1]

We also know that it was probably in this year that Chénier wrote a poem on the ascent made in a balloon by the brothers Montgolfier. This took place in June 1783 and they gave further demonstrations in August and November. On 14 February 1784 de Brazais wrote to Le Brun:

> Vous ne m'avez point envoyé comme je vous en avais prié, quelques vers de Chénier sur le Ballon Aérien. J'ai grande idée de sa conception. Si je pouvais oser me mettre de société avec vous deux, je dirais former un triumvirat qui puisse servir de modèle, un jour, ainsi que nos maîtres qu'il faut tâcher d'atteindre . . . De grâce envoyez-moi quelque chose de vous et de Chénier. Des nouvelles d'*Alphonse*. J'ai pour lui déjà une certain vénération. Son destin étonne mon génie.[2]

Two important points emerge from this letter. The first is that Chénier was writing a poem about the Balloon, which according to de Brazais's implied description was, perhaps, not just a short work. De Brazais only asks for a part of it to see ('quelques vers') and in speaking of its 'conception' is referring to its plan. Secondly, he asks for 'des nouvelles d'*Alphonse*'. This remark suggests that Chénier had already embarked on his ambitious didactic poem *L'Amérique*, in which one of the main characters, who was to relate parts of the narrative, was the poet 'Alfonse'. While it has been assumed that Chénier had already begun or conceived *L'Amérique*, such assertions have been made without

---

[1] D22, p. 701 (*Apologie*).   [2] Le Brun collection, BN, NAF 917,24.

evidence.[1] The first and only proof we have is that of de Brazais, which at least establishes that the poem was begun by 1783. If this is so, *Hermès* was also begun by then, for in *L'Amérique* Chénier was to take for granted certain scientific facts which he would have previously expounded in *Hermès*.

But at this point it is also possible to advance another hypothesis. It has been assumed that the poem on the 'Ballon Aérien' is lost: but it seems to me that it has been preserved, or that the substance or part of it has been preserved, among the fragments of *L'Amérique*. The passage in question is that which, precisely, was to be related by Alfonse:

AMÉR.

Le poète Alfonse, à la fin d'un repas nocturne en plein air, prié de chanter, chantera un morceau astronomique: quelles étoiles conduisirent Christophe Colomb.

'O nuit . . . ô ciel . . . ô enthousiasme, enfant de la nuit . . .'

Then follows the magnificent passage, beginning:

> Salut, ô belle nuit, étincelante et sombre,
> Consacrée au repos, ô silence de l'ombre
> Qui n'entends que la voix de mes vers, et les cris
> De la rive aréneuse où se brise Thétis.
> Muse, Muse nocturne, apporte-moi ma lyre.
> Comme un fier météore, en ton brûlant délire,
> Lance-toi dans l'espace; et pour franchir les airs,
> Prends les ailes des vents, les ailes des éclairs,
> Les bonds de la comète aux longs cheveux de flamme.
> Mes vers impatients élancés de mon âme
> Veulent parler aux Dieux, et volent où reluit
> L'enthousiasme errant, fils de la belle nuit.[2]

When we come to analyse what, at first sight, is a hymn to Enthusiasm, we see many other things that it is at the same time. In the first place, though it is an 'astronomical' piece, it has nothing to do with Columbus: it is not the explorer who is in question here, but the poet. However, unlike traditional invocations to the Muse, the poet does not ask for his inspiration to descend on him; rather, he takes off like a spirit into the sky. What has happened in writing this poem is one of those extraordinary moments of synthesis: the poet has brought together

[1] F36, p. 195: 'Dès 1780 le poète débutant pensait déjà à un poème sur le Nouveau Monde.'

[2] Taken from the manuscript (BN, NAF 6849,134) and not from Dimoff, D13, t. ii, p. 105.

in a few lines his reading of Alonzo d'Ercilla (one of the sources he quotes for his *L'Amérique*); his study of astronomy which has already led him to begin an Epistle to the astronomer Bailly; and finally, the elation of the Montgolfier experiment. It cannot be said that the fragment on Enthusiasm is actually the poem about the balloon mentioned by de Brazais, but it is obvious that it could not have been written independently, and that the poems are related.

Thus it is now possible to see that, already in 1783–4, Chénier was working on a very broad front. He had begun collecting material for his *Hermès* (to which we shall return later), a poem in which he was to survey the whole range of human knowledge from antiquity to the present day. He had begun work on *L'Amérique* which, besides celebrating the discovery of the New World, was to contain a survey of the geography of the whole globe ('absolument toute la géographie du globe aujourd'hui connue') and the social history of man and his institutions. At the same time he planned to write, together, a series of poems on modern love (his Elegies) as well as the classical poems which have since come to be known as the *Bucoliques*. This second ambition had crystallized in a poem he wrote when he was nineteen, that is to say, some time between October 1780 and October 1781:

> Quand à peine Clothon, mère des destinées,
> A mes trois lustres pleins ajoute quatre années,
> Mon cœur s'ouvre avec joie à l'espoir glorieux
> De chanter à la fois les belles et les Dieux.
> Né citoyen du Pinde, et citoyen du Gnide,
> Avide de plaisirs, et de louange avide,
> Aux antres d'Apollon pontife initié,
> Aux banquets de Vénus convive associé,
> Au temple de Paphos, sur la lyre d'Orphée,
> Mes chants vont à Vénus consacrer un trophée.
> Peuple, sur nos climats le printemps ramené
> A fait luire son front de rose couronné:
> Ses yeux de la Déesse ont ramené l'empire;
> Connaissez son génie aux feux qu'elle m'inspire;
> Tant que la lyre d'or va chanter sous mes doigts,
> D'un silence sacré favorisez ma voix.
>
> (Dim. III, 3)

Although Dimoff prints this poem as a Prologue to the *Élégies*,[1] it is obvious from the fourth and ninth lines that the poet is referring

---

[1] D13, t. iii, p. 3.

to *Bucoliques* as well as elegies. The second line mentions his age: three 'lustres' meaning fifteen, with scarcely four more added; that is to say that he was in his nineteenth year but not yet nineteen. The remark about spring in the tenth line helps us to date the poem spring 1781.

Finally, it is not unlikely that he was already beginning the long didactic poem, *L'Invention*, which was to express his *ars poetica*. This poem shows every kind of uncertainty as to what poetry is or is not, while at the same time serving as a plea for what he hoped to achieve through his *Hermès* and *L'Amérique* as well as in some of the *Bucoliques*. The composing of *L'Invention* was probably spread over a number of years, and it is likely that Chénier finished it (if he regarded it as finished) only when he was living in London between 1787 and 1790.

It was long thought that after his convalescence the poet made a tour through both Switzerland and Italy with the two Trudaine brothers: for instance, his nephew wrote, 'En 1784, après avoir éprouvé une crise de la maladie dont il était atteint, il fit un voyage avec les frères Trudaine, d'abord en Suisse, puis en Italie.'[1] However, Dimoff suggested that there must have been two separate tours, one to Switzerland between 19 September and November 1784, the second, to Italy, in 1785. This argument was based on the dates when the Trudaines appear to have been on leave.[2] It is now known that Chénier wrote to Lavater on 26 October 1784, thanking him for the reception he had given the group in Zürich; so Dimoff's assumption was correct.

With great ingenuity, Dimoff traced the possible itinerary of the three companions, by supposing that they followed a popular guide, William Coxe's *Lettres sur la Suisse* which had been translated and enlarged by Ramond de Carbonnières. It is the more likely that they used this book, as Ramond dedicated a copy of it to Mme de Sérilly, François de Pange's cousin. This would take them on a 'picturesque' tour from Schaffhausen to Geneva. However, Chénier's letter to Lavater implies the contrary, for after seeing Lavater in Zürich they then went on to Constance, Schaffhausen, and Basel. Thus it is quite possible that they started from Geneva, striking East towards Mont Blanc, then northwards up the Rhone valley.

If Chénier wrote any 'Swiss' elegies or epistles during his travels, they have not survived, but there are various echoes of this experience in later works. An epistle addressed to the Trudaines looks back

[1] D7, t. i, p. xxxi.   [2] F34, t. i, p. 137.

nostalgically to the country which had become, for him, the ideal of the 'simple life' and to which he dreamed of retiring and living in peace:

> Eh! qu'il eût mieux valu naître un de ces pâsteurs
> Ignorés dans le sein de leurs Alpes fertiles
> Que nos yeux ont connus fortunés et tranquilles! . . .

> Hasly! frais Élysée, honneur des pâturages,
> Lieu qu'avec tant d'amour la Nature a formé
> Où l'Aar roule un or pur en son onde semé . . .

> Là je verrais, assis dans ma grotte profonde,
> La génisse traînant sa mamelle féconde,
> Prodiguant à ses fils ce trésor indulgent,
> A pas lents agiter sa cloche au son d'argent,
> Promener près des eaux sa tête nonchalante,
> Ou de son large flanc presser l'herbe odorante . . .

Here, then, is Hasly, and the river Aar, then Appenzel, with all the poet's emphasis laid on the pastoral existence sentimentally popularized by Rousseau and Gessner, the Swiss poet whose influence on Chénier and his contemporaries was so lamentable. Fortunately, Chénier was equally sensitive to the 'horridness' of the Alps, and this poem ends on a more masculine note:

> Je veux, accompagné de ma Muse sauvage,
> Revoir le Rhin tomber en des gouffres profonds,
> Et le Rhône grondant sous d'immenses glaçons,
> Et d'Arve aux flots impurs la Nymphe injurieuse.
> Je vole, je parcours la cime harmonieuse
> Où souvent de leurs cieux les anges descendus
> En des nuages d'or mollement suspendus,
> Emplissent l'air des sons de leur voix éthérée.
> O lac, fils des torrents, ô Thoun, onde sacrée!
> Salut, monts chevelus, verts et sombres remparts
> Qui contenez ses flots pressés de toutes parts!
> Salut, de la nature admirables caprices,
> Où les bois, les cités, pendent en précipices!

It is clear from all this that we need not read Coxe or Ramond to understand where Chénier went: he has told us himself. Also, it is a mistake to imagine that Chénier was indifferent to what he saw, or recorded it in conventional terms. J. Fabre says of him that he had 'les yeux curieusement fermés au pittoresque réel de la route',[1] during

---

[1] F36, p. 46.

his journey to Italy; but it is evident from the above passage that he saw things as a poet sees them, not merely through literary reminiscences or with the practical eye of the professional traveller. It is enough to pick on one or two expressions such as 'cime harmonieuse', 'monts chevelus', 'sombres remparts', or the magnificent last line 'Où les bois, les cités, pendent en précipices', to feel the genuine impression that Switzerland made on him.

We have already mentioned his contact with the theologian Lavater, who later invented the theory of 'Physiognomy' which was to influence Gall. Unfortunately, his letter to Lavater does not tell us much: it is politely self-effacing, and, referring to his vocation as a poet, he wrote, 'Mais quoique j'aime l'art, je ne m'aveugle pas sur ma faiblesse à y atteindre.'[1] François de Pange made the same pilgrimage to Zürich in 1786, writing to Chénier, 'Il [Lavater] a autant de mémoire que tous ceux qui vous connaissent. Je lui ai parlé de vous et de M. de Trudaine. Il s'est rappelé avec plaisir les moments qu'il a passés auprès de vous.' More important, Lavater sent Chénier a manuscript of some forty pages, containing a translation into French of the philosopher's rather dull reflections on travel.[2] Further, Chénier was influenced by Lavater's famous theory of Physiognomy, in which he likened the heads and characters of human beings to certain animals. At the end of his *Essai* (Des Lettres et des Arts) Chénier argued that 'les ouvrages ont une physionomie; ils font connaître non seulement les humeurs et le caractère, mais même la figure'. From this he went on to speculate on the physical appearance of such writers as Plutarch, Newton, Locke, and Pope, affirming also that 'rien de commun, de bas ni d'impudent n'était sur le visage de Corneille ou de Milton'.

But Lavater's influence on Chénier did not end there. It contributed something essential to his satirical work; for, when in the *Ïambes* and his political essays he described the Jacobins as *tigres, dogues, vipères, loups, panthères*, he was closely reflecting Lavater's theory of psychophysical types.

[1] F34, t. i, p. 140. See also H1, p. 14, and C. E. Engel, *RDM*, 1 mai 1962, letter from Chénier to Lavater dated 26 octobre 1784.
[2] BMC 11811.

3

PASSION AND REVOLT

ALTHOUGH, both before and after his visit to Switzerland, Chénier was working hard, reading everything he could lay hands on in Greek, Latin, French, Spanish, and Italian, ranging from poetry to philosophy, astronomy to history and linguistics, his private life was just as unsettled as it had been before he joined the army.

Unfortunately for Chénier, who regarded himself as an expert in matters of love ('Je suis né pour l'amour, j'ai connu ses travaux'), he was destined to be a frustrated lover, like Keats, whom he so strongly resembles as a man and as a poet. It was part of their personal tragedy that, while gifted to the point of genius in their command of language and their faculty for synthesis, they could never reconcile their physical impulses with a proper understanding of the other sex, until it was too late. Whereas Keats's destiny foundered on a tardy but genuine affection for Fanny Brawne, so Chénier's amorous adventures led him finally to a deep but unsatisfactory affection for an ailing woman, Fanny Lecoulteux. Keats wrote in 1818: 'I am certain I have not a right feeling towards Women—at this moment I am striving to be just towards them but I cannot—is it because they fall so far beneath my Boyish imagination? . . . When I am among Women I have evil thoughts, malice, spleen—I cannot speak or be silent—I am full of Suspicions and therefore listen to nothing—I am in a hurry to be gone—You must be charitable and put all this perversity to my being disappointed since Boyhood. Yet with such feelings I am happier to be alone among crowds of men, by myself or with a friend or two.'[1] Both these poets, with all their capacity for sensitive feeling, squandered themselves on erotic adventures (offset, of course, by their powerful urge for friendship) before experiencing an enduring but impossible affection.

The women in Chénier's life were numerous, but few of them who are celebrated in the Elegies can be identified. There are a few poems written for and about a mysterious person designated as D.z.n., and a large number of poems for 'Camille'. But the import is the same in

---

[1] *Letters of John Keats*, ed. H. B. Forman, O.U.P., 1942, p. 192.

all of them, for Chénier constantly wrote as a man devoured by jealousy and frustration, repeatedly tricked and disappointed by women who would not take him seriously. Most of the elegies are of the same tone and quality, whoever inspired them, and perhaps it would not make much difference to our knowledge of the poet if the women could be identified.

It would be tempting to identify D.z.n. with Mlle Dozon, the famous opera-girl who married the actor Chéron. However, it is plain from the elegy 'Île charmante, Amphitrite, ta mère' that it could not be she, for she was born in France. Jean Fabre has recently suggested that the letters D.z.n. stand for *d'Azan*:

Je propose de lire D'Azan. Des géographes anciens donnaient le nom d'Azania à la côte de Mozambique et certains voyageurs modernes appellent d'Ajan ou d'Azan la partie de l'Océan indien où se trouvent les îles de France, Bourbon et Madagascar.[1]

It so happens that the woman whom Chénier addressed in some of his elegies as 'Camille' was born on the Ile Bourbon. Michèle de Santuary was the wife of an old man, M. de Bonneuil, who was master of the household of Monsieur, the king's brother, and very rich. The Bonneuils had a fine estate at Bonneuil-sur-Marne, near the forest of Sénart, on the road to Melun. Madame de Bonneuil was some ten years older than Chénier and had many lovers. She had three beautiful daughters, one of whom married the poet Arnault, and another the politician Regnault de Saint-Jean d'Angély, both of them subsequently, like Chénier, members of the Club des Feuillants.

When Madame de Bonneuil was arrested in 1793 and imprisoned in Sainte-Pélagie, the warrant contained the information that she was born in the Île Bourbon, was forty years of age, and described her as follows: 'Taille de 5 pieds, cheveux et sourcils châtain, yeux bruns, nez et bouche moyenne, visage et menton rond, front élevé.' Her Paris house was in the rue Neuve-Sainte-Catherine, which means that she must have been a fairly close neighbour of the Chéniers, before the Revolution.

Although Gabriel de Chénier rejected the idea that Madame de Bonneuil and Camille were the same person, while Becq de Fouquières suggested that only one of the elegies was destined for her and that the name 'Camille' was applied by Chénier to many different women,

[1] F34, p. 45. This identification enables Fabre to date the D.z.n. poems before the Camille cycle, arguing, 'Le choix d'un prénom, Camille, marque en quelque sorte, de la part de Chénier, une prise de possession.'

there is evidence that this is not the case. Madame de Bonneuil's son-in-law, Arnault, related in his *Mémoires d'un sexagénaire* that Chénier had loved her 'to the point of despair', referring to Madame Regnault as 'la fille d'une dame que votre frère André a éperdument aimée'.[1] It is not at all surprising that Chénier could love such a person, who was not only beautiful but gifted: she painted well, and sang to her own accompaniment on the harp, and from all accounts was a highly sensitive and cultured woman.

Although it was common in the eighteenth century for poets to write and publish very personal tributes to or complaints about their mistresses, Chénier's poems for Madame de Bonneuil are exceptional for their time, and are closer in spirit to the cycles written in the sixteenth century by Ronsard and Desportes. What makes this group of elegies highly original is their extraordinary range. Unlike Keats, who in his poetry showed but little sense of humour, Chénier gave full rein not only to his eroticism and jealousy, but also to his wit. Writing only for himself and for his friends, he did not hesitate to present himself in what others might have considered as the ridiculous position of the unwanted lover, and this he did not only with occasional melancholy and bitterness, which are to be expected, but with considerable humour.

There can be little doubt that the group of poems about D.z.n. were written at the beginning of Chénier's liaison with Madame de Bonneuil, and that D.z.n. is none other than Camille. It is surprising that in addition to his location, *d'Azan*, M. Fabre did not turn to internal evidence, for in the elegy beginning

> Hier en te quittant, enivré de tes charmes,
> Belle D.z.n. . . .

Chénier as much as indicates the forest of Sénart and Bonneuil-sur-Marne where, near her or in her absence, he walked incapable of thought or poetry; like a wounded beast:

> Tel que le faon blessé fuit, court, mais dans son flanc
> Traîne le plomb mortel qui fait couler son sang,
> Ainsi là, dans mon cœur, errant à l'aventure,
> Je porte cette belle, auteur de ma blessure.
> *Marne, Seine*, Apollon n'est plus dans vos forêts,
> Je ne le trouve plus dans vos antres secrets.
> Ah, si je vais encore rêver sous vos ombrages,
> Ce n'est plus que d'amour . . .

[1] F3, t. ii, pp. 178–9.

It is clear that, at first, Chénier was so dazzled by Madame de Bonneuil, and so perplexed by her mercurial nature, that he despaired of
being loved in return and tried to cure himself by avoiding her: but

> Si de livres, d'écrits, de sphères, de beaux-arts,
> Contre elle, contre lui je me fais des remparts,
> A l'aspect de l'Amour une terreur subite
> Met bientôt les beaux-arts et les Muses en fuite.

It will be noticed, already, that Chénier tried to avoid the seriousness
of his predicament by giving his lament a humorous turn. And
already, in the elegy to insomnia, beginning 'O nuit, nuit douloureuse,
ô toi, tardive aurore', we see the birth of that frantic jealousy and
suspicion which is more than a literary pose in the elegies:

> Dieu d'oubli, viens fermer mes yeux. O Dieu de paix,
> Sommeil, viens, fallût-il les fermer pour jamais.
> Un autre dans ses bras! ô douloureux outrage!
> Un autre! ô honte, ô mort, ô désespoir, ô rage!

He describes her changeable nature already:

> Souveraine au milieu d'une tremblante cour,
> Dans son léger caprice inégale et soudaine,
> Tendre et douce aujourd'hui, demain froide et hautaine . . .

While not setting too high a value (as Sainte-Beuve did) on all these
elegies, we must read them for the unexpected beauties they contain,
unforgettable lines rising spontaneously out of their conventional
context, lines which leap fifty years ahead to serve as a model for
another generation, such as, in the same elegy that we have been
quoting, the magnificent verse:

> Dans l'âme d'un poète un Dieu même respire.

It was only after the conquest of D.z.n. that Chénier, still anxious
to conceal her name, began to address her as Camille: there can be no
ambiguity about this, as two notes which are drafts for poems read:

AUTRE.

Seul, rêvant et passant le temps, suivant mon usage, à calculer les moments
où je l'ai vue et ceux où je la verrai, découragé, tout à coup je vis l'Espérance
. . . Elle me dit . . .

AUTRE.

O Espérance, tu es la première des Déesses . . . tu ne trompes point . . .
etc. . . . etc. . . . Tu m'avais dit que je fléchirais D' . . . et en effet (Jouissance).

The Camille cycle of elegies consists of ten completed poems. Some of them are very close in spirit and tone to the *Bucoliques*. There was an artificial grotto on the Bonneuil estate, in the eighteenth-century taste, to which the lovers sometimes repaired; it is celebrated in the classical style:

> Va, sonore habitant de la sombre vallée,
> Vole, invisible Écho, voix douce, pure, ailée,
> Qui, tant que de Paris m'éloignent les beaux jours,
> Aimes à répéter mes vers et mes amours:
> Les cieux sont enflammés; vole, dis à Camille
> Que je l'attends; qu'ici, moi, dans ce bel asile,
> Je l'attends; qu'un berceau de platanes épais
> La mène en cette grotte, où, l'autre jour, au frais,
> Pour nous, s'il lui souvient, l'heure ne fut point lente.
> Va: sous la grotte; ici; parmi l'herbe odorante
> D'où l'œil même du jour ne saurait approcher,
> Et qu'égaye en courant l'eau, fille du rocher.

Such verses show Chénier at his best, not merely making a statement but making a poem, an epigrammatic poem with a suave movement and melody which no poet of his century could rival. But at the same time, though he was obviously, in many of these poems, trying to write a kind of novel about Camille, a story of frustrated love, which he did his best to make impersonal and anonymous by transforming Madame de Bonneuil into Camille, he could not long escape into classical mythology, and the poems are full of genuine evidence about his own personality.

The first of the Camille elegies reflects a Rousseauistic love of solitude and reverie, and at the same time a very personal sense of isolation which owes nothing to literature and is the dominant sentiment of all the elegies:

> Ah, portons dans les bois ma triste inquiétude.
> O Camille! l'amour aime la solitude . . .

Like many a lover before and after him, in the absence of his beloved, Chénier had recourse to his imagination:

> Je la feins quelquefois attachée à mes pas;
> Je l'égare et l'entraîne en des routes secrètes.
> Absente, je la tiens en des grottes muettes . . .

The second elegy, which we have already quoted, not only achieves the independence of the poem from personal feeling but (like the lines above) tells us that the lovers retired for privacy to a little grotto on her estate. One of the most informative of the elegies reveals that, in her turn, Camille had gone on a journey, leaving the disconsolate poet alone in her country house waiting for her return. To his astonishment and delight she had taken the trouble of writing to him: 'O lignes que sa main, que son cœur a tracées', etc.[1] He relates the violent and tender scenes that had taken place between them:

> Mais pleurer est amer pour une belle absente;
> Il n'est doux de pleurer qu'aux pieds de son amante,
> Pour la voir s'attendrir, caresser vos douleurs
> Et de sa belle main vous essuyer vos pleurs;
> Vous baiser, vous gronder, jurer qu'elle vous aime,
> Vous défendre une larme et pleurer elle-même.

The eighteenth-century idea of sensibility did not exclude tears, and those critics who tend to regard Chénier as an effeminate poet lose sight of the fact that the open expression of the passions and emotions was less frowned upon then than it is now: there was indeed no barrier between the 'honnête homme', giving free rein to his emotions in the Age of Reason, and the romantic hero, alternately weeping and raging in the poems of Lamartine and Musset. In both cases the test for the critic lies in an estimate of sincerity, the most evasive of all the tasks of criticism. In Chénier's case we have not to forget that at the same time as these Elegies he was also writing an 'Art of Love' and that the reader might expect to find some hesitation between how Chénier the man actually behaved, and the way in which he thought a lover ought to behave. The problem is further complicated by his poetic artifice; for example the lines quoted above are partly taken from Propertius:

> Felix, qui potuit praesenti flere puellae:
> Non nihil adspersis gaudet amor lacrymis.

When, later in the same poem, he reproaches Camille for spending late nights dancing, gossiping, and drinking in society, at the expense of her health ('Mais, dieux! puisses-tu voir sous un ennui rongeur / De ta chère beauté flétrir toute la fleur / Plutôt que d'être heureuse à grossir tes conquêtes'), he is transposing Malherbe's 'Et vos jeunes beautés flétriront comme l'herbe'. Thus the proper reading of Chénier's elegies is a real challenge to the reader: they contain personal experience, often related in the style and imagery of classical sources,

---

[1] D13, t. iii, pp. 63–65.

but at the same time the personal experience is often deflected by the
intention of describing the behaviour of lovers in general. This does
not mean that he was insincere: it means that—like Baudelaire writing
for Madame Sabatier or Jeanne Duval—he was as much intent on
creating poems as on expressing his own tortured feelings.

However, in spite of this defence, it has to be admitted that Chénier's
elegies are largely narrations, and, though they are far more concentrated than the elegies of Le Brun (in which many parallels may be
found), not one of them has the sharp outline or depth of, say, Baudelaire's *La Béatrice*. Whereas Chénier's poems are descriptive and often
over-diluted because they are explicit (i.e. the theme of jealousy is
announced and embroidered on), Baudelaire's theme is implicit and
obliquely expressed: the whole of the poet's anguish, in Baudelaire's
case, is delivered without explanation in a brutal picture of treachery:
he saw

> La reine de mon cœur au regard nonpareil,
> Qui riait avec eux de ma sombre détresse
> Et leur versait parfois quelque sale caresse.

But such dynamic concentration is not to be found or even looked for
in Chénier's time, and he failed to find it in his elegies, while achieving
it brilliantly in many of the less personal *Bucoliques*. In other words
he was not capable of what G. Poulet calls 'distance intérieure', or impersonal vision in describing his own experiences, as Baudelaire was.
But the same objection may also be made against his Romantic successors, none of whom had the same impersonal power as Baudelaire.

That Chénier's offers to be the 'slave' of Madame de Bonneuil were
not insincere, and that his jealousy had an authentic foundation in love,
is also shown in this same elegy, which proves that his unhappy state
was the more painful because he had at some time imagined himself to
be her sole lover:

> Ah! ce n'est pas aimer que prendre sur soi-même
> De pouvoir vivre ainsi loin de l'objet qu'on aime.
> Il fut un temps, Camille, où plutôt qu'à me fuir
> Tout le pouvoir des Dieux t'eût contrainte à mourir.

So the poet's possessiveness was not merely a pretence, but (as in the
case of the poems written some years earlier for Lycoris) both arose
from his love and was one of the constant characteristics of his nature.
Asked by Madame de Bonneuil whether he had any particular wish, he
answered:

Et puis d'un ton charmant ta lettre me demande
Ce que je veux de toi, ce que je te commande.
Ce que je veux? dis-tu. Je veux que ton retour
Te paraisse bien lent; je veux que nuit et jour
Tu m'aimes! (Nuit et jour, hélas, je me tourmente.)
Présente au milieu d'eux, sois seule, sois absente;
Dors en pensant à moi; rêve-moi près de toi;
Ne vois que moi sans cesse, et sois toute avec moi.

By now the reader has probably made up his mind whether Chénier loved Madame de Bonneuil or not. The fourth elegy brings, to me at least, further conviction that he did; for it describes an angry scene followed by his submission, a submission which is extraordinary in a man of his pride:

Je viens lui pardonner; et c'est moi qu'elle accuse.
C'est moi qui suis injuste, ingrat, capricieux,
Je prends sur sa faiblesse un empire odieux;
Et sanglots et fureurs, injures menaçantes,
Et larmes, à couler toujours obéissantes;
Et pour la paix il faut que d'avoir eu raison,
Confus et repentant, je demande pardon.
O Camille, Camille . . .[1]

At the same time there was another side to his nature, to which he occasionally yielded like a shame-faced boy: in Camille's absence, or when she was cold towards him, he would escape with his friends into the company of lighter women. The fifth elegy, one of the finest he ever wrote, is, in spite of its light-heartedness and wit, a work in which his character is stripped bare. It begins with a triumphant *allegro*, not only throwing light on the easy manners of the period, but rejoining for a moment the pagan joy of the sixteenth century:

Et c'est Glycère, amis, chez qui la table est prête?
Et la belle Saxonne est aussi de la fête?
Et Rose qui jamais ne lasse les désirs,
Et dont la danse molle aiguillonne aux plaisirs?
Et sa sœur aux accents de sa voix la plus rare
Mêlera, dites-vous, les sons de la guitare?
Et nous aurons Julie, au rire étincelant,
Au sein plus que l'albâtre et solide et brillant?
Certe en pareille orgie autrefois je l'ai vue,
Ses longs cheveux épars, courante, demi-nue:

[1] D13, t. iii, p. 66.

En ses bruyantes nuits Cithéron n'a jamais
Vu Ménade plus belle errer dans ses forêts.
J'y consens. Avec vous je suis prêt à m'y rendre . . .

This lyrical *élan* is at once broken by the thought of Camille:

Allons. Mais si Camille, ô Dieux, vient à l'apprendre!
Quel orage suivra ce banquet tant vanté
S'il faut qu'à son oreille un mot en soit porté!

Thus an element of comedy is introduced into this account of a young man's prank, followed by a description of Camille's jealousy—as merciless as his own—and the scenes between them, and the extraordinary confession,

Que dis-je? sa vengeance ose en venir aux coups.
Elle me frappe. Et moi, je feins dans mon courroux
De la frapper aussi, mais d'une main légère,
Et je baise sa main impuissante et colère,
Car ses bras ne sont forts qu'aux amoureux exploits.

So far it is evident that all this violence is not much more than the play of love; the sense of comedy is preserved, though by now it is thin, and there follows a passage of deep psychological significance which reveals more of Chénier than perhaps he was aware of:

La fureur ne peut même aigrir sa douce voix.
Ah, je l'aime bien mieux injuste qu'indolente.
Sa colère me plaît et décèle une amante.
Si j'ai peur de la perdre, elle tremble à son tour,
Et la crainte inquiète est fille de l'amour.
L'assurance tranquille est d'un cœur insensible.
Loin, à mes ennemis une amante paisible.
Moi, je hais le repos. Quel que soit mon effroi
De voir de si beaux yeux irrités contre moi,
Je me plais à nourrir de communes alarmes.
Je veux pleurer moi-même, ou voir couler ses larmes;
Accuser un outrage, ou calmer un soupçon,
Et toujours pardonner ou demander pardon.[1]

'Moi, je hais le repos.' Robert Mauzi, in his thesis 'L'Idée du bonheur au XVIIIᵉ siècle', has, with great penetration, seized on this expression of Chénier's as a key to the *inquiétude* and fundamental unbalance of the eighteenth-century sensibility, of which exuberant rococo art was the natural outcome.[2] Chénier was constantly stretched on the rack of

[1] D13, t. iii, p. 68. [2] R. Mauzi, *L'Idée du bonheur au XVIIIᵉ siècle*, Colin, 1960.

opposing desires: if he yearned for calm, for all the peace and solitude of 'mon Louvre sous le toit', he also needed to live violently in the domain of the sensations; his stoicism was a mask which every now and then he had to throw off, like his purity, in an access of violence. This disequilibrium explains why, in spite of his repeated statements during the Revolution that he was above the *mêlée* and wanted to have nothing to do with politics, he was unable to still his sharp tongue and was not content until he had condemned himself to the scaffold.

The poem ends, after this intimate confession, with an outburst of Gallic humour which goes far beyond the Pléiade and reminds us of much medieval French verse, including certain passages of Villon. The poet and his friends, while he was describing his scenes with Camille (another eighteenth-century weakness which is repugnant to modern taste—we are equally nauseated by Des Grieux constantly narrating the latest stage of his love, to his friend), have by now reached their destination, the house of Glycère where the table is spread for supper:

> Mais quels éclats, amis? — C'est la voix de Julie.
> Entrons. Oh quelle nuit! joie, ivresse, folie!
> Que de seins envahis et mollement pressés!
> Malgré de vains efforts, que d'appas caressés!
> Que de charmes divins forcés dans leur retraite!
> Il faut que de la Seine, au cri de notre fête,
> Le flot résonne au loin de nos jeux égayé,
> Et qu'en son lit voisin le marchand éveillé
> Écoutant nos plaisirs d'une oreille jalouse,
> Redouble ses baisers à sa trop jeune épouse.

The astonishing thing about this poem, so spontaneous, so thoroughly knit together into an unbreakable unity, is that it contains a tissue of reminiscences, ranging from La Fontaine and Molière to Moschus, Propertius, Apuleius, Ovid, Horace, and Statius: even the line 'Le flot résonne au loin, de nos jeux égayé' has its source, which is in Propertius:

> Dulciaque ingratos adimant convivia somnos,
> Publica vicinae perstrepat aura viae.

Even more astonishing is the inability of critics to read their texts properly: how could Moland assert, in the light of such a poem as this, that the poetry of Chénier 'never smiles'?[1]

The sixth elegy is also a comedy, in which the lover, having sworn never to see Camille again, goes for a walk with his friend, but cannot

[1] D8, t. i, p. xv: 'André n'avait point de gaieté. . . . Dans toute son œuvre il n'y a pas un sourire.'

resist taking the walk as near to her house as possible—'Passons devant ses murs . . .' There is the same comic element, also, in the seventh elegy, when the poet goes to see Camille unexpectedly and another favourite has to depart in haste, while there is an amusing touch in the way he notices the cynical laughter of the concierge. The eighth elegy again hesitates between disgust and the desire for self-humiliation: the poet dreams of an idyllic existence in which (like Proust) he will imprison his beloved and look after her, making the bed and doing the housework and cooking, combing her hair and attending to her: 'c'est moi qui ferai tout'. Yet another light is thrown on Chénier during this period, by the ninth elegy, in which he tries to drown his despair in drink—which in his poor state of health was a form of suicide. Though he loves Camille no more, every glass of wine, whether Andalusian, Madeira, Bordeaux, or Cyprus, merely forms her image more clearly in his mind. But is there not a real tragedy of the emotions beneath this traditional farce?

> Ah, je l'aimais alors! Je l'aimerais encore,
> Si de tout conquérir la soif qui la dévore
> Eût flatté mon orgueil au lieu de l'outrager;
> Si mon amour n'avait qu'un outrage à venger;
> Si vingt crimes nouveaux n'avaient trop su l'éteindre;
> *Si je ne l'abhorrais.* Ah, qu'un cœur est à plaindre
> De s'être à son amour longtemps accoutumé,
> Quand il faut n'aimer plus ce qu'on a tant aimé!
> Pourquoi, grands Dieux, pourquoi la fîtes-vous si belle?[1]

And in spite of this 'Si je ne l'abhorrais' the submission begins all over again, in a way which the reader no longer finds comic, but painful:

> Riez, amis, nommez ma fureur insensée.
> Vous n'aimez pas, et j'aime; et je brûle, et je pars
> Me coucher sur sa porte, implorer ses regards . . .

If we are forced, in the end, rather impatiently to ask why in his peculiar way Chénier was so obstinately attracted to a woman who so humiliated him, the answer is to be found in the Epistles. If in one of the elegies ('Je suis né pour l'amour . . .') he talked, not for the first or last time, of suicide,

> Et, de mes yeux séduits plaignant la trahison,
> M'indiquaient l'hellébore, ami de la raison . . .

in the *Épître aux deux Frères Trudaine*, beginning

[1] D13, t. iii, p. 77.

Amis, couple chéri, cœurs formés pour le mien
Je suis libre, Camille à mes yeux n'est plus rien . . .

we find him dreaming of another escape, a second visit to Switzerland.
But a fundamental reason—apart from her beauty—why Chénier was
so attached to her, was because she was intelligent and appreciated and
encouraged his work. This is seen in the Epistle to Abel de Malartic
(beginning 'Pourquoi de mes loisirs accuser la langueur?'). Replying
to Malartic, who accuses him of laziness and blames Camille for it, he
replies that in his youth he was writing heroic poetry

— J'animais aux combats ma lyre turbulente, —

but after meeting Camille he could celebrate only her, not because he
willed it but because she transformed the world for him:

Tout pour elle a des vers. Ils renaissent en foule;
Ils brillent dans les flots du ruisseau qui s'écoule;
Ils prennent des oiseaux la voix et les couleurs,
Je les trouve cachés dans les replis des fleurs . . .

Unfortunately the only love-poems that have survived from the
Camille cycle are negative, and perhaps were not intended for Camille's
eyes: those that she received from him have passed into oblivion. But
she did inspire him and help him to write:

Elle me fait chanter, amoureuse Ménade,
Des combats de Paphos une longue Iliade;
Et si de mes projets le vol s'est abaissé,
A la lyre d'Homère ils n'ont pas renoncé.
Mais en la dépouillant de ses cordes guerrières
Ma main n'a su garder que les cordes moins fières.

In other words, Abel de Malartic forgot—as modern critics of Chénier
tend to forget—that there is not only the Homer of the *Iliad*, but the
Homer of the *Odyssey*, the Homer who wrote the only great epic of
love and eroticism. Whatever there may be of purely literary inspiration in the elegies that have survived, the accents of truth are, I think,
very moving in the positive picture of a cultured and appreciative
Camille given in this Epistle:

Hier, entre ses bras, sur sa lèvre fidèle,
J'ai surpris quelques vers que j'avais faits pour elle,
Et sa bouche, au moment que je l'allais quitter,
M'a dit: 'Tes vers sont doux, j'aime à les répéter'.

Here in four lines is described one of the purest and the rarest of

pleasures to which any poet can aspire: to know that the works of his
mind vibrate in the heart of the woman he loves.

After being the mistress of an indigent poet, Madame de Bonneuil
had a long liaison with the politician, Cazalès. Chénier's friend Montlosier makes a reference to him, without mentioning his name, in
a note which he wrote in exile:

> Madame de Bonneuil, son amie [i.e. l'amie de Cazalès] était venue à
> travers beaucoup de dangers le voir à Londres. Depuis longtemps, c'est-à-
> dire depuis le commencement de leur liaison, j'avais été mis en confidence
> par Madame de Bonneuil elle-même de ses sentiments, et du nouvel entraîne-
> ment dont Cazalès était l'objet. Je dis nouvel entraînement, *car elle avait
> sacrifié pour cela d'autres rapports qui étaient déjà anciens.*[1]

Cazalès was just as jealous of Madame de Bonneuil's friendship with
Montlosier as Chénier had been jealous of her in the past. A note adds:

> Madame de Bonneuil, née Santuary, était comme sa sœur Mme d'Épre-
> mesnil, une créole de l'île Bourbon et 'une des personnes les plus régulière-
> ment jolies', dit d'Espinchal [*Journal inédit*]. Incarcérée pendant la Terreur,
> sauvée par Thermidor, elle passa à l'étranger. Avant la Révolution elle avait
> été maîtresse d'André Chénier, qui l'a célébrée dans ses poèmes sous le nom
> de Camille.

The date of Mme de Bonneuil's death is not known.

If Chénier was unfortunate in love, he found much consolation in
his widening circle of friends. The list of aristocratic families in which
he moved at this time is too long for quotation. At the famous
suppers chez Grimod de la Reynière, Chénier was seen by Rétif de la
Bretonne in the company of Pons de Verdun, Fontanes, Sébastien
Mercier, the chevalier de Castellane, and the comte de Narbonne who
was later to become a Girondin minister. He was friendly with the
marquis de Moriolles, at whose house the chevalier de Florian offered
him a poem in Spanish.[2] Moriolles was a cousin of de Brazais, and was
friendly with both Chénier and Cazalès, so it is quite likely that
Chénier was well acquainted with his rival for Camille's affections.
Unfortunately, de Moriolles does not mention Chénier in his
memoirs.

The Trudaines were already following their father's example by

---

[1] F72.
[2] The poem may be seen in D7, t. i, pp. xxxvi–xxxvii. The manuscript at Carcassonne
carries the note by Chénier, 'Ces vers du chevalier de Florian m'ont été donnés par lui,
hier mardi, 7 février 1786, après dîner chez le marquis de Moriolles.'

becoming known as patrons of the arts, and they had taken under their protection the brilliant young painter Louis David, from whom they commissioned both the 'Three Horaces' and 'The Death of Socrates'. 'Chénier de Saint-André', as he now called himself, rapidly became a close companion and admirer of David: it is said that it was Chénier who advised David on the pose to be taken by Socrates in his famous painting. Chénier gave it a dramatic turn by insisting that Socrates should not hold the cup of hemlock in his hand, but calmly address his disciples while the cup is held by his waiting slave.[1] David made a portrait of Chénier at this time. Though the attribution to David of the portrait in the Carnavalet Museum has recently been contested by Gabriel Sarraute in his *Essai d'iconographie*, it is a fine work in David's style, and anyone who has seen both must recognize it as a companion piece to David's portrait of Marie-Joseph Chénier which is now at Versailles.[2] The friendship between the poet and the painter lasted for some ten years, and was broken only when they took different paths during the Revolution, David, who became the official painter of the Convention, not only supported the Jacobins but was friendly with some of the most odious of them, such as Chénier's enemy Collot d'Herbois. Even then, though towards the end of his life Chénier is supposed to have referred to him as 'le stupide David', he wrote an article on historical painting in 1792 in which, in spite of their political enmity, he described David as one of the greatest historical painters of all time.[3]

In 1785 Chénier began a friendship with another painter, the beautiful Marie Cosway, wife of the miniaturist Richard Cosway. Chénier wrote two poems for her, full of admiration and respect for her talents and her beauty, and later, in London, he was a frequent visitor to the Cosways' house in Pall Mall. At the same time he met the poet Niemcewicz, one of her admirers, and the great Polish poet and politician wrote on one of his manuscripts 'Niemciewicz sera toujours ami de Saint-André'.[4] We must close the list with the names of the countess of Albany and her companion, the Italian poet Alfieri.

---

[1] The anecdote given by C. Blanc in *L'Histoire des peintres* is as follows: 'Dans son tableau de la *Mort de Socrate*, David avait d'abord représenté Socrate tenant la coupe que lui offrait l'esclave en pleurs. "Non, non," lui dit André Chénier, "Socrate ne la saisira que lorsqu'il aura fini de parler."'

[2] See F97, p. 319. This portrait was unpopular with the Chénier family, who regarded the face as too square.   [3] See below, p. 229.

[4] The manuscript (BMC 11816) is of a poem, in Niemcewicz's hand, attributed by G. de Chénier to the Polish poet, and by Dimoff to A. C.

She had been the wife of the last of the Stuarts, while Alfieri was the greatest Italian poet of his day. This friendship, as we shall see, was both firm and intimate, and only the separation that came about through the events of the Revolution could end it. We shall find the countess writing to him in 1790 a delightfully cheerful and personal letter in which she chaffs him for eating too much.[1] As for Alfieri, he was already full of republican principles, and, like Chénier, was to adopt more moderate opinions only after mob-rule began and it became evident that France was not ripe for democratic government. At this time Alfieri was writing a book on 'The Prince and Letters' which he showed to Chénier, on whom it had a certain influence, for we find him more than once repeating Alfieri's thesis that literature and the arts can thrive only where there is political liberty. Alfieri also addressed to Chénier a long epistle in verse.[2]

Meanwhile, towards the end of 1786 (probably from September to December),[3] Chénier and the Trudaines set off for another tour, this time in Italy. It appears from Chénier's numerous verses on the subject that the original intention was for them to cross the Mediterranean, visiting Greece and even Constantinople, the place of his birth; but that another bout of sickness obliged him to cut the journey short and return to France. In an Epistle probably intended for the brothers de Pange,

> Vous restez, mes amis, dans ces murs où la Seine
> Voit sans cesse embellir les bords dont elle est reine,

he made it clear that he was travelling for his health:

> Moi, l'espoir du repos et du bonheur peut-être,
> Cette fureur d'errer, de voir et de connaître,
> La santé que j'appelle et qui fuit mes douleurs . . .

and gave some idea of what he hoped to see abroad:

> Marseille où l'Orient amène la fortune,
> Et Venise élevée à l'hymen de Neptune,
> Le Tibre, fleuve-roi, Rome, fille de Mars,
> Qui régna par la glaive et règne par les arts;
> Athènes qui n'est plus, et Byzance ma mère;
> Smyrne qu'habite encor le souvenir d'Homère.
> Croyez, car en tous lieux mon cœur m'aura suivi,
> Que partout où je vais vous avez un ami.[4]

[1] See below, pp. 90–91.
[2] *Del Principe et delle Lettere* did not appear until 1795. For Alfieri's poem (1789) see below, p. 81.
[3] F34, t. i, pp. 192 et seq.   [4] D13, t. iii, pp. 10–11.

It is amusing and touching to see how, in this last line, Chénier was quoting the words from Montesquieu with which he had astonished his old abbé when he was fourteen: 'Sois sûr qu'en quelque lieu du monde où je sois, tu as un ami fidèle.'[1] It also emerges from this poem that Chénier was hoping to be away from France for two years:

> Si je vis, le soleil aura passé deux fois
> Dans les douze palais où resident les mois,
> D'une double moisson la grange sera pleine,
> Avant que dans vos bras la voile nous ramène.

We do not know how long the absence lasted, but there are fragments about the Beaujolais region, about 'les beautés de Marseille', about Nice, 'cette ville où les étrangers . . . les orangers . . . etc.', which were to produce a poem based on a sonnet by Petrarch, as well as others about Naples and Rome. There is evidence, also, that Chénier was at this time trying to escape from the bondage of Camille:

> Partons, la voile est prête, et Byzance m'appelle.
> Je suis vaincu, je fuis. Au joug d'une cruelle
> Le temps, les longues mers peuvent seuls m'arracher.
> Ses traits que malgré moi je vais toujours chercher,
> Son image partout à mes yeux répandue,
> Et les lieux qu'elle habite, et ceux où je l'ai vue,
> Son nom qui me poursuit, tout offre à tout moment
> Au feu qui me consume un funeste aliment . . .

All that remains from this journey are some interesting fragments of elegies, some of which Chénier marked 'Élégies italiennes'. These show that, whatever his state of health, Chénier remained as passionate and self-indulgent as ever: like Boswell he was obsessed by women, constantly making good resolutions which he could not keep:

> Tel j'étais autrefois et tel je suis encor,
> Quand ma main imprudente a tari mon trésor,
> Ou la nuit, accourant au sortir de la table,
> Si Laure m'a fermé le seuil inexorable,
> Je regagne mon toit. Là, lecteur studieux,
> Content et sans désirs, je rends grâces aux Dieux . . .

Then he goes on to describe how these good intentions are quickly broken as soon as he has some money in his purse.

Another of the Italian Elegies is a kind of prayer for calm and wisdom in which the poet even looks forward enviously to old age:

---

[1] See above, p. 14.

> . . . Pour chercher les beaux-arts,
> Des Alpes vainement j'ai franchi les remparts;
> Rome d'amours en foule assiège mon asile.
> Sage vieillesse, accours, ô Déesse tranquille,
> De ma jeune saison éteins ces feux brûlants.

At the same time it is questionable whether these elegies have to be taken literally: this poem is followed by a prose note to indicate its further development: 'Eh bien, allons, conduis-moi aux pieds de . . . Je ne refuse aucun esclavage . . . Conduis-moi vers elle, puisque c'est elle que tu me rappelles toujours . . . Allons, suivons les fureurs de l'âge . . . Mais puisse-t-il passer vite! Puisse venir la vieillesse . . . La vieillesse seule est heureuse (contredire pied à pied l'élégie contre la vieillesse . . .).' All this might have been taken only as a literary exercise were it not for the energetic and voluptuous elegy for 'la belle Romaine':

> Oh, c'est toi. Je t'attends, ô ma belle Romaine.
> Chez toi, dans cet asile où le soir nous ramène,
> Seul je mourais d'attendre et tu ne venais pas.
> Mon cœur en palpitant a reconnu tes pas . . .
>
> Ces glaces, tant de fois belles de ta presence,
> Ces coussins odorants, d'aromates remplis,
> Sous tes membres divins tant de fois amollis,
> Ces franges en festons que tes mains ont touchées,
>
> Ces fleurs dans ces cristaux par toi-même attachées,
> L'air du soir si suave à la fin d'un beau jour,
> Tout embrasait mon sang; tout mon sang est amour . . .

However much Chénier lamented the ardours of his youth it is evident that his travel to Italy was not wasted. He returned from it, as Dimoff has pointed out, with an increased knowledge of and enthusiasm for painting and sculpture, while he perfected his knowledge of Italian to the point of being able to write poems in that language. Further, it was probably at this stage of his life that he began to learn Arabic, and began writing his biblical poem, *Susanne*, which like all his major projects remained unfinished: a note written at this time reads: 'Je vais achevant mon Hermès . . . Surtout les champs de tel et tel pays m'ont vu travailler avec délices mon poème de *Susanne*.' He also wrote, at this time, a fine piece about Rome, which, for some reason, he decided to include in his poem *L'Amérique*: it begins:

> Que ton œil voyageur de peuples en déserts
> Parcoure l'ancien monde et traverse les mers,

> Rome antique partout, Rome, Rome immortelle
> Vit et respire, et tout semble vivre par elle . . .

The Italian tour ended with a powerful elegy celebrating his return, written with such ease and strength that we see how, at the age of twenty-four, Chénier was now fully in possession of his medium:

> Ainsi, vainqueur de Troie et des vents et des flots,
> D'un navire emprunté pressant les matelots,
> Le fils du vieux Laërte arrive en sa patrie,
> Baise, en pleurant, le sol de son île chérie . . .

He continues by defending his elegies as a means of direct personal expression:

> Il est bien doux d'avoir dans sa vie innocente
> Une muse naïve et de haines exempte,
> Dont l'honnête candeur ne garde aucun secret . . .

And of the thoughts and loves of his youth he writes, with an endearing simplicity,

> Tous sont divers, et tous furent vrais un moment.

This elegy concludes with a reference to the failure of his brother Marie-Joseph's play, *Alzémire*, which was booed off the stage in November 1786: though Chénier describes himself as one

> Dont la main est sans tache et n'a connu jamais
> Le fiel dont la satire envenime ses traits,

it is characteristic that on his return, instead of finishing the works he had begun, he set about writing a long satirical poem, on the lines of the *Dunciad*, which was to be called *Les Cyclopes littéraires* or *La République des lettres* and which was a violent attack on the literary pundits and poetasters of his time.

There is little doubt that Marie-Joseph's first setback, which came about in spite of the support of Palissot and other influential writers, was a decisive moment in André Chénier's career. If, as a man, he was still immature and on his return from Italy was again dominated by his irrational attachment to Camille, the defeat of *Alzémire* helped him to crystallize certain aspects of his thought. It is evident from *La République des lettres* that, in attacking the Academy, he was striking with an almost republican conviction against one of the typical abuses of the *ancien régime*, which showered honours on hacks and noble amateurs while genuine writers—Gilbert, Malfilâtre, and of course the two young Chéniers themselves—had to live and write on a pittance.

In spite of the generous help of the Trudaines, he also denounced the system of patronage without which it was then almost impossible for a young man to write at all.

A further consequence, for Chénier, of his brother's temporary defeat was that if he ever had any intention of publishing his own poems he now put that thought aside, though by now he must have completed many pieces in the *Bucoliques*.

The year 1787 was thus to be an important one for Chénier, who was by now approaching his majority (twenty-five) and, looking round for some possible occupation, must have seen many a path closed to him.[1] The Trudaines had managed to buy themselves places as legal counsellors to the Paris Parliament, although they were under the required age for that office. What could Chénier do? During the months when he was looking out for work his political feelings crystallized in two poems which stand out from his previous manner. The first, an eclogue, *La Liberté*, to be found in the *Bucoliques*, is a discussion between a goatherd and a shepherd, one of them happy and prosperous because he is free, the other leading practically the same pastoral existence but morose and sickly because he is a slave. Biographers have, I think, tended to read too much into this poem. Chénier wrote several fragments about slaves, and in *La Liberté* the goatherd is such a churl that it would be going too far to identify him with the poet himself. When the shepherd tries to cheer him, offering him his flute, he replies:

> Je hais tous vos plaisirs, les fleurs, et la rosée,
> Et de vos rossignols les soupirs caressants.
> Rien ne plaît à mon cœur, rien ne flatte mes sens.
> Je suis esclave.

And he even adds to this:

> Comme moi je voudrais que tu fusses esclave.

The shepherd is not, then, Chénier lamenting his own fate, but the poem as a whole is obviously an illustration of the theories of Alfieri's *The Prince and Letters*, which has already been mentioned. Chénier

---

[1] A further reason for seeking work was that his father appears to have had a serious illness in 1787. Marie-Joseph wrote an epistle to his father, in that year, beginning with the lines

> Le ciel a tout à coup fermé le précipice;
> A nos larmes, mon père, il est enfin propice;
> Tes jours dans les douleurs à demi consumés
> Par les soins de Geoffroi sont enfin rallumés.

PLATE 2

A supposed portrait of André Chénier, by Louis David?
Musée Carnavalet

wrote in one of his elegies 'Qui ne sait être pauvre est né pour l'esclavage', and this admirable sentiment is repeated at length in the *Essai sur la décadence des lettres et des arts*: 'Que j'aime le sage qui se plaît dans sa médiocrité, qui goûte trop son bonheur pour y songer, qui n'aime point les grands, etc.' But in *La Liberté* the slave is, precisely, a man who cannot accept his condition because it is not freely chosen but inflicted upon him. In *La République des Lettres* occurs the isolated line 'Les arts indépendants veulent une âme libre'. Then in *L'Invention* he wrote of Homer and Virgil

> Mais leurs mœurs et leurs lois, et mille autres hasards
> Rendaient leur siècle heureux plus propice aux beaux-arts.

The influence of society on literature was the main theme of Chénier's *Essai*, and it is quite likely that his relationship to Alfieri resembled that of Baudelaire to Poe: that is to say, that he had already reached these conclusions independently before meeting the Italian poet. This is stated clearly towards the end of the *Essai*: though in the context in which the statement was placed he was speaking about 'l'imitation inventrice':

> Je veux de plus que l'on sache qu'avant que cet ouvrage entièrement fait fût entièrement écrit, Vittorio Alfieri d'Asti ... me lut ses trois livres du *Prince et des Lettres* qui n'étaient pas encore imprimés. Comme l'unanimité de sentiments et d'opinions avait été la première cause qui nous lia d'amitié, je ne fus pas si étonné que flatté de voir souvent une honorable ressemblance entre ce que j'avais écrit et ce que j'écrivais.[1]

This means that Chénier had already written some of *L'Invention*, and of the *Essai sur la décadence des lettres et des arts* and *La République des lettres*, before meeting Alfieri in 1786.

In any case, *La Liberté* reflects the thought of Rousseau as much as Alfieri's, for Rousseau had maintained that 'C'est la force et la liberté qui font les excellents hommes; la faiblesse et l'esclavage n'ont jamais fait que des méchants'. But Chénier gave as powerful a portrait of the tyrant as of the slave:

> Oui, donne et sois maudit; car si j'étais plus sage
> Ces dons sont pour mon cœur d'un sinistre présage.

---

[1] See D22, p. 691. An examination of Alfieri's book shows that there was no plagiarism on Chénier's part. Alfieri wrote in a ferociously sarcastic style, pushed almost to the point of ridicule, arguing that Princes should keep artists in complete slavery in order to get the best out of them, and that tyranny is the only paying proposition. Only in their central thesis, that great art can only be created by free men, did the two writers meet.

De mon despote avare ils choqueront les yeux.
Il ne croit pas qu'on donne; il est fourbe, envieux;
Il dira que chez lui j'ai volé le salaire
Dont j'aurais dû payer les chevreaux et la mère,
Et, d'un si beau prétexte ardent à se servir,
C'est à moi que lui-même il viendra les ravir.

La Liberté is a curious illustration of how Chénier was able to imitate perfectly an ancient form, while modernizing it by turning it to a satirical purpose and giving it a political edge applicable to his own time. If it has been greatly praised, it is, however, as much for historical as for aesthetic reasons: it really stands out as a false note in its context of the *Bucoliques*. It is interesting to see that the poem was written in three days, from the 10th to the 12th of March 1787, at a time when the poet's political views were hardening, towards the Left.[1]

The much more important poem, *Hymne à la Justice*, was written at about the same time as *La Liberté*, before Chénier went to England. His manuscripts show that it was to form part of a series of 'hymns' including those to Poverty and Necessity. Another, the *Hymne au Temps*, was to be not so much about Time as about the period he was living in. ('Ne point parler de faux, ni de tous ces autres emblèmes antiques . . . Tâcher d'en inventer de nouveaux . . . Tu révèles les crimes cachés, tu fais connaitre l'innocence.') To this group should be added *La France libre*, a poem obviously begun, though it remains unfinished, early during the Revolution, for it contains references to the constitution-maker, Sieyès, and also to Mirabeau.

If we anticipate, it is because the *Hymne à la Justice* not only is the first of Chénier's important political poems (unless parts of *La République des lettres* are to be counted as such) but was written at a time when the first murmurs of revolution were beginning to be heard all over France. Calonne had been appointed Finance Minister in 1785, but in spite of his genuine desire for reform he was dismissed in 1787. Such was the state of France at that time that the Assembly of Notables had to be called in 1787, leading to the appointment of Brienne in the same year. During Chénier's absence in London, Brienne was dismissed in 1788 and replaced by Necker. Already in 1787 there were wild rumours that the States-General would be called, and there were outbursts of violence in the provinces. We have not to forget, either, that Chénier had recently crossed France from one end

[1] Becq de Fouquières (D6) pointed out that the 10th of March 1787 was a Saturday, and the 12th a Monday.

to the other, and that the signs of oppression and unrest which he mentions in the *Hymne à la Justice* were something that he had seen with his own eyes.

The *Hymne à la Justice* has a lyrical impulse which is the only saving grace of any political commentary in verse. There had been nothing to compare with it in French poetry since Ronsard's *Discours des misères de ce temps*, for such works as Voltaire's *Désastre de Lisbonne* are much more generalized.

The draft of the poem begins with a prose note:

A la Justice

J'ai dit: O vierge adorée, en quels lieux te chercher?... Parler ensuite des innocents accusés et condamnés, des hommes éloquents qui les défendent et qui encourent l'inimitié des juges ignares et pervers. Finir par: Non, je ne veux plus vivre...

This last line was completed in the poem as 'Non, je ne veux plus vivre en ce séjour servile'; in other words, when Chénier left France to work in the French Embassy in London it was not only because a good job offered itself, but out of disgust with his own country.

The poem begins with a fine tribute to France:

> France, ô belle contrée, ô terre généreuse,
> Que les dieux complaisants formaient pour être heureuse,
> Tu ne sens point du nord les glaçantes horreurs,
> Le midi de ses feux t'épargne les fureurs...

He celebrates various beautiful provinces, Beaune, Provence, Aquitaine, and the fine rivers and canals, and even the roads—the best in Europe at that time, as they are now—which had been built by an ancestor of the Trudaines:

> L'indomptable Garonne aux vagues insensées,
> Le Rhône impétueux, fils des Alpes glacées,
> La Seine au flot royal, la Loire dans son sein
> Incertaine...
> Et ces vastes chemins en tous lieux départis,
> Où l'étranger, à l'aise achevant son voyage
> Pense au nom des Trudaine et bénit leur ouvrage.

After praising the courage and industry of the French peasantry, the tone suddenly changes:

> J'ai vu dans tes hameaux la plaintive misère,
> La mendicité blême et la douleur amère.

> Je t'ai vu dans tes biens, indigent laboureur,
> D'un fisc avare et dur maudissant la rigueur.

He goes on to condemn the same evils that Arthur Young noted during his travels in France before the Revolution:

> Tu vois sous les soldats les villes gémissantes,
> Corvée, impôts rongeurs, tributs, taxes pesantes,
> Le sel, fils de la terre, ou même l'eau des mers,
> Source d'oppressions et de fléaux divers;
> Vingt brigands, revêtus du nom sacré du prince,
> S'unir à déchirer une triste province,

and continues on a prophetic note, two years before the event,

> O sainte Égalité, dissipe nos ténèbres,
> Renverse les verrous, les Bastilles funèbres . . .

It is evident from certain passages in the poem that Chénier had no new ideas about how the peasants' lot could be changed, beyond applying the doctrine of the Physiocrats (deriving from Shaftesbury and Bolingbroke) which was a popular theory at that time: he invoked two great Ministers who believed in these measures but had been dismissed from office:

> Malesherbes, Turgot, ô vous en qui la France
> Vit luire, hélas, en vain, sa dernière espérance,
> Ministres dont le cœur a connu la pitié,
> Ministres dont le nom ne s'est point oublié.
> Ah, si de telles mains, justement souveraines,
> Toujours de cet empire avaient tenu les rênes!
> L'équité clairvoyante aurait régné sur nous,
> Le faible aurait osé respirer près de vous . . .

It is after this invocation to Malesherbes and Turgot—he had already met Malesherbes, and they were to meet again in dramatic circumstances when Chénier acted as his secretary in preparing the defence of Louis XVI a few weeks before his death—that Chénier introduced a more personal note into the poem:

> *Non, je ne veux plus vivre en ce séjour servile;*
> J'irai, j'irai bien loin me chercher un asile,
> Un asile à ma vie en son paisible cours,
> Une tombe à ma cendre à la fin de mes jours . . .
>
> Où mon cœur, respirant un ciel étranger
> Ne verra plus des maux qu'il ne peut soulager,

> Où mes yeux éloignés des publiques misères
> Ne verront plus partout les larmes de mes frères . . .

This is a beautiful poem, well constructed, with an energy and sweetness that fully match the importance of its theme. Political poetry,
directly written, can be the dullest of literary productions, and it can
only survive when thought is, as it were, embalmed in lyricism: this is
the case with Burns and Blake, with Byron and Hugo, with Auden's
wonderful poem, *Spain*, which is a classic of our literature. In spite of
its imperfections I would make the same claim for Chénier's *Hymne
à la Justice*, which has been adversely criticized by J. Fabre.[1] These
imperfections are in neither the conception of the theme nor its structure, for these are perfect: it has an impeccable balance between description, political commentary, and personal expression: the transitions of
tone are well calculated, and didacticism never runs away with the
fundamental elegiac manner. The faults are minor ones, faults of slack-
ness and even incorrectness: for instance he speaks of an '*amas* de
fleuves'—a heap of rivers—whereas he could as well have written
nombre instead of *amas*. Apart from this and other small faults, for
instance an occasional tendency to use banal epithets—*fer intrépide*,
usurpateur *avide*—in order to make a rhyme, it is a beautiful poem.
It contains perhaps the loveliest praise of Provence that has ever been
written by any French poet:

> La Provence odorante et de Zéphire aimée
> Respire sur ses mers une haleine embaumée,
> Au bord des flots couvrant, délicieux trésor,
> L'orange et le citron de leur tunique d'or;
> Et plus loin, au penchant des collines pierreuses,
> Forme la grasse olive aux liqueurs savoureuses,
> Et ces réseaux légers, diaphanes habits,
> Où la fraîche grenade enferme ses rubis.
> Sur tes rochers touffus la chèvre se hérisse,
> Tes prés enflent de lait la féconde génisse,
> Et tu vois tes brebis, sur le jeune gazon,
> Épaissir le tissu de leur blanche toison.

'J'irai, j'irai bien loin me chercher un asile'—certainly the 'bien loin'
does not quite indicate the exile in London which was now awaiting
Chénier. He might have been thinking of going to Constantinople, or
to Smyrna (where he had an uncle), or perhaps to the Île de France to

---

[1] F36, p. 216, speaks of 'la véhémence du ton, la grandiloquence du style, l'incohérente
banalité des images'—a most surprising judgement.

join his sister. What is certain is that if Chénier had published his *Hymne à la Justice* he would have been famous overnight, and perhaps thrown into the Bastille. Maybe he was afraid of sacrificing the career that was now opening to him, in the service of the very government he so much condemned?

4

THE CHEVALIER IN LONDON

(1787–90)

IN the meantime, while still, so far as is known, the slave of Madame de Bonneuil, Chénier had been making many new friends, some of whom were to have an influence on his later destiny. Some were only superficial acquaintances—the marquise de Clermont-Tonnerre, the princesse de Chalais, the comtesse d'Argenson, Madame de Luynes, the comtesse Beauharnais, the dukes of Mailli and Montmorency, and Count Potocki. Then there were such writers as Beaumarchais, Pelletier, Mercier, Joubert, Rivarol, Condorcet, Chamfort, who moved in the same social circles and with some of whom he was to have further relations during the Revolution.

Of the new friends who really counted for his later life, one was Françoise (Fanny) Lecoulteux (also spelt Lecouteulx), the daughter of Madame Pourrat, whom he met in the summer of 1787 through the intermediary of François de Pange.[1] They had a house at Passy and a château at Voisins. Madame Lecoulteux was happily married and was not in good health: her children and herself were to die of tuberculosis. It was this beautiful, delicate woman who was to become the last and truest love of his life. At the same time, also through de Pange, he was introduced to the beautiful Madame de Beaumont, daughter of the statesman Montmorin who was to be one of Louis XVI's ablest ministers. Chénier's friendship with her became so strong that he used to submit his poems to her criticism, and gave her copies of them: their friendship appears to have reached its height in the year 1791.[2] One of Montmorin's daughters had recently married the chevalier de La Luzerne, French ambassador to the United States. It is said that Madame de Beaumont introduced Chénier to La Luzerne —a sickly man, not much older than the poet himself—who was

---

[1] However, G. Walter (F101), p. 274, speaking of their relationship in 1793–4, states: 'Ils se connaissent déjà depuis une bonne dizaine d'années.'

[2] On Mme de Beaumont see Bardoux (F6b). Her closest friends in the 1780's were the Trudaines and de Panges, who introduced Chénier to her. In her turn she took him to the Pourrats' salon (p. 19). For their later friendship, see ch. 5 and p. 81, ibid.

about to be appointed Ambassador to London. La Luzerne invited Chénier to accompany him as his secretary, and the poet accepted. This phase in his career completes in an extraordinary way the intellectual and social formation which brings him so close to the poets of the Pléiade.

It was, indeed, time that André Chénier decided on a career. Though he had already written an enormous amount he had not published a line, and in this sense had not justified himself in his own eyes or those of his parents. On the other hand his friends were all placed and mounting in the hierarchy, as it then was. His brothers, after many difficulties, had steady careers before them. His younger brother, Marie-Joseph, had written two plays and his name was already well known in Paris. It did not matter that his work was superficial and for the most part a cheap imitation of the tragedies of Voltaire: Marie-Joseph, one of the shallowest writers who ever put pen to paper, knew how to take the easiest roads to the easiest forms of success. And now, after many years of work, old Louis de Chénier, that admirable and unselfish toiler, had produced his history of the Moors, in three volumes—a work unique at that time—only to see it fall flat, for neither the government nor the public were any longer interested in Morocco at a time when all eyes were turned towards America and England, and when the first throes of revolution were already being felt in France itself. 'André must work', must have been his conclusion.

Thus it was that on the 6th of December 1787 Chénier set out from Calais on a stormy day, to sail to Dover. He was not—nor is anyone at that time of the year—a good sailor, and he wrote a poem about the occasion which reminds us of a sonnet on the same subject by Rupert Brooke:

> Ainsi, lorsque souvent le gouvernail agile
> De Douvre ou de Tanger fend la route mobile,
> Au fond du noir vaisseau sur la vague roulant
> Le passager languit, malade et chancelant.
> Son regard obscurci meurt. Sa tête pesante
> Tourne comme le vent qui souffle la tourmente;
> Et son cœur nage et flotte en son sein agité,
> Comme de bonds en bonds le navire emporté.
> Il croit sentir sous lui fuir la planche légère.
> Triste et pâle, il se couche, et la nausée amère
> Soulève sa poitrine, et sa bouche à longs flots
> Inonde les tapis destinés au repos . . .

Thus, 'triste et pâle', Chénier arrived in London after a nerve-racking experience (which perhaps helped him in writing *La Jeune Tarentine*, *Dryas*, and so many other lovely *Bucoliques* on the theme of death by water), to add to his manuscript the note 'Fait en partie dans le vaisseau, en allant à Douvres, couché, souffrant. Écrit à Londres le 10 décembre 1787'.

Not much is known about Chénier's stay in England. The Ambassador did not arrive at the Embassy at 31 Portman Square until the middle of January 1788, so Chénier had about a month in which to settle down, as well as preparing for the Ambassador's arrival. On the 4th of February he wrote to his younger brother Marie-Joseph, expressing his satisfaction at being in London, and praising the work of Shakespeare. Part of Marie-Joseph's reply, dated 13 February 1788, runs as follows:

Vous vous plaisez à Londres, et je m'y attendais. Je voudrais bien un jour pouvoir vous aller embrasser dans cette belle ville, avant de vous revoir à Paris. . . .

Vous me paraissez indulgent pour Shakespeare; vous trouvez qu'il a des scènes admirables. J'avoue que, dans tous ses drames, je n'en connais qu'une seule qui mérite à mon gré ce nom, du moins d'un bout à l'autre: c'est l'entretien de Henri IV mourant, avec son fils, le prince de Galles. Cette scène m'a toujours paru parfaitement belle. Ailleurs, et dans la même pièce, il y a des morceaux qui unissent la noblesse à l'énergie; mais il m'a paru qu'ils étaient courts. Dans *Jules César*, par exemple, la scène vantée de Brutus et de Cassius, avant la bataille de Philippes, est, selon moi, très-vicieuse. . . .

Vous voyez que j'aime à vous rendre compte de mes travaux; j'espère que vous en userez de même: vous savez combien je suis sensible aux marques de votre amitié, et combien vous devez compter sur la mienne: un des grands plaisirs que je puisse avoir, est de recevoir de temps en temps de ces beaux vers que vous savez faire. Adieu, prenez soin de votre santé, qui est précieuse aux lettres et à tous ceux qui vous connaissent. . . .

Since Shakespeare has been mentioned, we might note that André Chénier, perhaps over-influenced by his brother, hesitated more than once in his estimate of our greatest poet. In *L'Invention* he paid tribute to the originality of the English poets:

> Ce n'est qu'aux inventeurs que la vie est promise :
> Nous voyons les enfants de la fière Tamise,
> De toute servitude ennemis indomptés ;

but went on to condemn the lack of decorum of our poetry as 'transports déréglés, vagabonde manie'. In the *Essai sur les lettres et les arts* he wrote of the Greeks, 'Ce ne sont pas là de ces convulsions barbares de Shakespeare', and went on to praise Young before condemning most of our poets in a few lines: 'mais la plupart de ces poètes du Nord, surtout Anglais, se tourmentent toujours, en toute occasion.' However, he paid Shakespeare the compliment of adapting a few lines from *Henry IV*: a task which he accomplished so beautifully that it might serve as a model of what poetic translation should be:

> She bids you on the wanton rushes lay you down
> And rest your gentle head upon her lap,
> And she will sing the song that pleaseth you
> And on your eyelids crown the god of sleep,
> Charming your blood with pleasing heaviness;
> Making such difference 'twixt wake and sleep,
> As is the difference 'twixt day and night,
> The hour before the heavenly-harnessed team
> Begins his golden progress in the east.

> Viens, là sur des joncs frais ta place est toute prête.
> Viens, viens. Sur mes genoux viens reposer ta tête.
> Les yeux levés sur moi, tu resteras muet,
> Et je te chanterai la chanson qui te plaît.
> Comme on voit, au moment où Phœbus va renaître,
> La nuit prête à s'enfuir, le jour prêt à paraître, . . .[1]

Unfortunately for Chénier, he was soon to discover what it meant to be only the Ambassador's private secretary, and not an official member of the diplomatic corps. He had hardly the status which, today, would be held by a third or fourth secretary, and most of his time seems to have been spent in copying documents, arranging the Ambassador's time-table, organizing receptions, keeping visitors in conversation while the Ambassador was busy or absent, taking messages, and in general acting as his A.D.C. His superiors were MM. Aragon and Nettement, and the Minister, François Barthélemy. Aragon has related that on one occasion Chénier was so indignant at being kept 'doing nothing' that he refused to draw his salary and received a written rebuke, though worded in a kindly manner, from La Luzerne, who no doubt pointed out that he had engaged the poet in order to afford him leisure in which to write.[1] Nettement, who after

[1] For the complete text, see my arrangement of *La Chanson des yeux* in D25, p. 24.

[2] This anecdote cannot be traced to its source. It was first told by Sainte-Beuve in his essay on 'Mathurin Régnier et André Chénier' (G68) in 1829: 'La fierté délicate d'André Chénier était telle que, durant ce séjour à Londres, comme les fonctions d'attaché n'avaient

the Revolution wrote several literary works, never mentioned Chénier. However, Barthélemy, the nephew of the famous Barthélemy who wrote the *Voyage du jeune Anacharsis en Grèce*, seems to have had a great affection for Chénier, and mentioned him in his memoirs as being a close friend. We shall see later that between Chénier and Barthélemy, who became during the Revolution one of the greatest ambassadors that France has ever had, relations were not broken when Barthélemy achieved power, and that there were probably some important exchanges between them over the incident of the Suisses de Châteauvieux.[1] It is to be noted, also, that Chateaubriand claims in his *Mémoires d'Outre-Tombe* that his brother Jean-Baptiste knew Chénier in London, but I have been unable to find any other evidence of this.[2] There is evidence that Chénier was friendly with the consul-general, Hermann, against whom in 1790 there was, on the part of some rival, a plot to oust him from his post.[3]

The only solution for Chénier in his boredom was to work, as well as seeking lighter distractions of the kind he had known in Paris. Though he probably read Thomson and Young (of whom he translated or adapted certain lines) in French, he read in English Spenser, Pope (no doubt to help in composing *L'Invention*), and above all, Milton, the English poet whom he most prized, and to whom in his *Susanne* he paid the fine tribute: 'Grand aveugle dont l'âme a su voir tant de choses.' Had he ever finished it, *Susanne* would certainly have been a Miltonic poem, for the Christian epic was practically defunct in France in the eighteenth century, and he had no other models but Milton. Another draft reads 'Imiter Milton et les livres juifs',[4] and yet another: 'Il n'y a qu'à faire guider les infâmes vieillards par Bélial, le Dieu de la débauche, que Milton peint dans cette énumération des anciens Dieux de l'Orient. Admirable morceau.'[5] He carried his admiration for Milton so far as to speak in the *Essai* of his personal

rien de bien actif et que le premier secrétaire faisait tout, il s'abstint d'abord de toucher ses appointements, et qu'il fallut qu'un jour M. de La Luzerne trouvât cela mauvais et le dît un peu haut pour l'y décider.' Becq de Fouquières (D6), p. xxx, wrote, 'C'est M. Aragon, premier secrétaire de M. de La Luzerne, qui a raconté ce fait au beau-père de M. Gérusez.' However, Gérusez made no mention de cette story in his book on the Revolution (see G32).

[1] See below, Chapter 11.

[2] F34, t. i, p. 104. The story is unlikely: the ambassador had two secretaries (Nettement and Chénier) until summer 1790, then two in 1791. J.-B. Chateaubriand must have come to Portman Square after Chénier.

[3] Mentioned in a letter to A.C. from the comtesse d'Albany, 5 mai 1790, BMC 11816. 'L'intrigue contre M. Hermann est un peu assoupie ... etc.' See D7, t. i, p. lxiv.

[4] D13, t. ii, p. 148. [5] Ibid., p. 163.

beauty: 'rien de commun ni d'impudent n'était sur le visage de Corneille ou de Milton.'[1] Similarly he spoke of Pope as 'le grand Pope', setting his *Essay on Man* far above Voltaire's imitation of it.

At the same time he did some research on the English Constitution which was perhaps intended to form part of a work to which he himself gave the English title 'History of the Royal Power in Europe: History of the Prerogative'. These notes were either intended for his *Hermès*, or were passed to de Pange, who later published a pamphlet on the subject. It was while he was in England, also, that he applied himself to Arabic and Spanish and compiled notes on *L'Espagne et ses superstitions*: he was also intending to write some 'Spanish elegies'. Meanwhile he was collecting the fine Oxford and Cambridge annotated editions of the classics, which are now in his library at Carcassonne. He met a number of learned men, including Dr. Priestley and the theologian and philosopher Dr. Price to whom he later referred in his political articles during the revolution. He was probably in correspondence, also, with English scholars: one of the addresses noted in his papers is a certain Mr. Charles Curtis, then living at 8 Clarendon Street in Oxford.[2] There is direct evidence, also, that he was working on his *Bucoliques* at this time, for he had obtained the works of Sannazar, whom he mentioned under his Latin name Actius. Sannazar was the first poet to have written what Chénier called 'Idylles maritimes', and it was under his influence and that of Lucian that Chénier was now writing some of the best of the *Bucoliques*, those, including *La Jeune Tarentine*, which treat of death by drowning.

In the summer of 1788 La Luzerne, who was already in uncertain health, went to France for his leave but did not take Chénier with him. The poet then spent some time at the sea-side, maybe at Brighton or Hastings, which were then popular, or on the Isle of Wight where La Luzerne had friends. A short poem is all that commemorates this event:

> Et moi, quand la chaleur, ramenant le repos,
> Fait descendre en été le calme sur les flots,
> J'aime à venir goûter la fraîcheur du rivage,
> Et bien loin des cités, sous un épais feuillage,
> Ne pensant à rien, libre et serein comme l'air,
> Rêver, seul, en silence, et regardant la mer.

---

[1] D22, p. 693.
[3] BN, NAF 6851, folio 288, also gives a drawing of a wind-chart for Mr. Curtis, with explanations in Latin. Another English address (NAF 6851, no number) is that of a Dr. Warner, Barnard's Inn, written on a blank visiting-card.

Another poem written in the same year, on Embassy paper, expresses not only his nostalgia for the liberty he had before going to England, but his feeling that his abilities were being wasted in humble employments, and his impatience with the pretentious people with whom he had to deal: he refers to his job and the boring receptions he had to attend and envies those who can live to themselves:

> Il ne faut point qu'il dompte un ascendant suprême,
> Opprime son génie et s'éteigne soi-même
> Pour user sans honneur et sa plume et son temps
> A des travaux obscurs tristement importants;
> Il n'a point pour pousser sa barque vagabonde
> A se précipiter dans les flots du grand monde . . .

It irked him to

> Trahir la vérité pour avoir du repos,
> Et feindre d'être un sot pour vivre avec les sots.

Chénier evidently felt himself an outsider in London. Being French and, though he had a ready tongue, at a loss how to entertain the young débutantes to whom, in any case, he was no doubt not properly introduced, and perhaps feeling that his clothes were not up to the occasion, he could only stand aside and be overcome with depression in the midst of the brilliant company surrounding him:

J'ai été à ce bal où toutes ces belles Anglaises . . . . Je les regardais sans rien dire. . . . Je portais envie à ceux à qui elles parlaient et de la main de qui elles acceptaient des oranges, des glaces. . . .[1]

Not, however, that he failed to appreciate the 'belles Anglaises', to whom he dedicated an unprintable poem in Greek. He even concluded that 'aucune autre contrée ne nourrit de plus belles jeunes filles que l'Angleterre', though his relations with them, however intimate, were not with the exquisite representatives of high society, but with anonymous young ladies of Ranelagh or Vauxhall, whom he named simply Caroline, Aglaé, and Byblis. One has only to read the Journals of Boswell to understand the adventures to which a spirited young man was driven in London in those days, for the favours of eligible young ladies were closely guarded at that time. Chénier was the kind of impoverished lone wolf who was carefully scrutinized and barred by attentive chaperones.

No, it was not easy, even for a man who had been welcome at the tables of the most distinguished families in France, to establish himself

[1] D13, p. 159.

socially in London in the 1780's. The menfolk all belonged to a club: after returning from their activities in the City, or in the House, they repaired to their clubs for a while, and there was no set time for dinner. This meant that the hopeful guest could not, as in Paris, arrive in time for the *apéritif* in the expectation of being invited. The only solution was to join a club oneself, and this Chénier apparently did. We do not know which one it was, though it was probably the one to which Dr. Priestley and Dr. Price belonged. The only house at which Chénier could count on a warm reception was that of the Cosways, the spacious and elegant Schomberg House, in Pall Mall, where he might meet a few artists. They held 'Musical evenings' which were attended by such personalities as Horace Walpole, the Duchess of Devonshire, the Countess of Aylesbury, the Marquis of Townshend, Lord Erskine, and Lord Sandys: but this does not mean that they took any interest in him.

There was, indeed, only one bright moment for Chénier in this year, but he reacted to it in a negative way. Palissot published a work *Mémoires pour servir à l'histoire de notre littérature*, in which the Chénier family was mentioned. André Chénier must certainly have been pleased at Palissot's praise of his father's work: 'Le Travail de M. de Chénier est un véritable service qu'il a rendu à sa patrie. C'est à l'administration juste et éclairée qui lui avait donné sa confiance, de le récompenser d'une manière digne d'elle.' Of course the Administration turned a deaf ear to the claims of the worthy man. Then, after some praise of Marie-Joseph, the promising playwright, Palissot paid the following tribute to André Chénier himself:

C'est à son insu que nous nous permettons de le révéler à la renommée, persuadé qu'il voudra bien nous pardonner de le comprendre dans cette espèce de tableau de famille que nous venons de tracer, et dont nous aurions trop de regret de l'exclure, en cédant à sa modestie. Avec moins d'empressement de se produire, et un désir de gloire non moins vif peut-être que son frère, mais auquel il sait commander, jusqu'à présent il ne paraît occupé, si nous l'osons dire, qu'à méditer sa réputation dans le silence. Qu'il me permette cependant l'expression du plaisir que nous ont fait le peu d'ouvrages qu'il a bien voulu nous communiquer. Peut-être avons-nous été moins frappé des talents qu'ils annoncent pour la poésie que d'un caractère de pensée mâle et profonde, qui ne peut appartenir qu'à l'homme de génie.[1]

It would be going too far to say that Chénier was irritated with this left-handed compliment in which, while speaking of his 'genius',

[1] G62, t. iii, pp. 123–4.

Palissot suggested that he had written but little and that his capacities as a poet were secondary to his powers as a thinker. In any case, he reacted rather ungraciously, sending Palissot a letter in which he criticized in detail Palissot's treatment of the *Encyclopédie*. Palissot was at some haste to defend himself, in a letter which gives us some idea of the nature of Chénier's objections.[1] Chénier appears to have reproached the critic with 'confusing the wasps with the bees' and writing too often 'in order to take his revenge'. In particular, as Palissot's answer shows, the young poet must have defended not only Voltaire but the whole of the *Encyclopédie*, especially Diderot, whom Palissot called 'une tête exaltée qui se perd continuellement dans le brouillard'. Among their contemporaries, Chénier defended Suard (one of the great journalists of the period, who later became editor of *Le Journal de Paris*: it is said that it was at Suard's that Chénier met Fanny Lecoulteux), Morellet, and, surprisingly, Marmontel. After replying carefully to Chénier's protests, Palissot ended with the tribute: 'Ce que je peux vous dire avec vérité, c'est que, de tous nos jeunes gens de lettres, vous êtes un de ceux que je distingue le plus, et dont l'estime me flatte davantage.'

Perhaps Palissot's letter came at a time when Chénier was too depressed to appreciate it; when, alone and discouraged as the winter set in, he was passing through one of those phases of spleen or melancholia to which he was prone and which, of course, were fashionable in those days when melancholy was a recognized form of sickness. He had, in any case, at all times a tendency to feel himself an outcast, an outsider, and now he expressed those feelings which were to return to him years later when in prison:

> Sans parents, sans amis, et sans concitoyens,
> Oublié sur la terre et loin de tous les miens,
> Par les vagues jeté sur cette île farouche,
> Le doux nom de la France est souvent sur ma bouche.
> Auprès d'un noir foyer, seul, je me plains du sort,
> Je compte les moments, je souhaite la mort.
> Et pas un seul ami dont la voix m'encourage;
> Qui près de moi s'asseye, et, voyant mon visage
> Se baigner de mes pleurs et tomber sur mon sein,
> Me dise: 'Qu'as-tu donc?' et me presse la main.

This could not be because his friends were neglecting him: the situation was probably the reverse, as the painter David wrote to

[1] The 'Lettre de Palissot à M. de Saint-André' is given in E2, pp. cix–cx.

Mrs. Cosway: 'C'est parce que je me connais paresseux que je pardonne à Monsieur Saint-André de ce qu'il ne m'écrit pas: j'espère qu'un jour il lui prendra le même remords qu'à moi. Dites-lui bien des choses de ma part et combien je regrette de ne plus le voir. La maison de Monsieur Trudaine est triste depuis qu'il n'y est plus.'[1]

Things were no better for Chénier in the following year, for in April 1789 he went and sat down in Hood's Tavern and wrote several pages of bitter reflections about his solitude: 'Mais ici je suis seul, livré à moi-même, soumis à ma pesante fortune, et je n'ai personne sur qui m'appuyer. Que l'indépendance est bonne! Heureux celui que le désir d'être utile à ses vieux parents et à toute sa famille ne force pas à renoncer à son honnête et indépendante pauvreté!'[2] There is some contradiction here, for Chénier had never been independent, and, spoilt no doubt by the social status he had enjoyed in Paris, he did not realize that 'independence' involves earning one's living. But his lack of logic arose from the anguish of frustration:

'Je sais bien qu'il ne m'arrive rien dont mon honneur puisse être blessé; je sais bien aussi que rien de pareil ne m'arrivera jamais, car cette assurance-là ne dépend que de moi seul. Mais il est dur de se voir négligé, de n'être point admis dans telle société qui se croit au-dessus de vous; il est dur de recevoir, sinon des dédains, au moins des politesses hautaines; il est dur de sentir ... Quoi? qu'on est au-dessous de quelqu'un? — Non; mais il y a quelqu'un qui s'imagine que vous êtes au-dessous de lui.'

So he went on, spending a fruitless hour and a half in vague expression of his tortured feelings, without ever coming to the point. It is possible, from internal evidence ('La triste circonstance qui m'a fait dîner ici tout seul' and 'Il est triste de se voir négligé, de n'être point admis dans telle société qui se croit au-dessus de vous'), that he had received some social rebuff, and M. Dimoff suggested that, for once, he had perhaps been excluded from the Ambassador's table. All this might imply that there was some weakness of character in Chénier: he was weak in small matters, but strong enough when his strength was required. This is shown by a letter which he wrote to his father not long after, on the 21st of April 1789: in it he described how he had paid a debt incurred by his brother-in-law, because the creditor would otherwise have put the matter in the hands of the French embassy.[3] He also expressed his wish to protect his sister, and added that there was no

[1] F104, pp. 35–36.
[2] The complete text of this important statement is given in Appendix B below.
[3] D22, pp. 784–5.

urgency for her to repay him. As for his recent state of melancholy, he told his father: 'Il n'y a aucun refroidissement entre l'Ambassadeur et moi. La réflexion qu'il m'a faite était plutôt une marque d'estime qu'un reproche; j'en ai jugé ainsi par le ton. L'attachement qu'il me témoigne me paraît peu susceptible de diminution; car il est moins fondé sur des séductions momentanées que sur la connaissance de mon caractère.' His father must have mentioned something about his work, for André wrote: 'Quant à ce que vous me dites sur le sacrifice de mon indépendance; vous voyez bien que je l'ai fait. Ce désir-là, quoique bien vif, a cédé à celui de pouvoir un jour être utile à ma famille, et mon sacrifice est d'autant plus méritoire qu'en renonçant à l'indépendance je n'ai pas cessé d'en sentir le prix.' What emerges from this is that Chénier must have taken his father into his confidence and sent him a letter containing some of the reflections he had written in Hood's Tavern, but since then he had come to a more rational view of his relations with the Ambassador. He also mentioned that he was invited, that same night, to a reception and ball which was being given to celebrate George III's projected visit to Hanover: the letter ends with his sending his 'respects' to his mother, and the signature 'Chénier de Saint-André'.

Chénier must, at that time, have been pouring out his wounded feelings to others besides his father, for Alfieri wrote him a long epistle in Italian verse, dated 29 April 1789. It begins, 'La voici donc enfin ta douce lettre, cher Chénier, cette lettre si longtemps attendue et que j'aurais souhaitée un peu plus longue', and contains not only references to Chénier's melancholy, but an effort to rouse him by turning his mind to politics:

J'apprends qu'elle est pour toi plus amère que l'absinthe, cette Londres où tu te trouves étranger: et véritablement c'est le supplice de Mézence, que d'habiter chez une nation où personne ne vous favorise des beaux liens de la joyeuse amitié. Ah! tu as bien raison de dire qu'elle a des clous de fer,
La Nécessité, déesse inexorable, seule divinité à qui le tyran cède aussi quand elle devient géante.
De ce que je dis, un bel exemple est donné maintenant par les Français, qui sont voisins de la liberté, précisément parce qu'ils ont usé la servitude.
Ici maintenant on n'entend plus qu'un seul cri; grands et petits, hommes et femmes, militaires et prêtres, tous les Parisiens *solonisent* [sic].
On n'entend que ce cri: les États! et si le souffle répond au désir, je crois que le règne des soldats touche à sa fin.
... En attendant, chasse tes sombres pensées. Toi qui es né pour écrire, ne pense qu'à écrire ...[1]

[1] Given in Italian in D7, pp. liv–lvii, and in French translation in G6, pp. 21–23.

Chénier's exile in London was favourable to his studies, and there is evidence that more than one of the *Bucoliques* were written while he was there. But his more personal poems show a bleak anguish in which his thoughts turned only too often towards suicide. It was not enough to distract his mind by collecting notes for a history of Christianity, or for a treatise on the royal prerogative. He felt incurably alone and his solitude was no doubt increased, after Palissot's remarks or imaginary slights from other sources, by the feeling that he had done little to justify all the years of independence which had already been given him in order to write. He was now twenty-seven, but does not seem to have been emotionally mature. His mercurial character, as in the past, drove him from one extreme to another. This longing for death is forcefully expressed in a fragment of an elegy written at this time, and which might well have accompanied his letter to Alfieri. It is a revealing document rather than a good poem:

> O nécessité dure! ô pesant esclavage!
> O sort! je dois donc voir, et dans mon plus bel âge,
> Flotter mes jours, tissus de désirs et de pleurs,
> Dans ce flux et reflux d'espoir et de douleurs!
>
> Souvent, las d'être esclave et de boire la lie
> De ce calice amer que l'on nomme la vie,
> Las du mépris des sots qui suit la pauvreté,
> Je regarde la tombe, asile souhaité;
> Je souris à la mort volontaire et prochaine;
> Je me prie en pleurant d'oser rompre ma chaîne;
> Déjà le doux poignard qui percerait mon sein
> Se présente à mes yeux et frémit sous ma main,
> Et puis mon cœur s'écoute et s'ouvre à la faiblesse …

The 'weakness' which held him back was the thought of his family and friends, as well as 'mes écrits imparfaits', but it is interesting to notice how, even while describing this 'weakness', Chénier finds strength:

> Et puis mon cœur s'écoute et s'ouvre à la faiblesse;
> Mes parents, mes amis, l'avenir, ma jeunesse,
> Mes écrits imparfaits; car à ses propres yeux
> L'homme sait se cacher d'un voile spécieux …

In spite of the intimate notes of the beginning, with its reminiscences of *Hamlet*, Catullus, and Homer, the poem achieves a typically eighteenth-century character by moving into the third person, and being more concerned with Man than with the poet's own situation. Though it is a 'cry from the heart' it turns into a moral reflection and ends with an epigram:

> Il a souffert, il souffre; aveugle d'espérance
> Il se traîne au tombeau de souffrance en souffrance,
> Et la mort, de nos maux ce remède si doux,
> Lui semble un nouvel mal, le plus cruel de tous.

This was one of the first poems to reveal Chénier's name to the world, as it was printed by Chateaubriand in 1802, a fact which suggests that Madame de Beaumont had a manuscript copy of it. But though at first sight it contains all the germs of the 'mal du siècle' which Chateaubriand and the next generation were to celebrate, Chénier wrote with more conviction about the things to be lived for than of the reasons for suicide. He certainly suffered from no small disadvantages—ill health, poverty, social inferiority, solitude, and exile—but in another fragment he put an energetic end to all these speculations:

> Je vis. Je souffre encor. Battu de cent naufrages,
> Tremblant, j'affronte encor la mer et les orages,
> Quand je n'ai qu'à vouloir pour atteindre le port.
> Lâche! aime donc la vie, ou n'attends pas la mort.

The temptation to suicide did not return to Chénier again until 1794, when he was in Saint-Lazare, and it is striking to notice how, by comparison with the above statement ('Je vis. Je souffre encor') he had matured by then, writing in the last *Iambe*, 'Je souffre, mais je vis!'

Fortunately for the poet, he was given a long leave of four or five months in the summer of 1789. By now he knew too much about his functions at the Embassy—'travaux tristement importants'—to worry unduly about losing his appointment owing to the turn of events: indeed he probably thought that radical changes in the government of France would improve his position. In any case he now came into contact with the authorities at the Ministry of Foreign Affairs, in Paris, for when he returned to London in mid-November he carried with him the new secret cypher with which he had been entrusted.[1]

The exact date when Chénier arrived in Paris is not known. Events were moving swiftly. The States General met on the 5th of May, then, after some wrangling between the three Estates and the monarchy, the

[1] Letter from the Ambassador, dated 24 Nov. 1789: 'J'ai reçu le même jour le chiffre que vous m'avez envoyé par M. de Saint-André et la lettre que vous m'avez écrite.' *Archives du Ministère des Affaires étrangères, Corresp. politique, Angleterre*, vol. 571, folio 181.

Tennis-Court oath was taken at Versailles on the 20th of June. Under this oath, the Third Estate refused to disband until a new constitution was drawn up. The Bastille fell before the mob on the 14th of July. On the 4th of August came the 'abolition of privileges', while on the 6th of October the royal family was brought back to Paris and practically imprisoned in the Louvre.

Meanwhile Louis Chénier had drawn up, with André's help, one of those innumerable *cahiers* in which the wishes of the people were expressed. It contains certain principles to which the poet was to remain faithful till the end of his life. The Cahier is dated 18 April 1789, and entitled *Idées pour un Cahier du Tiers-État de Paris*. It has usually been attributed to Louis de Chénier, for it was printed only with the signature 'M. de Chénier', and until recently all the poet's biographers admitted that André had a hand in its composition. However, G. Walter has argued that it might have been drawn up by Marie-Joseph, as a list of notabilities, circulated not long after, mentioned 'De Chénier, poète tragique, qui vient de donner un Cahier de doléances, rempli d'excellentes vues'.[1] The fact that M. Walter suggests that Marie-Joseph had issued this list himself, out of vainglory, would not affect his argument. But the Chéniers were constantly confused with each other: André had to protest about being mistaken for Marie-Joseph in 1792, while at his trial in 1794 he was confused with Louis-Sauveur. While it is unlikely that André Chénier was responsible for the Cahier, it was probably a family document, in which André had his share, drawn up by Louis de Chénier: the conceit of Marie-Joseph would never have allowed him to omit his Christian names from the title-page, had the work been his own.

This brochure of twenty-eight pages contains many suggestions which were to be given effect during the Revolution, such as equality of taxation, the suppression of sinecures, the marriage of priests, suppression of monastic oaths, and the withdrawal of legislative power from the monarchy. An item which could quite well be a contribution from Marie-Joseph is the abolition of the censorship, for which he was already fighting, though later in his life he was to make the censorship more severe. There are some ideas which André Chénier was later to defend as a journalist: for instance the selection of juries on the same basis as in England; the abolition of the death penalty; toleration of all religions; defence of the property of monks and religious orders, and the total separation of the Paris administration from the Assembly.

[1] F101, p. 114.

At least three out of these five points would never have been proposed by Marie-Joseph.

In August (1789) Marie-Joseph came into the limelight through his struggle with the censorship, when his play, *Charles IX*, in which he hoped to 'avenge the nation' and hold up 'that monster, Charles IX, to public execration', was heard and forbidden by the royal censor, and thus excluded from the Théâtre Français. In passing, we note that the censor at that moment was Suard, a friend of André Chénier's. Marie-Joseph, nothing daunted, had the play read in a *salon* with the Duke and Duchess of Orleans present. Marie-Joseph was already in league with the then unknown Collot d'Herbois, Fabre d'Églantine, Camille Desmoulins, and Danton, two of whom were later to become his brother's most dangerous enemies. Meanwhile, Marie-Joseph issued a number of brochures and articles attacking the censorship, then on the 19th of August he and his friends created a disturbance at the Théâtre Français during a performance of Molière. Finally the mayor and municipality of Paris agreed to listen to his play. It was shown at the Théâtre Français on the 4th of November with the great Talma in the chief part.[1] Its success was such that it was considered to be a great blow to the French monarchy. His brother André probably saw the play before leaving for London.

Louis-Sauveur Chénier was also making trouble at this time. Though he was a lieutenant in the regular army, after the fall of the Bastille he distributed pamphlets, which he had written himself, exhorting the troops to slaughter the aristocracy.[2] According to his own account of the affair, Louis-Sauveur had sold all his possessions in April, raising a sum of 4,873 *livres*, with the object of rallying soldiers to his ideas.[3] This account is hardly to be trusted, as his own father said of him, 'Je ne sais ce qu'il pense, ni s'il pense.' Although André Chénier, like his friends and brothers, welcomed the Revolution, his subsequent writings about army discipline suggest that he must have viewed Louis-Sauveur's activities with distaste.

To complete the picture, his friends the Trudaines and François de Pange were writing pamphlets, attending meetings, and cutting the ground from under their own feet as fast as they could. We shall turn

---

[1] See H. F. Collins, *Talma*, Faber 1964, ch. 8.

[2] *Lettre à M. le comte de Mirabeau*, sur les dispositions naturelles nécessaires et indubitables des officiers et des soldats français et étrangers. 25 juin 1789.

[3] In a letter dated 23 mai 1791 (reprinted in *Le Cabinet historique*, 1862) Louis-Sauveur claimed to have distributed, by hand, 210 of these leaflets and to have taken part in the attack on the Bastille.

to this aspect of the matter at a later stage. Is it true to suggest, as one biographer has done, that Chénier never understood the real meaning of the Revolution because he had not taken part in its beginnings?[1] It is certainly true that his absence in France during the critical eighteen months before, means that he missed everything that could not be learnt through the written word. However, he probably returned to Paris in June 1789 to attend the elder Trudaine's wedding, which was on the 13th of June. He was in France during the first memorable five months of the Revolution, then was absent again for part of 1790. On the other hand he must have heard and witnessed many things behind the scenes, in London, and especially the reaction of the English upper classes and politicians. He saw the first wave of emigrant nobles making themselves ridiculous and unpopular in English society, and could test his own feelings and ideas alongside his liberal colleague, the Minister Barthélemy, who because of La Luzerne's failing health had his hand on every aspect of policy that came through the Embassy. And, for that matter, he must have seen and heard much that went on behind the scenes when he was in Paris, for de Pange and the Trudaines were at the very centre of events.

It must, then, have been with mixed feelings that Chénier returned to London in November. Although he was against the old social order, he had a hatred of anarchy and was already distressed at the way the mob was taking matters into its own hands. During his remaining few months in London, at his friends' request he began working out the moderate constitutional stand that he was to take publicly in 1790 and from which he was never to depart.

Immediately after arriving in London he wrote his father a letter which gives an interesting picture of the state of mind that must have prevailed at the Embassy, where the whole staff, with the possible exception of La Luzerne himself, at once welcomed and feared the Revolution. This letter is dated 24 November 1789 and signed 'Chénier de Saint-André':

Je suis arrivé ici le 19, mon très cher père, après un voyage qui n'a rien eu de remarquable, et le plus douloureux passage de mer que j'aie encore eu. Je n'ai pas tardé à regretter Paris; car ici les inquiétudes sur nos affaires ne sont pas moindres et sont plus désagréables, parce qu'elles sont plus vagues, et qu'on est plus longtemps à savoir à quoi s'en tenir. Ajoutez que les mauvaises nouvelles sont toujours grossies et exagérées, non seulement par la mauvaise

[1] F101, p. 185: 'Il ignorait, malheureusement (et son absence en ces mois d'hiver 1789–1790 qui virent la crystallisation des partis politiques en France pourrait lui servir d'excuse), que l'impartialité était devenue un simple paravent derrière lequel se cachaient les royalistes les plus authentiques.'

volonté des Anglais, mais encore plus par la plupart des Français qui sont ici, et qui ne voient pas que leur odieuse animosité envers leur patrie les rend méprisables et ridicules. . . .[1]

Chénier goes on to tell how letters dated the 19th and 20th, sent 'par courrier extraordinaire', announced that all Paris was in flames. This, of course, was completely untrue, but it was typical of the kind of propaganda sent abroad by the die-hards in order to sway English opinion.

At the same time, things were not going well at home. The family was divided politically, Madame Chénier, Louis-Sauveur, and Marie-Joseph being at the extreme Left, almost to the point of anarchy, while Louis and André were moderates.[2] Now the Assembly was threatening to reduce or stop all pensions that had been granted under the old régime. As from the 1st of January 1790 the elder Chénier's pension was to be reduced to 3,000 *livres*, and André wrote to him expressing anxiety on this score on the 19th of January, advising his father to draw up a statement about his position. Though Chénier and his friends, later on, failed to give enough attention to the economic aspects of the Revolution, he saw at this stage that financial reform was the key to the situation: 'Plaise au ciel que les affaires s'arrangent, ce qui ne peut guère avoir lieu que par les Finances, qui vont bien lentement. Outre la honte qu'entraînerait une faiblesse, quelles horribles convulsions n'en seraient pas la suite dans Paris! car les provinces s'en ressentiraient moins. Mais il est sûr que Paris serait un enfer pendant quelque temps.'[3] Recent events had sobered and matured Chénier, and now, instead of lamenting over his own destiny, he was giving more thought to others: the letter contains an expression of his joy at the success of Marie-Joseph's play, which was still running, and mentions that M. Dutens was subscribing for two copies. He also mentioned the pamphlet which François de Pange had just published, *Réflexions sur la Délation et sur le Comité des Recherches*, which he called 'un écrit plein de justice, de noblesse, de raison et d'éloquence, et qui ne peut déplaire qu'au faubourg Saint-Antoine'.

In reply to this letter, his father said that he was in straitened circumstances and must raise money at once. André replied (29 January 1790)

---

[1] D22, p. 786.
[2] As Louis put it to his daughter, 'Votre mère a renoncé à toute son aristocratie et est entièrement démagogue, ainsi que Joseph. Saint-André et moi, nous sommes ce qu'on appelle *modérés*, amis de l'ordre et des lois. G . .. [Louis-Sauveur] est employé dans la gendarmerie nationale, mais je ne sais ce qu'il pense, ni s'il pense. Constantin trouve que rien n'a changé.' D6, p. xxv.
[3] D22, p. 786.

that he himself was in difficulties, for not only had he no money, but he had contracted debts in the previous year and owed it to his friends who had stood caution, not to make any new debts till the old ones were paid. One has only to glance at the endings of the poet's letters to feel the depth of sympathy that existed between them: he would end with his 'respectueuse tendresse', or 'je vous embrasse de tout mon cœur', or 'je vous embrasse aussi tendrement que je vous aime et respecte'. Now he hastened to correct his father's accounts, saying: 'Dans l'état de votre fortune que vous m'avez envoyé, vous avez marqué au nombre de vos dettes les petits secours que j'ai eu le bonheur de pouvoir vous procurer parfois. C'est très bien fait pour l'exactitude du compte, mais hors de là vous ne devez point faire entrer tout cela au nombre de vos dettes.'[1] One cannot but admire Louis de Chénier's scrupulous honesty, which impelled him to count his son's gifts among his owings. André now raised the sum of 2,400 *livres*, which he repaid to de Pange in December of the same year. This was about the amount required for his father to free himself of debt, after which he could manage to make ends meet on his reduced pension. In the same letter, however, the son scolded his father, who had lost confidence in himself and, in the spirit of King Lear, was proposing that his children should take over his finances: 'Quant à la proposition que vous faites de laisser administrer votre modique revenu par vos enfants, je la désapprouve sous tous les points de vue possibles. Comment avez-vous pu avoir une pareille idée?' The poet was now self-supporting and could thus speak his mind, when invited to do so. There follows a painfully revealing sentence, which is a criticism of his mother: 'Vous avez donc oublié que si vos affaires sont en si mauvais état, c'est parce qu'elles ont été bien longtemps administrées *pour* vos enfants, et pour des personnes qui méritent encore plus qu'eux-mêmes le titre d'enfants.' The ebullient Madame Chénier had been living on the level of a minor aristocrat for over twenty years, and it is astonishing that the family had ever been able to make ends meet since they left Constantinople. The poet's advice was that his father should show his accounts to Bailly, who was then Mayor of Paris. In the meantime he would sell some of his personal effects to help his father: 'Pour cette année en vendant le peu que j'aurais d'effets ou bijoux non nécessaires, je pourrais vous aider à compléter cette somme', that is to say, the tax that had to be paid on the original pension of 6,000 *livres*. Like his father, Chénier was unselfish in money matters: one of his first acts on being appointed to the

[1] D22, p. 788.

Embassy had been to send a very fine clock to his uncle and aunt at Carcassonne, where it can now be seen in the museum. He would have no hesitation in asking, also, 'cent louis' from his friends, for 'j'ai vécu et je vivrai toujours de façon à mériter qu'on me rende service, et par conséquent à ne pas baisser les yeux en le demandant'. This suggests that, while accepting his friends' hospitality for long periods, he had always taken care to repay whatever sums they lent to him.

His next letter to his father, dated London, 5 March 1790, deals only with the political situation.[1] He was already turning against Burke: M. Fox et M. Sheridan parlent de notre révolution avec louange, et M. Burke avec dénigrement.' He was also using what small influence he had to help his father, for a letter of 19th of March shows him arranging a meeting between Louis de Chénier and the Ambassador's mother.[2] Perhaps the intention was to ask her to intercede with Montmorin, La Luzerne's father-in-law, who at that time had considerable influence over the Treasury: 'Le vicomte de La Luzerne écrit dans ce moment à sa mère. Il m'assure que l'entretien que vous désirez avoir avec elle ne souffrira aucune difficulté. Je ne lui ai point donné la lettre que vous m'adressiez pour qu'il la montre à la comtesse de La Luzerne; j'ai cru que cela pourrait avoir auprès d'elle un air d'apprêt et d'arrangement qui pourrait n'être pas bon.' Tactfully, the poet had put his finger on one of the reasons why his father had never received any advancement since being Consul-General in Morocco. His father, though he was probity itself, had perhaps a slightly obsequious manner when addressing his superiors. No doubt he was inclined to give too long an account of his troubles and requirements; otherwise it is difficult to understand why Vergennes, a former ambassador to Turkey, and the elder Trudaine, who was genuinely interested in him, were unable to help him.

It is not known exactly when Chénier finally returned to France, but his nephew Gabriel asserted that it was in June 1790. This is probably true. When Chénier's name was set on the list of members of the 'Société des amis de 1789', it was with the mention 'en Angleterre', and the list was drawn up on or about the 12th of April. A letter written to him on the 5th of May by the countess of Albany also proves that he was still in London then. This letter (which is in the Carcassonne library) bears only the simple date 'le 5 mai' and was for a long time attributed to the year 1791 because of a reference it contains to Paoli.[3]

---

[1] Ibid., p. 789.   [2] Ibid., p. 790.
[3] BMC 11816/488/339, folio 5.

However, Paoli was also in France in 1790: he was presented at Court in April, then received by the Assembly in a special session on the 22nd of the same month. One of the most interesting facts that emerges from the countess's letter is that Chénier appears to have written to the Corsican leader, for she writes: 'J'ai eu soin de remettre votre lettre au bon général Paoly, qui a plus l'air d'un bon homme que d'un héros, cependant on le regarde comme tel à Paris, il a fait son salamalec à l'assemblée législative où son discours a été vivement applaudi.' It is easy to see why Gabriel de Chénier dated the letter 1791: because of the reference to the *legislative* assembly. But the fact that the countess goes on to say that Paoli was taken under the wing of La Fayette seems to confirm that this must have been in 1790, for it was then that La Fayette organized Paoli's reception. This is altogether a delightful letter: it contains some lively remarks about Chénier's liking for food and drink:

> ... Notre liberté s'établit lentement, je crois que nous serons encore long-temps sous l'anarchie, c'est une belle et bonne chose que cette liberté mais il est bien dur de la voir prendre possession d'un pays.
>
> Quel spectacle affligeant elle occasionne; toutes les choses, même les meilleures du monde, doivent être vues de bien loin; la comparaison n'est pas sotte; mais pour vous qui êtes gourmand elle ne vous déplaira pas; c'est comme un bon dîner qui a un coup d'œil excellent sur la table; mais si on l'avait vu préparer il aurait dégoûté. Je crois qu'il en est de même de la liberté. A propos de dîner je crois que vos maux viennent de trop manger, vous êtes gourmand, l'ambassadeur fait bonne chère, vous êtes faible, vous vous y livrez, de là dérivent tous les petits maux et les grandes mélancolies dont vous souffrez; la sobriété préserve de cela, elle tient le cœur content et l'esprit joyeux; l'esprit et le cœur dépendent beaucoup du physique, ne vous dé-plaise, nous ne sommes pas aussi spirituel que bien vous croyez, aussi donc pour être maître de ce physique il faut de la sobriété; je vois ici toutes les objections que vous avez à me faire car je connais votre penchant naturel pour la bonne chère ....

The countess went on to say that as her name was on the 'red book' she was in danger of losing her pension and might have to escape to England. Actually, as can be seen from Alfieri's memoirs, the couple spent all 1790 in France, and left for England towards the end of April 1791—yet another fact which helps us to date this letter 1790. She ended her letter on a cheerful, intimate note: 'Si vous arrivez bientôt vous me trouverez encore à Paris, attendant les décrets de vos légis-lateurs sur ma fortune. S'ils me traitent mal j'aurai un peu moins de serviteurs et de coursiers, mais j'aurai toujours des anchois et de l'huile de Provence à vous donner, et un dîner bien sobre qui vous remettra l'estomac.'

It has already been mentioned that Chénier was a member of the 'Société de 1789'. This club was limited to 660 members, of whom a select group of 89 formed the core. It contained not only the Chénier circle, but La Fayette, Bailly, Mirabeau (for whom Chénier had great admiration—he probably knew him), Roederer, who was later to be one of Chénier's friends, La Rochefoucauld, who in 1792 was to direct one of the last plots to save the royal family, Dupont de Nemours, and the philosopher Chamfort. When Chénier returned to France in June 1790 it was in order to write, on this society's behalf, one of the most important pamphlets of the French Revolution.

PART II

THE WORK, DOWN TO THE REVOLUTION

5

HIS VIEWS ON POETRY

So far we have had many glimpses of Chénier's work before the Revolution, but for the most part it has been used to throw light on his biography and has not been discussed for its own sake. Chénier was, perhaps, slow to develop as a man, and only reached his full intellectual and moral stature during his struggle with the Jacobins. But although the Revolution was needed to bring out his powerful gifts as a polemist, and also helped him to find new methods of expression in verse, his views and capacities as a poet had already won him respect. If he was, as Palissot suggested, 'nursing his reputation in secret', he was, so far, not the kind of poet whose work or ideas would have brought about a complete revolution in poetry. Rather, he had gifts which were enabling him to fulfil, in his practice, a neo-classical theory of poetry which was little more than wishful thinking and, until he appeared, a pretentious mask behind which third-rate minds could easily masquerade as poets.

Chénier did not come to destroy the old poetic but to explore it in depth and, where possible, to justify it through works. It is a common error in criticism to imagine that what a poet writes about his art is of prime importance, and that his theoretical statements about the nature or craft of poetry are to be taken as doctrine. They are always interesting, but they are not indispensable. Every poem embodies and illustrates a theory of poetry and tells us what must have been the poet's idea of poetry at the time when he wrote it. In this respect Chénier's explicit theory of poetry is less impressive than his actual practice, partly because almost all his writings about poetry are unfinished works.

Another difficulty in appreciating Chénier's statements about the art of poetry, or in relating them to the poetry he wrote, is that we do not know the exact date when they were written. Dimoff suggested that the three main works under consideration (*L'Invention, La République des lettres*, and the *Essai*) were conceived between 1786 and 1788, but elsewhere described the *Essai* as the first of them.[1] He also said that the *Essai* was written in London.[2] Internal evidence, however, would suggest a different order. *L'Invention*, a didactic poem of 392 lines, reflects the correlation *amour–poésie* which was the basis of the elegies from 1781 onwards. Parts of it are also an obvious attempt to justify the modernism of *Hermès* and *L'Amérique* and could be dated from 1783. There are some of the stronger passages, such as that beginning 'Sous l'insecte vengeur envoyé par Junon', which have not only the power of maturity, but do not properly fit into the poem and are of later conception. I would conclude that the bulk of *L'Invention* as we know it was written before Chénier went to London; that is to say between 1783 and 1787. One of the reasons for thinking this is that, surprisingly, it contains little reflection of the awakening to social problems reflected in his *Hymne à la Justice* in 1787, as one might expect of a finished 'Art poétique'. It contains a reference to Bailly's work on astronomy, but that does not necessarily mean the *Traité de l'Astronomie indienne et orientale* of 1787, but probably Bailly's earlier work on astronomy of 1781.

As for *La République des lettres*, a large bundle of fragments in the manner of the *Dunciad*, this could not have been begun before Chénier's trip to Italy, for until then he regarded satire as an unworthy pursuit. It was probably begun at the end of 1786 or early in 1787, and was intended as an attempt to defend his brother, who was having trouble with the critics. The dismissal of any but political satire stated in the *Épître sur ses ouvrages* was also a signal that the *République des lettres* (or *Les Cyclopes littéraires* as it was originally called) was soon cast aside. The similarity of the attacks on the Academy and on gentlemen-scribblers, as well as critics, in the *Essai*, suggests that the fragments of the *République* might have found their way into the essay at a later stage. The *République des lettres* was most likely abandoned as soon as Chénier went to London and was no longer living in the milieu it describes. It can thus be dated 1786–8.

As for the *Essai*, it contains some ideas formulated before 1785, some of them already versified in *L'Invention*. These ideas he took

---

[1] F34, t. i, p. 407.   [2] Ibid., p. 281.

more seriously when he met Alfieri in 1786 and found that they were in agreement about the relationship between literature and society. It would be then that he had the idea of writing, alongside *L'Invention* and the *République*, a prose work comparable with Alfieri's *The Prince and Letters*, some of which he had seen in manuscript. He continued writing it in London in 1788–90. Parts of it may be dated as late as 1792–3, such as the mention of the Avignon massacres. The *Essai* is thus the most serious and most mature of all these projects, and may be dated 1786–93.

The *Épître sur ses Ouvrages* was dated 1787 by Dimoff, and 1791 by Gabriel de Chénier. We are inclined to think that the prose draft was written in 1787, while its gay and jovial style also suggests a pre-Revolutionary work. All the dates we have given imply that the *Essai* is the centre of Chénier's thought about poetry, and although it is an unfinished work, the others that we have mentioned have to be read in relation to it.

However, the title of the poem, *L'Invention*, a key-word in his aesthetic, suggests that, had it been finished, it would have contained the essence of his poetic theory. Some critics have assumed that it was intended to be part of his didactic poem, *Hermès*, and in any case it does contain an apology for the modern pseudo-epic. The basis of *L'Invention* lies in a note in which he wrote, 'Côtoyer toujours les anciens auteurs — Sur des pensers nouveaux faisons des vers antiques'.[2] But, unfortunately, as even a superficial examination of his manuscripts would show, Chénier's method of composition, according to which he always wrote short fragments which he afterwards tried to piece together into a whole, resulted in this case in a piecemeal work which does not logically hold together. His poetic impulse rarely, at any time, took him as far as a hundred lines: quite a number of the elegies and epistles, as well as the famous last *Ïambe*, consist of eighty-eight lines, and perhaps this was his chosen optimum. The one thing which holds *L'Invention* together, though it gives the impression of having been written in fragments over a long period, is the epigraph *audendum est* which reappears several times in the form 'osons'. The central problem of *L'Invention* may be reduced to the paradox: imitate the Ancients, but dare to be new and original. In order to dispose of this paradox, Chénier had to re-define the words invention and imitation. The poem begins with praise of Homer and Virgil as 'inventors'

---

[1] F 34, t. i, pp. 216–17, and D7, t. i, p. lxvi.
[2] BN, NAF 6849, 5, v.

while carefully mentioning the special conditions in which they wrote: they lived in an age that provided them with

> ... un ciel pur, les plaisirs, la beauté,
> Des mœurs simples, des lois, la paix, la liberté,
> Un langage sonore aux douceurs souveraines.

This theory was more fully developed in the *Essai*, in which Chénier argued that great literature could only come from free men living in a free society. After asserting (line 19) 'Ce n'est qu'aux inventeurs que la vie est promise' he went on to explain that invention does not mean that the poet should offend 'truth, common sense and reason' by writing in the undisciplined manner of the English. According to him, the inventor is he who not only describes what all men experience and understand (Pope's 'What oft was thought but ne'er so well expressed') but has also the special gift of perceiving true analogies and making a synthesis of them:

> Ainsi donc, dans les arts l'inventeur est celui   45
> Qui peint ce que chacun peut sentir comme lui,
> Qui, fouillant des objets les plus sombres retraites,
> Étale et fait briller leurs richesses secrètes;
> Qui, par des nœuds certains, imprévus et nouveaux,
> Unissant des objets qui paraissent rivaux,   50
> Montre et fait adopter à la nature mère
> Ce qu'elle n'a point fait, mais ce qu'elle a pu faire;
> Car le fécond pinceau qui, sûr dans ses regards,
> Retrouve un seul visage en vingt belles épars,
> Les fait renaître ensemble, et par un art suprême,   55
> Des traits de vingt beautés forme la beauté même.

At first sight there is nothing particularly original in these lines. Line 46 comes, with some modification, from Pope and Horace. Line 47 is based on Phaedrus ('rara mens intelligit / quod interiore condidit cura angulo'); line 56 is from Socrates (Xenophon, *Memorabilia*, III. x) and the same notion is to be found in a letter from Raphael to Castiglione. Where Chénier appears to be more original is in lines 49–50, where he went to the heart of metaphor and, in a few words, expressed a theory of imagination which was to receive its full development in the thought of Coleridge. A similar theory was expressed by Vico, but there is no evidence that Chénier knew of it. Vico's theory of language is based on the nature of metaphor: he pointed out, for instance, that man tends to name the things in nature from the parts of his own body, and sometimes uses the opposite device. Thus we speak of the neck of a bottle or of a mountain-pass, or the mouth of a river, the eye of a needle, the skin on milk, the head of a nail, and so on. It is perhaps for this reason that poetry is most moving when inanimate things are compared or identified with living things, as in Baudelaire's 'Comme un visage en pleurs que les brises essuient / L'air est plein du frisson des choses qui s'enfuient'. Chénier's work was consistently metaphoric, his analogies being made with little or no explanation: he understood, like Mallarmé, that poetry must be and not merely explain. As he went on to say (line 49), originality lies not only in perceiving hitherto unknown analogies, but in giving them new expression. His theory of poetry is essentially a theory of style.

What Chénier had to say about the poetic genres is of no interest to us today, and is only part of the conventional theory of his time. We cannot sympathize with him when he asserts that the greatest achievement for a poet would be to guide his Muse through 'les sentiers confus d'une vaste épopée' (l. 84). It is this part of the poem (ll. 57 ff.) which amounts to a defence of his own unfinished enterprises, *Hermès*, *L'Amérique*, and *Susanne*. The tragedy of eighteenth-century poetry is that so many talented men frustrated their gifts because this gigantism and academic theory of genres oppressed them: they were destroyed by it as many poets are today by an oppressively narrow concept of Tradition. Chénier was very much of his time in this respect, classifying his works not according to their quality but by the yardstick of Kinds. This is, perhaps, why he failed to realize that he had, himself, made a most important contribution to the genres, his invention of the 'little epic', as Hugo was later to call it. Maybe he never understood that his short *Bucoliques* were more original, concentrated, and beautiful than his more grandiose projects. *L'Invention* thus tells us as much about Chénier's conventional prejudices as about his originality.

Much attention has been given, in France, to the passage (ll. 96–130) in which Chénier, after arguing that our world is not the same as that of the Ancients ('Tout a changé pour nous, mœurs, sciences, coutumes'), evoked the names of modern thinkers such as Torricelli, Newton, Kepler, Galileo to indicate that we know more than the Ancients, and should thus imitate their style, nor their ideas. All this is rather a bore to us, today, even when the gap has widened between what have been called the Two Cultures. However, it does enable us to see Chénier as one of the last of the humanist tradition, before the 'dissociation of sensibility' had set in. But though it is easy enough to quote Condillac, or various articles from the *Encyclopédie* and put them alongside isolated lines in Chénier's work, his arguments are just another instance of the enormous gap there really was between poetic theory and practice in his time. There is all the difference in the world between poetry in which the present state of knowledge is reflected as part of the background of man's actions, and the verse-treatise, from Le Brun's *De la Nature* and Delille's *Les Jardins* to Hugo's *Le Télégraphe*. Le Brun had already written in one of his odes (L, xxi)

> Soyez donc, Ombres immortelles,
> Mes guides, et non mes Modèles;
> Qu'un autre rampe à vos genoux:
> Il est une Gloire plus sûre;
> Vous n'imitiez que la Nature
> Et je l'imite comme vous.

But in spite of all the self-satisfied nonsense that was written about 'Nature' in the eighteenth century, there was never a period when poetry was further away from nature. The most that can be said about Chénier in this respect is that he was closer to 'nature', including human nature, than any of his contemporaries. In saying 'Volons, volons chez eux retrouver leurs modèles' he was certainly seeking, in his way, the secret springs of poetry. He believed that the Ancients could guide us to the essence of things because, as he wrote in the *Essai*, 'Chez les anciens l'homme n'était pas habitué, façonné à une multitude d'institutions arbitraires et absolument éloignées de la nature, était plus lui-même, plus nu.'[1] Rightly or wrongly he saw them as free; living when 'Chaque homme ose être un homme et penser au grand jour' (l. 162). Putting aside all arguments about the Ancients, behind this statement we see Chénier as the logical culmination of Renaissance thought. He would not have agreed with Auden's statement that 'the poet is the only free man'.

It is in the same passage (ll. 153–84) that Chénier worked towards a few lines which were later to become a kind of manifesto:

> Allons voir au théâtre, aux accents d'Euripide
> D'une sainte folie un peuple furieux
> Chanter: *Amour, tyran des hommes et des dieux.*
> Puis, ivres des transports qui nous viennent surprendre,
> Parmi nous, dans nos vers, revenons les répandre;

---

[1] D22, p. 645.

> Changeons en notre miel leurs plus antiques fleurs;
> Pour peindre notre idée empruntons leurs couleurs;
> Allumons nos flambeaux à leurs feux poétiques;
> Sur des pensers nouveaux faisons des vers antiques.   (176-84)

It is true that the idea in the famous line 'Pour peindre notre idée empruntons leurs couleurs' had already been expressed by Voltaire in his essay on epic poetry: 'Il faut peindre avec des couleurs vraies comme les anciens, mais il ne faut pas peindre les mêmes choses.'[1] But there is more in Chénier's lines than meets the eye. While his 'new ideas' would largely be those of the *Encyclopédie* he was more original in his conception of 'vers antiques'. He did not see classical poetry only as something full of wisdom and restraint, as Boileau did: we have to note such expressions as *sainte folie, ivres, transports, surprendre, doux*. He had said earlier, 'l'âme est partout' and he saw the poet, like Éluard more recently, not as he who is inspired, so much as he who inspires. It is especially the emotional impact of the Ancients that he wanted to restore to poetry, and he was, quite rightly for a stylist, groping towards a theory of effects. One of the strangest things about *L'Invention* is all that he leaves out; for instance at no stage did he try to offer a history of poetry (as Boileau did): this was no doubt to be reserved for the *Essai*.

It is most difficult to give any coherent account of this highly incoherent poem. The reader is constantly seduced away from his thought by the rare beauty of language, for parts of *L'Invention* surpass, in this respect, anything that has ever been written about poetry, at least in French. The originality of *L'Invention* lies, more than anything, in the fact that Chénier so often managed to write real poetry about poetry. Section III (ll. 185-248) contains a number of these seductive passages: for instance in lines 209-22 he goes far beyond his intention, which is to refute La Bruyère's notion that 'tout est dit':

> Cette reine des cœurs, à la touchante voix,
> A le droit en tous lieux de nous dicter son choix,
> Sûre de voir partout, introduite par elle,
> Applaudir à grands cris une beauté nouvelle,
> Et les objets nouveaux que sa voix a tentés
> Partout, de bouche en bouche, après elle chantés.
> Elle porte, à travers leurs nuages plus sombres,
> Des rayons lumineux qui dissipent leurs ombres,
> Et rit quand, dans son vide, un auteur oppressé

---

[1] *Poétique de M. de Voltaire*, 1761, p. 75.

Se plaint qu'on a tout dit et qu'on a tout pensé.
Seule, et la lyre en main, et de fleurs couronnée,
De doux ravissements partout accompagnée,
Aux lieux les plus déserts ses pas, ses jeunes pas
Trouvent mille trésors qu'on ne soupçonnait pas.

It is in passages such as this that thought becomes a pretext for pure poetry. It is followed at once by a remarkable lyric flight which strains far beyond the didactic intention which prompted it: neither Boileau nor Pope, had they been capable of writing it, would have inserted into a treatise on poetry such a remarkable passage as this, in which Chénier, through his image of the fly in amber, comes closer to a definition of the relationship of art to life than he could have done in any statement of the question in prose:

Elle seule connaît ces extases choisies,
D'un esprit tout de feu mobiles fantaisies,
Ces rêves d'un moment, belles illusions,
D'un monde imaginaire aimables visions . . .

Seule, de mots heureux, faciles, transparents,
Elle sait revêtir ces fantômes errants;
Ainsi des hauts sapins de la Finlande humide,
De l'ambre, enfant du ciel, distille l'or fluide,
Et sa chute souvent rencontre dans les airs
Quelque insecte volant qu'il porte au fond des mers;
De la Baltique enfin les vagues orageuses
Roulent et vont jeter ces larmes précieuses
Où la fière Vistule, en de nobles coteaux,
Et le froid Niémen expirent dans ses eaux.
Là les arts vont cueillir cette merveille utile,
Tombe odorante où vit l'insecte volatile;
Dans cet or diaphane il est lui-même encor,
On dirait qu'il respire et va prendre l'essor.   233–50.

The description of how amber is formed (taken from the Ancients) is, of course, odd and incorrect, but this takes nothing away from the importance of the passage: if the insect is a symbol of the 'extase choisie', then poetry becomes the timeless vehicle of living things, the privileged moments of insight and of transcendence which great minds are supposed to know.

Another highly original and beautiful movement develops between lines 264 and 284. Chénier firmly believed in the unity of the arts, and though this idea has dominated European art at certain moments—for instance in the work of Leonardo—it was generally neglected in the eighteenth century. After proclaiming that 'tous les arts sont unis' he took sculpture as his symbol of all of them, using an analogy between poetry and sculpture which was to return to him several times in his later work, and chiefly in the fine *Ïambe*, 'La Fête de l'Être suprême'. This remarkable movement arises out of a banal exhortation to young poets to work hard ('Qui que tu sois, enfin, ô toi, jeune poète, / Travaille . . .'):

> Aux antres de Paros le bloc étincelant
> N'est aux vulgaires yeux qu'une pierre insensible.
> Mais le docte ciseau, dans son sein insensible,
> Voit, suit, trouve la vie, et l'âme et tous ses traits.
> Tout l'Olympe respire en ses détours secrets . . .

It goes on to show how the gods and heroes lie dormant in the uncut stone, waiting for the artist's hand to bring them to life, then ends with the superb lines:

> Dieu tout entier habite en ce marbre penseur.
> Ciel! n'entendez-vous pas de sa bouche profonde
> Éclater cette voix créatrice du monde?

As usual, Chénier's beautiful lines stand in a context which in itself is disappointing, and seem to emerge in spite of the commonplace notion —that hard work, as Eliot has since reminded us, is at the basis of all poetic activity—which he was anxious to present. He shows no concern (if we looked at the passage more closely) with the metaphysical questions beneath what he is saying; for instance, the relation of beauty, or imagination, to the material world. The passage takes us a long way into Chénier's mind, however, for it shows that he had a basically aesthetic attitude to the world. Though he was not so conscious of this as Mallarmé was, already before him he saw matter, and human experience, as something waiting to become art. This fine passage was probably written at a fairly late stage in Chénier's development, for it has a parallel in a prose passage in the *Essai*.[1] In those pages he rejected the idea that knowledge and craftsmanship are enough. The Greeks made man in the image of God, and they could not do this by mere labour: 'Ce n'est point là qu'ils sont; c'est dans l'imagination brûlante, c'est dans la sublime pensée.' The poet's labour is necessary, but he has to have in the first place an exceptional sensibility:

[1] D22, pp. 650–2.

. . . si l'idée ou la vue de la beauté allume tes sens et te met hors de toi; si tu aimes à t'enfoncer dans les bois, seul, errant comme un insensé, et ruminant dans ton cerveau les brûlants tableaux des poètes et répétant les vers où respirent, où se meuvent les héros, les géants, les dieux . . . si, toujours mécontent de ce que tu viens de faire, une ardente inquiétude te fait toujours chercher quelque chose au delà, viens, viens, travaille; c'est toi qui feras des chefs-d'œuvre; c'est toi qui ressusciteras ce bel art, cet art divin, si mal connu parmi nous.

It is precisely this 'inquiétude', this spiritual and intellectual uneasiness, that makes Chénier a forerunner of modern Romanticism, and justifies Hugo's remark that he was 'romantique parmi les classiques'.

In the few lines after this Chénier returns to his views about how to imitate the Ancients in a creative way: 'Et sans suivre leurs pas imiter leur exemple' (l. 238). As P. Dimoff has shown, this formula was not new, but was probably taken from Young's *Conjectures on Original Composition.*[1] But once again, after this flat writing, the tone rises and brings us to the highest point in *L'Invention*, the movement which begins:

> Sous l'insecte vengeur envoyé par Junon,
> Telle Ïo tourmentée, en l'ardente saison,
> Traverse en vain les bois et la longue campagne
> Et le fleuve bruyant qui presse la montagne;
> Tel le bouillant poète en ses transports brûlants,
> Le front échevelé, les yeux étincelants,
> S'agite, se débat, cherche en d'épais bocages
> S'il pourra de sa tête apaiser les orages,
> Et secouer le Dieu qui fatigue son sein.
> De sa bouche à longs flots ce Dieu dont il est plein
> Bientôt en vers nombreux s'exhale et se déchaîne:
> Leur sublime torrent roule, saisit, entraîne
> Les tours impétueux, inattendus, nouveaux,
> L'expression de flamme aux magiques tableaux
> Qu'a trempés la nature en ses couleurs fertiles,
> Les nombres tour à tour turbulents ou faciles:
> Tout porte au fond du cœur le tumulte et la paix,
> Dans la mémoire au loin tout s'imprime à jamais.
> C'est ainsi que Minerve, en un instant formée,
> Du front de Jupiter s'élance toute armée,
> Secouant et le glaive et le casque guerrier,
> Et l'horrible Gorgone à l'aspect meurtrier . . .
>   (341–62)

[1] F34, t. i, p. 354.

The fact that this brilliant movement is immediately followed by a few
deadly platitudes about language shows that the poem was not
finished, for the last lines (363–92) do not connect logically with
what preceded them. The passage we have just quoted lays a stress on
inspiration which appears to be completely at odds with most of
L'Invention; for here, as in Valéry's *La Pythie* which is on the same
theme, the poet is represented as a kind of victim. It is indeed a pity
that *L'Invention* is so incoherent, so far from being a finished work,
and that a few remarkable lyrical passages are lost to most readers
because of their dull context. Perhaps one of the reasons for this (apart
from the poet's early death) is that Chénier was not sure how he would
present it. Perhaps it was not intended, in any case, to be self-contained,
for in the *Essai* he remarked 'tout cela peut être traité soit en prose, soit
en vers, dans cette espèce de roman sur la perfection des arts'.[1] The fact
that he was hoping to write a work in both prose and verse, for which
a model already existed in Voltaire's *Le Temple du Goût*, suggests that
L'Invention would have been cut up into small pieces which would
have been distributed through the *Essai*, perhaps together with some
fragments of *La République des Lettres*.

Chénier's *Essai*, as we shall call it (for the long title 'Essai sur les
Causes et les Effets de la Perfection et de la Décadence des Lettres et
des Arts' was only given to it by Abel Lefranc in 1899),[2] made him
a pioneer in speculations on the relationship between literature and
society, of which important exponents have been Madame de Staël,
Hegel, Comte, Taine, Marx, Engels, and Plekhanov. Unlike some of
his successors, he never lost sight of the fact that the writer is an
individual, with his own capacities, as well as a social creature; nor did
he allow his concern for the present state of society and the arts to
falsify his historical sense. His *Essai* is a remarkable bridge between
two eras, condemning the reign of privilege and pointing forwards
towards liberalism; making no extravagant claim for the artist as
a special kind of man, but relating his role in society to the health or
corruption of its institutions, balanced by the moral probity of the
artist himself. Unfortunately, his *Essai* did not reach the public until
over a hundred years after his death. The result was that the first in the
field was Madame de Staël, with her erratic and often ignorant *De la
Littérature considérée dans ses rapports avec les institutions sociales*,
which appeared in 1800. Hers was a hasty, slipshod composition,

[1] D22, p. 692.   [2] E4.

written in that assertive and torrential style which had as bad an influence as many of her theories. Lacking Chénier's capacity for either close study or synthesis, she applied, with less discrimination than he, Montesquieu's theory of the influence of climate on institutions and manners. With her usual unscrupulousness she was content to grind her own axes, without admitting her ignorance of large areas of her subject: her theory of the 'perfectibility of man', which has much to be said for it, though it led to a conception of 'progress' in the nineteenth century which is disastrous when applied to the arts, forced her to conclude that the Romans, and their culture and institutions, were superior to the Greeks. The Nordic literatures were 'superior' to the Latin ones, because the northern writers were, supposedly, more respectful towards women. If she did much to restore medieval literature to its proper place, it was at the expense of the classics. Being a polemicist and not a poet, she asserted that political liberty set polemics and 'éloquence' above 'poésie d'imagination'. But her general thesis, the intimate connexion between the arts and prevailing institutions, was little different from Chénier's, except that he had the sense to see that the artist can also be an active force by entering into opposition; in other words, the correlation between literature and institutions can never be exact. It is a matter for debate whether Madame de Staël was right in undermining the classical ideal of beauty, substituting for it woolly notions of relativism which have bedevilled criticism ever since. Had the early Romantics not been brought up on the classics, she would have produced an even greater lowering of standards and values than actually took place.

Where Madame de Staël's book was compelling, though it is an odd mixture of sound and shallow ideas, Chénier approached the same task with greater learning and greater seriousness of mind. Though his might appear to be the last and noblest defence of the classical canon, the old rhetoric, it pointed into the future by its emphasis on a free society and the individuality of the artist. Better grounded than Mme de Staël in aesthetics, he had a clearer notion of what is or is not a work of art. Though written in a very personal manner, his is a more objective document than hers. Had it appeared at the right time, it would have given the same check to the romantic fallacies as Coleridge's thought did in England.

Though we have more than once suggested that Chénier was, in some ways, slow in maturing, the *Essai* shows a full intellectual maturity, as well as being written in a precise and modern French which is a model of the expository style. Begun as early as 1785 (when he was only twenty-three), there is evidence that he was still working on it down to the time of his imprisonment in 1794. Like Pascal's *Pensées* it is only a bundle of fragments. Chénier was, by nature, incapable of writing a book from the beginning, and wrote bits which were to be fitted in here and there. The *Essai* as it stands consists of about seventy closely printed pages, ranging from short notes or jottings to long and carefully composed passages, all of which it is not difficult to fit into the ambitious pattern he had laid down.

The *Essai* begins with a long introduction which gives the basis of his theory and also contains some interesting personal remarks. The very first sentence comes as a challenge, for in a few words it resumes the essence of the philosophy of the Encyclopaedists: 'Il n'y a de bonheur, pour aucune espèce vivante, qu'à suivre ce à quoi la nature la destine.'[1] He did not fall into the primitivism of Rousseau, or imagine that man is naturally good; but saw man endowed with faculties that lead him to live as a social being, and ceaselessly to strive after the creation of a society based on equity and justice. Nor did he fall into the error or regarding man as a passive creature or instrument. Though expounding republican and libertarian sentiments, he did not abandon the idea of an élite, for 'Quelques-uns, plus grands que tous, n'ont que le pur enthousiasme de la vertu; d'autres y joignent le désir de la gloire'.[2] These exceptional men—like Hugo's 'Mages'—are those fitted to guide and improve others, through good actions and good works. The good book acts as a leaven in society: 'Souvent un bon livre est lui-même une bonne action; et souvent un auteur sage et sublime, étant la cause lente de saines révolutions dans les mœurs et dans les idées, peut sembler avoir fait lui-même tout ce qu'il fait faire de bien.'[3] Here, then, we have Shelley's 'unacknowledged legislator'. Like many of his contemporaries, Chénier had an exaggerated idea of the power of the written word: we shall find him, in 1791, declaring that all the good and bad done during the Revolution had been the result of published works.

After describing how in young societies literature is an integral part of an accepted way of life, and therefore of direct public utility, he suggested that this state of the arts can only continue so long as institutions are good. The identification of the writer with society fails, when society fails. As soon as there is privilege, tyranny, greed, when 'un petit nombre se partage tout', institutions will be flouted. The writer

---

[1] D22, p. 621.   [2] Ibid., p. 621.   [3] Ibid., p. 622.

is then thrust into a defensive position: some will have the courage to protest, but more will sell their pen and soul to the highest bidder. One or two 'esprits généreux' will become enemies of that society and work for its overthrow. At this point Chénier made one of those personal statements which suddenly bring his subject alive:

Pour moi, ouvrant les yeux autour de moi au sortir de l'enfance, je vis que l'argent et l'intrigue étaient presque la seule voie pour aller à tout; je résolus donc, dès lors, sans examiner si les circonstances me le permettaient, de vivre toujours loin de toutes affaires, avec mes amis, dans la retraite et dans la plus entière liberté. Choqué de voir les lettres si prosternées et le genre humain ne pas songer à relever sa tête, je me livrai souvent aux distractions et aux égarements d'une jeunesse forte et fougueuse; mais, toujours dominé par l'amour de la poésie, des lettres et de l'étude, souvent chagrin et découragé par la fortune ou par moi-même, toujours soutenu par mes amis, je sentis au moins dans moi que mes vers et ma prose, goûtés ou non, seraient mis au rang du petit nombre d'ouvrages qu'aucune bassesse n'a flétris. Ainsi, même dans les chaleurs de l'âge et des passions, et même dans les instants où la dure nécessité a interrompu mon indépendance, toujours occupé de ces idées favorites, et, chez moi, en voyage, le long des rues, dans les promenades, méditant toujours sur l'espoir, peut-etre insensé, de voir renaître les bonnes disciplines, et cherchant à la fois, dans les histoires et dans la nature des choses, *les causes et les effets de la perfection et de la décadence des lettres*, j'ai cru qu'il serait bien de resserrer en un livre simple et persuasif ce que nombre d'années m'ont fait mûrir de réflexions sur ces matières.[1]

We know that Chénier's awakening to social problems must have come as soon as he entered the army at the age of twenty-one. It is curious to see that his first reaction had been to withdraw from public life and that, at the same time, he implies that the turbulence and errors of his youth had something to do with his disgust with society. His idea of literature—or rather of his own productions—was of something untainted by that decadent society, though not necessarily 'committed'. In working on his *Essai* he must have seen it, in his mind, as a contribution to the Revolution, one of those 'good actions' that committed literature might become. He did not ask on what his 'independence' was based, but perhaps took it for granted that society owes a poet his living. It is noticeable, too, that Chénier took the same stand of impartiality and independence in literary matters as he was to take in his politics:

Sûr de n'avoir jamais ni la richesse au prix de la liberté, ni l'amitié ou la familiarité des princes et des grands, ni les éloges privés, ni l'association à

[1] Ibid., p. 625.

aucun musée ou académie, ou autre confrérie savante, ni enfin aucune espèce
de récompense royale ou littéraire; déterminé à ne point vivre partout où
la pensée ne sera point libre; à ne connaître de guide que la raison, de maître
que la justice, et de protecteur que les lois, je puis, autant que ma nature
m'aidera, chercher la vérité sans déguisement, la trouver sans que des
préjugés me l'obscurcissent, et la dire sans que ni désir, ni espérance, ni
crainte, viennent altérer ma franchise ou la rendre muette.[1]

After saying that he would aim at nothing but a 'nerveuse et succulente
brièveté' he paid tribute to Montaigne, Montesquieu, and Rousseau,
'des hommes que l'on ne peut surpasser dans l'art d'écrire'.

The plan of the *Essai* is so ambitious that even with a 'succulent
brevity' it would probably have run into a work of two or three
volumes. His survey of the question would have been far more logical
and thorough than Madame de Staël's book, and (to judge from the
parts he completed) more copiously illustrated. It would have been in
three parts, with an Introduction and Conclusion:

> Causes qui favorisent les lettres:
> > du climat; des lois; des mœurs et usages; des circonstances locales et
> > momentanées.
> Influence d'une bonne littérature.
> Causes qui nuisent aux lettres:
> > des associations littéraires; qu'il est faux que la protection des princes
> > ait fait du bien aux lettres; qu'il est faux que la politesse et l'élégance du
> > style et du langage naissent dans les cours.
> Histoire du style et du goût.
> Influence d'une mauvaise littérature.
> Exhortation et examen des circonstances présentes.

Chénier completed only half a dozen pages of the first part. The first
chapter, 'Des Lois', argued that 'Il ne peut y avoir que des talents
oisifs et inutiles dans la tyrannie, encore moins dans l'aristocratie, et
que tous les talents sont de l'essence de la démocratie, vraie république'.[2]
Like Alfieri, Chénier conveniently forgot that enlightened patrons of
the arts may exist even under a despotism, and that some artists have
found more freedom in that way than if they worked as free-lances
or depended on the whims of a twentieth-century French or British
government or local council. However, Chénier was also aware that
Demos can become a despot, and he saw that in certain states of society
it is likely that many different conditions may coexist—for instance
artists may be advanced by a combination of royal tyranny, aristocracy,

---

[1] D22, p. 626.   [2] Ibid., p. 630.

and public (democratic) opinion, so that good and bad men may come
to the top together. He was, in any case, bourgeois enough to think
in terms of men 'coming to the top' or into prominence. He was also
conscious that even in the perfect democracy or republic a privileged
caste would either survive or be created, either as relics of an aristocracy
or out of public gratitude. We have only to look at the societies around
us today to see that he was right. He admitted, even, that it was
possible for a 'tyrant' to be 'un homme sage et éclairé' and to favour
the best men, but that the greatest obstacle to this is the aristocracy,
who will always resent the honours shown to men of humble birth.
We see, also, from his reflections on monarchy, how the independence
and originality of Chénier's thought on the subject enabled him to
avoid the almost irrational over-simplification of many of his successors, and in reading these remarks we can understand how, during the
Revolution, his awareness of the relativeness and complexity of social
conditions made it impossible for him to accept the slogans of those
who thought they could discover the just State overnight:

> Comme la plupart des monarchies de l'Europe moderne sont une espèce
> de mélange . . . où la tyrannie n'est pas extrême, où l'aristocratie est dans les
> mœurs, les coutumes et les idées, plutôt que dans les lois et les constitutions,
> où le peuple a conservé quelque espèce de droits et de titres, et est encore un
> peu plus que rien . . . ce triple esprit a agi; nous voyons les trois effets
> ensemble . . . c'est-à-dire que d'un côté les nobles s'indignent que la porte des
> honneurs puisse s'ouvrir aux plébéiens, et de l'autre, tantôt les rois, tantôt
> le cri de la faveur publique élèvent des hommes dignes et indignes. Cela
> nous a fait grand bien . . ., etc.[1]

It was such reflections as these that led him to believe that talent would
best flourish in a democracy. Napoleon was to prove him right, for
his slogan 'la carrière ouverte aux talents' did not prevent him from
persecuting some of his best writers. We can see, however, that
Chénier's openness of mind was forcing him into a Utopian position.
Whereas Alfieri, Madame de Staël, Marx, and many others tended to
see the social problem in black and white, Chénier took into account
the possibility of the benevolent despot, an enlightened aristocracy,
and the mass of 'the people' who can 'govern as a single tyrant'. He
was to see this last condition after the 10th of August 1792, when
the 'democratic' Convention crushed all independent thought. But
Chénier's 'democracy', we feel, is something that might exist in the
pages of Montesquieu and Rousseau, but not in this world: the artist

[1] Ibid., p. 630.

has not been noticeably happier in Switzerland or America than elsewhere, because aristocracy is quickly replaced by the even crueller
tyranny of cash. The Marxist state might correspond, in theory, to
Chénier's ideal, but nowhere has his vision of the tyranny of a pseudo-
democracy been more fully realized than in Russia.

The third chapter, 'Des Mœurs et Usages', consists of only a few
fragments, but here again the originality of Chénier's approach is
apparent. Instead of taking the typical Rousseau-istic example of the
negro, or the American Indian, to illustrate his idea of the primitive-
ness of manners in a society, he took that of the ancient Greeks, and
was to have given his passage of verse describing the combat of the
Lapiths and Centaurs (the climax of *L'Aveugle*) to show how even
the common convention of hospitality may be disregarded.[1] We cannot help reflecting that it might be in some so-called primitive community, for instance an African tribe, that Chénier would have found
instances of a very highly organized society, in which a strict code of
manners is observed and the artist fulfils his natural functions by
common consent. It is likely, however, that he would have sought this
in some Greek city-state. The only other interesting remark in this
chapter is concerned with Semantics, for he observed that every nation
tends to draw a system of local metaphor from its own manners and
customs, and that these cannot be translated into other languages,
whose system is bound to be different. Of this he gave a recondite
example, the Japanese use of the word 'kawakiri', meaning a cauterizing
medicine, as a synonym for income-tax. He went on to describe how
lying, which is gross and stupidly obvious in primitive societies,
becomes deceptively elegant and persuasive when society is more refined. It is difficult to see where such thoughts would have led Chénier,
but the indications are that this chapter would have developed a theory
of the relationship between society and language, and, consequently,
literature.

Chénier put most of his work into the second part of his Essay,
where he began to come to grips with his subject. His first attack was
on what he called 'Associations littéraires' or academies which, as he
put it, imagine that they can confer genius on their members. He began
by describing how, as a child, he had pretended he was a priest celebrating Mass in his home-made 'chapel' (see p. 8 above). Playing on
the word 'chapelle', which in French means a literary clique, he drove
home his point with 'Un poète . . . Une académie . . . O la ridicule

[1] D22, p. 633.

chapelle! les hommes qui devraient être sages et qui . . . imaginent de faire la roue et d'aller à cheval sur un bâton.'[1] He abandoned the solemn tone of his early chapters, to indulge his wit at the expense of the 'secrétaire perpétuel' of the Academy, saying, 'Il se croit le secrétaire perpétuel du genre humain.' In making fun of academic criticism he advanced some of his own views about style, which could well be taken to heart even today, not only in academies but in most universities:

> Si l'ouvrage est en vers, ils observent gravement que quelquefois il n'y a point de repos après l'hémistiche. S'il est en prose, ils examinent combien on y rencontre de vers alexandrins. Et ils sont trop sévères critiques pour pardonner un si horrible défaut.
>
> Irez-vous leur dire qu'il n'y a qu'un sot qui abandonne une expression franche, naïve, pittoresque, parce qu'elle se trouve former une phrase coupée en deux moitiés de six syllabes chacune? Mais, pour les convaincre, il faudrait leur apprendre *que c'est aux pensées à créer le style, qu'elles ont leur expression propre que le génie rencontre toujours sans le chercher jamais*, et que toutes ces conventions académiques qui réduisent tout à un mécanique arrangement de paroles font de l'art d'écrire un amusement puéril et méprisable. . . .[2]

Chénier was well in advance of his contemporaries in his onslaught on the Academy which, of course, was much more fully developed in his *La République des Lettres*. We know now that the French Romantics had first to fight the Academy before they could impose their new literary ideas and manner and that afterwards, when they themselves became academicians, they found it almost impossible to reform it from the inside, because even academic power corrupts. If Chénier was at all a pre-romantic, it was especially in personalizing style by declaring it to be inseparable from thought, and in stressing the right to individuality. Though Buffon had announced that 'le style, c'est l'homme' he was not, like Chénier, prepared to throw overboard the whole critical apparatus of pseudo-classicism, which, like the State, was based on the idea of authority. As we shall see, Chénier was thinking many years ahead—and thinking dangerously, perhaps— when he declared in *La République des Lettres* that 'Nul n'est juge des arts que l'artiste lui-même' (see below, p. 120). An essential novelty of Chénier's *Essai* is the extent to which it disregards authority and ready-made recipes, in order to consider both society and literature from the point of view of the individual writer. It is not surprising,

---

[1] Ibid., p. 635.   [2] Ibid., p. 636.

then, that his diatribe against the Académie led him to the conclusion that 'l'institution des académies est une des choses qui, nécessairement et par leur nature, ont été, sont et seront les plus nuisibles aux progrès et à l'honneur des lettres'. It is quite possible that Chénier was also influenced by what he saw or heard of the intrigues and disputes, as well, of the Royal Academy of Arts which was founded in Britain in 1768.

Chénier wrote nothing of his chapter on royal patronage, but in 'L'Influence des Cours' (part II, chapter iii) took a stand against patronage in arguing that, as the courtier has to please his 'master', the king, so, in his turn, the writer or artist is forced to please the courtier, taking his place in a kind of hierarchy of servility. Even when the artist revolts, as in the case of Aristotle and Theocritus, or John Gay on whom Chénier wrote at some length, it is usually not for good aesthetic or moral reasons but because he has not been paid or flattered enough. His revolt is therefore just as foolish as his subjection. But here again we see Chénier's good sense, for instead of arguing that the writer must therefore avoid the court, he suggests instead that he should keep his independence: 'Que j'aime le sage qui se plaît dans sa médiocrité, qui goûte trop son bonheur pour y songer, qui n'aime point les grands et qui en parle fort peu, qui sait vivre avec eux sans les rechercher, se passer d'eux sans les fuir . . .'[1]

Chénier made most progress with his 'Histoire du Style et du Goût' (chapter iv), which contains some thirty pages of observations. It is made up of so many fragments that it is not possible to give a consecutive account of its argument: all that can be done is to draw attention to items that throw light on his poetic theory. It starts, surprisingly, with praise of the Bible, which Chénier regarded as a collection of poems: 'Ce recueil renferme les ouvrages d'un grand nombre de poètes qui, tous, avaient leur génie particulier . . . digne d'être connu.' He went on to argue that it was only by some accident of history that they were taken as doctrinal books 'et devinrent le seul code du genre humain'. He reproached Voltaire for having failed to appreciate them, perhaps because he was incapable of liking 'la poésie haute et sublime'.[2] He called for a new edition of these books 'tels qu'ils sont' and praised the scholarship of such biblical commentators as Richard Simon, Schultens, and Bishop Lowth. Rousseau, of course, had already written in general terms about the 'poetry' of the Bible, but Chénier's theory of its being a collection of poems was not only original (however unsound it may be) but surprising for a disciple of the

---

[1] D22, p. 638.   [2] Ibid., p. 642.

Encyclopaedists, who had done their best to demolish any faith in
the Scriptures, while paying no attention to their literary qualities.
D'Holbach, for instance, had mocked the Bible as 'un roman oriental,
dégoûtant pour tout homme de bon sens', and this was the general
opinion of the 'philosophes'. But Chénier's scholarly taste instinctively
led him in the direction that Renan was later to follow.

Turning to ancient Europe, it is clear that Chénier placed the
Golden Age in the past, before the Romans and Carthaginians disturbed the Greek way of life.[1] He saw the ancient Greeks as open and
unspoilt ('Les anciens étaient nus . . . leur âme était nue'), whereas
modern man has become a slave to habits, conventions, and institutions
which cramp imagination. So their language was rich and poetic as
they were: 'Langue grecque: beaucoup d'épithètes y sont des tableaux
tout entiers.' His admiration for the Greeks led him to scorn much of
modern literature: his prejudice in their favour was such that he
described them as 'nés pour les beaux-arts plus que nul peuple au
monde', they could write with 'une sensibilité intéressante et douce qui
vous émeut, qui vous pénètre'—'leurs expressions sont vraies, humaines, nées dans l'homme et doivent toucher tous les hommes'.
Against them he set Shakespeare's 'barbarous convulsions' and 'ces
idées énormes et gigantesques' of the Northern poets which, according
to him, depress the spirits without touching them.[2] Here his standpoint
is the very opposite of Madame de Staël's, though, perhaps, equally
unjust. He thought that Young often spoke 'le vrai langage de la
passion' but contrasted the gloom, mingled with grotesque humour,
with which Northern poets write about death, with the Greeks' attitude to it: 'Ils attendent la mort couronnés de roses, sans se travailler
pour lui rire au nez.' It is noticeable that, had it been finished, Chénier's
Essai would have had more to say about poetry than about anything
else, and that in this respect it would have been very complete and
detailed: he noted, 'Faire entièrement, avec soin, toute l'Histoire de
la littérature grecque, surtout poétique', and gave some indications
how this would have been done.[3] It is doubtful whether any French
poet or critic, before or after Chénier, ever wrote of things Greek with
such passion or such beauty: one of the finest moments in the Essai
is when, with the kind of upsurge of feeling that we sometimes find in
Pascal or Chateaubriand, he tried to express his admiration for Greek
sculpture.[4] It is all very well to seek out sources, as some of Chénier's
critics have so devotedly done, but rather than debate whether or not

[1] Ibid., p. 645.   [2] Ibid., p. 647.   [3] Ibid., p. 649.   [4] Ibid., pp. 650–1.

he had read Winckelmann (for instance) it is surely more important
to see that Chénier wrote of the classics, not with the modest pen of the
scholar, but with the same lyrical warmth as Chateaubriand or Walter
Pater. Without going into details, it is also significant that Chénier
had little or nothing to say of the thought or the mind of the Greeks:
he was the first critic to dwell rather on their sensibility, which he
described variously as unspoilt, interesting and gentle, or 'tender',
and on their 'imagination brûlante'. The mental picture he had of
Greek poetry and art was thus far different from that of scholars either
then or now. Unabashed by the centuries of academic awe that sur-
rounded his name, he was able to bring Homer himself down to human
terms, admiring his 'noble, majestueuse, attachante, *naïve simplicité*'.
For him, the true Greek 'genius' lay in this gift of sensibility, and he
argued that decadence came with scholarship—'l'érudition prit la place
du génie'—and wit: 'Les Grecs, toujours portés à la subtilité d'esprit,
dès qu'ils eurent perdu leur génie, n'ayant point perdu leur activité
d'esprit, ne furent plus que de pointilleux sophistes.'[1] Whether he was
right or not, this fits in logically with his main thesis, for, according
to him, the decline of sensibility came with the subjection of Greece
to foreign powers. His tribute to Greek art and literature is the very
basis of his view of modern literatures, for 'Les premiers anciens inven-
taient, nos grands hommes étaient obligés de réparer'.

As his *Bucoliques* form the centre of Chénier's work, it is interesting
to see that he was well informed about the nature of bucolic poetry as
a whole: 'En parlant des Églogues de Virgile imitées de Théocrite, et
que les poésies bucoliques ne sont originairement que des scènes de
comédie, et que *versibus alternis opprobria rustica fudit* fut l'origine de la
comédie; et la poésie pastorale et la comédie viennent d'une même
source...'[2] It was thus with a full knowledge of what he was doing
that Chénier brought comedy into his pastoral poems, as well as making
them as dramatic as he could. That he was aware of the implications of
this theory is shown by his subsequent criticism of the *favole bosche-
reccie* of the Italians, and of the degenerate French pastorals and 'ber-
geries'. This passage is followed immediately by an important statement
which explains the essential purity of his own work, even when it is
erotic:

Les élégiaques anciens, simples, naturels, passionnés, d'une nudité décente
... comparés à ces fades et énigmatiques subtilités appelées galanteries, qui
rendent la plupart de nos écrivains érotiques si fastidieux pour tous les

[1] D22, p. 655.   [2] Ibid., p. 660.

lecteurs qui joignent à un esprit droit et juste *une sensibilité vraie et une âme ouverte* à tout ce que les passions ont de doux ou d'orageux.[1]

In stressing this union of intellect and sensibility he was defining not only his ideal of the elegiac poet but also his ideal reader. The implied rejection of the rococo mannerism which destroyed French poetry at the roots in the eighteenth century, explains better than anything in the *Essai* what Lacretelle meant in writing about him, 'Frondeur du goût efféminé qui lui paraissait dominer notre poésie devenue froidement coquette, il voulait la ramener aux beautés fortes et sévères qu'il avait étudiées dans leur source primitive.'

Among the seventeenth-century writers he gave priority to the genius of Corneille, Racine, Molière, and La Fontaine. He dismissed such writers as Quinault and Perrault with contempt. He was not a typical 'modernist', treading blindly in the steps of La Motte and Fontenelle, for while he granted them certain qualities, he condemned them as second-rate minds: 'L'un et l'autre étaient nés sans le talent, sans le génie des beaux-arts, absolument inhabiles à la poésie, par conséquent sans aucune justesse de goût pour apprécier ces sortes d'ouvrages, et pourtant avec la fureur de s'en occuper.'[2] His most damning comment on these two enemies of the 'ancients' is that they knew no Greek.

Chénier's reflections on literary fashion, which begin by showing how Racine was for long compared unfavourably with Corneille, and Voltaire with Crébillon and J.-B. Rousseau, until now young poets were brow-beaten by excessive esteem for Voltaire in his turn, lead to some sustained criticism of Voltaire which gives us a clear idea of Chénier's independence and originality. He had no respect for the *Henriade*, saying that 'ce grand homme n'a pas été trop modeste, quand il a dit qu'il avait fait un poème épique avant de savoir ce que c'était'.[3] Chénier's criticism is almost Romantic, because the whole weight is brought to bear on Voltaire's character, which to Chénier appeared to be unworthy of a great writer. He accused Voltaire of toadying to the great, then taking spiteful revenge: 'J'y vois un égoïsme intolérant, un amour-propre bilieux et colère qui lui montre des ennemis partout.' The vicious strain in his character prevented him from being a poet: 'Chez lui, tous les genres de poésie deviennent la satire.'[4] That is, when he was not busy writing verse to flatter not only kings and princes but their mistresses as well: Chénier called him 'ce philosophe parasite',

---

[1] Ibid., p. 661.   [2] Ibid., p. 664.   [3] Ibid., p. 665.   [4] Ibid., p. 667.

and went so far as to say, 'Tout cela me montre un homme que je n'aurais pu estimer et avec qui je n'aurais guère aimé de vivre.' He could not understand how the same writer could pour contempt on 'les vertus austères et mâles' with one hand, yet also produce works in praise of virtue and liberty. While admitting that Voltaire was endowed with 'des talents faits pour atteindre aux plus hauts points de perfection dans les arts' he blamed him for taking the easiest way in everything, 'se contentant de cueillir les filets précieux qui brillaient à la surface'.[1] Voltaire's poem on *La Loi naturelle*, he says, in spite of its noble subject, 'ne fut qu'un croquis informe, sans plan, sans suite, sans liaison, écrit d'un ton absolument indigne de la noblesse et de la majesté du sujet'. As for his prose works, with the exception of 'un petit nombre d'articles fort beaux' he gave out nothing but 'un puéril amas d'opuscules, où d'intéressantes questions de science ou de politique sont décidées avant d'être entamées'. Voltaire's reputation as a 'philosophe' was gained largely by a sparkling, light style 'qui amuse et étourdit le lecteur et lui fait perdre avec joie autant de temps à les lire que l'auteur en perdit à les composer'.

Chénier's objections to Voltaire are necessarily sketchy, and would have needed more development to be satisfying. He was obviously in a dilemma about Voltaire, being conscious of his claim to greatness but just as conscious of his enormous weaknesses as a writer and thinker. People were then too close to Voltaire to see him in his proper perspective, and for the most part they were still too close to him during the nineteenth century, when his reputation underwent an eclipse. What is particularly surprising is that Chénier, with his advanced political views, should have succeeded in dissociating Voltaire the writer from the genius of the Revolution who was entombed in the Pantheon. But Chénier was closer to the truth than his contemporaries, for Voltaire has never been taken seriously as a poet outside France, while he has no standing as a philosopher in the proper sense of the term—and the proper sense of the term is certainly not that of the so-called 'philosophes' of eighteenth-century France. The reasons why Chénier comes so close to the truth, though his particular statements would have to be modified or substantiated in every direction, is that his critical principle of moral responsibility and integrity is sound and unassailable. Chénier showed very ably, at the end of his commentary, that only a lack of moral scruple could enable Voltaire to rehabilitate Pedro the Cruel (of Castile) whom he, Chénier, described as 'un des

[1] D22, p. 669.

plus odieux tyrans qui ont déshonoré le trône'. There is no doubt that Chénier could have furnished more detail of this kind in support of his analysis, which is one of the most penetrating attacks that have ever been made on the great Voltaire. It would be underestimating Chénier's critical powers, however, to say that he merely approached writers from the standpoint of their individuality. That his discovery of the principle of moral integrity as a necessary part of the critical canon was no accident is seen not only in his approach to Voltaire but in his eulogy of Cicero, to whom he gave equal attention in a very carefully-written part of the same chapter. In the case of Cicero he reached the opposite conclusion, finding in him a perfect balance between his character and his works. It is as though, bearing Plutarch in mind, he was setting these two contrasting portraits of Voltaire and Cicero side by side.

Chénier completed only a small part of his fifth chapter ('Influence d'une mauvaise littérature') but there is enough to show that he was unhindered by any traditional taboos. For instance, he criticized Aristotle, because part of his work had become a basis for Scholasticism, which Chénier regarded as harmful. Pascal was criticized for lending his powers to unworthy purposes, using reason to destroy reason: 'Il y a en effet des endroits éloquents, mais combien c'est peu de chose que de l'éloquence employée à soutenir du ton le plus arrogant les plus impitoyables sophismes.' Valéry has since attacked Pascal on much the same grounds.

Chénier began two chapters of his third part ('Examen des circonstances présentes'), which promised to be the most interesting. The first of these chapters is, in the main, an attack on artificiality and preciosity, and on the false values which he had also condemned in his *République des Lettres*. In revolt against the conventional standards of his century, he was its only writer to demand 'natural' writing as well as rejecting all rule-of-thumb methods of criticism (such as 'Cela n'est pas français; cela ne se dit pas; cela est inexact'), many of which are still in force today. It was here that he had a sudden insight into the metaphorical nature of poetry, and poetic language as a language of analogy, which he expressed in another way in a brilliant passage of *L'Invention* (see p. 95 above). He was well on the way to formulating Coleridge's theory of Imagination (as opposed to Fancy) in dismissing those who are 'toujours incapables de sentir ces grands mouvements de l'âme qui seuls font inventer les expressions sublimes, de saisir *ces nombreux rapports des choses entre elles* et qui frappent une imagination sensible et lui inspirent *ce langage ardent et métaphorique qui donne la vie à tout*, et par qui *les objets s'éclairent les uns les autres*'.[1] There is a weight of thought behind this statement which shows that Chénier had, already, a sufficient philosophical background for developing, had he lived, that theory of analogy which was to be formulated best by Baudelaire and to make the fortune of French Symbolism. It would be a mistake to consider this short statement as a kind of accident, for it is really the basis for the theory of *naïveté* which Chénier developed more fully in the second chapter, which follows. Repeating Horace's *Homo sum* . . . he suggested that when writers have not seen 'les vrais rapports des choses' they turn to imaginary relationships between things, then draw false conclusions from them: the poetic world is thus reduced and 'on a fait des crimes des choses qui sont dans la nature et qu'elle prescrit'. His idea of nature was not, then, the false eighteenth-century picturesque, but the real world of the philosopher and (for that matter) the scientist. But it is natural that a poet should then pursue his argument on the terrain of what is the real world of the sensibility, of the emotions, of the imagination, and this Chénier did in a remarkable way. Perhaps it is unfortunate that he chose the words 'naïf' and 'naïveté' as the basis for his demonstration; but he made it abundantly clear that he was using the words in their proper sense, meaning what is unchangeably true and almost primitive in nature; not 'une franchise innocente et presque enfantine à dire de petites choses'. What he was seeking was (for instance) the sublime simplicity of Shakespeare's phrase 'Prithee, undo this button' on the lips of King Lear as he dies. In a few phrases Chénier was demolishing the neo-classical idea that a proper knowledge and command of Rhetoric is all that is needed for fine writing; in his view the very opposite is the case:

> . . . La naïveté est le point de perfection de tous les arts et de chaque genre dans tous les arts. Vous pouvez avoir un beau choix de mots, des phrases bien arrondies, des périodes sonores et harmonieuses; si vous n'êtes point naïf, vous ne toucherez point. L'oreille retiendra vos sons, l'âme ne retiendra point vos pensées; elles n'iront point jusqu'à l'âme, elles se perdront dans l'oreille. Vous serez comme le poète Rousseau, toujours pompeux et jamais sublime.[2]

He went on to argue that, from nobility down to intimate tenderness, everything depends on this 'naïveté' of feeling and expression: without it, the writer cannot write well, nor can the reader touch a genuine

---

[1] D22, p. 676.   [2] Ibid., p. 681.

experience. We are here in the presence of new and stirring thoughts which might have changed the whole course of French poetry. They point to Baudelaire's protest, 'Ne méprisez la sensibilité de personne. La sensibilité de chacun, c'est son génie.' In his insistence on the effect produced by a work of art, Chénier was feeling towards that theory of effects which was to be so well elaborated by Baudelaire and Valéry. But what is striking and convincing is the demonstration that Chénier then proceeded to give of his theory, taking his examples from Dante, Corneille, Racine, Homer, Terence, Sophocles, Tacitus; and, among the French, 'notre divin La Fontaine', Montaigne, Rousseau, and Montesquieu. Chénier's theory of the sublime was based on completely opposite premisses to those which were then in vogue, and which identified it with the grandiose, the grandiloquent; taking the example of Dante's description of the fate of Ugolino and his children, he wrote:

C'est la naïveté sublime, c'est ce malheureux père qui, entendant murer la tour, regarde ses quatre enfants sans dire un seul mot; c'est son expression: '*Si dentro impietrai*'; c'est l'étonnement de ces quatre enfants qui ignorent la cause de ce regard effaré: '*Tu guardi si, padre: chè hai?*' C'est le désespoir avec lequel il se mord les mains; c'est le cri déchirant de Graddo, qui expire de faim à ses pieds: '*Padre mio, chè non m'aiuti?*' Voilà des traits pour lesquels on pardonne des volumes d'absurdités.[1]

Similarly, in considering the best of Corneille and Racine, Chénier found this 'sublime naïveté' not in long speeches of noble rhetoric, but in those moments to which great art inevitably leads, when human passions and dilemmas are suddenly reduced to their simplest terms, when speech comes nearest to a kind of silence which penetrates the soul of the reader or spectator. Chénier is one of the very few French critics ever to have appreciated the proper value of understatement, which is the more likely to be reached, the more a writer knows and has experienced but can never fully express: he praises what is not the result of artifice but of inner necessity, the writer who 'sans apprêt, dit à mesure qu'il pense, écrit comme malgré lui, et pressé de l'abondance de ses idées semble contraint de leur ouvrir une issue et de les répandre dans un ouvrage; quiconque enfin, dans la moindre chose qu'il dit, montre une vaste connaissance, une infaillible érudition de la nature, une profonde et naïve expérience du cœur humain'. Of course, Chénier was expressing his ideas in his usual urbane, unprofessional way; but it is, precisely, in terms of *experience* that modern criticism

[1] Ibid., p. 682.

has made its most useful contribution to the understanding of the arts. Abandoning the current recipes for fine writing, Chénier was well on the way to a theory of communication; for he never lost sight of the reader, at the receiving end, who is brought to life only by what is universal: 'Il y a des sentiments si purs, si simples, des pensées si éternelles, si humaines, si nôtres, si profondément innées dans l'âme, que les âmes de tous les lecteurs les reconnaissent à l'instant; elles se réunissent à celle de l'auteur, elles semblent se reconnaître toutes et se souvenir qu'elles ont une origine commune.'

Another most interesting theory, developed in this chapter, is that there are ideas which are so universal that they come to be held in common by all writers. It then becomes logical to assume that, in the same way, there is a certain universality or continuity in style: there must be expressions which are nobody's—or everybody's—property. Chénier was quite frank about his theory of creative plagiarism which he developed so brilliantly in his *Épître sur ses Ouvrages*, and insisted that every writer should nourish his work from what was well done in the past: thus, 'recueillant dans ses souvenirs et dans ses lectures quelques beautés qui se trouvent devant lui, [il] grossit son fleuve déjà grand, et mêle de l'or avec de l'or'.[1] What Chénier was really driving at in this part of the *Essai* was a theory of Tradition. He had, over a century before them, a theory of tradition which was close to that of Pound and Eliot, though he would probably not have agreed with Eliot that the 'individual talent' should efface itself before tradition. Chénier saw the writer as an individual talent nourished and sustained by tradition, but not sacrificed on the altar of the past. Chénier was also breaking away from the neo-classical theory of tradition (as a series of abstract rules and precepts laid down successively by Aristotle, Horace, Malherbe, Boileau, Longinus, and the rest) by seeing it as, rather, a collection or body of works, all giving life to each other: 'Ainsi cette *filiation de bons ouvrages*, quoiqu'elle rende le talent plus épineux, bien loin d'en tarir la source, l'entretient et la reproduit. . . .' Thus he could conclude, 'Et toujours cette sorte d'*imitation inventrice*, dont j'ai parlé, enrichit les auteurs les plus justement renommés pour leur originalité.' We can see at once how mature and balanced was Chénier's approach to one of the most disputed problems in criticism. All that has gone before also throws an enormous light on the nature of his own poetry, and particularly of his *Bucoliques*, poems which are always striving towards such simplicity and directness that, at first sight,

[1] D22, p. 689.

the uninformed reader might be deceived in regarding them as shallow or merely charming or moving, whereas they are often most natural when they are most learned, most touching when the poet has most carefully weighed the value of a rhythm or a nuance, and most profound when they are most close to the common stuff of human experience. While we cannot expect all Chénier's statements on poetry to be new, it is certain that his thoughts on invention, creative imitation, analogy, and 'sublime naïvety' were no accidents, but arose from his own poetic practice; and they are all the more valuable and acceptable for that. But he was correcting terms and ideas which were commonplace, rather than seeking to create a revolutionary aesthetic: it was by being so much a man of his time that he was able to go beyond it.

Chénier's *Essai* gives a remarkable picture of self-awareness and honesty, of striving towards a sincere knowledge of his own position as a poet, which is characteristic of the highest minds. This work also goes far beyond the kind of treatise that was the delight of French intellectuals before him, in the very manner in which it is written; in which learning is carried so lightly, in which he created a passionately persuasive style which is, none the less, muscular, nervous, concentrated, and highly modern. If his final portrait of the poet is thoroughly classical in its stress on intelligence, will, and insight, it is also written in a French of a strength and purity which belong to no age, but seem to touch the very essence of the language:

Il a un regard clair et vaste; tout est lumineux et clair autour de lui; il dispose de sa matière à volonté; il choisit ses campements; il arrange son armée, la réunit, la divise, la ralentit, l'accélère à son gré; il n'oublie aucun de ses acteurs; il les place chacun dans le poste qui leur convient le mieux; il change de style en changeant de personnage; il a toujours l'œil sur chacun et sur tous; soit qu'il resserre ses forces, soit qu'il les étende, il les fait toujours avancer ensemble. Il est vrai, sûr, infaillible comme la nature; il crée, il imite en tout l'ouvrage de Dieu.[1]

It is not only beautifully written; it is remarkably suggestive. Chénier's ideal poet comes close to Leonardo da Vinci, as seen through the eyes of Paul Valéry.

Before approaching the finest of Chénier's epistles, (the *Épître sur ses Ouvrages*) we propose to take from *La République des Lettres* one or two remarks which throw some light on his position fairly early in

[1] Ibid., p. 684.

his career. The first of these comes at the end of a kind of prayer to 'le
Dieu des vers' in which he praised Boileau, Voltaire, Racine, and others:

> Donne-moi, d'un poète, esprit, gloire, génie,
> Tout, excepté pourtant l'enfantine manie
> De tel qui . . .
> A tout heure est poète et n'est rien que poète.[1]

Chénier was out of sympathy with the pretensions of the professional
or drawing-room poets of his age who were more concerned with
social success than with hard work. (The bardic pretensions of that
time are summed up in the behaviour of Southey, who suffered from
a large carbuncle on his head, as a result of wearing a crown of laurels
throughout his tour in Scotland.) Chénier meant that a poet is a poet
when he is writing, but otherwise must be and live as other men. He
meant also that poetry cannot be regarded as a profession, and that
a poet may also be a useful citizen and a man of action. At the same
time the poet is in a privileged position so far as his work is concerned,
for the poet contains a critic: Chénier put this point in a challenging
way in the statement 'Nul n'est juge des arts que l'artiste lui-même.'[2]
This notion is expressed in a strong passage in which the critic, whom
he regarded as an impotent person incapable of writing creatively himself, is compared with a deaf man listening to Cimarosa, or a blind man
in front of a Raphael or a Titian.[3] Without entering into an argument
over the most debatable point in criticism, what is interesting here is
that Chénier was anticipating the Romantic view of the supremacy of
artist over critic, which for over a hundred years has created a gulf
between poets and their public. Experience has shown that poets are
no more indulgent to each other than lay critics are towards them:
Coleridge would perhaps have written less severely against Wordsworth's theory of poetic diction had he not been a poet himself; and
no academic critic would have dismissed Milton as T. S. Eliot did. But
there are times when the artist has to assert his rights, and nobody did
this more strongly than Chénier, at a time when it was needed, in his
savage attack on critics and academicians. Otherwise, in his attacks on
patronage, rich amateurs, and the snobbery of letters which was never
worse than at the close of the old régime, there is little that is worth
saving from his *République des Lettres*, though there are one or two
flashes in it—for instance 'Les arts indépendants veulent une âme
libre'[4]—which relate it to *L'Invention* and the *Essai*.

---

[1] D13, t. ii, p. 209.   [2] Ibid., p. 211.   [3] Ibid., p. 212.   [4] Ibid., p. 234.

His *Épître sur ses Ouvrages*, written in a delightfully good-natured and urbane style, is one of Chénier's most pleasing compositions. It was probably begun in 1787 and has a lightness of touch which is rarely to be found in his later works. The prose draft, addressed to de Pange, is highly whimsical and amusing, and could have been written by Charles Lamb. While giving a description of his methods of work it also reveals what a lively and charming companion he must have been, and explains why his friends were so attached to him:

De Pange, tu es parti pour la Suisse. . . . Je m'ennuie de ne plus te voir et j'attends avec impatience le moment où nous nous retrouverons chez toi en Champagne. L'ami près de son ami est content et ne songe à rien. Mais quand son ami est parti, il le regrette. Il en parle à ses Muses consolatrices et il écrit en vers à son ami. . . . Eh bien! que t'apporterai-je? Tu sais combien mes Muses sont vagabondes — Elles ne peuvent achever promptement un seul projet; elles en font marcher cent à la fois. Elles font un pied à ce poème-ci, une épaule à celui-là. Ils boitent tous et ils seront sur pied tous ensemble. Elles les couvent tous à la fois: ils sortiront de la coque à la fois, ils s'envoleront à la fois. . . . Souvent tu me crois occupé à faire des découvertes en Amérique, et tu me vois arriver une flûte pastorale sur les lèvres; tu attends un morceau d'Hermès et c'est quelque folle Élégie. . . . C'est ainsi que je suis maîtrisé par mon imagination. Elle est capricieuse et je cède à ses caprices. . . .[1]

He goes on to compare his imagination to a hobby-horse, travelling where it wills, or himself to a potter—'et l'argile que j'avais amollie et humectée pour en faire un pot à l'eau, sous mon doigt capricieux devient une tasse ou une théière'. But, he says, while always doing something new, he never gives up his earlier projects but returns to them all sooner or later.

The *Épître* in verse is a more serious presentation of the same theme, yet it loses nothing of this joviality. It begins with a dismissal of satire on the grounds that it is a waste of time to write literary satire against second-rate writers: this means that he must have abandoned the *République des Lettres* fairly early. But this was not because matter for satire was lacking in France:

Aux reproches sanglants d'un vers noble et sévère
Ce pays toutefois offre une ample matière:
Soldats tyrans du peuple obscur et gémissant,
Et juges endormis aux cris de l'innocent;
Ministres oppresseurs, dont la main détestable
Plonge au fond du cachot la vertu redoutable . . .

[1] Ibid., t. iii, p. 200.

Thus he was conscious of the need for social and political satire, but on a grand scale, directed against social evils, though he was not yet committed and was content to leave that task to others:

> Ainsi donc, sans coûter de larmes à personne,
> A mes goûts innocents, ami, je m'abandonne.
> Mes regards vont errant sur mille et mille objets.
> Sans renoncer aux vieux, plein de nouveaux projets,
> Je les tiens; dans mon camp partout je les rassemble,
> Les enrôle, les suis, les pousse tous ensemble.

As we have seen (p. 119) this military image was more forcibly developed in the *Essai*. Now he breaks off to pursue the image of the sculptor, with whose methods of creation he compares his own:

> S'égarant à son gré, mon ciseau vagabond
> Achève à ce poème ou les pieds ou le front;
> Creuse à l'autre ses flancs, puis s'abandonne et vole
> Travailler à cet autre ou la jambe ou l'épaule.
> Tous, boiteux, suspendus, traînent: mais je les vois
> Tous bientôt sur leurs pieds se tenir à la fois.

Then comes a lively dialogue between the poet and the patron of letters, who is astonished that he produces nothing: the virtuoso replies in that beautiful passage in which the poet compares himself with the foundryman making bells: the range of Chénier's gifts is nowhere better illustrated than in this sudden shift from comedy into poetry of a very high order, in which description is based on observation, and in which an Homeric analogy is fully developed:

> 'Eh bien! nous lirez-vous quelque chose aujourd'hui?
> Me dit un curieux qui s'est toujours fait gloire
> D'honorer les neuf Sœurs, et toujours, après boire,
> Étendu dans sa chaise et se chauffant les pieds,
> Aime à dormir au bruit des vers psalmodiés.
> — Qui, moi? Non. Je n'ai rien. D'ailleurs je ne lis guère.
> — Certe, un tel nous lut hier une épître!... et son frère
> Termina par une ode où j'ai trouvé des traits!...
> — Ces messieurs plus féconds, dis-je, sont toujours prêts.
> Mais, moi, que le caprice et le hasard inspire,
> Je n'ai jamais sur moi rien qu'on puisse vous lire.
> — Bon! Bon! Et cet Hermès, dont vous ne parlez pas,
> Que devient-il? — Il marche, il arrive à grands pas.
> — Oh! je m'en fie à vous. — Hélas! trop, je vous jure.
> — Combien de chants de faits? — Pas un, je vous assure.

— Comment?'
         Vous avez vu sous la main d'un fondeur
Ensemble se former, diverses en grandeur,
Trente cloches d'airain, rivales du tonnerre?
Il achève leur moule enseveli sous terre;
Puis, par un long canal en rameaux divisé,
Y fait couler les flots de l'airain embrasé;
Si bien qu'au même instant, cloches, petite et grande,
Sont prêtes, et chacune attend et ne demande
Qu'à sonner quelque mort, et du haut d'une tour
Réveiller la paroisse à la pointe du jour.
Moi, je suis ce fondeur: de mes écrits en foule
Je prépare longtemps et la forme et le moule,
Puis sur tous à la fois je fais couler l'airain:
Rien n'est fait aujourd'hui, tout sera fait demain.[1]

These two pictures of himself, the one comic, the other serious, correspond to all that we know of Chénier's mercurial and ardent nature,
from which hard but fitful work and the elaboration of great designs
were not excluded. Though he made light of his method, it is one
which has been followed by some of the greatest poets; but it requires
a longer life than Chénier's in order to bear fruit: this light-hearted
epistle assumes a tragic undertone now, when we can see how many
noble tasks were left undone.

In the last part of the epistle Chénier described with verve and
obvious enjoyment his system of 'plagiarism' which so closely resembles that of the Renaissance poets:

Souvent des vieux auteurs j'envahis les richesses.
Plus souvent leurs écrits, aiguillons généreux,
M'embrasent de leur flamme et je crée avec eux . . .

He boasted that any critic accusing him of plagiarism would be even
more surprised, were the poet to show him exactly what he had taken
and transformed, weaving it like invisible threads into the fabric of
his own work:

Que ne vient-il vers moi? Je lui ferai connaître
Mille de mes larcins qu'il ignore peut-être.
Mon doigt sur mon manteau lui dévoile à l'instant
La couture invisible et qui va serpentant,
Pour joindre à mon étoffe une pourpre étrangère.

[1] D13, t. iii, pp. 204–5.

He admits stealing not only thoughts, images, words, and lines, but even prose which he converts into poetry:

> Tantôt chez un auteur j'adopte une pensée,
> Mais qui revêt, chez moi souvent entrelacée,
> Mes images, mes tours, jeune et frais ornement;
> Tantôt je ne retiens que les mots seulement,
> J'en détourne le sens, et l'art sait les contraindre
> Vers des objets nouveaux qu'ils s'étonnent de peindre.
> La prose plus souvent vient subir d'autres lois
> Et se transforme, et fuit mes poétiques doigts;
> De rimes couronnée, et légère et dansante
> En nombres mesurés elle s'agite et chante.[1]

He then goes on to compare himself with a gardener, grafting the classics on to a fresh stem:

> Des antiques vergers ces rameaux empruntés
> Croissent sur mon terrain mollement transplantés.
> Aux troncs de mon verger ma main avec adresse
> Les attache, et bientôt même écorce les presse.
> De ce mélange heureux l'insensible douceur
> Donne à mes fruits nouveaux une antique saveur.

Here, in a homely image, Chénier has restated the meaning of 'Sur des pensers nouveaux faisons des vers antiques', and there is no better definition of the strange quality of his own work, especially in the *Bucoliques*, than 'antique saveur'. The poem ends with a cheerful mockery of the critics:

> Le critique imprudent, qui se croit bien habile,
> Donnera sur ma joue un soufflet à Virgile.
> Et ceci (tu peux voir si j'observe ma loi)
> Montaigne, il t'en souvient, l'avait dit avant moi.

This is satire at its best, for the satirist must always demonstrate—or cunningly conceal—examples of his meaning when dealing with literary questions. The example he is giving of how to turn prose into verse is taken from Montaigne: 'Je veux qu'ils donnent une nazarde à Plutarque sur mon nez, et qu'ils s'eschauldent à injurier Senecque en moi.'

This epistle is not only a sustained work of Wit in its highest form: its enormous variety of imagery is most unusual for the period in which it was written. It is as highly personal as any of the *Élégies*, and

---

[1] D13, t. iii, pp. 205–6.

is remarkable, after the pompous admonitory tone in which critics had written ever since Malherbe and Boileau, for its conversational verve and its downright assertion of the writer's independence. Chénier is an unusual example of a mind dominated by classical discipline, yet at the same time vibrating with a restlessly passionate temperament and a strong tendency to revolt and individualism. We are bound to describe as a complete poet a man who was capable of writing deliberately according to what can only be called a recipe (as Valéry said, 'le poète se fait des *recettes*') and who at the same time vaunted the powers of spontaneity and inspiration, writing in one of the *Élégies*:

> L'Art, des transports de l'âme est un faible interprète:
> L'art ne fait que des vers, le cœur seul est poète.

But it is precisely because these qualities of intellect and temperament clashed and merged that he has his place in the great lineage that runs from Racine and La Fontaine down to Valéry. The foolish dispute over whether Chénier was classical or romantic is nothing more than an unconscious tribute to his generous gifts.

6

THE ELEGIES

It has already been seen that Chénier never formulated a complete theory of poetry, and that it should be easier to draw from his poems themselves a satisfactory idea of his gifts and his intentions. The numerous elegies that have been drawn on in the first part of the present study not only throw a great deal of light on Chénier's life and character: when we come to analyse their themes and range we find that they deal mainly with love, jealousy, melancholy, friendship, and poetry, while often containing 'asides' in the form of descriptions of nature or moral or pseudo-philosophical reflections. But did Chénier actually bring anything new to this form of poetry?

The elegy had widened its range considerably, between Boileau's rather narrow definition of it and the time when Chénier chose it as a favourite form of expression. Boileau placed the elegy a little higher only than the eclogue, and reserved it mainly for the expression of sorrow and love:

> D'un ton un peu plus haut, mais pourtant sans audace,
> La plaintive élégie, en longs habits de deuil,
> Sait, les cheveux épars, gémir sur un cercueil.
> Elle peint des amants la joie et la tristesse;
> Flatte, menace, irrite, apaise une maîtresse.
> Mais, pour bien exprimer ces caprices heureux,
> C'est peu d'être poète, il faut être amoureux.[1]

So far as Chénier's range is concerned, it has to be noted that already before him Colardeau had introduced satire into the elegy; Parny (*Poèmes érotiques*, 1778) had presented his elegiac poems practically in the form of a novel (as Chénier's 'cycles' might have become); Bertin, in his *Amours* (1780), claimed that they were practically 'l'histoire fidèle de ma vie', while Gilbert, Léonard, and Thomas had extended the elegy as a direct form of personal utterance.[2] Thus, by the time Chénier appeared, Boileau's limited definition of the elegy had already been exploded. Chénier's elegies reflect all these new develop-

---

[1] Boileau, *Art poétique*, ii.   [2] See G66.

ments as well as the pastoral influences of Young, Thomson, and Gessner. At the same time he very much widened the range of classical sources and gave the French elegy a new dimension of scholarship. But his main contribution was his own distinctive voice and manner.

As can be seen from his epistle to Le Brun and de Brazais, written in 1782, Chénier's early elegies have behind them the naïve theory, based on Boileau, that only lovers can write poetry, and that the prime function of the elegy is to expound the passions:

> Aimer, sentir, c'est là l'ivresse vantée
> Qu'aux célestes foyers déroba Prométhée.
> Calliope jamais daigna-t-elle enflammer
> Un cœur inaccessible à la douceur d'aimer?
> Non; l'amour, l'amitié, la sublime harmonie,
> Tous ces dons précieux n'ont qu'un même génie:
> Même souffle anima le poète charmant,
> L'ami religieux et le parfait amant.[1]

Le Brun had expressed the same idea in one of his Odes, entitled 'Que l'amour est le plus puissant mobile de la valeur et du génie',[2] but although Chénier's early confusion between poetry and experience was rather limited and juvenile, it will be noticed that friendship played a vital part in it. His youthful identification of poetry with the passions comes close to the Romantic fallacy that the poet has to drain life of every sensation in order to write. That he was as near to this Romantic heresy, deriving from Rousseau, as he was to the *Encyclopédie*, is shown by his oft-repeated confession that his affairs with Lycoris and Camille had made him incapable of writing heroic verse, and that 'au flambeau de l'Amour j'ai vu fondre mes ailes'. Like Icarus he had fallen from his high ideal and could write of nothing but love and jealousy:

> Les forêts d'Idalie ont des routes si belles!
> Là, Vénus, me dictant de faciles chansons,
> M'a nommé son poète entre ses nourrissons . . .

[1] D13, t. iii, p. 183.
[2] But with a grotesque pompousness, so unlike Chénier's natural warmth, Le Brun writes:
> Oui, chastes Nymphes de Mémoire!
> Le tendre Amour donne à la Gloire
> Un vol encor plus généreux:
> L'Amour seul, inspirant Orphée,
> Sut nous élever un Trophée
> Jusqu'au Rivage ténébreux.

These lines illustrate how classical allusion destroyed true metaphor in the eighteenth century, reducing poetry to a kind of crossword puzzle to amuse the snob.

Thus the obsessions of the heart prevented him from carrying out his most important plans, to which he returned during his stay in London, then at intervals during the Revolution. It was perhaps the pernicious influence of Le Brun, in the first place, that had tempted him to set 'love' so high that it had a destructive effect on his work.

A second element in his early theory and practice was his stress on the 'naïf'. He wrote on his return from Italy (see above, p. 63) that this was to govern his personal elegies:

> Il est bien doux d'avoir dans sa vie innocente
> Une muse naïve et de haines exempte,
> Dont l'honnête candeur ne garde aucun secret . . .

This Rousseau-istic notion of 'honnête candeur' points already to that orgy of self-revelation which reached its height later in Musset and Baudelaire. But the maturer Chénier, developing in such a way that nothing of his past experience was wasted, most convincingly extended this theory of naïvety in an entirely different direction, by relating it also to heroic and tragic poetry (see above, pp. 116–17).

Enough has already been quoted from his elegies (in Part I of the present work) to give some idea of their bearing on his life, as well as their qualities of sensibility and wit. Though they show great variety of tone and style, ranging from the tragic to the comic and from straight description to acute irony, one of the apparent limitations of his work down to 1790 is that he used no other form but the alexandrine couplet. Maybe he did try his hand at Pindaric odes and other forms that were then fashionable, but if so, they have not come down to us. He had, perhaps, too strong a prejudice in favour of the alexandrine. Though he admired Petrarch and Shakespeare and Malherbe, he despised the sonnet and translated one of Zappi's sonnets into couplets. There is only one fragment of an elegy written in quatrains. It was only with the *Jeu de Paume* (1790–1) that he broke away from the alexandrine to choose an amazing nineteen-line stanza for which his previous work had in no way prepared him.[1] The other Odes that came after it show that he had to serve a hard apprenticeship to freer forms before achieving his extraordinary mastery of the *ïambe*. It is tempting to say that the elegies would have gained by being written in a variety of verse-forms, and to observe that, as they stand, they are indistinguishable from the epistles. But that would be an over-statement. There is a much greater monotony in (for instance) the

[1] See below, pp. 230–4.

elegies and other poems of Parny, which are written for the most part in
octosyllabics and decasyllabics. These forms allow of far less internal
variety than the alexandrine as Chénier handled it. Parny, on the
contrary, showed his limitations very clearly by shunning the alexandrine: this noble form, comparable with the heroic couplet as used
by Dryden and Pope, was considered the supreme test for French
poets: in the eighteenth century, in particular, any poet who used it
was at once measuring himself against Racine and Corneille. Voltaire
was right in saying 'L'hexamètre est plus beau, mais *parfois* ennuyeux'.
Marmontel remarked in his *Éléments de Littérature* (1787), 'Dans nos
vers la monotonie a deux causes: l'une, parce qu'on ne se donne pas
assez de soin pour en varier les césures; l'autre, parce que, dans nos
poèmes héroïques, les vers sont rimés deux à deux.'[1] Chénier used
every possible device for avoiding these two types of monotony. His
abuse of the *enjambement* and *rejet* enabled him constantly to lengthen
or shorten his line while ostensibly obeying the law of the cesura,
though he often violated that also.[2] He indulged in a bold fragmentation of the line, as in 'Allons, jeune homme, allons, marche; prends ce
flambeau'. His abuse of the overflow or enjambment led to a constant
fragmentation of the couplet (a point to which prosodists, too concerned with single lines, give little attention). French prosodists are
not familiar with the notion of counterpoint; but an analysis of a simple
short passage like the following shows how Chénier's lively manner of
setting the natural speech-rhythm against the numbering of verse
overcomes the convention of the couplet; just as Marx advanced the
paradox that, at a certain point, the State 'disappears', so, in good
verse, versification can disappear:

> Sois tendre, même faible; on doit l'être un moment;
> Fidèle, si tu peux. Mais conte-moi comment,
> Quel jeune homme aux yeux bleus, empressé, sans audace,
> Aux cheveux noirs, au front plein de charme et de grâce . . .
> Tu rougis? On dirait que je t'ai dit son nom.
> Je le connais pourtant.

The truth is that, here, we have the alexandrine as it was adapted to
comedy by Molière. This extract is not intended to be high poetry,
and its familiar tone and syntax take the reader's attention away from
the rhymes; yet this is done without any violation of the strictest
classical rules. More often, Chénier will break the monotony by

[1] See Yves Le Hir, *Esthétique et structure du vers français*, PUF, 1956, p. 102.
[2] For instance, in *L'Aveugle*.

combining an enjambment with a splitting of the next couplet, giving
his meaning in three lines instead of two:

> Mon âme comme un songe autour de ton sommeil
> Voltige. En me lisant demain à ton réveil
> Tu verras, comme toi, si mon cœur est paisible.

It was in drawing attention away from the structure, not only of the
line but of the couplet itself, that Chénier avoided the monotony of
close rhymes. Another way of doing this was by a practice which was
not then approved of—the use of internal rhyme:

> . . . Du sein de vos *feuillages*,
> D'.z . ., fantôme aimé, m'environne, me suit
> De *bocage* en *bocage*, et m'attire et me fuit.

Internal rhyme, alliteration, assonance; Chénier spontaneously used
all these devices, not merely to avoid monotony, but because of the
ever restless movement of his thought and emotions. In this respect
his versification, when we also take into account the enormous variation in the length of his phrases, clauses, periods, is more fluid than
that of his Romantic successors, with the exception of Hugo. Even
Baudelaire's versification is more conventional than that of Chénier,
often falling into a heavy rhythm, or drawing undue attention to the
rhyme by its chiming richness. When we add to this Chénier's rapid
changes of tone (for instance in the elegy 'Animé par l'amour', which
starts with a triumphant assertion of youthful sensuality, then lingers
on the quiet pleasures of old age) we begin to see the extent to which
his poetry, though written in alexandrines, is so nervous and alive.
His versification was as supple and modern as that of Lamartine or
Vigny, having all the harmony of the former and the vigour of the
latter.

There is little point in returning to those elegies which have already
been discussed. Of those remaining there are two, among the finest,
which illustrate two main manners of Chénier's early work. The first
of these, *La Lampe*, is the only one of the elegies which is entirely
classical in spirit and presentation. As the prose draft contains the note
'Bois, malheureux Gallus' it is evidently a poem belonging to the
Lycoris cycle and written in about 1782, when he was aged twenty.
Chénier began by adapting an epigram from Asclepiades which he
found in Brunck's *Analecta*. This epigram treats of unfaithfulness but
does not tell the same story as *La Lampe*; it runs:

> Et toi, lampe nocturne, astre cher à l'amour,
> Sur le marbre posée, ô toi qui jusqu'au jour
> De ta prison de verre éclairas nos tendresses,
> Tu fus le seul témoin de ses douces caresses.
> Mais, hélas, avec toi son amour incertain
> Allait se consumant et s'éteignit enfin;
> Avec toi les serments de cette bouche aimée
> S'envolèrent bientôt en légère fumée.

La Lampe in its completed form deals with jealousy in a more detached, impersonal way than the other elegies. The poem was written in three stages: first the translation of the above epigram, with a few notes on Asclepiades; then a few fragments of verse linked by a prose narration, and finally the complete poem into which the prepared fragments were inserted in their proper place. Even in the elegies Chénier did not always start at the beginning, but used his fragments as what Paul Valéry called 'islands' round which he constructed his work.

The complete poem, then, is a dialogue between the lover and the lamp which had witnessed the treachery of his mistress until she blew it out. Though Chénier mentioned Asclepiades, Sainte-Beuve pointed out that it owed more to Meleager: at the same time it contains reminiscences of Propertius, Racine, and La Fontaine. Only a poet in complete possession of his craft could have so woven these elements together as to make a poem so tightly constructed and with such a firm narrative line that it is hard to quote any part of it outside its context. The tone is ostensibly tragic, but the general effect is one of comedy. Yet the irony is so traditional—so hackneyed, in fact—that it is hard to define how he made it new:

> Tu l'embrasses, tu pars, tu la vois endormie.
> A peine tu sortais, que cette porte amie
> S'ouvre: un front jeune et blond se présente, et je vois
> Un amant aperçu pour la première fois.
> Elle, alors, d'une voix tremblante et favorable
> Lui disait: 'Non, partez; non, je suis trop coupable.'
> Elle parlait ainsi, mais lui tendait les bras ...

The poem is not only light and unpretentious: although the theme is erotic it is handled with a delicacy unusual for Chénier's time. It belongs to a long European tradition of light verse, going back to La Fontaine and Chaucer, and beyond that to Greece.[1] It is obviously not

---

[1] See above, p. 55.

a personal poem, but rather a literary exercise; yet it is possible that in his comic theme, ending with the Lamp's advice to blow out his love as his mistress had blown on the flame, Chénier was able to express some of his own frustration in an elegant manner:

> Je cessai de brûler. Suis mon exemple. Cesse.
> On aime un autre amant. Aime une autre maîtresse.
> Souffle sur ton amour, ami, si tu m'en crois,
> Ainsi que pour m'éteindre elle a soufflé sur moi.

Chénier's elegies, for the most part, are intimate and personal, even though at times they appear to be too close to a fashionable convention. But *La Lampe* is the only one which, perhaps, shows something of his apprenticeship to La Fontaine, and, in this case, the La Fontaine of the *Contes*. A comparison of it with any of the *Contes* would show that Chénier's poem is superior to them: it has none of the fabulist's lapses of taste, and is written with a passionate movement, tempered though it is with the same kind of wit that is found in La Fontaine or Boccaccio, but without any of the asides and superfluous detail in which his predecessors indulged.

It is a pity that Chénier did not attempt this kind of impersonal narrative more often, for such bitter, witty moments of comedy are the most modern quality in the elegies as a whole, anticipating, even, the familiar tones and wry humour of Laforgue and the Eliot of *Prufrock*. That this is no exaggeration may be seen from such elegies as *La Porte* (to give it a title). In this poem the poet begins by intending to lie all night weeping on his mistress's doorstep. Alternately cursing and blessing her, the poem ends with a finely concentrated movement:

> J'admire seulement qu'à ce sexe imbécile
> Nous daignions sur nos vœux laisser aucun pouvoir;
> Pour repousser ses traits, on n'a qu'à le vouloir.
> Ingrate que j'aimais, je te hais, je t'abhorre . . .
> Mais quel bruit à sa porte? . . . Ah! dois-je attendre encore?
> J'entends crier les gonds . . . On ouvre . . . C'est pour moi . . .
> Oh! ma Camille m'aime et me garde sa foi . . .
> Je l'adore toujours . . . Ah! Dieux! ce n'est pas elle.
> Le vent seul a poussé cette porte cruelle;
> L'ingrate de mes maux n'a point eu de pitié . . .
> Je lui dois bien ma rage et mon inimitié.
> Vent jaloux, pour jouer ma cruelle espérance,
> Avec sa perfidie es-tu d'intelligence?

It is not easy to see where Chénier found this manner, but obviously behind it lie Molière and Marivaux, or perhaps memories of the comic opera. The comparison with Eliot and Laforgue might surprise some readers, but one has only to look at Laforgue's *Derniers Vers* and Eliot's *Prufrock* or *Portrait of a Lady* to see that we are on familiar ground. What is unusual for Chénier's period is to see the elegy become a vehicle for dramatic comedy of this kind. Also unusual is the use of the internal dramatic monologue, full of questions and answers. The fragmentation of these thirteen lines, recalling certain moments in Molière and La Fontaine, shows a technique which we meet only in Byron and Browning, in English, and Laforgue in French, before we come to Eliot and Valéry. We have here also a sustained example of Chénier's success in annihilating versification. Rhymes apart—and they count for nothing here—it is good modern prose. We have already noticed this extraordinary talent for dramatic writing, accompanied by a startling change of tone, in the *Épître sur ses Ouvrages* (above, p. 122). But the quality which most recalls Laforgue and Eliot is its irony, of the kind which Irving Babbitt described as 'romantic irony', that is to say, an irony directed at the poet's own self, destructive of the ego. The eighteenth-century French writers generally lacked this capacity for self-criticism and were afraid of appearing ridiculous: Rousseau was always on his dignity when attacking himself, and Diderot was one of the few who had an inkling of this kind of humour. It is a paradox to say that Chénier's auto-humour appears modern because it was learnt from Montaigne.

At the other extreme from *La Lampe* and the comic elegies lies the intimate elegy 'O jours de mon printemps', which is the centre of the whole collection and comes nearer to Chénier's conception of elegiac poetry as 'extases choisies'. It was Sainte-Beuve who first took up this beautiful expression, 'extases choisies', and applied it to the elegies. In its context (*L'Invention*, line 231) it is applied to all poetry and not only to this particular kind:

> Elle seule connaît *ces extases choisies*,
> D'un esprit tout de feu mobiles fantaisies,
> Ces Rêves d'un moment, belles illusions,
> D'un monde imaginaire aimables visions,
> Qui ne frappent jamais, trop subtile lumière,
> Des terrestres esprits l'œil épais et vulgaire.

Chénier is close to Shelley and Keats in this idea that poetry may capture or express 'privileged moments' which are lost to other people.

The stress here, however, does not seem to be exactly on privileged moments of everyday experience, but on dreams, illusions, and the workings of the imagination. While the term 'extases choisies' may aptly describe Chénier's elegies, the intention behind this passage points to something different—the roving and inquiring mind of the Poet.

The elegy 'O jours de mon printemps' was probably begun in 1787 and finished later, in London: its recapitulation of the past suggests that it must have been written at a crisis in the poet's career, when he looked back on his youth and forward to a life of different responsibilities and interests. It opens with a fine, fluid movement which shows to perfection his talent for making an old theme new:

> O jours de mon printemps, jours couronnés de rose,
> A votre fuite en vain un long regret s'oppose.
> Beaux jours, quoique souvent obscurcis de mes pleurs,
> Vous dont j'ai su jouir même au sein des douleurs,
> Sur ma tête bientôt vos fleurs seront fanées.
> Hélas! bientôt le flux des rapides années
> Vous aura loin de moi fait voler sans retour . . .

These lines are very characteristic of Chénier in the way they appeal, almost in spite of the reader's intelligence, by their cunning exploitation of the gentler sounds and rhythms of the French language, with their internal rhymes and half-rhymes placed with absolute naturalness and grace. This is the *bel canto* of the Renaissance, forgotten in France for two hundred years before Chénier recaptured it. The whole of this poem is built up on a very limited number of rhymes, or rhymes so closely related to each other that they follow like echoes:

> . . . D'avoir su se bâtir, des dépouilles des fleurs,
> Sa cellule de cire, industrieux *asile*
> Où l'on coule une vie innocente et *facile*;
> De ne point vendre aux grands ses hymnes *avilis*,
> De n'offrir aux talents, de vertus *annoblis* . . .

But criticism would be an easy matter if it were no more than the counting of such tricks. What is demonstrable from the above, is that it is poetry which demands to be read aloud; it has a strong physical claim to existence. The same demand is made by its slow, majestic movement, for the melancholy of the mood and tone is also implicit in the rhythm:

> Soit sur ces bords heureux, opulents avec choix,
> Où Montigny s'enfonce en ses antiques bois,

> Soit où la Marne lente, en un long cercle d'îles,
> Ombrage de bosquets l'herbe et les prés fertiles,
> J'ai su, pauvre et content, savourer à longs traits
> Les Muses, les plaisirs, et l'étude et la paix.

This dignified movement is matched by equally dignified sentiments, such as we expect in a poem that dwells on the pleasures of solitude and friendship, and the consolations to be drawn from the arts and an intimate circle of highly cultured minds:

> Qui ne sait être pauvre est né pour l'esclavage . . .
>
> Une pauvreté libre est un trésor si doux,
> Il est si doux, si beau, de s'être fait soi-même,
> De devoir tout à soi, tout aux beaux-arts qu'on aime . . .
>
> Je n'ai point fait ramper vos lauriers trop jaloux.
> J'ai respecté les dons que j'ai reçus de vous . . .

In this elegy, which touches so gently but deeply on so many themes, Chénier wrote with a restrained grace and dignity that mark him off from his Romantic successors, though we often find in him, particularly in his style, intimations of Lamartine, Musset, or Vigny. These personal elegies on solitude and friendship are more serious and masculine than the love-poems. Why? Is it, possibly, because underneath all the 'galanterie' of the eighteenth century love was fundamentally cheapened, whereas disinterested friendship was never more exalted than at that time? Or is it because friendship brought out Chénier's finer qualities, in which the unison of heart and head was achieved while the negative feelings of jealousy and envy were excluded? We shall find, later, that there were unsatisfactory moments in Chénier's odes for Fanny Lecoulteux: for him, love was unease, a violent or gentle torment, but never peace. It is perhaps no accident that the flowering of his powers came to the full in the *Iambes*: are we to conclude that he was more gifted in the expression of the negative emotions than in other directions? That this interpretation would be going too far is shown in the success of these elegies on friendship and nature.

Entertaining and often touching as the love-cycles are, they tend to show minor aspects of the poet's character, minor aspects of his talent. On the other hand the rest of his elegies show us rather more of his youthful outlook on the world; yet they point in the same direction, to a surprisingly unbalanced and mercurial temperament, constantly changing in thought and tone. For instance, in an elegy addressed to de Pange ('De Pange, le mortel dont l'âme est innocente'), he started with the intention of writing in a flippant way about Venus and the pleasures of love. Then the tone suddenly hardens as the poet reflects on mortality and the onset of old age:

> Humains, nous ressemblons aux feuilles d'un ombrage
> Dont au faîte des cieux le soleil remonté
> Rafraîchit dans nos bois les chaleurs de l'été.
> Mais l'hiver, accourant d'un vol sombre et rapide
> Nous sèche, nous flétrit; et son souffle homicide
> Secoue et fait voler, dispersés dans les vents,
> Tous ces feuillages morts qui font place aux vivants.
> La Parque sur nos pas fait courir devant elle
> Midi, le soir, la nuit, et la nuit éternelle;
> Et par grâce, à nos yeux qu'attend le long sommeil,
> Laisse voir au matin un regard du soleil.

This solemn, responsible tone, and this kind of slow reflection, so carefully worked out as art that the last line rejoins the second ('soleil . . .'), are lacking in the love-poems. It detracts nothing from the passage to know that part of it was adapted from Mimnermus (in the *Analecta*), on which Chénier grafted an image from the *Iliad*. Seeking, in the Ancients, thoughts that appealed to him, he could clothe them with beauties of his own ('Midi, le soir, la nuit, et la nuit éternelle', or 'un regard du soleil').

In another elegy (beginning 'O Muses, accourez . . .'), in which he expressed his desire for a quiet, rustic life, occur the lines:

> Venez. J'ai fui la ville aux Muses si contraire,
> Et l'écho fatigué des clameurs du vulgaire.
> Sur les pavés poudreux d'un bruyant carrefour
> Les poétiques fleurs n'ont jamais vu le jour.
> Le tumulte et les cris font fuir avec la lyre
> L'oisive rêverie au suave délire . . .

The eighteenth century, still believing in the truth of Boileau's epistle 'Sur les embarras de Paris', had no notion that city life might inspire a new poetry. Chénier followed Horace and Boileau in expressing nostalgia for the quiet life, while spending much of his time in quest of social excitement. The unusual—almost Mallarméan—line 'L'oisive rêverie au suave délire' is not only beautiful for its sound and concentration, but is remarkable because it pin-points this tension between repose and movement.[1] There could be no greater contrast than between *rêverie* and *délire*, unless it be the strange choice of epithet, *suave*, to qualify the latter word. The poems that have been classified (by Dimoff) as 'Souhaits d'une vie indépandante et paisible' contain many surprises of this kind. Treating the conventional theme of the rusticated poet, content with his cottage existence (Pope's longing for 'these chicks mine own'), Chénier writes:

> . . . Quand pourrai-je habiter un champ qui soit à moi?
> Et, villageois tranquille, ayant pour tout emploi
> Dormir et ne rien faire, inutile poète,
> Goûter le doux oubli d'une vie inquiète?

While the latinism 'inutile' has a charm of its own, it is the sharp contrasts in these elegies—here between 'oubli' and 'inquiète'—which gives them life. But in spite of his repeated craving for peace and solitude Chénier seems to have had, like Keats, the kind of mind that no retreat could have appeased. This fluidity he defined on many occasions. After his return from Italy he wrote in *Le Retour*:

> . . . De ses pensers errants vive et rapide image,
> Chaque chanson nouvelle a son nouveau langage,
> Et des rêves nouveaux, un nouveau sentiment:
> *Tous sont divers, et tous furent vrais un moment.*

Chénier was a man who had no centre and who viewed himself as something of a chameleon, until his thought was crystallized by politics. He was aware that, although he had given much attention to philosophy, he was slow in adopting a philosophical position, and perhaps for him, as a poet, it was necessary to keep a more open mind than his thoughtful friend François de Pange, to whom he left the task of speculation, whether it be on Hindu religion or the 'dream' of Descartes:

> Ou comment dans sa route, avec force tracée,
> Descartes n'a point su contenir sa pensée?

Chénier knew that his quest was not so much for thought as for poetic excitement, and that his favourite task was to listen to the past, to abandon himself to the incantations of the old poets who inspired his *Bucoliques*:

> Consumant ma jeunesse en un loisir plus vain,
> Seul, animé du feu que nous nommons divin,
> Qui pour moi chaque jour ne luit qu'avec l'aurore,

[1] See above, p. 54.

> Je rêve assis au bord de cette onde sonore
> Qu'au penchant d'Hélicon, pour arroser ses bois,
> Le quadrupède ailé fit jaillir autrefois.

While he was content with beauty, he left to de Pange the pursuit of truth, knowing only too well that he, Chénier, could not obey the dictates of his own reason:

> Sois heureux, et surtout aime un ami qui t'aime.
> Ris de son cœur débile aux désirs condamné,
> De l'étude aux amours sans cesse promené,
> Qui, toujours approuvant ce dont il fuit l'usage,
> Aimera la sagesse et ne sera point sage.

He wrote elsewhere 'Toujours vrai, son discours souvent se contredit', as though believing, like Montaigne (from whom he learnt so much of his self-indulgence), that his very inconsistencies were proof of a generous and open-minded attitude towards all things. Thus, for every statement he made about his desire for solitude it would be possible to show a statement to the contrary, such as (in 'J'ai suivi les conseils . . .'):

> Non, mon cœur n'est point né pour vivre en solitude:
> Il me faut qui m'estime, il me faut des amis
> A qui dans mes secrets tout accès soit permis;
> Dont les yeux, dont la main dans la mienne pressée
> Réponde à mon silence, et sente ma pensée.

As a young man, on the way to Italy, he imagined himself as a Roman and as a man of action:

> J'aurais, jeune Romain, au sénat, aux combats,
> Usé pour la patrie et ma voix et mon bras.

In the early elegy, 'Tel j'étais autrefois et tel je suis encor', he admitted that all his resolutions to study in quiet were broken as soon as the opportunity for excitement came along:

> Adieu les grands discours, et le volume antique,
> Et le sage Lycée, et l'auguste Portique . . .

Chénier himself defined his elegies as having 'Le rire sur la bouche et les pleurs dans les yeux', and part of their charm is to see him torn between 'folles orgies' or fits of jealousy and the desire to hurl himself into action of any kind, and the longing for some too-true-to-be-good wife such as he described in an amusing passage of the Epistle to

Trudaine. This contains a highly rococo description of the cheese which his rustic spouse would make for him:

> Une rustique épouse et soigneuse et zélée,
> Blanche (car dans l'ombrage au sein de la vallée
> Les fureurs du soleil n'osent les outrager),
> M'offrirait le doux miel, les fruits de mon verger,
> Le lait enfant des sels de ma prairie humide,
> Tantôt breuvage pur, et tantôt mets solide
> En un globe fondant sous sa main épaissi,
> En disque savoureux à la longue durci;
> Et cependant sa voix simple et douce et légère
> Me chanterait les airs que lui chantait sa mère.

It would be too easy to laugh at the contrast between this picture of the obedient housewife, making cheese and singing folk-songs, and the poet's admiration for the 'amoureux exploits' of Camille, all beauty and violence. While it would be hard to decide now much of these two extreme positions came from literature, and how much from the heart, much of the honesty of Chénier's elegies, which are so attractive in their openness, comes of his being equally concerned with destructive passion and with a deep human desire for enduring love, simple in its truth and sublime in its permanence. Despite the rococo unease of the passions as Chénier described them, how often do his poems end with this longing for an almost animal affection, for that security of the heart and senses that life refused him; it is what he wished for his friends when he was only nineteen or so:

> Et quand la mort viendra, qu'une amante fidèle,
> Près de vous désolée, en accusant les Dieux,
> Pleure, et veuille vous suivre, et vous ferme les yeux.

Few things are so banal, in literature, as the description of happiness when it is directly presented. Chénier rose to this challenge many times in the *Bucoliques*, but there are also many occasions in the elegies and epistles where he did so. For instance, the home-coming scene was a set piece for eighteenth-century poets, but few are so fresh, so genuine as the one he wrote for de Brazais when he was only twenty-one:

> Qu'il est doux, au retour de la froide saison,
> Jusqu'au printemps nouveau regagnant la maison,
> De la voir devant vous accourir au passage,
> Ses cheveux en désordre épars sur son visage:
> Son oreille de loin a reconnu vos pas,
> Elle vole et s'écrie et tombe dans vos bras,

Et sur vous appuyée et respirant à peine,
A son foyer secret loin des yeux vous entraîne.
Là, mille questions qui vous coupent la voix,
Doux reproches, baisers, se pressent à la fois.
La table entre vous deux à la hâte est servie.
L'œil humide de joie, au banquet elle oublie
Et les mets et la table, et se nourrit en paix
Du plaisir de vous voir, de contempler vos traits.
Sa bouche ne dit rien, mais ses yeux, mais son âme
Vous parlent . . .

There are, then, moments when Chénier was really speaking for
himself, as well as 'making a poem'. Boissy d'Anglas wrote, after the
poet's death, of his fundamentally melancholy nature. Chénier's lines
on melancholy in 'O Muses, accourez' ring true. They contain the
essence of the eighteenth-century picturesque, against which the mood
is set, but are none the less intensely personal:

Douce mélancolie, aimable mensongère,
Des antres, des forêts déesse tutélaire,
Qui vient d'une insensible et charmante langueur
Saisir l'ami des champs et pénétrer son cœur,
Quand, sorti vers le soir des grottes reculées,
Il s'égare à pas lents au penchant des vallées,
Et voit des derniers feux le ciel se colorer,
Et sur les monts lointains un beau jour expirer.
Dans sa volupté sage, et pensive et muette,
Il s'assied, sur son sein laisse tomber sa tête.
Il regarde à ses pieds, dans le liquide azur
Du fleuve qui s'étend comme lui calme et pur,
Se peindre les coteaux, les toits et les feuillages,
Et la pourpre en festons couronnant les nuages.

Chénier has often enough been praised for his sensitiveness to nature,
but on the whole his reactions tend to remain generalized, though, at
times, smell, taste, and vision are acute. In the above passage, both
vision and feeling are vague and imprecise until the words 'Il s'assied',
after which the reader is aware that a real experience is being described.
As Gaëtan Picon has remarked, though Chénier's themes are often
conventional he shortened the distance that there then was between
poetry and experience. The same effort of focusing experience was
made by Wordsworth; but Chénier was less exact. In portraying
nature, Chénier tended to write impressionistically, evoking fluidity
and light, rather than defined forms. He achieved more sharpness of

outline in the *Bucoliques* than in the elegies; perhaps because nature, in these elegies, is a setting for solitude, melancholy, introspection, whereas in the *Bucoliques* it was a setting for dramatic events.

The first generation of Romantic poets tended to prize above all the poetry of introspection, and naturally regarded Chénier's elegies as his most original work; yet we have to be careful in repeating their judgements, as it is not always clear whether they distinguished between his modern and ancient elegies. It was Hugo who started this tendency in 1819, writing that 'C'est surtout dans l'élégie qu'éclate le talent d'André Chénier. C'est là qu'il est original.'[1] Sainte-Beuve, who saw in these elegies a pretext for his own musings under the name 'Joseph Delorme', went far towards defining that originality in describing Chénier's elegies as 'élégies d'analyse'.[2] Perhaps he was right, but not in the sense in which we should be inclined to take the expression. He wrote in his *Pensées de Joseph Delorme*, 'Lorsqu'en effet ce grand poète ne traite pas des sujets grecs . . . il nous offre le plus parfait modèle de l'élégie de l'analyse, si l'on peut ainsi s'exprimer. Il nous peint la nature avec curiosité, quoique sans minutie, et nous révèle son âme dans ses dispositions les plus délicates, mais sans tomber dans la psychologie.'[3] But Chénier was far from being an analytical *paysagiste*. He almost never evoked a landscape for its own sake, but always as an incidental setting for mood or action. What he did analyse was jealousy and sensuality, in the Camille cycle of elegies; but the real point about all his analysis is that it was self-conscious, and that it did 'fall into psychology'. He was acutely conscious, always, of the distance between necessity and will, between ideals and realities, and though regarding himself as one who 'aimera la sagesse et ne sera point sage' he often analysed his torment. In the London elegies, though the problem has become a social one (see above, p. 82), the introspection becomes Hamletian, and it is in these that the analysis is taken the furthest, while being tempered by a tendency to generalize in the third person. We cannot help feeling that Sainte-Beuve was anxious to create a Chénier of his own, to justify his own activities as the poet of 'Joseph Delorme'. But however high we put the elegies, we cannot hesitate long before rating them below the *Bucoliques* and *Ïambes*, though there might be disagreement about the quality of the *Odes*. The elegies did not often achieve the seriousness of the other works: we tend to like them *because* they are immature, though it is true that they are saved by their qualities of analysis and self-awareness. So far as

---

[1] G40.   [2] G69, t. i, p. 217.   [3] Ibid.

the Camille and Lycoris cycles are concerned, we are more impressed
by their comic and ironical features than by their cunning adaptation
of the Anthology or by their sensual torment. What we admire in the
best of them is usually a perfect combination of high craftsmanship,
with a musical gift that creates a temporary magic, hovering round an
immaturity of the emotions. So far as the substance of the personal
elegies is concerned (we exclude for the moment the whole of the
Bucoliques, which are models of the elegiac mode) they often tail off
into epistles, as, for instance, in the otherwise admirable 'O muses,
accourez' which ends with digressions about Richardson's novels.

It is possible to read these elegies for other reasons than those which
moved the Romantic generation. There is, for instance, their purely
period quality, their historic charm, which makes much the same appeal
as antique furniture of the Louis XV or XVI styles. We might be as
moved as Chateaubriand and Hugo were, by the London elegies in
which despair is tempered by wit; in them Hamlet makes his first
appearance in French literature. We find it harder to tolerate his period
expression of jealousy, which is such a dull vice, and are grateful to
Chénier for having made fun of it at the same time; for it cannot be
denied that the poems that we quoted earlier from the Camille cycle
have the redeeming quality of intelligence, even in the midst of
emotional self-indulgence. And then the reader who is willing to spend
half an hour or so on the unfinished elegies can hardly come away
without finding that isolated lines, jotted down but never worked into
a poem, will follow him into the street and pester him in the bus:

> Je parcours ces déserts peuplés de ton image . . .
> Le serpent rajeuni dépouille ses années . . .
> Les serpents dévorants et les vastes baleines . . .
> Et la rose pâlit sur ta lèvre tremblante . . .
> Chaque instant de ma vie est abreuvé d'absinthe . . .

These lines and many others come as a caution, reminding us that we
are in the presence of a poet whose promise was unfulfilled. But,
finished or not, he left enough pieces in his workshop for some judgement to be made. One of the best of the personal elegies, on friendship,
is that beginning 'Quand la feuille en festons a couronné les bois'. It
was addressed to François de Pange. It contains, towards the end,
a miniature 'fête galante', a description of a picnic in the woods:

> Viens, viens, mon jeune ami, viens, nos Muses t'attendent;
> Nos fêtes, nos banquets, nos courses te demandent;

Viens voir ensemble et l'antre et l'onde et les forêts.
Chaque soir une table aux suaves apprêts
Assoira près de nous nos belles adorées,
Ou, cherchant dans le bois des nymphes égarées,
Nous entendrons les ris, les chansons, les festins;
Et les verres emplis sous les bosquets lointains
Viendront animer l'air, et du sein d'une treille
De leur voix argentine égayer notre oreille.

J. Fabre has made an interesting comparison of these lines with Baudelaire's adaptation of them, saying:

'Le vert paradis des amours enfantines' s'est peuplé des images que Baudelaire devait à Chénier:

> Les *courses*, les *chansons*, les baisers, les bouquets,
> Les violons vibrant derrière les collines,
> Avec les brocs de vin, *le soir, dans les bosquets* . . .
>
> Peut-on le rappeler, avec des cris plaintifs,
> Et l'*animer* encore d'une *voix argentine*,
> L'innocent paradis plein de plaisirs furtifs?

Fabre adds: 'Sa magie révèle sans doute ce qui manquait encore à Chénier: l'allusion au lieu du développement, les souvenirs devenus sortilèges, les mots talismans etc.'[1] Such criticism could open a large field of inquiry, It is true that there is too much expansion in the elegies; but the neo-classical tradition demanded that 'développement' should be such that the reader is not obliged to retrace his steps. The historical part of M. Fabre's remarks is, therefore, obvious. However, a very early poem of Chénier's is being compared with one of Baudelaire's maturity, and it is shown that the mature Baudelaire thought Chénier to be worth imitating. The art of 'allusion' was not unknown to Chénier, but there is more of it in the *Bucoliques* than in his modern elegies. The 'sortilège' or magic in evoking the past is to be found in certain other elegies, such as 'O jours de mon printemps'. Baudelaire, who knew as well as Chénier where to look for a lead or an inspiration, was fortunate in finding this passage, in which there is all the nostalgia and tenderness that set the tone of his own poem. Of course, he owed more to Chénier than these lines: for instance his *Épître à Sainte-Beuve* is an 'analytical elegy'. There is something of Chénier, also, in 'J'aime le souvenir de ces époques nues' and the beautiful *Paysage* which became the prologue to the *Tableaux Parisiens*. Looking at the two extracts quoted by M. Fabre, we see that Chénier's has a beauty of its

[1] F36, p. 214.

own which is not, like Baudelaire's, that of incantation. In Chénier's everything is seen through a mist, heard and seen from a distance in space ('Et les verres emplis dans des bosquets lointains'). In Baudelaire, things are seen through the distance of time and memory. Chénier's evocation, though warm, is rather like a faded pastel by Boucher, of the kind mentioned by Baudelaire in *Spleen*. What the two poets have in common, in all their work, is the same kind of nostalgic joy: we find it, in Chénier, in the early elegy beginning 'Animés par l'Amour', or in 'Reste, reste avec nous, ô père des bons vins', as well as in the Odes for Fanny Lecoulteux. The two poets also come together, at times, in their moments of violently expressed introspection: for instance, some of Chénier's London elegies—'Souvent, las d'être esclave et de boire la lie' or 'Souffre un moment encor; tout n'est que changement'—anticipate the negative but powerful tonality of Baudelaire's 'Spleen' poems. Though Baudelaire did not make much mention of Chénier in his criticism, he took his work seriously. In his *Salon* of 1845 he spoke of 'Prud'hon, ce frère en romantisme d'André Chénier'.[1] In his essay on Gautier, he attributed the success of the Romantic revival, in the first place, to Alfred de Vigny, saying of Chénier 'André Chénier, avec sa molle antiquité à la Louis XVI, n'était pas un symptôme de rénovation assez vigoureuse'[2]—no doubt meaning by that, that whatever was new in Chénier's work was not enough to detach it from the eighteenth century. In his uncompleted study of Villemain he came to Chénier's defence by qualifying Chateaubriand's comparison of him with Fontanes:

Nous n'hésitons à dire que l'auteur de *la Chartreuse* [etc.] offre quelques traits en commun avec l'originalité plus neuve et plus hardie de l'élégie sur *le Jeune Malade* et des stances à Mlle de Coigny. . . .[3]

Finally, in a letter to Sainte-Beuve, he said, 'Le mot *élégie analytique* s'applique à vous mieux qu'à André Chénier.'[4] All that we can deduce from these remarks is that Baudelaire always had a proper respect for the work of his predecessor. Chénier was one of the formative influences on Baudelaire, and it is chiefly in the poems of his first manner that his influence is to be felt.

Chénier himself made no extravagant claim for his elegies, but did seem to hope that they would last and be useful to other young people in love:

---

[1] Baudelaire, *Œuvres*, Pléiade, t. ii, p. 55.   [2] Ibid., p. 464.
[3] Ibid., p. 594.   [4] *Corresp. gén.*, Conard, t. v, p. 218.

Ainsi, que mes écrits, enfants de ma jeunesse,
Soient un code d'amour, de plaisir, de tendresse;
Que partout de Vénus ils dispersent les traits;
Que ma voix, que mon âme y vivent à jamais:
Qu'une jeune beauté, sur la plume et la soie,
Attendant le mortel qui fait toute sa joie,
S'amuse à mes chansons, y médite à loisir
Les baisers dont bientôt elle veut l'accueillir . . .

Qu'un jeune homme, agité d'une flamme inconnue,
S'écrie aux doux tableaux de ma Muse ingénue:
'Ce poète amoureux, qui me connaît si bien,
Quand il a peint son cœur, avait lu dans le mien.'

Of course, Chénier was hoping for too much. In spite of their occasional beauties, their tenderness, wit, and humour, they give a very incomplete picture of the affections and they hesitate too much between sincerity and a fashionable pose. A great deal of their undeniable charm comes from their immaturity, their breathless profusion, their frequent failure to come to grips with experience. The Chénier of the elegies was the poet of youth, as vehement and as sensuous as John Keats, and often as wrong-headed. The modern elegies give frequent glimpses of a true poet; but his full powers do not unite in them as they do in the *Bucoliques*, in which sensibility and imagination combine all the better because the poet's self is thrust into the background.

7

THE DIDACTIC AND NARRATIVE POEMS

As is normal in the case of writers who die young, his critics have given much attention to Chénier's ambitious projects, the unfinished *Hermès*, *L'Amérique*, and *Susanne*. But although he spent from seven to ten years collecting material for the first of these, and perhaps as much time on the second, and a year or two on the third, it seems unlikely that he would ever have finished them. Although it is sad to turn to a poet's manuscripts and find the ruins, or only the foundations, of large enterprises, we are obliged to judge them according to the quality of the fragments that were actually written, and not to indulge too much in speculation over what they might have become. In the case of Chénier, his reputation has been made without these works: the Romantics found enough to please them in the elegies and odes to enable them to acclaim his genius, while the Parnassians based his reputation on the *Bucoliques*, and a more recent tendency has been to thrust the *Ïambes* into the front place.

On the other hand, Émile Faguet thought that Chénier's work passed through three phases: the *Bucoliques*, the elegies, and the narrative and didactic poems.[1] Chronologically, he was wrong, and it might also be asked whether he was wrong in seeing the didactic work as the crown of Chénier's career. P. Dimoff has also lamented the unfinished *Hermès* and *L'Amérique*.[2] The abbé Venzac has been the only critic to say much in defence of *Susanne*.[3] Perhaps M. Dimoff's judgement was based more on what those works might have been or become, than what they are. M. Dimoff ended his impressive thesis at

[1] G21, chapters iii, iv, v, vi.

[2] Throughout his study of Chénier (F34) Dimoff accepted without question the poet's own valuation of these long works, though (livre iv, chap. i) he doubted whether they would ever have been completed.

[3] F96, p. 178: 'Mais, se portant d'un seul élan de Voltaire à Renan, devançant d'un siècle le mouvement des idées, dépassant la réhabilitation poétique ou romanesque du christianisme par le romantisme, réhabilitation pour son compte à lui déjà acquise dans ses poèmes de *l'Amérique* et de *Susanne*, André Chénier est, semble-t-il, le premier penseur français à demander de substituer à l'incompréhension et aux railleries de l'absolu, l'intelligence historique du christianisme.' *Susanne* is thus to be seen in the wider perspective of Chénier's modernism in religious matters.

the year 1790, in the belief that Chénier wrote nothing of interest afterwards: 'Mais il aura surtout recours à la prose, et ce sont, en définitive, ses articles du *Moniteur* et du *Journal de Paris* qui constitueront l'œuvre essentielle de ses quatre dernières années.'[1] On the other hand M. Dimoff was following in the steps of Sainte-Beuve and Becq de Fouquières in attaching special importance to Chénier's pseudo-epic works.[2] In doing so, all these critics were only sharing the view of Chénier's friends, and of the poet himself. Chénier was long at the feet of Le Brun and de Brazais, because the first was engaged on a gigantic poem about *La Nature* which would have presented Buffon's view of the world, while de Brazais was laboriously composing *L'Année*, a Thomsonian poem on which he spent forty years. The epistles of Chénier show that his friends were very concerned about the progress of *Hermès*, and he himself described it as 'ma plus belle espérance'.

When we look at the facts, we find that the three great poems were hardly begun. In the state in which the poet left them they can scarcely be described as significant ruins. *Hermès* consists of fifty pages, mainly of prose notes. *L'Amérique* reaches fifty-five pages, mostly of prose notes. *Susanne* covers about twenty pages, mostly in prose.

Considering that *Hermès* would have begun by describing 'the system of the earth, though not of the world; Man from the beginning of his savage state down to the foundation of societies; Societies, Politics and Morality, the invention of the Sciences. System of the world'— then we have a physical picture of how far Chénier was, with his sixteen pages of verse, from having seriously begun writing his poem, which according to Dimoff would have filled twelve thousand lines. I say, 'seriously begun writing', because he had certainly seriously begun work on the poem: that is to say, he had read and digested many of the learned works which were a necessary basis for such a vast enterprise. As they stand, the main value of these three poems is that they gave some direction to Chénier's reading, and thus became an important part of his self-education. Some idea of the vast extent of his reading may be gained by reference to Dimoff and Fabre.

Turning to *L'Amérique* we see that here again, although in a

---

[1] F34, t. i, p. 277.

[2] Sainte-Beuve, G68 (*Quelques docs. inédits*): 'La partie la plus riche et la plus originale des manuscrits porte sur les poèmes inachevés: *Susanne, Hermès, l'Amérique*. . . . Je m'attacherai ici particulièrement au poème *Hermès*, le plus philosophique de ceux que méditait André, et celui par lequel il se rattache le plus directement à l'idée de son siècle.' See also Becq de Fouquières, G6, ch. iv.

different and more attractive form, Chénier would have had to give almost a history of the civilized world, together with a history of man's inventions, explorations, and religions. In addition he would have had to create all sorts of striking tales and episodes. Of all this, he only managed to write ten pages of verse. As for *Susanne*, we have the usual impressive programme in prose, for a poem in six books or 'Chants', of which only five pages of verse were actually written.

It is surely not enough to suggest that the Revolution and the poet's political activities alone prevented him from advancing these three important works. It is more likely that, having formed such ambitious projects, each of which demanded great reading before he could profitably put pen to paper, Chénier was seduced by the pleasures of scholarship, and would perhaps have remained so had not the Revolution obliged him to write articles, as well as hymns, odes, and *ïambes*. The most we can say of these long poems, by way of speculation, is that if he had finished any of them and lived to have it published under the Empire, it would have had more life in it than anything that was produced at that time. It would have brought him a pension and other honours. But would fame of that kind have been any more solid than the ephemeral glory of Delille, Chênedollé, Baour-Lormian, and Lemercier?

Looking at the fragments of these three poems as they stand, it is noticeable that Chénier was always prompt to write his prologues and epilogues, but slow to come down to the real task before him. This is understandable, for his was a lyrical genius, and he naturally delighted in the flight of imagination that prologues and epilogues allow. The first few lines of *Hermès*, in which he described the existence of rich and poor side by side, are rather loosely written and unoriginal:

> Dans nos vastes cités, par le sort partagés,
> Sous deux injustes lois les hommes sont rangés.
> Les uns, princes et grands, d'une avide opulence
> Étalent sans pudeur la barbare insolence;
> Les autres, sans pudeur vils clients des grands,
> Vont ramper sous les murs qui cachent les tyrans . . .

These Rousseau-istic sentiments are badly expressed: there is no 'law' dividing society in this way. All the more astonishing, then, is the remarkable passage that follows, in which the poet is represented as a Seer (a 'voyant'): the poetic impulse is so authentic, the language raised to such a point of incandescence, that any scepticism we might have about his didactic poem is suddenly overcome:

Heureux qui sait aimer ce trouble auguste et grand:
Seul, il rêve en silence à la voix du torrent
Qui le long des rochers se précipite et tonne;
Son esprit en torrent et s'élance et bouillonne.
Là je vais dans mon sein méditant à loisir
Des chants à faire entendre aux siècles à venir;
Là, dans la nuit des cœurs qu'osa sonder Homère,
Cet aveugle divin et me guide et m'éclaire.
Souvent mon vol, armé des ailes de Buffon,
Franchit avec Lucrèce, au flambeau de Newton,
La ceinture d'azur sur le globe étendue.
Je vois l'être et la vie et leur source inconnue,
Dans les fleuves d'éther tous les mondes roulants;
Je poursuis la comète aux crins étincelants,
Les astres et leurs poids, leurs formes, leurs distances;
Je voyage avec eux dans leurs cercles immenses.

This exercise in the grand manner shows how completely Chénier had
not only mastered the old rhetoric but was so at home in it that he
could at the same time hint at scientific knowledge and imitate the
classical 'afflatus' without falling into the Miltonic style. The positivistic
pupil of the Encyclopaedists could yet compare his verses with
thunderbolts: 'J'y rapporte des vers de nature enflammés, / Aux purs
rayons des Dieux dans ma course allumés.' Hinting, also, at his second
work, *L'Amérique*, he evoked it in such massive, resonant terms that
the reader's imagination is again stirred in advance:

Je dirai l'Amérique à l'Europe montrée;
J'irai dans cette riche et sauvage contrée
Soumettre au Mançanar le vaste Marañon . . .

Such lines give us a clue to Chénier's inner conception of the modern
pseudo-epic, far more than any of his ambitious descriptions of its
content could do. In the fragments given above there is a pride and
vigour of tone of an entirely different quality from what we meet in
his other work. The alexandrine, so often relaxed in the elegies, so
suavely musical in the *Bucoliques*, is here tightened and hammered into
a hard instrument of dynamic force. Had Chénier been able to keep up
this density, this noble rhetoric, he would have produced a poem unique
in French literature, anticipating the final style of Hugo. But this is
unlikely: some of the other fragments fall into the usual bathos of the
eighteenth century, as in this passage which, according to Chénier's
note, has something to do with the Ethiopians:

> Il croit (aveugle erreur) que de l'ingratitude
> Un peuple tout entier peut se faire une étude,
> L'établir pour son culte, et de dieux bienfaisants
> Blasphémer de concert les augustes présents.

There are as many clichés here as there are lines—'aveugle erreur',
'dieux bienfaisants', 'de concert', 'augustes présents'. As for their
meaning, M. Dimoff tells us that 'Il s'agit de Diodore de Sicile et de
l'explication qu'il nous donne des coutumes religieuses de certaines peu-
plades éthiopénnes.'[1] Even this explanation leaves us unenlightened.
It is plain that in a didactic poem the information needed by the reader
has to be given in the poem, and not in notes. This kind of obscurity
does not suggest that Chénier had 'l'esprit didactique'. The same conclusion is forced on us by other fragments, such as Chénier's rendering
of Lucretius's praise of Epicurus.

This does not mean, however, that Chénier might not have written
some interesting didactic passages when he came to handle more
modern ideas. What has been said so far is directed against the mere
information and literary reminiscence that the poem was obviously to
contain. His own personal didacticism would no doubt have had more
vitality: for instance he left two lines of his own on superstition, which
are so concentrated as (once more) to remind us of Mallarmé:

> Partout sur des autels j'entends mugir Apis,
> Bêler le dieu d'Ammon, aboyer Anubis.

Some of the prose drafts might have been developed in an original
manner, for instance:

> L'homme juge toujours des choses par les rapports qu'elles ont avec lui.
> C'est bête. . . . Le jeune homme se perd dans un tas de projets comme s'il
> devait vivre mille ans. . . . Le vieillard, qui a usé la vie, est inquiet et triste. . . .

But in spite of Chénier's cry, towards the end of his life, 'O mon fils,
mon Hermès, ma plus belle espérance!' we might ask whether the poet
really had such confidence in his project, and whether, if he had, it
would not have reached a much more advanced state than it actually
did? There is one passage which throws some doubt on his own belief
in this work:

> Il faut que le sage magicien qui sera un des héros de ce bizarre poème ait
> passé par plusieurs métempsychoses, propres à montrer allégoriquement
> l'histoire de l'espèce humaine. . . .

[1] D13, t. ii, p. 47.

The idea of introducing a character of the type of Tiresias was a good one, but it is strange that, in his notes, there is little or no sign of concentration on what the characters in the poem were to be. It is strange also that, while he was so eager to criticize religions and attack superstition, Chénier should have to invent a 'wise magician' or that he should describe the work as 'this odd poem'. It suggests that a fundamental uncertainty, rather than the harrassing circumstances of his life, explains why such a vast project was doomed to come to nothing. It is hard to see how his 'deathless magician' fits in with such items as 'Exposé du contrat social et des principes des gouvernements — très rapide'. Indeed it would be a simple enough matter to show that the plan as well as some of the detail of *Hermès* was not satisfactory. It would also be simple to show that Chénier, so adept at exploiting other people's ideas, was not always so good at exploiting his own. For instance, there is a highly original note on philology, written in beautiful prose, which is full of poetic insight and imagination:

Format[ion] des langues

Sons, accents, organes naturels. Les mots. Rapides Protées, ils révèlent la teinture de tous nos sentiments, ils dissèquent et étalent les moindres de nos pensées *comme un prisme fait les couleurs*.

Unfortunately, this brilliant observation on the influence of language on thought, expressed so powerfully through the image of the prism, did not find its way into the rather dull sequence of seventy-five lines in which Chénier described the evolution of writing from the papyrus to the printed book. His image is a most striking example of how scientific knowledge was impinging on the liberal arts in the eighteenth century; but perhaps Chénier was unaware of this. Our criticism is that, like his contemporaries, Chénier failed to realize the difference between didactic poetry based on original observation (such as the above image), and that which is no more than an account of the present state of knowledge on a given subject.

Hermès contains some things which are positive and enduring, and in which Chénier's powers are seen to be very great. The generations have not ceased to marvel at the fragment describing Orpheus, which is a masterpiece of concentration and harmony:

> Ainsi quand de l'Euxin la Déesse étonnée
> Vit du premier vaisseau son onde sillonnée,
> Aux héros de la Grèce, à Colchos appelés,
> Orphée expédiait les mystères sacrés

Dont sa mère immortelle avait daigné l'instruire.
Près de la poupe assis, appuyé sur sa lyre,
Il chantait quelles lois à ce vaste univers
Impriment à la fois des mouvements divers;
Quelle puissance entraîne ou fixe les étoiles,
D'où le souffle des vents vient animer les voiles,
Dans l'ombre de la nuit, quels célestes flambeaux
Sur l'aveugle Amphitrite éclairent les vaisseaux.
Ardents à recueillir ces merveilles utiles,
Autour du demi-dieu les princes immobiles
Aux accents de sa voix demeuraient suspendus,
Et l'écoutaient encor quand il ne chantait plus.

This is poetry worthy of the great ideal that Chénier had set himself, written in a natural, easy movement throughout. It represents eighteenth-century poetry in its purest state. The only conventional poetic diction is in the expressions 'célestes flambeaux' and 'aveugle Amphitrite'—the stars, lighting up the sea at night. For the rest it has an epic dignity and creates an enchanted atmosphere, perfectly illustrating Chénier's remark (in the *Essai*), 'Comme un philosophe se vantait de le pouvoir, avec de la matière et du mouvement, *il fait un monde.*'

Another fine sustained passage is that in praise of the legislators, a sequence of about seventy lines beginning:

Descends, œil éternel, tout clarté, tout lumière,
Viens luire dans son âme, éclaire sa paupière,
Pénétrer avec lui dans le cœur des humains,
De ce grand labyrinthe ouvre-lui les chemins . . .

If we can accept T. S. Eliot's argument (the very opposite of Edgar Allan Poe's) that in a long work in verse it is a mistake to have too much concentrated poetry, and that some dilution is necessary, then this movement would be easy to defend. Chénier himself did not believe that poetry should remain long at the same intensity, the same heat, and criticized those who look only for the purple passage:

Un morceau est beau dans un auteur, on ne cite que ce morceau tout seul. . . . Voltaire, d'autres, apprennent cette manière commode de juger . . . qui plaît beaucoup aux gens qui veulent juger de tout sans rien lire. . . . On dit 'Le quatrième livre de l'*Énéide* est admirable . . .' mais on devrait remarquer que les anciens écrivent tout comme il convient, changent de ton, etc. . . .[1]

However, there is a great difference between changing tone and style according to the requirements of the subject, and Eliot's apology for

[1] In the *Essai*, D22, p. 647.

the prosaic. Though Chénier's lines about the legislators are acceptable in their argument, there is a steady decline from the superb opening, as he enters into detail. It may be questioned whether poetry is the proper medium for close reasoning of the kind we meet here:

> Quand d'un crime léger la mort est le salaire,
> Tout grand forfait est sûr. Débile à se venger
> La loi ne prévient plus même un crime léger.
> La balance est en nous. Le pouvoir d'un caprice
> N'a point fondé les droits, la raison, la justice.
> Ils sont nés avec l'homme et ses premiers liens.

I do not know who goes to poetry for such neat formulas as 'la nature du crime en indique la peine', but apparently Chénier was less old-fashioned in this than he looked, since, as Claudel has pointed out, the Napoleonic Code contains such near-alexandrines as 'Tout condamné à mort aura la tête tranchée'. It is a fact, however, that the history of poetry does not bear out Eliot's assertion, and that lukewarm poetry, dealing in a near-prose style with ideas—of the kind that is being written now by our younger poets—does not long survive.

That Chénier did not intend his poem to contain much dilution of this kind, however, is shown by the astonishing fact that he originally intended to bring into it such intense writing as the passage on the Lapiths and Centaurs which he ended by inserting into *L'Aveugle*. It is fascinating to see that this great narrative passage was not written for its own sake, but in order to condemn the primitive manners of the Ancients:

> Les hommes ont toujours les mêmes passions, mais chaque siècle a ses mœurs et dans chaque siècle les mêmes passions ont une nouvelle manière de se montrer. Jadis quand la société avait moins appris à avoir de l'empire sur soi, les rivalités étaient sanglantes, rarement une fête finissait sans voir briller le fer et les coupes servir d'armes.
> *C'est ainsi que l'Olympe*, etc.

This opens up interesting possibilities. Was *L'Aveugle* in its entirety intended to form an episode of *Hermès*? Would Chénier have brought into it other long poems such as *Le Mendiant*, in order to draw a moral conclusion? Is it possible that the *Bucoliques*, or many of them, would have found a place in the structure of *Hermès*? We cannot know this, but, if so, *Hermès* might, after all, have become a poem of unusual originality. It is quite certain that some of the notes in *Hermès*, apart from the one given above, do point to this possibility; for instance the whole theme of his fine eclogue, *La Liberté*, is given in a note for the third Canto:

Il n'y a qu'un peuple vertueux, qui puisse être et rester libre. Pour goûter la liberté il ne faut pas aimer le repos et la mollesse. L'esclavage est plus paisible que la liberté.

Be that as it may, apart from some of the prologue and the lines celebrating Orpheus, the most authentic part of *Hermès* is the so-called 'epilogue' which Chénier wrote during the Revolution. It has to be noted that this could never have served as an epilogue for the completed poem; it is, rather, an elegy in which the poet laments an unfinished work. We shall return to these lines later. For the moment it is necessary to take up a statement which occurs in the third line:

> O mon fils, mon Hermès, ma plus belle espérance,
> O fruit des longs travaux de ma persévérance,
> Toi, l'objet le plus cher des veilles de dix ans,
> Qui m'as coûté des soins et si doux et si lents ;
> Confident de ma joie et remède à mes peines ;
> Sur les lointaines mers, sur les terres lointaines,
> Compagnon bien-aimé de mes pas incertains,
> O mon fils, aujourd'hui quels seront tes destins ? . . .

The third line originally read 'veillé pendant sept ans'. In spite of the assertions of some critics, the only definite evidence we have of the date Chénier began this poem points to 1783. If, in 1790 or 1793, Chénier could refer to it as 'ma plus belle espérance' and suggest that it had been his constant occupation, it is incredible that he should be referring to the poem in the state in which it has survived, and it is likely that far more of it was written than has come down to us.

Sainte-Beuve, who in 1839 gave a fairly long analysis of *Hermès*, did not make any extravagant claim for it, but regarded it as the work in which Chénier came closest to reflecting the thought of his century. This article ('Quelques documents inédits sur André Chénier') brought a witty reply from Alfred de Vigny, though he was one of Chénier's most consistent admirers: 'Vous m'avez vraiment consolé de sa mort, puisqu'il est vrai que *ce qu'il avait là* était cette grosse chose nommée *Hermès*. Il allait se gâter, on le savait bien là-haut, et l'on a mis un point à sa phrase quand il a fallu.'[1]

According to Faguet, *Hermès* 'eût été vraisemblablement le plus beau poème philosophique de la langue française';[2] but Jean Fabre

[1] Cit. by M. Allem in G68, p. 240.   [2] G21, p. 136.

remarks on this statement, 'Faguet l'affirme et reconnaît à ce chef-d'œuvre tous les mérites, sauf celui d'exister.'[1] But in any case *Hermès* had no definite theme or structure and could never have become much more than an anthology of accepted ideas, with here and there some stray diamond lost in a prosaic paste. This does not mean, however, that we must dismiss *Hermès* in reflecting on Chénier's numerous gifts. Unfinished and perhaps unfinishable, none the less the manuscripts that remain, the seventy or so pages of notes and drafts, form a kind of Journal of the poet's ideas which is of the greatest interest. It is lively, entertaining, naïve. We see the humanist, regarding man's progress in transforming the world as a series of 'miracles': 'Prenons-le au commencement, et tout ses miracles vont nous passer en revue.' The poet's world is alive, like that of Swedenborg: 'il faut magnifiquement représenter la terre sous l'emblème métaphorique d'un grand animal qui vit, se meut, etc.' His theory of utility, the interdependence of all things on each other, so banal in itself, takes on charm and colour when, like some Orpheus, he asks questions of nature: 'Rien n'est fait pour soi seul. . . . Toi, arbre ou fleuve, réponds, pourquoi tu fais ceci ou cela? — Je le fais pour . . . — Et toi telle autre chose, pourquoi? — Je le fais pour . . . .' Believing that 'l'homme seul est perfectible' he is not discouraged by the thought that prolonged error cannot be set right: 'cela n'empêche que l'âme et le jugement du genre humain entier ne soit porté à la vertu et à la vérité, *comme le bois d'un arc, quoique courbé et plié un moment, n'en a moins un désir invincible d'être droit et ne s'en redresse pas moins dès qu'il le peut.*' At every turn these notes show poetic thinking of a high order; Chénier thinks spontaneously in metaphor, turning his very platitudes into fresh discoveries: 'Il est tourmenté par une passion; une autre passion vient la combattre, et lui mettre *un frein qu'elle a beau mordre et blanchir d'écume.*' Sometimes we feel that his reflections are autobiographical: '. . . plus on est né un personnage, plus on a de passions ardentes et plus on peut avoir eu une jeunesse fougueuse et des égarements terribles.' However, the facts that Chénier's notes are interesting, and that, very often, we see that his vivid imagination might have succeeded in animating ideas which at first sight are not very promising for poetry, do not remove our doubts as to the fundamental error that underlay his project. It was natural for the eighteenth-century poets to think that, as they were living in a privileged 'age of reason', the time had come for a 'poetry of reason'. But the time had gone when one man could hope to dominate existing

knowledge, or when it was in any way necessary to versify it. Wordsworth managed to make the didactic poem acceptable, because he took
himself as its centre; but Chénier was still too bound by neo-classicism
to start from his own self. Chénier was the victim of a fashionable
fallacy in thinking, in the first place, in monumental terms, and in
imagining that no more than an historical framework was sufficient to
give form to a poem. While there is evidence that his imagination
would have solved, beautifully, many a problem of detail, it is only too
obvious, from his notes, that he had failed to *imagine* the work as
a whole. Poetic creation must, especially in a long work, rely very
strongly on the shaping power of will, on a kind of intellectual vitality
or toughness; but if it is not conceived through an initial act of imagination and seen as a single, unique thing from the very outset, then
knowledge will drive out intuition, and the poet will end by using his
precious gifts for their own destruction.

The same cannot be said of *L'Amérique*. The subject was both well
defined and modern, while Chénier had found a method of presentation which was completely original and which could have bound the
work into a proper unity. The true act of imagination which should lie
behind any poem or play or novel involves the discovery not only
of an idea but of its essential form, and it is best when such discovery
is spontaneous. Chénier instinctively found this form: 'Il faut tâcher
d'inventer quelque chose dans le goût du bouclier d'Achille et d'Énée
pour y représenter les points cardinaux de l'histoire du monde.'
L'Amérique could thus have become a genuinely heroic poem, and not
merely versified history or philosophy. He also had the intention of
allowing his characters to speak, instead of speaking *ex cathedra* himself: 'Comme les personnages d'Homère entremêlent dans leurs discours des récits des choses qui leur sont arrivés dans leur jeune âge,
ainsi on peut mettre dans la bouche de quelques personnages du poème
des allusions un peu détaillées de quelques révolutions intéressantes.'
Just as important was his realization that, for his modern poem, he
must invent a mythology of his own: 'Il faut que j'invente entièrement
une sorte de mythologie probable et poétique avec laquelle je puisse
remplacer les tableaux gracieux des anciens.' Further, his ideas on
religion had broadened since he conceived his *Hermès*. Whereas
Hermès was to condemn superstition (and, by implication, all religion)
he now wrote: 'Il faut dans cet ouvrage que chaque nation ait son Dieu,
comme de raison. Mais le poète les admettra tous. Il peindra les
cérémonies de toutes les religions avec une indifférence et une égalité

parfaites.' That Chénier was far from hostile to religious matters is shown by several notes:

— Et ces prêtres barbares après cela vont à l'autel, entrer à l'autel de Dieu . . . et consacrer la sainte hostie . . . Dieu s'indigne de voir le pain devenir lui-même entre leurs mains sacrilèges.

— Peindre une procession . . . les moines de différentes couleurs . . . de différents habits . . . les surplis, les cierges . . . Traduire quelquefois transitoirement par allusion, par prétérition, quelques prières de l'Église. . . .

— Ne pas oublier les fêtes de l'Église dont plusieurs sont intéressantes, comme Noël, le dimanche des rameaux, le vendredi saint, et plusieurs histoires du Nouveau Testament, la femme adultère, la Samaritaine, le Samaritain charitable. . . . Quoi qu'on en dise, toutes ces fables ont leur prix sans valoir peut-être celles d'Homère. Encore ce dernier point peut-il être contesté.

— Parmi les cérémonies catholiques qu'il faut peindre, ne pas oublier les Cendres . . . et: *aperite portas, principes, vestras* . . . et les rogations . . . et les enterrements . . . baptêmes . . . viatique . . . extrême-onction. . . .[1]

It is interesting to see that the only alternative that Chénier could find, at that stage, to classical mythology was the 'merveilleux chrétien' over which the French ancients and moderns had fought.

While it is admitted that according to his plans Chénier had more chance of writing a great poem in *L'Amérique* than in *Hermès*, we are again brought down to earth once we turn from his prose notes, which are always interesting, to consider what he actually achieved. The few historical fragments that he completed—the crowning of Henry VI at Vincennes, the short description of Henry V, the sixteen lines about the St. Bartholomew massacres—are banal. But there are four other passages which are equal to anything in *Hermès*: these are the ten lines beginning 'Plus beau que ce coursier, ce superbe Cyllare'; the tribute to Rome which we have already quoted (see pp. 62–63); the magnificent 'Enthousiasme, enfant de la nuit' which has already been discussed (see p. 41), and the more conventional portrait of the poet as seer, beginning:

> Le poète divin, tout esprit, tout pensée,
> Ne sent point dans son corps son âme embarrassée.
> Il va percer le ciel aux murailles d'azur,
> De la terre, des mers, le labyrinthe obscur . . .

Chénier took the precaution of adding a note, 'Il faut mettre ceci dans la bouche du poète (qui n'est pas moi).' Without that note it could be

---

[1] *L'Amérique*, section IV ('Mythologie et Religions').

reproached against him that he did not believe this kind of thing, and that it is merely fine writing for its own sake, pure poetry. Blake, Hugo, Nerval, could write in this way because they really believed that the poet has a divine mission; but Chénier had no 'mystique' or metaphysic to justify such a flight, interesting only because it shows how the eighteenth-century poets took no trouble to reconcile their encyclopaedist, rationalist philosophy with a posturing that was taken direct from the Ancients. Fact and fiction would have lived uneasily together in *L'Amérique*.

As for *Susanne*, which was to be written in six books or cantos, it is by no means easy to judge at what stage in his career Chénier began to write it. Dimoff has argued that it must have been late in 1786, when Chénier went to Italy,[1] on the evidence of a draft for an 'élégie orientale' which begins:

> Trop longtemps le plaisir, égarant mes beaux jours,
> A consacré ma lyre aux profanes amours.
> J'ai trop chanté de vers, trop suaves peut-être,
> Que l'œil de la Pudeur n'a point osé connaître.

— Mais aujourd'hui que mon âge a commencé de se calmer, que les belles m'inspirent des fureurs plus tranquilles, je puis sans interruption chanter sur un ton plus austère ... Je vais achevant mon *Hermès* ... Surtout les champs de tel ou tel pays m'ont vu travailler avec délices à mon poème de *Susanne*. ... O Pudeur, vierge sainte, c'est pour toi que je fais cet ouvrage. ...

Dimoff classified this draft, in his edition, with the 'Voyage en Italie: projet de voyage en Orient';[2] but there are reasons for suggesting that he was wrong. The Italian elegies (so far from being calm and chaste) are clearly marked 'élég. ital.', while the one that has just been quoted is marked 'élégie orientale'. Though it is true (or may at least be assumed) that Chénier was hoping, in 1786, to go as far as the Middle East, there is evidence that he did not begin to take an interest in oriental languages and literatures—Arabic, Persian, Hindu, and Chinese—until he was in London.[3] It was certainly not in 1786 that he regarded his youthful spirits as becoming more calm! It seems far more likely that the desire to write a biblical poem, *Susanne*, was inspired by his discovery of Milton, when he was in London, and that,

---

[1] F34, t. i, pp. 192, 197.
[2] D13, t. iii, p. 32.
[3] Dimoff's hypothesis (F34, t. i, pp. 180–2) that Chénier took up oriental studies in 1785–6, an interest stimulated by François de Pange, has no evidence for it; whereas it is known that it was in London that Chénier read Jones's *Persian Grammar* and certain oriental works, while drafting 'oriental elegies'.

subsequently, he thought of it as a work to be written in honour of Fanny Lecoulteux, who was not only devout, but a model of chastity.[1]

There are other acceptable reasons why Chénier should have taken chastity as his theme, and chosen the story of *Susanne*. His friend de Brazais suddenly destroyed an erotic work, *Psyché*, which he had begun in 1787, and began to write a poem on the Messiah. If Chénier might seem to be speaking out of character in exclaiming 'O Pudeur, vierge sainte, c'est pour toi que je fais cet ouvrage!' yet, in his elegies, he more than once revealed his uneasy conscience at his way of life: like Boswell or Keats he was torn between natural desires and a sense of guilt. And then he had found in Milton a divine poet whom he could admire as much as Dante, calling him 'Grand aveugle dont l'âme a su voir tant de choses'. There was also a negative reason why he might be tempted to write a biblical epic: his reaction against Voltaire, whom he accused of debasing sublime themes. Though he never mentioned *La Pucelle*, his condemnation of the *Henriade* was so complete that he could have had nothing but contempt for that occasionally witty mock-epic which represents all that is most regrettable in the nature of Voltaire.

All these good reasons for writing *Susanne*, however, do not make a poem; and of the three verse passages which Chénier completed, only the invocation to the religious Muse, with its fine tribute to Milton, will bear scrutiny. While the two other completed passages are merely dull and show nothing of that narrative gift which is so evident in the *Bucoliques*, the invocation is well written and shows not the slightest hint of any fault of tone, such as would point to the poet's insincerity:

> O fille de là-haut, organe du génie,
> Voix sublime et touchante, immortelle harmonie,
> Toi qui fais retentir les saints échos du ciel
> D'hymnes que vont chanter près du trône éternel
> Les jeunes séraphins aux ailes enflammées;
> Toi qui vins sur la terre aux vallons Idumées
> Répéter la tendresse et les transports si doux
> De la belle d'Égypte et du royal époux;
> Et qui, plus fière, aux bords où la Tamise gronde,
> As, depuis, fait entendre et l'enfance du monde
> Et le chaos antique et les anges pervers,
> Et les vagues de feu roulant dans les enfers,
> Et des premiers humains les chastes hyménées,

[1] However, H1, p. 15, also suggests that Chénier showed some of *Susanne* to Palissot in 1787.

Et les douceurs d'Éden si tôt abandonnées;
Viens, coule sur ma bouche, et descends dans mon cœur.
Mets sur ma langue un peu de ce miel séducteur
Qu'en des vers tout trempés d'une amoureuse ivresse
Versait du sage roi la langue enchanteresse;
Un peu de ces discours, grands, profonds comme toi,
Paroles de délice ou paroles d'effroi,
Aux lèvres de Milton incessamment écloses,
Grand aveugle dont l'âme a su voir tant de choses.

There is no need to suggest that because Chénier embarked on writing a biblical poem, he was therefore a Christian. Though we cannot agree with Rivarol or Chênedollé that he was an atheist, 'athée avec délices'—in any case Chênedollé never met Chénier and his statement was never corroborated by any of his contemporaries—he was certainly not a Christian.[1] However, L. Joubert pointed out that *Susanne* went against 'tous ses préjugés philosophiques'; J. Haraszti affirmed that Chénier was a Christian; C. Kramer spoke of his 'inquiétude toute moderne et même chrétienne', while both Barbey d'Aurevilly and Maurras remarked on the religious undercurrent in the *Ïambes*.[2] It would be dangerous to argue, from the numerous religious references in his poems, that Chénier was even a deist. So far as *Susanne* is concerned we must remember Coleridge's argument that poetry may be dissociated from beliefs. What Chénier possessed in an exceptional measure was a proper respect for human beings and for moral values. Though he was anti-clerical at the beginning of the Revolution he wrote a public plea for indulgence towards the clergy, and for tolerance towards all religions. Though he regarded religion as 'superstition' he did not reject Christ, though he questioned his divinity:

A Dieu ne plaise que je veuille, comme plusieurs ont fait, insulter par une risée barbare aux angoisses et à la mort d'un homme qui, à travers les puérilités et les extravagances que ses absurdes historiens lui attribuent, souvent avec quelque vraisemblance, fait cependant briller un caractère de douceur et de philanthropie, qui ne fut accusé d'aucun crime, et qu'un lâche gouverneur laissa traîner au supplice quoiqu'il le jugeât innocent.[3]

Maurras asked the question whether Chénier's religious outlook

[1] Note the excellent article by Venzac on this problem (G72). He suggests that the expression 'athée avec délices' (first printed by Sainte-Beuve who attributed it to Rivarol) could have been first used by Joubert. My own view is that Chénier was no atheist, but that the expression applies perfectly to Marie-Joseph Chénier.

[2] For these remarks see G34, also G72.

[3] D22, p. 724.

did not undergo some change while he was imprisoned in Saint-La-zare.[1] He must have still been engaged on his *Histoire du Christianisme* at an advanced stage of the Revolution, as he mentioned it in connexion with the Avignon massacres.[2] One of his objects was to defend the Ancients against modern commentators, and this he did by describing the Platonism of the early Fathers and quoting Justin Martyr, 'qui, dans sa seconde Apologie, dit expressément que Socrate avait en partie connu le Christ'.[3] His history of Christianity was hostile to religion, however, and on every page there is the same appeal to fact and reason: he accused Pascal of arrogance and condemned him for indulging in 'le dur plaisir d'humilier l'espèce humaine devant les chimères qu'elle-même inventa dans son délire'.[4] There is no sign of a possible con-version in any of his writings. The most that can be said is that he was interested in religious questions as he was interested in everything else, but in a spirit that looked forward to the scientific agnosticism of the nineteenth century.

The imperfection of these three major projects that we have been discussing, *Hermès*, *L'Amérique*, and *Susanne*, has led us away from the task of aesthetic appreciation; but the point to be stressed is that these works were unfinishable, or, at least, that Chénier was not the man to finish them. Chénier appears to have confessed this himself, in a statement about *L'Amérique* which he made in his *Essai*:

Outre beaucoup d'hommes médiocres, deux poètes célèbres se sont occupés de cette matière [le Nouveau Monde], savoir Alexandre Tassoni, en Italie, et monsieur . . . chez nous. J'ignore pour quelle cause le premier n'a point poussé son ouvrage au delà du premier chant. Pour monsieur . . . c'est bien dommage qu'avec de si grands talents il n'ait point exécuté une si belle entreprise. Nous aurions un poème à opposer aux anciens. Mais, comme nous le lui avons ouï dire plusieurs fois, son dessein, en commençant, n'était point d'achever cet ouvrage.

J. Fabre has suggested that Chénier was speaking of himself.[5] As for *Hermès*, he 'wrote it off' during the Revolution and worked on his *Buco-liques*. Perhaps the fact that the *Bucoliques* did not tie him down to any fixed plan enabled him to express his lively but fitful genius more directly through them than he could have done through any other medium.

[1] G55, p. 481: 'Les cachots de la Terreur ont pu et dû changer quelque chose à sa philosophie. On le peignait athée avec délices. Mais les *Ïambes* laissent filtrer une invoca-tion au *grand Dieu des armées*. Quelque ironie douloureuse qu'on y découvre, cela n'a plus rien d'athée.'
[2] D22, p. 725.   [3] Ibid., p. 727.   [4] Ibid., p. 725.
[5] F36, p. 198. See also Van Tieghem, 'Un Monsieur mystérieux', in *RHLF*, 1928.

8

THE *BUCOLIQUES*

CHÉNIER's *Bucoliques* is the only great collection of lyrical poems
to have been written in French between La Fontaine's last collection
of *Fables* in 1693 and Lamartine's *Les Méditations* in 1820. This may be
said although Chénier's poems were grafted on a tradition of pastoral
poetry which was already in decline and is now extinct. Chénier himself
headed most of these manuscripts with the abbreviation Βυκ or Βουκ
and in doing so was relating his works directly to that of such poets
as Moschus, Bion, Theocritus, Callimachus, and Virgil, for whom the
term referred to poems dealing mainly with 'the care of flocks, and the
pleasures and activities of rural life'. His poems bear little relationship
to eighteenth-century pastoral verse: nowhere did he mention or
imitate such poets as Desforges-Maillard, Dorat, Colardeau, Berquin,
or Léonard, whose work we have examined from this point of view.
He sometimes wrote at the top of his poem, both *Βyx* and *Ydille*,
using the latter term in its proper acceptance, which in French meant
no more than 'a short poem'. If his work occasionally felt and suffered
from the more recent influence of Young, Thomson, Gessner, and
Barthélemy, this influence was so slight (indeed Barthélemy's *Voyage
du jeune Anacharsis* (1788) came too late to affect the essential nature
of his work) as to be of no significance. Indeed one of the most surprising aspects of the *Bucoliques* is that they rarely bear the stamp of
the century in which they were written. His local colour is hardly ever
touched by eighteenth-century anachronism. The conventional poetic
diction is less obtrusive than in any of his contemporaries, while his
latinisms are often little different from those used by the Romantics
or the Parnassians. These poems also turn away from his century
because, for the most part rejecting the flat narrative style, he turned
away from purely descriptive and narrative pastoral to create what we
can only call 'dramatic lyrics'. The dramatic quality of his poems sets
him apart as the last, and perhaps the only, disciple of La Fontaine. It
might be said that in their dramatic quality the *Bucoliques* stand half-
way between La Fontaine and Valéry.

Unfortunately the *Bucoliques* remain almost inaccessible to the average modern reader, since Heredia's fine edition of 1906 has long been out of print. P. Dimoff's edition is so arranged—the poems being split up into as many as ninety-seven groups—as to form a useful book of reference rather than a readable text. In the Pléiade edition, prepared by G. Walter, the arrangement is no more satisfactory: his system of isolating 'finished' from 'unfinished' poems does not hold; for it is often hard to tell whether a poem was finished or not, while some of Chénier's finest poetry is to be found encrusted in passages of prose. One way of approaching these poems, however, is to regard the *Bucoliques* as a kind of poet's workshop. For that reason we do not propose to follow the printed editions, but to make a rapid journey through the manuscripts as they stand today, even if this might not be the order in which the poet left them: for some disturbance certainly occurred among them at the hands of Latouche, their first editor, in 1819, and of the poet's nephew, Gabriel de Chénier.

It is with some emotion that those who care for poetry first cast their eyes on any poet's manuscripts, appreciating the careful or rapid hand, the corrections, hesitations, and decisions which show the poet in the process of communing with his own mind. We see him prompting himself with all kinds of suggestions and alternatives; reminding himself that this or that had already been better expressed by some other poet; and sometimes crossing a fragment out and starting again, or striking his pen through the whole manuscript, writing a date on it and stating, triumphantly, 'C'est fait'. In Chénier's case it is particularly moving to find, on the back of a poem, the address of a friend in London, Paris, or Oxford, or the words, evidently written in prison, 'J'ai peur de perdre mon papier'. But it is not our intention to offer thrills of this kind, though it would not be difficult in Chénier's case to dramatize his manner of composition. All we can do is to forget the arbitrary arrangements that have been made of his works, and see them in the chaotic state in which he left them to posterity—a state which justifies his frequent laments at his slow progress and wayward mind, or his too optimistic comment, 'Rien n'est fait aujourd'hui: tout sera fait demain.'

Opening the first set (NAF 6848) of Chénier's five collections of manuscripts, we find over two hundred folios of different dimensions, ranging from scraps no bigger than a visiting-card to large quarto or foolscap sheets. Sometimes they are pale blue, or grey, or brownish; sometimes with fox-marks caused by drops of water or wine. The writing is usually very small and neat, or even compressed so that a magnifying-glass is needed. He would usually fold his paper perpendicularly and write in a thin, cramped column. We are told that he always carried paper and pen about with him, and wrote wherever the fit seized him. Each folio may contain, on both sides, anything from one to nine or ten bits of different poems; though sometimes, when the writing is proud and steady, we are in the presence of a fair or final copy. We have entered a personal world—not the orderly, scholarly, catalogued world of poetry that we find in printed books in which, so to speak, the poem's nakedness has been made decent and sociable; but a spontaneous, intimate world in which ideas and feelings, pictures and music, prose and verse are alive and writhing under a man's hand, trying to assume an independent and enduring life of their own.

The first manuscript (folio 5) is a fragment of his greatest poem, *L'Aveugle*. The blue paper, measuring only twenty-two by seventeen centimetres and folded vertically, carries on it, full of corrections, the famous forty-four lines narrating the combat between the Centaurs and Lapiths which, as we have already seen, Chénier had at first intended to use in his *Hermès* (see above, p. 153). In this passage, Chénier concentrated over three hundred lines from Ovid's *Metamorphoses*. This almost excessive concentration, which recalls certain passages in Shakespeare, is the first enduring quality of his work, and it is fitting that it should be demonstrated in its extreme form, in the first document that comes to hand. This piece bears no title but the word *Bουκ* followed by Chénier's terse note, *employé*. Yes, employed to some purpose, as it became the splendid finale of one of the finest narrative poems in the French language, the first of the 'little epics' which inspired Hugo to create his *Légende des Siècles*. Becoming used to the writing, we look more closely and read the first few lines:

> c'est ainsi que l'Olympe et les bois de Pénée
> virent ensanglanter les banquets d'hyménée
> quand Thésée, au milieu de la joie et du vin . . .

Looking at the various editions, we see that they all read:

> Enfin, l'Ossa, l'Olympe et les bois de Pénée
> Voyaient ensanglanter les banquets d'hyménée . . .

As no other manuscript of the poem has been found, either this change was made by Chénier in an amended version, or it was made by

Latouche. We grow more conscious of the difficulties of making a sound edition when we notice that the Pléiade text absent-mindedly leaves out a whole line in the same sequence ('D'un érable noueux il va fendre sa tête'). Our disappointment grows when, thumbing rapidly through the collection, we realize that except for these forty-four lines, the manuscript of *L'Aveugle* which came into Latouche's hands in 1819 is for ever lost, for his papers were destroyed or stolen by the Germans in 1871.

Chénier's own corrections are not very spectacular. The rather abstract description, 'l'affreux Macarée', is improved into 'le noir Macarée'. The poet wrestled unsatisfactorily with the problem of expressing piebaldness, hesitating between 'dont les crins affectaient, de taches colorés' and 'qui portait sur ses crins, de taches colorés'. Without hoping to learn too much from the poet's amendments, we notice already a tendency to modify his draft, perhaps as he was going along, in the direction of increased intensity, and more correct and less precious syntax. We also notice, from the start, that Chénier rarely used a capital letter at the beginning of a line. In his manuscripts, this makes the poems look less formal, more modern, and contributes to a livelier movement, especially as he was very sparing in his use of punctuation. He often used full stops where Dimoff inserted commas: where Chénier wrote

> L'insolent quadrupède en vain s'écrie; il tombe.

Dimoff gives

> L'insolent quadrupède en vain s'écrie, il tombe;

Indeed, Dimoff (*Œuvres d'A.C.*, vol. 1) admits, in his footnotes, to making twelve changes of punctuation in twenty lines (221–41), but the authority of his edition is such that everyone has imitated him since. Literally hundreds of commas and semi-colons have been added to Chénier's poems by his editors, and whereas he hardly ever used an exclamation-mark they have rendered him a poor service in throwing in so many. This has been done on the pretext that Chénier's punctuation is eccentric; forgetting that the modern system of French punctuation dates from the late nineteenth century only, and that any poet's punctuation is placed, not for correctness by schoolroom standards, but in order to mark pauses for the voice, or to clarify the sense, or to bring out some nuance in movement. As we read on we become convinced that what is really required is a facsimile edition of these manuscripts.

Turning to the next page, we become aware of Chénier's range. The brutal, heroic world of the Centaurs suddenly disappears. Here, on a narrow strip of pale blue paper, are six different pieces, all pressed together. The first piece bears the title *Aglaé*, though in the first edition Latouche gave it the title *Euphrosine*, while Heredia called it, simply, *Douze ans*:

> Ah, ce n'est point à moi qu'on s'occupe de plaire.
> Ma sœur plus tôt que moi dut le jour à ma mère.
> Si quelques beaux bergers apportent une fleur
> Je vois qu'en me l'offrant ils regardent ma sœur.
> S'ils vantent les attraits dont brille mon visage
> Ils disent à ma sœur *C'est ta vivante image.*
> Ah, pourquoi n'ai-je encor vu que douze moissons?
> Nul amant ne me flatte en de douces chansons.
> Nul ne dit qu'il mourra si je suis infidèle.
> Mais j'attends. L'âge vient. Je sais que je suis belle.
> Je sais qu'on ne voit point d'attraits plus désirés
> Qu'un visage arrondi, de longs cheveux dorés,
> Dans une bouche étroite un double rang d'ivoire,
> Et sur de beaux yeux bleus une paupière noire.

We may savour Chénier's quaint eighteenth-century spelling a little, before we feel the poem: he wrote *plutôt*, *j'attens*, *bleux*. The poem shows the poet's touch at its lightest: he could write better about a child's jealousy than about his own. It is typical of the large number of poems in which he dealt, sensitively and with such insight, with childhood and adolescence. The thought is so real, so alive, because it is all expressed in the present; yet it is not a spoken monologue, but the girl's inward thoughts. Nobody else in the eighteenth century ever wrote like that, with such naturalness, delicacy, and understanding, with such slow and suave musicality. It has the logical directness of good prose. There is not a single stylized trick in it, not a single eighteenth-century inversion, not a single cliché or hint of poetic diction. It has the simplicity and depth of Wordsworth at his best. There is no intervention, on the poet's part, between the girl and the reader: nothing dims the immediate presentation of simple feeling. The *Bucoliques*, of course, are supposed to be about Greece, and this frightens readers away; but we see from this that such themes are universal and do not even need local colour to support them. Analysis does not reveal why the human imagery of the last two lines lingers in the memory; whether it is the music or the picture which does the work, reminding us at the same time of Baudelaire.

Immediately after it is another item, reading simply 'Une petite fille de 10 ans qu'on appelle enfant et qui se fâche'. This is not quite the same idea as in the poem above, but this 'quadro' sets the reader musing, realizing suddenly that the frequent mention of children of all ages in Chénier's poems, even in the most ambitious such as *L'Aveugle* and *Le Mendiant*, is not just an ornament but a characteristic device. It helps to fill out the pastoral setting, and creates an atmosphere in which innocence and good faith lead naturally to belief, while this attentive audience of children enables the poet to write in direct speech.

The next piece on this folio takes us into another aspect of Chénier's world, for it contains the prose draft of *Le Mendiant*, one of those 'honnête homme' poems very much to the taste of the eighteenth century. The story of how the beggar Cleotas is given hospitality by the wealthy Lycus on his daughter's tenth birthday ends with one of those typical recognition-scenes which tend to amuse the modern reader: we find, afterwards, that Lycus had formerly been Cleotas's slave. But it describes the same world of impeccable and sublime charity as that of *L'Aveugle*. Though some critics have thought that Chénier could not 'invent' in the proper sense of the term, and that he always needed someone else's work on which to hang his own, on the contrary the very first words of his draft strike us as full of invention. Chénier does not only think of a story: like Chekhov he has the gift of finding the kind of significant detail which brings story, setting, and characters immediately to life:

La fille de Lycus âgée de 8 ans va mangeant un gâteau le long du bois . . . il en sort un pauvre qui lui demande l'aumône. A cette Voix, effrayée, elle s'enfuit en courant . . . Mais il la presse en 2 ou 3 vers touchans, elle se rassure revient et lui donne son gâteau et lui dit: ne pleure pas . . . viens ce soir à la maison de mon père — c'est Lycus, et je te donnerai encore des gâteaux . . .

This is only the beginning of a very long prose draft (about thirty lines) for a poem which was to work out to 336 lines. What strikes us in the beginning of the draft is the presentation of the little girl, with the emphasis on her only treasure, a piece of cake. However, there is one of those small disappointments in store for us, which we can only know when we have had access, in this way, to the author's spontaneous thoughts. In the poem, of which the manuscript is lost, the girl is no longer eight years old, but ten. What we miss is that cake which the poet mentioned thrice in his first draft—'va mangeant un gâteau le long des bois'—'et lui donne son gâteau'—'je te donnerai encore des gâteaux'. The Chekhovian touch is lost. Nor, at the feast in the evening, is there any mention of cake at all: the uninvited guest is told 'Sieds-toi. Vois, l'on apporte et la table et le pain'. Bread, followed by

> Et les fumantes chairs et les disques d'airain,
> Et l'amphore vineuse et la coupe aux deux anses.

These two lines show some of the linguistic weaknesses from which Chénier ought to have been free by 1788 or 1789—for this poem was written in London, probably, since some of the lines are close to the prose of Barthélemy's *Voyage du jeune Anacharsis*, published in 1788. Perhaps these two lines are not merely precious, but an attempt at local colour; it is certain, however, that Barthélemy did not improve Chénier's poem, but led him away from his own more direct manner. Quite apart from Chénier's failure to follow his own first intuition (the detail of the cake), *Le Mendiant* has none of the concentration of *L'Aveugle*: it is a pleasing enough tale, but too close to the sentimentality of its time. In it, however, we are fully in Chénier's ancient world, in the paradise of the Golden Age when, if there were suffering and poverty, beggars and slaves, feelings were prompt and deep, hospitality was sacred and immediate, destiny guided the honest man to his salvation, and wrongs were put right. He was creating that Homeric climate in which what W. B. Yeats called 'the ceremony of innocence' was not a fiction.

The same folio (7) contains other surprises. Here, item 4, is a bit of the prose draft for *L'Aveugle* itself:

des petits garçons rencontrent dans la forêt un aveugle . . . ils lui donnent l'un son pain l'autre ses pommes l'autre ses olives et du pain à son chien . . . ils le font chanter . . . il leur chante . . . et puis ils le ramènent au village qui vient au-devant de l'aveugle et lui fait fête . . .

There is the whole of the draft as it stands, before adding to it other pieces which are to be found elsewhere. It contains the essence of the great poem, and we shall return to it in a moment to see how it was transformed, in his mind, from just another story about a blind beggar into the powerful tale he made of it. Here we have a blind man and his dog, and a few children. Asked to sing, he is then given the honour of hospitality. We note exactly the same kind of homely details as in the draft of *Le Mendiant*, and are touched in the same way by the children's gift of what they have in their hands, and especially by the offering to the dog. Nothing could be more ordinary, or more swiftly evoke 'the ceremony of innocence'. This time, turning to the text (the manuscript being lost, except, as we have stated, the forty-four lines about the Centaurs) we see with satisfaction that Chénier has used this detail in the poem; yet the offerings are on a grander scale and, though in keeping with the pastoral atmosphere, less homely:

> Ils versent à l'envi sur ses genoux pesants
> Le pain de pur froment, les olives huileuses,
> Le fromage et l'amande et les figues mielleuses,
> Et du pain à son chien entre ses pieds gisant.

The simple bread has been 'improved' (*pur froment*) and we see, not for the last time, the accomplished gourmet who made our mouths water in the elegies, and whom the Countess of Albany reproached for being too fond of food: the 'olives huileuses' and 'figues mielleuses' are the gifts of a sensualist, as eager to evoke rich tastes as John Keats. Charles Chassé has remarked in an amusing book (*Style et physiologie*) that 'André Chénier se montrait novateur lorsqu'il parlait en vers de "la mielleuse banane"'.[1]

Logically, after his prose outline, Chénier ought to have jotted down the first lines of his poem. But his mind did not work in that way. Instead, the next item on the sheet is a note for another poem, which has not survived, and which was probably suggested by Sappho:

... vois-tu sur la colline ... vois-tu ceci ... vois-tu cela ... Si tu veux m'aimer tout cela sera à toi ...

> Mon amour aime-moi. Sur l'herbe chaque soir
> Au coucher du soleil nous viendrons nous asseoir.

Je te ferai ceci ou cela pour te plaire.

Immediately after this, at the foot of the page, comes another bit of the draft for *L'Aveugle*. What happened is that Chénier must have suddenly had another idea about the poem, for the prose fragment we gave above (p. 168), ending with the words 'et lui fait fête', had a cross added against it, and beside the cross the words 'C'est Homère', obviously squeezed in afterwards. The note at the foot of the page reads:

Avant de chanter il caresse les petits garçons il leur dit: 'Sans doute ... vos visages sont doux autant que votre voix ... Venez ici que je vous tâte ...

[1] C. Chassé, *Style et physiologie*, Albin Michel, 1928, p. 137.

'Toi le plus grand de tous, je me confie à toi.
Assieds-moi sur la pierre et veille auprès de moi.
Prends soin du vieil aveugle . . .'   (Sophocle, v. 21)

It is plain that the identification of the blind beggar with Homer was a brilliant afterthought, though in one of the other collections there is a third prose note, which might have something to do with it, for it completes the same story. This is in NAF 6852, folio 94:

Homère chantant dans un village et des hommes et des femmes et des enfans lui donnant des fruits, et d'autres hommes et d'autres femmes accourant pour l'entendre.

It is a great pity that the verse manuscript has been lost. Millevoye printed some fragments of it in 1812–13,[1] but apart from the lines 213–56 on the Centaurs, we have to rely on Latouche's version.

L'Aveugle is so well known as to need little comment. It is now generally accepted that the battle of the Centaurs was added to the manuscript as a further afterthought, and as Heredia put it, after ending at the lines 'Ainsi le grand vieillard en images hardies / Déployait le tissu des saintes mélodies', the poet felt that some stronger climax was needed, and 'C'est alors qu'après avoir refait le premier vers pour le raccorder aux précédents, il y intercala ce prodigieux combat des Lapithes et des Centaures qui laisse le lecteur avec l'impression d'un éblouissement de foudre'.[2] Thus a simple tale was raised to the level of an extraordinary display of virtuosity, by the simple device of tacking on to it a passage that was intended for *Hermès*.

In its final form the poem is superbly constructed, starting as naïvely as *Le Mendiant*, with a rustic background in which a castaway, thrown overboard because he could not pay his fare, makes his way into the village. Although the old man is so impressively handsome that the children wonder whether he is a god, a simple form of dramatic irony is built up and kept until the last line, indeed the last word, of the poem.

An important aspect of *L'Aveugle* which deserves discussion, though so far it has not received any, is that apart from the homely tale and the patient evocation of the Golden Age, Chénier was also (from line 141 onwards) engaged on the formidable task of evoking, by example, all the different kinds or genres of poetry:

---

[1] Millevoye's second book of elegies also contains his poem *Homère mendiant* which, though he did not acknowledge it, was based on both *Le Mendiant* and *L'Aveugle*.
[2] D12, p. xvii.

> La voix me reste. Ainsi la cigale innocente
> Sur un arbuste assise, et se console et chante.
> *Commençons par les dieux*: Souverain Jupiter . . .

Then, after singing the gods, he sings of men:

> De là, portant ses pas dans les paisible villes,
> Les lois, les orateurs, les récoltes fertiles . . .

Then come rustic pleasures:

> Puis aussi les moissons joyeuses, les troupeaux
> Bêlants et mugissants, les rustiques pipeaux,
> Les chansons, les festins, les vendanges bruyantes,
> Et la flûte et la lyre et les notes dansantes . . .[1]

Then the dead:

> Puis il ouvrit du Styx la rive criminelle,
> Et puis les demi-dieux et les champs d'asphodèle,
> Et la foule des morts, vieillards seuls et souffrants,
> Jeunes gens emportés aux yeux de leurs parents,
> Enfants dont au berceau la vie est terminée,
> Vierges dont le trépas suspendit l'hyménée . . .

There is no need to continue this enumeration, once it is seen that the whole of Homer's song is a kind of *toccata*, a rapid improvisation in which all the kinds of poetry are honoured in short, evocative pictures. This is not only the poetry usually associated with the name of Homer, but all poetry, including the didactic poetry of Lucretius, the pastoral and ode, the epic, elegy, and every known form. This toccata, which makes up the body of Chénier's poem, then opens out into one sustained example, as if by way of demonstration—the short heroic episode of the Centaurs. Alfred de Musset cleverly imitated Chénier's idea in one of his best poems, *La Nuit de Mai*, when after touching on all the genres he developed the fable or parable of the Pelican.

One of the striking things about Chénier's toccata is the way in which it describes so many of the themes and poems which make up his own *Bucoliques*. If the *Bucoliques* were to have been welded into a single poem, the key to how it would have been done lies in *L'Aveugle*. It could without difficulty have been expanded into a very long and varied work by bringing into it, in the same way as the Centaurs episode,

---

[1] A variation introduced by Becq de Fouquières is 'les *noces* dansantes'—but the word *notes*, more original, is given in the first editon (D1).

such works as *La Jeune Tarentine*, or the procession of Bacchus, the death of Hercules, the pieces about Proserpine or Medea, or his many descriptions of rustic customs, banquets, lovers, and children—in a word, all those traditional themes which make up Chénier's own picture of the ancient world.

Chénier reproached himself, and has been reproached by others, for writing little heroic poetry and contenting himself with following the minor instead of the greater poets. It might be replied that all his life a poet is trying to write one poem, and that if he wrote one in which his genius was fully expressed, he would have no need to write another. The episode of the Centaurs and the fragment on the death of Hercules are enough to prove that Chénier was an epic poet of the highest genius, just as the first part of *L'Expiation* would be a sufficient claim for Hugo. Although Chénier (despite his reference to Sophocles, or a possible source in the *Hymn to Apollo* of Herodotus) based this major episode in *L'Aveugle* on Ovid, his narrative is in the best ancient tradition of heroic poetry, and at the same time in the best modern tradition. It is in the best ancient tradition because the episode springs naturally from its context, and because it is self-explanatory. It is in the best modern tradition because it has that concentration—almost excessive—which since Baudelaire has become one of the marks and requirements of great poetry. This concentration exists, here, at every level. First it is to be seen in lines of extraordinary density, worthy of Mallarmé, such as 'Le peuple monstrueux des enfants de la Nue' or 'L'héréditaire éclat des nuages dorés'. Sainte-Beuve had an interesting comment to make on the latter line. Pointing out that the Centaurs were sons of the clouds, he wrote, 'Ce vers est exprès tourné au faste, à l'ampleur, et il exprime à merveille l'orgueil du monstre, fier à la fois de sa naissance et de sa crinière.'[1]

This concentration is also achieved through the vigorous use of names. This device is used not only for evocatory purposes but also to people the scene and create the impression of an enormous number of combatants, though only about twenty are actually mentioned:

> Sous l'effort de Nessus la table du repas
> Roule, écrase Cymèle, Évagre, Périphas.
> Pirithoüs égorge Antimaque, et Pétrée,
> Et Cyllare aux pieds blancs, et le noir Macarée . . .

This piling up of names, sometimes repeated in different forms (for

---

[1] G68, 'Un Factum contre A.C.'

instance 'le fils d'Égée'), contributes also to the movement, and this movement is made shockingly brutal by the frequent rupture of the alexandrine. Sometimes, without breaking the rules, Chénier manages to transform the alexandrine into a new instrument, merely by the way he bends it to his meaning, rather than allowing its conventional structure to influence the sense. Take, for example, the line 'L'insolent quadrupède en vain s'écrie; il tombe.' The syllables can be taken in groups of 3/3/2/2/2, or 3/3/4/2. It is not this, however, which makes the line effective, but the way in which the last two words, *il tombe*, remain alone, producing a wonderful demonstration of imitative harmony—or rather, reproduction of movement at its best. This line strikes me as a very high point of art, for the disposition of the words could not be more intelligent: additional weight is given to the word *insolent* by placing it before the substantive, and the verb *s'écrie*, coming after the adverb as it does, is so placed as to obtain a rising tone which immediately drops with the verb that follows it, *il tombe*. At the risk of trying the reader's patience, we pass on to realize that the two verbs had to be placed together for their full effect, and that if the poet had written 'S'écrie en vain, il tombe', which the versification would admit and syntax would approve, this sublime line would become entirely banal.

Perhaps it is wrong to analyse individual lines in this way; but in any case Chénier's work is so full of beauties of this kind that it is necessary to draw attention to his craftsmanship from time to time. Yet poetry is not a matter of individual lines, as Arnold thought, but of massive effects, and here, too, Chénier, whose versification has more than once been described as eccentric (Hugo spoke of his 'coupes barbares'), proves himself over and over again to be one of the most cunning and conscious artists who ever handled French verse. Barbarous, yes, according to the old academic standards; but with that kind of daring barbarism which pointed forward to Nerval, Mallarmé, and Valéry. He was the first French poet, emerging from neo-classicism, to prove that what are commonly regarded as errors may be exploited as devices. For instance, he used the device of the *rejet* and *enjambement*, which had been condemned since Malherbe, to convey an impression of multiple and intensely brutal activity in the Centaurs passage. The violence done to the versification is justified, as it accompanies a series of destructive acts:

> Le quadrupède Hélops / fuit. / L'agile Crantor,
> Le bras levé, / l'atteint. // Eurynome l'arrête:

> D'un érable noueux il va fendre sa tête,
> Lorsque le fils d'Égée, // invincible, / sanglant,
> *L'aperçoit*, / à l'autel prend un chêne brûlant,
> Sur sa croupe indomptée, / avec un cri terrible
> *S'élance*, / va saisir sa chevelure horrible,
> *L'entraîne*, / et quand sa bouche ouverte sans effort
> *Crie*, / il y plonge ensemble et la flamme et la mort.

The syncopated effect is produced not only by the use of enjamb-ment but by the breaking down of other lines into uneven parts: the first line really has a *coupe* 7/5 or would otherwise have to be read 6/1/5, while others, though outwardly correct, are more fluid and suggest speed: for instance it would be foolish to read the fourth line as 'L'aperçoit, à l'autel // prend un chêne brulant', for everything after the word *aperçoit* makes up a single group, that is to say an autonomous breath-group, sense-group, and rhythm-group all at once. The same applies to the line 'S'élance, va saisir sa chevelure horrible', which deliberately repeats the same pattern, perhaps in order to show that the first specimen was no accident. Throughout the passage the dominating principle has been to place the verbs in a strong position, either at the centre or the end of the line, or, in defiance of the rules, in the boldest possible use of enjambment which involves placing the verb at the beginning of the next line, which is here done in four lines out of nine. No French poet before Chénier had practised syncopation to this extent, almost, in the process, discovering free verse. Though so much of the force of the Centaurs passage comes from the energetic use of verbs and staccato phrasing, Maurras has remarked that the fifty or so lines 'ne font qu'une seule phrase, presque trop courte, et sublime de bout en bout'.[1] This statement appears incomprehensible, since in fact the passage is divided into so many short sentences; but what Maurras no doubt meant is that the whole action is so coherent, so powerfully unified in spite of the ruptured, jerky movement, and so many diverse acts are so carefully dovetailed, flowing one into the other, that it produces an overall effect or illusion of being a single, spontaneous linguistic act, that is to say a phrase. Before leaving this remarkable episode, we recall that it condenses into forty-four lines some 325 lines from Ovid.[2] In other words, in addition to the enjoy-ment and effort of writing his own intensely muscular version, Chénier enjoyed the intellectual excitement of competing with a great poet.

---

[1] G55, p. 459.
[2] Ovid, *Met.* xii, but also Homer, *Od.* xxi, Hesiod, *Scut. Herc.* 178; Virgil, *Georg.* ii.

It is not hard to understand why Chénier rarely, after this experience, reached anything like its intensity and compactness before he came to compose the last *Ïambes*. This episode of the Centaurs has a demoniacal quality which he could hardly have attempted a second time without giving the impression of self-parody.

A further interesting feature is Chénier's consistent use of the present tense, not only in *L'Aveugle* but in most of the *Bucoliques*. This is a characteristic which sets him apart from his later disciples, the Parnassians. Of course the French language lends itself naturally to this, and it is not uncommon for narrative passages, even in novels where the past tense dominates, to be written in the present. But Chénier did not use the present only in describing the Centaurs' battle. *L'Aveugle* began with a hesitation between the past and present. The first movement started in the past ('Trois pasteurs . . . le suivaient') but the narrative tense changed already at line 17 ('Mais il entend leurs pas'), where it was not strictly necessary, and remained in the present down to line 75. Then, when the blind man related his adventures (line 76) he did so in the past ('Des marchands de Cymé m'avaient pris chez eux'). The Centaurs passage was carried in the past tense for four lines (213–18) before Chénier, to stimulate the reader's excitement, moved into the present tense and then maintained it. The Parnassians made little of this art of variation, which keeps narrative alive and the reader alert, and much of the honourable dullness of their work, fine as it is at its best, comes from a monotonous use of the past tenses of the verb, though there are some outstanding exceptions to this in Leconte de Lisle.[1] Whence this difference of time and atmosphere? To explain it we need only to turn back to the commentary on Malherbe which Chénier wrote when he was nineteen, and recall his insistence on 'tableaux *vivants*', 'la marche . . . *vive* et lyrique' or 'pleine de tableaux', 'images frappantes', 'la hardiesse et la force de l'expression'.[2] All these remarks point to a very dynamic conception of poetry, which demanded that an effect of immediacy be sought by every possible means: brevity, variety, concentration, and movement.

Folio 9 is marked *Ydille 3* and contains, this time in large writing, the eclogue *La Liberté* which we have already discussed.[3] The prose draft for this poem is only to be found much further on (folio 200) and reads:

Un jeune homme libre et un esclave se rencontrent . . . l'homme libre fait à l'autre avec ravissement la peinture des beautés de la nature dont ils

---

[1] For instance, 'Niobé' in *Poèmes antiques*.
[2] See above, pp. 19–21.   [3] See above, p. 64.

jouissent . . . l'esclave répond qu'il ne les voit point . . . le brusque . . . et oppose des malédictions còntre lui-même à toutes les extases de l'autre. Le Style de l'un est doux et fleuri celui de l'autre dur et sauvage.

It is surprising that all Chénier's editors begin this passage with the words 'un jeune berger', instead of 'un jeune homme'. In the manuscript the word *berger* is written above the word *homme* and neither is crossed out; but in the poem it is the goatherd, not the shepherd, who is the free man. There are some instructive changes in the manuscript: for instance the first draft of lines 47–48 read:

> N'est-il pas quelque baume ou quelques huiles pures
> Qui puissent/peuvent de ton âme assoupir les blessures.

In the corrected version the assertive tone is dropped, by changing the pronoun *ton* to *notre*:

> Il est des baumes doux, des lustrations pures
> Qui peuvent de notre âme assoupir les blessures?
> Et de magiques chants qui tarissent les pleurs?

The use of the learned word *lustrations* in place of *huiles* might offend some readers, who see in it nothing but pedantry. Apart from giving some local colour, for *lustrations* suggests oils with magic powers, the ritual of anointment, it smooths out the line by effacing the repetition of the ugly-sounding *quelques*. The editors (Dimoff and Walter) who have suppressed the two question-marks which are in the manuscript fail to see that they were there to increase the delicacy and tact of the speaker; grammatically, there is the word 'mais', understood at the beginning of the passage: the tone created by the question-marks is that of 'But maybe' or 'But surely there are . . .'. While carefully correcting his draft to convey this discretion in the goatherd's speeches, Chénier's effort in the shepherd's replies were bent in the other direction. For instance the final speech from the shepherd, as he ungraciously accepts gifts, began:

> Donne. Je les reçoi. Pourtant si j'étais sage . . .

This was changed to

> Oui, donne et sois maudit. Car si j'étais plus sage . . .

It was the 'republican sentiments' of the dialogue which enabled Lemercier to say in 1819 that this was the most original of Chénier's eclogues.[1]

---

[1] Népomucène Lemercier's paper on Chénier, which he read to the French Academy, was reprinted in the *Revue Encyclopédique* in October 1819. He found in Chénier's work 'Là, des incorrections sans nombre; ici, des beautés éparses mais éclatantes . . . une

Chénier probably wrote more of these conversation-pieces than the three which have survived. There is another, *Mnazile et Chloé*, on folio 12, which is marked *Idylle (dernière)*. We are set speculating why this was meant to be the last idyll and presumably the last of the *Bucoliques* and why Dimoff (following Sainte-Beuve) attached two fragments to it (from folios 19 and 146) which have nothing to do with this poem. It is, of course, possible that by 'dernière' Chénier meant the last-written idyll, and not necessarily that it was to be placed last. In any case this piece brings out another aspect of Chénier's genius, and of the *Bucoliques* themselves: we see that his collection was to include comedy, just as he had brought comedy into the elegies. This means that the *Bucoliques* would have had a human completeness and would not have been only a collection of heroic, grave, or elegiac works. Readers who expect the *Bucoliques* to be always on the level of high seriousness might wonder at this, but as we have shown (see above, p. 112) Chénier was conscious of the real meaning of the terms he used, and in his *Essai* stressed that 'la poésie pastorale et la comédie viennent d'une même source'. He broadened this to include 'tout ce que les passions ont de doux ou d'orageux', and this leaves room for *La Liberté* and more sombre works. In *Mnazile et Chloé* and *L'Oaristys* the touch is light, but the sensibility is most delicate without being effeminate or pretentious. Chénier's sense of humour is yet another gift which is absent from the Parnassians, whose work is 'ancient' in an academic sense: pastoral poetry did not smile again in France until Valéry's *L'Aurore*.

In *Mnazile et Chloé* Chénier cunningly interwove reminiscences from Virgil and Ovid with, perhaps, a memory of *A Comedy of Errors* and *A Midsummer-Night's Dream*. In this piece, which reminds us forcibly of situations in Marivaux and Musset, he showed his two lovers wandering through the wood, full of anguish and disappointment, then, on meeting, pretending to be there by accident. It ends:

CHLOÉ

Ah! je l'ai vu. C'est lui. Dieux! je vais lui parler!
O ma bouche, ô mes yeux, gardez de vous troubler.

tendance à traduire les idées en figures . . . une véhémence ambitieuse que n'éclaire point assez la sagesse . . . une témérité systématique'. Commenting on his style, he said, 'Il tourmente les périodes et multiplie les césures; il supprime les articles et les liaisons grammaticales; il rompt les vers par de brusques enjambements, les obscurcit et les embarrasse de trop d'incises; il dénature le sens des mots et jette l'incohérence entre les choses et les figures.' He thus brought out in a remarkable way all those characteristics which make Chénier's poetry modern.

MNAZILE

Le feuillage a frémi. Quelque robe légère . . .
C'est elle. O mes regards, ayez soin de vous taire . . .

CHLOÉ

Quoi, Mnazile est ici? Seule, errante, mes pas
Cherchaient ici le frais et ne t'y croyaient pas.

MNAZILE

Seul au bord de ces flots que le tilleul couronne,
J'avais fui le soleil, et n'attendais personne.

We are reminded of George Moore's remark on Laforgue, 'evanescent
as French pastry'. The poem is indeed slight, but the result of a very
sophisticated art. This short poem is very dryly written and resists the
temptation (to which eighteenth-century poets usually succumbed) of
declining into eroticism; it ends with that suggestion of modesty
together with coquetry which makes for wit and breaks off short of
sensuality. The same wit is to be seen in the famous *Oaristys* (of which
the manuscript has recently been discovered at Angers) in which, with
an even more successful mixture of humour and delicacy, the sensual
aspects of the wooing of Naïs by Daphnis are conveyed with astonishing purity. On this and many other occasions—for instance in his
poems on Bacchus and on Hylas—Chénier's personal contribution is
the way in which he eliminates all the grossness from his classical
sources: as though his conception of 'naïveté' involved absolute
innocence and purity. The *Oaristys* is original in another way—its
unusually free versification. The rhymes are disposed in a way which is
surprising for the eighteenth century and which recalls the fluid movement of La Fontaine which has never been recaptured since. It would
be tedious to examine the rhyme-scheme of these ninety-eight lines.
Heredia describes its system as 'vers irrégulièrement entrelacés, à rimes
redoublées'.[1] To give some idea of its complexity or irregularity, the
first three groups are arranged: abbacc/deeded/fggfgg. This liberty,
though some groups recur with the same organization, is characteristic
of the poem as a whole. Many of the rhymes, especially those in *ère*
and *aire*, are used over and over again at different stages, and on analysis the impression is that Chénier was trying to pack in as many
feminine rhymes as he could. The poem is, thus, written on very few
rhymes indeed, and the overall effect of the versification is not unlike

[1] D12, p. 208.

that of Valéry's *Narcisse parle* which I have described elsewhere.[1]
Altogether the three conversation-pieces, *La Liberté*, *Mnazile et Chloé*,
and *Oaristys*, form one of the most fascinating groups of poems in the
Bucoliques.

One of the poems most praised by the Romantic generation was *Le
Malade*, the drafts for which are to be found in folios 14, 15, and 16.
Chénier himself marked this *Ydille IV bis*, which implies that it must
have had a pendant, the word *bis* meaning that there were either two
parts of this fourth idyll or two poems on the same theme. One poem
which could have been the pendant of *Le Malade* is the story of the
love-sick girl, 'Jeune fille, ton cœur avec nous veut se taire', which is
usually (I think, wrongly; see below, p. 201) printed among the
elegies. A second possibility is *La Belle de Scio* (folio 95), the draft for
which was suggested to him by *Hamlet*:

Le jeune fille qu'on appelait la belle de Scio . . . Son amant mourut . . .
Elle devint folle . . . Elle courait les montagnes . . . (la peindre d'une manière
antique.) (J'en pourrai un jour faire un tableau, un quadro.) et longtemps
après elle on chantait cette chanson faite par elle dans sa folie:

> Ne reviendra-t-il pas? Il reviendra sans doute.
> Non, il est sous la tombe. Il attend. Il écoute.
> Va, belle de Scio, meurs. Il te tend les bras.
> Va trouver ton amant. Il ne reviendra pas.

Another possible pendant to *Le Malade* is that which is called *L'Amant
insensé*, though Chénier's own title for it (folio 177) was *Jeune homme
fou par amour*. This story is taken up on folio 182, beginning: 'Il est
fou, il est la fable de tous les jeunes Cnidiens', then moves into a passage
of verse beginning:

> Pour lui ce Praxitèle a de sa main savante
> Des antres de Paros fait sortir une amante . . .

It is the story of a young man who had a statue made in the image of
his beloved Cypris, and which he kissed and scolded. In other words,
the poem would have been a variation on the story of Pygmalion.
Chénier added the note: 'Peut-être espère-t-il qu'elle fera pour lui
ce qu'elle fit pour Pygmalion. Conter la chose comme Ovide. Elle vit
à la fois le ciel et son amant.' Chénier had in mind another poem on the
Pygmalion theme. He left a very long draft for an ambitious poem, *Le
Groupe de marbre* (folios 96, 97), in which, this time, a girl fell in love
with a statue; but, as her passion brought it to life and it embraced

[1] F. Scarfe, *The Art of Paul Valéry*, Heinemann, 1954, pp. 152–3.

her, she also was turned to stone. This is a remarkable variant on the Pygmalion legend—a theme which obsessed both painters and writers in the eighteenth century[1]—as well as anticipating Mérimée's macabre story *La Vénus d'Ille*. A further possible pendant to *Le Malade* is to be found in the fragment of an elegy beginning:

> Je t'indique le fruit qui m'a rendu malade;
> Je te crie en quel lieu sous la route est caché
> *Un abîme où déjà mes pas ont trébuché* . . .

It is hardly surprising that these strange lines should have inspired Paul Valéry, writing in *La Jeune Parque*, 'Non loin, parmi ces pas, rêve mon précipice.' Be this as it may, the examples we have given show that in the *Bucoliques*, as in the elegies, love is often treated as a destructive passion leading to sickness and death. Here we find not only the heritage of Racine, but evidence that Chénier was gripped by the same uneasiness as his contemporaries, for whom the aggressive positivism of the *Encyclopédie* could bring no solace to the sensibility.

It is not surprising that *Le Malade*, to which we now return, was frequently imitated by the first Romantic generation. Apart from the sickly vein in Musset's *Nuits* we have to count Belmontet's *Gilbert mourant*; Valéry's *Le Jeune Malade*; Madame Tastu's *La Jeune Mère mourante*, and Campenon's *La Sœur malade*.[2] Raynouard wrote of Chénier's poem in 1819, 'De pareils vers n'ont pas besoin d'être loués; malheur aux personnes auxquelles il faudrait en expliquer les beautés.'[3] Girardin called it 'Une véritable idylle de Théocrite retrouvée dans les cendres de Pompéii ou dans un manuscrit palimpseste'.[4]

Though the story of *Le Malade* might strike the modern reader as insufficiently masculine—the story of a young adolescent lying at the point of death because of his unrequited love for a girl to whom he has never spoken, and who is saved when she comes to his bedside— allowances have to be made for the theme, and are readily made because it is so beautifully written. In this respect it is superior to Keats's *Isabella*, which Keats himself described as 'mawkish', because it is so much better written than Keats's poem. The same flaw of self-pity is to be found, after all, in Valéry's different versions of *Narcisse*, and

---

[1] As J. Carr has shown in his article on the subject, 'Pygmalion and the Philosophes', in *Journal of the Warburg Institute*, xxiii, 1960.

[2] See G13, t. i, p. 214.

[3] In *Le Journal des Savants*, Nov. 1819.

[4] In *Cours de litt. dramatique*, t. iv ,1843.

the poet's task is to overcome the resistance of the modern mind by aesthetic persuasion.

The poem opens with a powerful invocation, spoken by the mother, full of authentic feeling:

> Apollon, Dieu sauveur, Dieu des savants mystères,
> Dieu de la vie et Dieu des plantes salutaires,
> Dieu vainqueur du Python, Dieu jeune et triomphant,
> Prends pitié de mon fils, de mon unique enfant . . .

Whereas in Valéry's *Narcisse* the lament is all introspective, coming from the sole character, Chénier's device of allowing the mother to speak first gains the reader's confidence and compels a serious reaction. We see, also, in this speech, how Chénier had mastered the devices of rhetoric, using them with such delight that they almost ran away with him. In the invocation to Apollo he seized the essence of prayer in the form of simple repetitions, with variations, such as

> Dieu *jeune*, viens aider sa *jeunesse*. *Assoupis*,
> *Assoupis* dans son sein cette fièvre brûlante . . .

or

> Ces *mains*, ces *vieilles mains* orneront ta statue.

But the greatest mystery, for the common reader, is to see how Chénier's art could transform prose into beautiful and apparently spontaneous verse. It is true that the prose itself was beautiful, to start with:

Ma mère, il est un lieu au bord de l'Érymanthe où les jeunes filles viennent danser. Il ne produit point de poisons ni de serpents et il n'y a point d'aussi beau lieu dans toute la nature. Il y a trois jours que j'y ai vu danser les jeunes filles. Je ne les y verrai plus. Oh, porte-moi au pied de l'Érymanthe, que je le revoie encore . . . que je voie la fumée sortir du toit de cette cabane où elle est assise auprès de son vieux père et charme ses derniers jours; que je la voie par-dessus la haie se promener en silence dans son jardin auprès du tombeau de sa mère . . . Oh que ses yeux sont doux etc. (2 vers) . . .

Here is the same passage, transposed into verse:

> O coteaux d'Érymanthe! ô vallons! ô bocage!
> O vent sonore et frais qui troublais le feuillage
> Et faisais frémir l'onde, et sur leur jeune sein
> Agitais les replis de leur robe de lin!
> De légères beautés troupe agile et dansante!
> Tu sais, tu sais, ma mère? Aux bords de l'Érymanthe,
> Là, ni loups ravisseurs ni serpents ni poisons.

O visage divin! ô fêtes! ô chansons!
Des pas entrelacés, des fleurs, une onde pure!
Aucun lieu n'est si beau dans toute la nature.
Dieux! ces bras et ces flancs, ces cheveux, ces pieds nus
Si blancs, si délicats! je ne les verrai plus.
O portez, portez-moi sur les bords d'Érymanthe,
Que je la voie encor cette vierge dansante!
O, que je voie au loin la fumée à longs flots
S'élever de ce toit au bord de cet enclos . . .
Assise à tes côtés, ses discours, sa tendresse,
Sa voix, trop heureux père, enchante ta vieillesse . . .

The writing is simple as can be, with only one surprise (the ellipsis behind 'Des pas entrelacés'). There is nothing here for the critic to seize on, except perhaps the historical fact that the whole charm of the piece lies in its supple movement, which has no parallel in the eighteenth century. It is already the insinuating rhythm of Lamartine and Musset, saying little, but in its unpretentious way rejuvenating the alexandrine, making a new instrument out of a measure which since Racine had, so to speak, been locked in a kind of arthritis. The writing is not 'modern' but is well ahead of its time. The fact that Chénier actually numbered this poem and placed it well to the front of the *Bucoliques* shows the importance that he attached to it, though today we find other pieces more satisfactory.

Next comes the exquisite *Lydé* (not the poet's title),[1] which is a girl's lament for an absent lover, followed by a response. It is followed by a mildly erotic piece which could have been inserted into *Hylas* or *Daphnis et Chloé*, relating the seduction of a boy by a nymph. On folio 21, which contains nine fragments, we find one of his pleasing little *quadri*:

On peut faire un petit quadro d'un jeune enfant assis sur le bord de la mer dans un joli pays où il jouera sur deux fluttes [*sic*] et les dauphins accourent vers lui.

This motif recurred frequently in Etruscan art; the poet had perhaps seen it in some mosaic during his visit to Italy. Slight as it is, this little *quadro* makes us reflect on the gratuitousness of Chénier's work. The poems of the *Bucoliques* are not there to argue or to prove anything but, it seems, for their own sake and, for the poet, for the sheer pleasure of making poetry. Other manuscripts, incidentally, come to our help in deciding on the meaning of the word *quadro*. While the

---

[1] Title given by Latouche (1819), who perhaps had another manuscript?

example given on p. 179 ('J'en pourrai un jour faire un tableau, un quadro') could feasibly refer to a drawing or painting, in all other cases
it seems to me clear that Chénier was referring to a story or poem.
Another reads 'Peindre une jolie petite jambe et un petit pied entouré
de la chaussure grecque', but the manuscript is clearly marked βυκ,
suggesting that by 'peindre' he only meant 'describe'. Yet another
runs as follows:

> Peindre l'Hyménée *croceo velatus amictu*, conduisant une jeune fille . . . ses
> vêtements . . . ses beaux yeux baissés vers la terre sous leur paupière noire
> et longue (ce peut être un jeune amant qui menace de la mettre dans cet
> état et sans répondre elle s'en ira en riant et en rougissant)

> Et sur ses blonds cheveux, en couronne brillante,
> Mêler la rose blanche et la rose sanglante
> Que les dieux du Liban virent naître jadis
> Des larmes de Vénus et du sang d'Adonis.

The ways of scholarship are surprising, for although the prose item
is on the same folio (120) as the lines of verse which accompany it,
P. Dimoff, who is one of the partisans of the idea that 'peindre' and
'quadro' actually referred to Chénier's intentions to make drawings
or paintings, separated the prose and verse by over 200 pages in his
edition. It seems to me that the word 'quadro' meant no more for
Chénier than a little picture or image in verse, or sometimes the prose
draft itself, intended either to stand alone or to be inserted into a longer
work. It has much the same meaning as the word 'tableau' in Chénier's
commentary on Malherbe. In the case of the boy with his music at-
tracting dolphins this is proved by the poet's immediate composition
of a few lines on the same theme:

> Deux fluttes sur sa bouche aux antres, aux Naïades,
> Aux Faunes, aux Sylvains, aux belles Oréades
> Répètent ses amours . . .

Damalis is a curious piece of thirty-eight lines, divided into two
sections of nineteen lines each, but joined exactly in the middle of the
poem. It is a kind of conversation-piece, each half of which is an epigram, the two neatly joined by a couplet on which the meaning turns:

> Qui prévient le moment l'empêche d'arriver;
> Qui le laisse échapper ne peut le retrouver.

This is one of the few pieces which are no more than drawing-room verse, the stock-in-trade of the period, at which Chénier did not excel.[1]

Perhaps because of the challenging nature of set themes, Chénier's powers often come out at their best when writing about the gods of antiquity. One of the finest of these pieces is *Bacchus*, which appears on folio 26. Already on folio 21 there occurred the isolated line 'Le Satyre au pied double et le jeune Sylvain', with the word *employé* written beside it. The line reappears, slightly changed, in the completed poem, and this suggests that Chénier's poem started with what Valéry called a 'vers donné' similar to the 'Pâle, profondément mordue' which inspired *La Pythie*. This close kinship to Valéry as a deliberate poet, a 'poète volontaire', is one of the most striking aspects of Chénier's genius.

Bacchus is a short but densely concentrated poem, highly pictural, plastic. The text we propose to give is that which Heredia built up from folios 22 and 26 together:

BACCHUS

> Viens, ô divin Bacchus, ô jeune Thyonée,
> O Dionyse, Évan, Ïacchus et Lénée,
> Viens, tel que tu parus aux déserts de Naxos,
> Quand tu vins rassurer la fille de Minos.
> Le superbe éléphant en proie à ta victoire
> Avait de ses débris formé ton char d'ivoire.
> De pampres, de raisins, mollement enchaînés
> Le tigre aux larges flancs de taches sillonnés,
> Et le lynx étoilé, la panthère sauvage
> Promenaient avec toi ta cour sur ce rivage.
> L'or reluisait partout aux axes de tes chars.
> Les Ménades couraient en longs cheveux épars
> Et chantaient Évoé, Bacchus et Thyonée,
> Et Dionyse, Évan, Ïacchus et Lénée,
> Et tout ce que pour toi la Grèce eut de beaux noms,
> Et la voix des rochers répétait leurs chansons,
> Et la rauque tambour, les sonores cymbales,
> Les hautbois tortueux et les doubles crotales
> Qu'agitaient en dansant sur ton bruyant chemin
> Le Faune, le Satyre et le jeune Sylvain,

---

[1] And yet these two lines seem to echo the popular eighteenth-century English song, 'Blow away the morning dew':

> If you will not when you may,
> You shall not when you will.

Au hasard attroupés autour du vieux Silène
Qui, sa coupe à la main, de la rive Indienne,
Toujours ivre, toujours débile, chancelant,
Pas à pas cheminait sur son âne indolent.

C'est le dieu de Nysa, c'est le vainqueur du Gange,
Au visage de vierge, au front ceint de vendange,
Qui dompt et sait courber sous son char gémissant
Du lynx aux cent couleurs le front obéissant.

Apollon et Bacchus, un crin noir et sauvage
N'a hérissé jamais votre jeune visage.
Apollon et Bacchus, vous seuls entre les Dieux,
D'un éternel printemps vous êtes radieux.
Sous le tranchant du fer vos chevelures blondes
N'ont jamais vu tomber leurs tresses vagabondes.

Chénier has handled the legend of Bacchus with impressive dignity. Rejecting the popular, degraded image of Bacchus as a creature sodden with the juice of the vine, he has chosen the most sober and noble elements in his legend and, while giving him all the names attributed to him by the ancients (in the first two lines), he has preferred to portray him as the young and pacific conqueror of India, who from compassion married the abandoned Ariadne and was regarded as not only the deity of harvests (for he was said to have invented the arts of agriculture) but also the deity of marriage. J. Fabre has shown how Chénier avoided the hackneyed rococo style in which Bacchus was usually portrayed in the eighteenth century, also contrasting Chénier's classical handling of the theme with Ronsard's baroque and fanciful treatment in his *Hymne de Bacchus*.[1] Where Ronsard revels in vulgar, exotic licence, in Chénier 'le désordre s'ordonne, la dissonance devient harmonie, la bacchanale se fait aimable, le délire sobrement triomphal'. This could not be better put. Fabre also shows how the composition in Chénier's poem is entirely linear, economical in both colour and form, and conceived something in the manner of a frieze. At the same time, while Chénier's serious treatment of his theme—so characteristic of the aristocratic poise of the *Bucoliques* as a whole—shows clearly that he was writing at the very highest level of the classical tradition, his success here comes of refinement rather than puritanism; for he hints at the other, Uncle Toby side of the picture in the drunken philosopher Silenus, following like a Sancho Panza on his donkey in

[1] F36, pp. 158-9.

the wake of Jupiter's son, Bacchus. We cannot but admire the majestic movement of this poem, so melodious although there is no sign of any straining for effect, so learnedly accurate in its detail, though with no trace of scholarly self-satisfaction.

There are four fragments on the same doubled sheet as *Bacchus*, including some lines about Ericthonus, inventor of chariots, and a very pleasing piece about Ariadne, who led Theseus out of the labyrinth after he slew the Minotaur:

> Là du sage Minos cette fille si belle,
> Le fil en main formait une danse nouvelle
> Quand du grand labyrinthe un jeune séducteur
> Eut vaincu par ses soins l'inextricable erreur.
> Le blond Thésée admire à sa brillante fête
> Et les vierges d'Athène et les vierges de Crète.
> Toutes, près d'Ariane en des détours légers
> Errent, du noir palais retraçant les dangers;
> Et leurs pas tortueux d'un confus labyrinthe
> Feignent de parcourir la ténébreuse enceinte.

This is only a minor and probably early piece, not highly serious because it describes a dance, not an event; but it is important for various reasons. Dimoff classified it, with the pieces about Pasiphaë, under his own rubric 'Danses, Sacrifices et Chants', but there are no other dances to accompany it. Surely it would be more satisfactory to group together all the pieces related to the legend of the Bull, such as those concerning Europa, Minos, the Minotaur, and Ariadne? There is, indeed, clear evidence that this is what Chénier intended doing, for in the draft of *Le Banquet des Satyres* (oddly classed by Dimoff in a section 'Fêtes, danses, jeux et sacrifices') he wrote (folio 159):

Des Nymphes des Satyres chantent dans une grotte qu'il faut peindre bien romantique, pittoresque, divine, en soupant avec des coupes ciselées, chacun le sujet représenté sur sa coupe: l'un 'Étranger, ce taureau, etc. . . .' l'autre, Pasiphaé, d'autres, d'autres.

Thus Chénier intended welding several tales together by the device of describing a goblet. Chénier's obsession with Naxos and Crete (quite apart from the intrinsic beauty of these legends) was natural enough, as it was from that part of the world that his mother's ancestors came. G. Venzac has argued very convincingly that the theme of Ariadne was that of the dance 'La Candiote', which the poet's mother used to perform for her guests.[1]

---

[1] F96, p. 32.

Hylas (folio 31) is another set piece which has been attempted by many French poets, including Ronsard, Parny, Volney, and Leconte de Lisle.[1] The episode in Ovid, describing how Hercules' boy, Hylas, was sent to fetch water and captured by the Naiads, is one which naturally lends itself to burlesque and sensuality, yet Chénier's version is tinged with melancholy and is a picture of entire innocence. Parny made of it nothing more than a thin anecdote:

> Trompons le temps par quelques jeux,
> Par des récits, par un conte frivole . . .

Making no attempt to evoke landscape or inner feeling, Parny rushed through the story: this is how he described how Hylas was drawn into the brook:

> Hylas arrive, une cruche à la main,
> Ne songe guère aux Nymphes qui l'admirent;
> Il s'agenouille, il la plonge, et soudain
> Au fond des eaux les Naïades l'attirent.

But Chénier's vision, and the amplitude of his verse, give new life and interest to a stock theme:

> Sur l'immobile arène il l'admire couler:
> Se courbe, et s'appuyant à la rive penchante
> Dans le crystal sonnant plonge l'urne pesante.
> De leurs roseaux touffus, les trois Nymphes soudain
> Volent, fendent les eaux, l'entraînent par la main
> En un lit de joncs frais et de mousses nouvelles . . .

Parny was writing in a would-be 'modern' way in his choice of diction; for instance he used the homely word 'cruche' which is in strong contrast to Chénier's 'urne pesante'. At first sight Chénier's vocabulary might look pedantic, until we see that it was strictly necessary. His Hylas was young and frail, and by stressing the weight of the ewer he gave beauty and outline to a simple action, the slowness and difficulty of which is underlined by the boy's gesture in leaning on the bank with one arm, holding the heavy urn in the other. Thus he showed an understanding of the movement from the inside, which completely escaped Parny.[2] At the same time it is curious that, in the

---

[1] See P. Moreau's interesting comparison of three versions in *Mélanges offerts à Joseph Vianey*, 1934.

[2] But the gesture is to be found in Ronsard:
> Tandis Hylas de la gauche s'appuye
> Dessus le bord, de l'autre tient la buye,
> Qu'à front penché laisse tomber en l'eau . . .

same poem, Chénier struck out some words ('d'Hercule insidieux rivaux') and wrote beside them the criticism '*maniéré*'. He was even more anxious than Parny to avoid mannerism; yet the mannerism in choosing the word 'urne' in preference to 'cruche' was entirely justified. All this shows that any assessment of poetic diction must take the context into account.

On folio 33 we find the last three lines of *Néère*, hastily scribbled; the rest of the poem is on folio 34. Heredia has already pointed out that Gabriel de Chénier (or whoever it was) made a mistake in arranging the two manuscripts in this order, as the two folios were originally one folded sheet. This lovely poem is an aria of anguish, written in three movements. First is the comparison of the dying girl with the swan, singing its last song:

> Mais telle qu'à sa mort pour la dernière fois
> Un beau cygne soupire, et de sa douce voix
> De sa voix qui bientôt lui doit être ravie,
> Chante, avant de partir, ses adieux à la vie —

lines which give the impression of being written in accentuated verse, so strong is their movement. Néère first addresses the Naiads and Nature, then finally her lover, Clinias. Part of the second movement anticipates a well-known effect obtained by Lamartine in *Le Lac* and by Musset in *Solitude*:

> O cieux, ô terre, ô mer, prés, montagnes, rivages,
> Fleurs, bois mélodieux, vallons, grottes sauvages,
> Rappelez-lui souvent, rappelez-lui toujours
> Néère, tout son bien, Néère ses amours . . .

This kind of numerical invocation was, of course, not unknown to the Ancients, while a French model for it is to be found in Ronsard:

> Je vous supply, ciel, air, vents, monts et plaines,
> Taillis, forêts, rivages et fontaines,
> Antres, prés, fleurs, dites-luy pour moi . . .

Ronsard's enumeration is cerebral, descending logically from *ciel* down to *fleurs*, and is strong rather than melodious. Chénier's series is less logical, but is arranged in such a way as to wring the maximum of music from the words. The last movement of this poem is the best, and is as sensitively written as anything to be found in Chénier. It shows that his masterpiece *La Jeune Tarentine* was no accident: indeed the reader who feels the latter poem to be hackneyed will find many of its virtues, unspoilt by popularity, in the conclusion of *Néère*:

O soit que l'astre pur des deux frères d'Hélène
Calme sous ton vaisseau la vague Ïonienne;
Soit qu'aux bords de Pœstum, sous ta soigneuse main
Les roses deux fois l'an couronnent ton jardin,
Au coucher du soleil si ton âme attendrie
Tombe en une muette et molle rêverie,
Alors, mon Clinias, appelle, appelle-moi.
Je viendrai, Clinias, je volerai vers toi.
Mon âme vagabonde à travers le feuillage
Frémira. Sur les vents ou sur quelque nuage
Tu la verras descendre, ou du sein de la mer
S'élevant comme un songe étinceler dans l'air,
Et ma voix toujours tendre et doucement plaintive
Caresser en fuyant ton oreille attentive.

This passage is full of poetic discoveries which go far beyond the poetic practice of Chénier's century. We have seen in *L'Aveugle* how he exploited the overflowing of the line to gain an effect of violence: now he uses the same device for the very opposite purpose, as no poet did before or after him, drawing the utmost pathos from the lengthening of his line:

> Mon âme vagabonde à travers le feuillage
> Frémira.

It is hardly surprising that Heredia wrote about this poem: 'Jamais poète n'a si magistralement manié l'alexandrin. . . . Il le pétrit, il le brise, il le renoue à son gré. On dirait qu'il le modèle. Le vers obéissant semble suivre la pensée, l'oreille, la vision du poète.'[1] The prolonging of the alexandrine follows not only the thought or the ear, but conveys an overwhelming yet trembling surge of emotion. And what a splendid contrast there is in the rise and fall of the next three lines, ending on an unforgettable image:

> Sur les vents ou sur quelque nuage
> Tu la verras descendre, ou du sein de la mer
> S'élevant comme un songe étinceler dans l'air . . .

Once more we are able to observe the working of Chénier's mind, for the image 's'élevant comme un songe' comes directly from Homer (*Odyssey*, XI. 207) and the image of the cloud is taken from the *Iliad* (XXIII) where the soul of Patrocles comes down to console Achilles. Chénier's peculiar gift was not merely to sense how to use reminiscences

---

[1] D12, p. xxx.

in a spontaneous way, but to be able to add to them and even surpass them, for it is surely the image 'étinceler dans l'air' which crowns and perfects this whole movement. We can also guess at a whole theory of the sublime, and of the emotions, behind these few lines, for to attribute to a girl the expressions which Homer reserved for his heroes shows Chénier's desire to raise common feeling to the heroic level. It may seem a paradox to say so: but in spite of its classical groundwork, this passage strikes one as essentially Shakespearian in its harmony, imagery, and immediacy of feeling.

We have already drawn attention (p. 186) to the short piece about Ariadne and its relation to the legend of the Bull which had its cult chiefly in Crete and Sicily before spreading over the Mediterranean, to degenerate into the *corrida* as it is today. Chénier was particularly interested in this theme and often returned to it, as we see in folios 38, 39, 40, 42, 69, 180, 187. The legends of Jupiter and Europa, Pasiphaë, the Minotaur, Minos, as well as the ritual sacrifices of bulls to Pluto and Persephone, form part of a folk-lore which is thoroughly represented in the literature and all the arts of antiquity. It is likely that Minos and his descendants wore the golden mask of the Bull when they went down to the temple below the palace, where rites were performed in which bulls, dancers, and acrobats took part. Needless to say, these themes have remained a challenge to poets and artists ever since, long after their religious meaning was lost.

Of Chénier's various attempts at describing the rape of Europa, the first, which is to be found in the six manuscripts 38–43, is very characteristic of his early work. The ninety-two lines are mainly a translation from a passage of Moschus which he found in Brunck's *Analecta*. Chénier's first version is sensitive enough, but for the most part he reduces the legend to a kind of fairy-tale or romance fit for the salon, and the choice of epithets makes for little more than prettiness. The Bull is described as follows:

> Sur tout son corps s'étend un blond et pur éclat;
> Une étoile d'argent sur son front délicat
> Luit; d'amour, dans ses yeux brille la flamme ardente;
> Un double ivoire enfin sur sa tête élégante
> Se recourbe; la nuit tel est le beau croissant
> Que Phoebé dans les cieux allume en renaissant.

These lines are written in an unoriginal, decadent, eighteenth-century style, in which mere epithets try to do the work and there is no genuine imagery, while the epithets are so dull and conventional—

'délicat', 'élégante'—that the bull does not come to life. Where the
original reads 'he licks the virgin's neck and his caress thrills her with
pleasure' Chénier writes, coyly, 'Sur ses pieds délicats sa langue se
promène.' The only successful moments are, first, when he leaves
Moschus and wrings some sweet notes from the French language—

> Il mugit doucement: la flûte de Lydie
> Chante une moins suave et tendre mélodie —

and at one point where the verse suddenly tightens into a line of epic
quality, when we suddenly feel the strength of the Greek language
piercing through the French:

> Rien qu'une mer immense et le ciel sur sa tête.

In his *Art d'aimer*, which we know to have been an early work,
Chénier left a further remark on the legend of Europa:

> Il faut qu'un amant sache prendre toutes les formes. . . . Exemples des
> métamorphoses des Dieux. . . . Après trois ou quatre, finir par raconter en
> douze ou quinze vers (c'est trop) l'enlèvement d'Europe, traduisant Ovide,
> I, ii et Moschus . . . d'abord elle a peur . . . Puis elle finit par s'asseoir sur
> lui.[1]

Then followed some of the weakest lines he ever wrote, in which the
ridiculousness of the first line, 'Jupiter quadrupède et sur l'herbe pais-
sant', seems to have escaped him. But it contains one very good line,
full of movement:

> . . . la vierge qu'il adore
> L'approche, fuit, revient, fuit et revient encore.

That short version is bad because it is nothing but narrative, an abridge-
ment of the story without any of the piquant and original detail of
which he later became a master.

In the end, after all these attempts, Chénier managed to write the
story in his own inimitable way (folios 159, 79, 43, 69). He obviously
intended writing a long poem, perhaps as important as *L'Aveugle*, in
which all the myths of the Bull would have been drawn together, as we
have shown in his prose draft for *Le Banquet des Satyres* (see p. 186).
After this he gave a short prose account of Europa (folio 79) which,
far from being dead narration, is already a species of poetic composition, inasmuch as the method of presentation is already fully there:

> Étranger, ce taureau que tu vois fendre les flots et nager vers Crète, avec

[1] BN, NAF 6849, folio 118.

une jeune fille qui tient sa corne, qui tremble, qui cherche à voir sa patrie, qui appelle ses compagnes,

> tactumque vereri
> Assilientis aquae timidasque reducere plantas,
> [Ovid, vi. 106]

Ce nageur mugissant, ce taureau, c'est un Dieu. . . . Dans ses traits de taureau, tu reconnais les traits de Jupiter. Amoureux d'Europe, de la fille d'Agénor, il est descendu au rivage de Phénice, beau, délicat, l'objet des vœux de toutes les génisses. La fille d'Agénor a osé s'asseoir sur lui. — Il s'est lancé dans les flots, il a déjà passé Chypre et Rhodes.

In the translation from Moschus which we considered earlier, the poet's efforts were directed chiefly towards an easy melody, but in the new version there is no concession of that kind. The overall structure is entirely original, the only *datum* being the traditional story itself. Now the emphasis is on vision, resulting in a series of vivid pictures. This time there is no sentimental comedy; the twenty-four lines are touched with melancholy as though the poet had at last *felt* this myth, and saw Europa in the grip of a destiny over which she had no control. Perhaps a masterpiece has been lost to us, as the whole prose draft is crossed out and the words 'c'est fait' written after it: this could mean that the whole of the *Banquet des Satyres* was actually completed. But this passage of twenty-four lines makes a satisfactory work in itself. It begins with a characteristic address in the second person, followed by a fluid, racy narrative:

> Étranger, ce taureau qu'au sein des mers profondes
> D'un pied léger et sûr tu vois fendre les ondes,
> Est le seul que jamais Amphitrite ait porté.
> Il nage aux bords Crétois. Une jeune beauté
> Dont le vent fait voler l'écharpe obéissante
> Sur ses flancs est assise, et d'une main tremblante
> Tient sa corne d'ivoire, et les pleurs dans les yeux
> Appelle ses parents, ses compagnes, ses jeux,
> Et redoutant la vague et ses assauts humides,
> Retire et veut sur soi cacher ses pieds timides . . .

It is only then that the poet reveals that he is describing a relief in bronze, and this device itself is handled with great skill:

> L'art a rendu l'airain fluide et frémissant;
> On croit le voir flotter . . .

Just as, in his portrayal of Bacchus, Chénier had defied the conventional treatment of the theme by his grave interpretation of it, so, in describing the Bull he puts aside the usual flippancy (and salaciousness) and reminds us of the stern god beneath the disguise:

> Dans ses traits déguisés, du monarque suprême
> Tu reconnais encore et la foudre et les traits.

Though this piece has not much more than its clean narrative line to recommend it, the poet has again successfully avoided the flippant or gallant tone of his sources. Perhaps he had seen or heard of the famous salt-cellar made for one of the Medici by Cellini? It is more certain that he had seen Veronese's painting, not when he made his first version from Moschus, but when he wrote this final version based on Ovid and Anacreon. It is yet another instance of the 'gratuitousness' of the *Bucoliques*: in this case a kind of superior entertainment, the poetry of a craftsman rejoicing in his plastic vision, his subtleties of versification, his dovetailing of sources. We feel, however, that for the poet it is not quite 'pure poetry' but a kind of spiritual exercise in which the artist is intent on self-discipline, self-perfection, preparing for the day when all his powers will be stretched in more exacting labours. It would not be easy to gather from the *Bucoliques* what was the author's personal view of existence, for he never took the obvious opportunities to draw a moral or to preach (incidentally, there are thousands of admirers of La Fontaine who, in reading his Fables, pay no attention to his moral conclusions). But although there is nothing explicit of this kind, familiarity with the *Bucoliques* does gradually give the reader some idea of an underlying point of view. Behind these poems there is a strong sense of destiny, fatalism, inevitability. The poems are constantly stressing the beauty of nature, love, existence, together with their impending destruction. If the ancient world as seen by Chénier was primarily aesthetic, and if he strove to convey it in vivid pictures and images as well as haunting, often melancholy music, it was not merely an artificial paradise, for violence, pain, and death played a very large part in it. There is, of course, a certain distance, for the 'I' of the poet never intrudes; this 'I' is always that of a character, whether legendary or created by him. These characters are rarely heroic, but his children, young girls, and young adolescents in love or at the point of death seem often to be under the shadow of a superior necessity. It might be argued that this tension between beauty and violence was not Chénier's but was implicit in the sources to which he turned. The answer to that objection is that he chose to turn to certain sources rather than others, and in many cases imposed his own interpretation on a theme which others saw only as stylized.

There could be no greater mistake than to think that Chénier was trying to portray some insipid Golden Age in his *Bucoliques*. They contain the same extremes of emotion as his elegies, or indeed his political journalism. It has already been noted that there is an almost diabolical energy in his description of the battle between the Lapiths and the Centaurs. In *Pasiphaé*, the companion piece to the poem about Europa, we again sense this satanic quality in his portrayal of murderous jealousy. While the poem is based on Virgil and Ovid, he goes beyond either in sharpening jealousy to the point of frenzy, showing first the destructive feelings in Pasiphaë's breast, then her excessive delight as she sacrifices her rival and casts her heart into the flames. This poem has, at times, a Racinian quality:

PASIPHAÉ

Tu gémis sur l'Ida, mourante, échevelée,
O reine, ô de Minos épouse désolée.
Heureuse si jamais, dans ses riches travaux,
Cérès n'eût pour le joug élevé des troupeaux.

Certe, aux antres d'Amnise, assez votre Lucine
Donnait de beaux neveux aux mères de Gortyne;
Certes vous élevez aux gymnases crétois
D'autres jeunes troupeaux plus dignes de ton choix.

Tu voles épier sous quelle yeuse obscure,
Tranquille, il ruminait son antique pâture,
Quel lit de fleurs reçut ses membres nonchalants,
Quelle onde a ranimé l'albâtre de ses flancs.

— O Nymphes, entourez, fermez, Nymphes de Crète,
De ces vallons, fermez, entourez la retraite,
Si peut-être vers lui des vestiges épars
Ne viendront point guider mes pas et mes regards.

Insensée! à travers ronces, forêts, montagnes,
Elle court. O fureur! dans les vertes campagnes
Une belle génisse à son superbe amant
Adressait devant elle un doux mugissement.

La perfide mourra. Jupiter la demande.
Elle-même à son front attache la guirlande,

L'entraîne, et sur l'autel prenant le fer vengeur:
— Sois belle maintenant, et plais à mon vainqueur.

Elle frappe, et sa haine, à la flamme lustrale,
Rit de voir palpiter le cœur de sa rivale.

Chénier's alexandrines fall naturally enough into quatrains. He has used every possible narrative device here: the first twelve lines are written in the second person, where Pasiphaë is seen and sized up from the outside. The fourth quatrain is in direct speech and spoken by her, then with the exception of lines 21 and 24 the rest is in conventional third-person narrative. There are two versions of the poem, of which this is the better. J. Fabre[1] has pointed out how Chénier quickly avoids straight narration and seeks the most vivid musical and plastic evocation. All his best narratives are like this, at once dramatic and lyrical. While poetry is not to be judged only by its intensity, the restlessness with which Chénier constantly moves from one person of the verb to another, or presents his subject simultaneously at different angles, gives a highly nervous tonality to his work. This may be due in part to his desire to cramp the story into as short a space as possible (one sometimes wonders, on looking at writers' manuscripts, whether their style is not often influenced by such physical factors as the size of the paper they have to hand), but the result is an exceptional vitality. At the same time Chénier's habit of rewriting his work also led to a kind of concentration that is almost a nuisance—a scholar's concentration—it was in the second version of this poem that he added the two lines

> Certes, aux antres d'Amnises assez votre Lucine
> Donnait de beaux neveux aux mères de Gortyne.

Such a couplet is a brain-twister for young readers or teachers, but the surprising thing is that Chénier was particularly pleased with himself on this occasion, adding the note, 'Amnise, fleuve de Crète où est l'antre de Lucine. V. Hom. *Odyss.* et Meursius, *Crit.* I. i. c. 6.' Another revealing point is that in his notes to this poem Chénier also mentioned the scholar Valkenaer. This shows that the Europa and Pasiphaë episodes were both written after 1788, either in London or Paris, as it was only while he was in London that Chénier discovered Valkenaer's works. Subsequently he described him in a Latin note as 'magnus Valkenarius' and became friendly with his son.[2] But what the two learned lines about Amnise and Gortyne suggest is that as Chénier

---

[1] F36, p. 164.   [2] D22, p. 753.

matured he not only sought more subtle effects but wanted his poetry to be more learned. This did not augur well for his poetry, but perhaps the *Ode au Jeu de Paume* halted that tendency, for there is no abuse of scholarship in his verse after that. There are only two classical references in the whole of *La Jeune Captive*.

Had Chénier completed his *Banquet des Satyres* he would no doubt have added the poem about the Minotaur to complete the story of Ariadne, and related something of the rape of Proserpine. There are two good passages on Proserpine, each complete in itself. The first (folios 26 and 187) was probably written in London, or later, as it is on the same sheet as the hymn to Bacchus (which might also have formed part of the *Banquet*). It has charm and originality, for Proserpine is depicted when she was a little girl, spoilt by the Cyclops:

> Tranquille, tu jouais avec leurs noirs cheveux.
> Ils riaient de te voir, de ta main enfantine
> Arracher la toison de leur vaste poitrine.

This kind of playful invention prevents the *Bucoliques* from being only a series of academic exercises. The other fragment is quite different, epigrammatic in quality and more serious in tone.

Of the other divinities and heroes celebrated by Chénier, there are three pieces on Diana, and pieces on Ceres, Venus, Minerva, Medea, Orpheus, and Hercules, and a long passage on the return of Ulysses. Altogether this gallery is much smaller than might be expected: does it mean, as some critics have suggested, that Chénier was not sufficiently interested in the heroic side of ancient poetry? Looking a little further, however, we find that there are numerous prose drafts or notes which imply that he had intended writing many more pieces about the gods. Jupiter would have been portrayed as an eagle in a piece about Ganymede (folio 197); he would have written about Apollo and Daphne (folio 184), while there are numerous notes, as well as passages of verse, about the nymphs, fauns, satyrs, naiads, sylphs, and all the lesser fry associated with the gods. On the whole we are obliged to conclude that the tales of the gods and heroes were certainly not Chénier's main preoccupation, for even with the drafts they occupy the smallest part of the *Bucoliques*. The chief explanation for this is, probably, that such tales are static: when the end of a story is already foreseen and has already been told by countless poets, little scope is left for originality except in matters of detail and interpretation—as in the description of *Bacchus*, for instance. While a large part of the

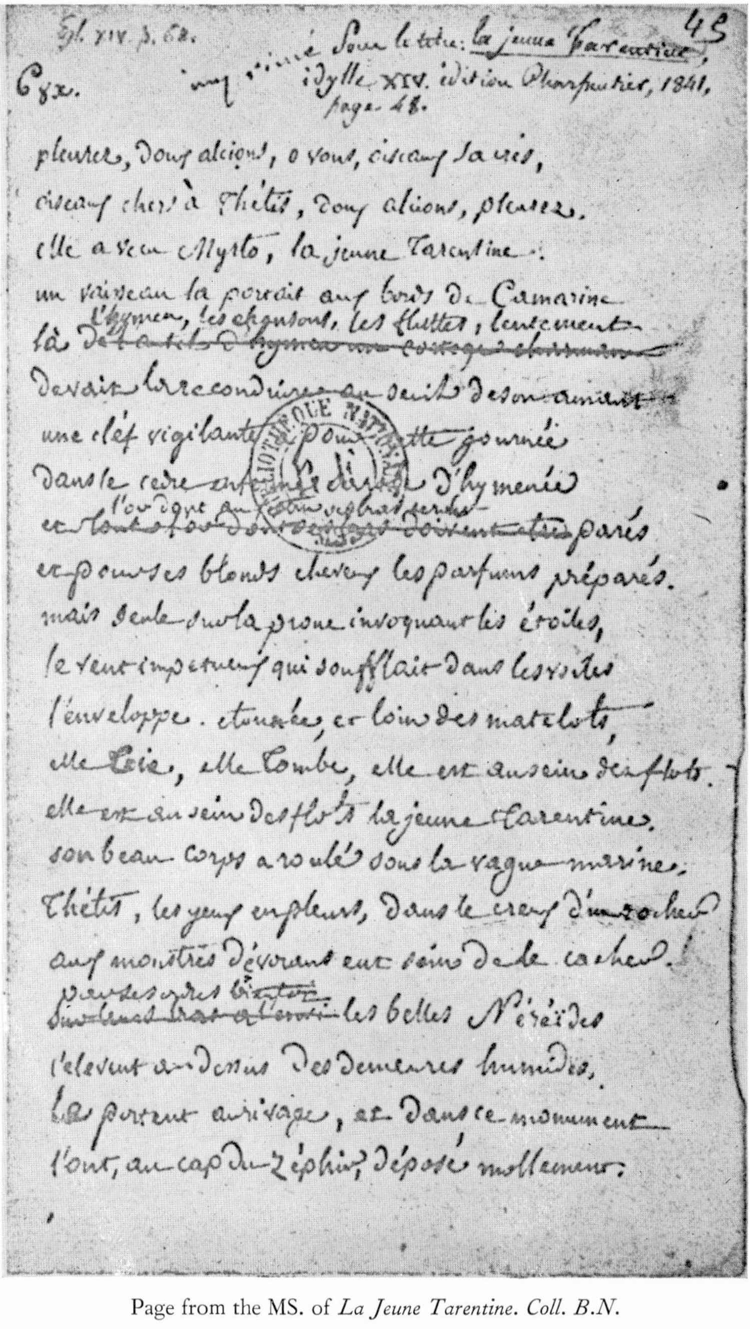

PLATE 3

[handwritten manuscript, largely illegible]

Épî. XIV. 3. 68.

68x.

...é Sous le titre: la jeune Tarentine,
Idylle XXV. édition Charpentier, 1841,
page 48.

Pleurez, doux alcions, ô vous, oiseaux sacrés,
oiseaux chers à Thétis, doux alcions, pleurez.
Elle a vécu Myrto, la jeune Tarentine.
Un vaisseau la portait aux bords de Camarine.
Là l'hymen, les chansons, les flûtes, lentement
devait la reconduire au seuil de son amant.
Une clef vigilante a pour cette journée
dans le cèdre enfermé sa robe d'hyménée
et l'or dont au festin doivent être parés
et pour ses blonds cheveux les parfums préparés.
Mais seule sur la proue invoquant les étoiles,
le vent impétueux qui soufflait dans les voiles
l'enveloppe. Étonnée, et loin des matelots,
elle crie, elle tombe, elle est au sein des flots.
Elle est au sein des flots la jeune Tarentine.
Son beau corps a roulé sous la vague marine.
Thétis, les yeux en pleurs, dans le creux d'un rocher
aux monstres dévorants eut soin de la cacher.
Par les ..... les belles Néréides
l'élèvent au-dessus des demeures humides,
les portent au rivage, et dans ce monument
l'ont, au cap du Zéphir, déposé mollement.

Page from the MS. of *La Jeune Tarentine*. Coll. B.N.

Bucoliques, on the other hand, is admittedly descriptive, the fact that Chénier was a creative poet and was not content to translate or imitate is shown by the considerable place that is given to narrative or dramatic elegies in which the poet could himself create a situation or a character.

To return to the manuscripts, *La Jeune Tarentine* is a perfect example of this creative turn of mind. It is with some emotion that we find this, perhaps Chénier's best-known poem, on folio 45. It bears no title, but was first published by his brother Marie-Joseph under the title 'Élégie dans le goût ancien' in 1798.

LA JEUNE TARENTINE

Pleurez, doux alcyons, ô vous, oiseaux sacrés,
Oiseaux chers à Thétis, doux alcyons, pleurez.

Elle a vécu Myrto, la jeune Tarentine.
Un vaisseau la portait aux bords de Camarine;
Là l'hymen, les chansons, les fluttes, lentement
Devaient la reconduire au seuil de son amant.
Une clef vigilante a pour cette journée
Dans le cèdre enfermé sa robe d'hyménée
Et l'or dont au festin ses bras seront parés
Et pour ses blonds cheveux les parfums préparés.
Mais seule sur la proue invoquant les étoiles,
Le vent impétueux qui soufflait dans les voiles
L'enveloppe. Étonnée, et loin des matelots,
Elle crie, elle tombe, elle est au sein des flots.

Elle est au sein des flots la jeune Tarentine.
Son beau corps a roulé sous la vague marine.
Thétis, les yeux en pleurs, dans le creux d'un rocher
Aux monstres dévorants eut soin de le cacher.
Par ses ordres bientôt les belles Néréides
L'élèvent au-dessus des demeures humides,
Le portent au rivage, et dans ce monument
L'ont, au cap du Zéphir, déposé mollement.
Puis de loin à grands cris appelant leurs compagnes
Et les Nymphes des bois, des sources, des montagnes
Toutes, frappant leurs seins, et traînant un long deuil
Répétèrent *hélas* autour de son cercueil.

Hélas! chez ton amant tu n'es point ramenée.
Tu n'as point revêtu ta robe d'hyménée.
L'or autour de tes bras n'a point serré de nœuds.
Les doux parfums n'ont point coulé sur tes cheveux.

Marie-Joseph, in printing his brother's poem, added to it the note:

Le jeune homme, auteur de ces vers, donnait aux lettres les plus grandes espérances, quand il fut assassiné par le tribunal révolutionnaire. Quelques morceaux de prose qu'il fit insérer dans le *Journal de Paris* en 1792, ont prouvé son courage et son talent politique. Les vers manuscrits qu'il a laissés et qu'il n'eut pas le temps de revoir, manquent trop souvent de correction et de pureté; mais on y trouve plus d'une fois le goût antique et le talent du poète.

Marie-Joseph, who had publicly announced in his poem 'La Calomnie' that he would 'raise an altar' to his brother's memory, went no further than printing this one poem, with, as Heredia pointed out, four misreadings and twenty-seven errors of punctuation. (The version given above is based on the manuscript and the version given by Heredia.) While it was generous of Marie-Joseph to praise his brother's journalism and political talent, which had come between them, it was an impertinence on his part to question the correctness or purity of André's work.

La Jeune Tarentine belongs to two categories of poems in the *Bucoliques*, the first of which is the halieutic poems and the series called *Idylles Marines*, and the second, a group of epitaphs and poems describing funeral rites. It is the best known of the marine idylls. Though it contains echoes of both Greek and Latin poets, in it we see him inventing his own story and the character Myrto, while following a traditional form of lyric. He shows all his narrative skill in using many different forms of presentation in such a short poem, reminding us of the roving camera in the modern film. There is nothing more complex yet more natural than the frequent, restless changes of tense here, which are all directed towards dramatizing the situation and extracting the utmost pathos from it. With the exception of one or two latinisms ('le cèdre', meaning coffer, or the odd ellipsis 'une clef vigilante') the vocabulary is simple and easy of access. The poet's deliberate change, on the manuscript, from 'doivent être parés' to the future 'seront parés' creates a sense of security and certainty which heightens the tragedy of the girl's death. One of the most striking changes of tense is at line 12:

> Le vent impétueux qui *soufflait* dans les voiles
> *L'enveloppe.*

It is not only the frighteningly brutal enjambment which accompanies the change of tense, that is interesting here: the transition would be difficult to justify were it not that the 'soufflait' refers to the very immediate past, only a second before the wind changed. With its repetitions and refrains, its dramatic structure, its gentle harmonies so expressive of emotion, the poem demands a chorus of female voices to bring out its total effect. What is most strange is that in spite of everything the poem is in no way painful: there reigns over it a kind of serene fatalism accompanied by consoling ritual—a perfect illustration of the 'Sunt lacrimae rerum, et mentem mortalia tangunt' of Virgil. It is this sense of inevitability together with compassion which raises the poem far above any possible accusation of sentimentality.

La Jeune Tarentine is a masterpiece of restraint, the poet's reward, in its grasp of the classical spirit, for his years of patient toil on what seemed to him more ambitious themes. While it vindicates entirely Chénier's theory of 'naïveté', its unique balance between craft and feeling sets it above the other Marine Idylls, though they all have something to commend them. *Amymone* (folio 126) relates much the same story, though tragedy is averted, while *Chrysé* (folio 47) is a lover's account of a nightmare in which he dreamed that Chrysé was drowned. *Dryas* (folio 138) relates the drowning of a man with almost brutal swiftness, and has not that aesthetic finish which protects the reader from a sense of frustration. But the thorough draft for *Les Navigateurs* (folios 187, 217, 218) shows that this would have been a long and ambitious work, probably the most important of the Marine Idylls.

The first inkling of *Les Navigateurs* is the brilliant line 'Les sommets de Naxos bruyants de bacchanales' which occurs in isolation on folio 187 and later found its way into the longer draft. The story as outlined by Chénier is simple: the sailors (about nine voices) are chatting together about their own experiences and villages, in a naïve way:

A — Enfin nous avons passé dans la nuit le cap de Malée. Les Dieux soient loués . . . J'ai fait un long voyage. Avant que nous nous embarquions tous ensemble à Syracuse, j'avais parcouru la côte de Marseille et Tyrrhénie etc. . . . Certes le monde est grand. Mais voici notre Grèce chérie . . . Et vous, compagnons, d'où veniez-vous quand nous nous sommes embarqués ensemble sur ce vaisseau?

B — Moi, j'ai été ici . . .

C — Moi, là . . .

D — Moi, j'ai été jusqu'à Tartessus, au-delà des colonnes d'Alcide, aux embouchures du Bétis . . . là . . . là . . . Ah, vous n'avez rien vu, vous tous . . . (Je brûle de me revoir à Lesbos, ma patrie . . .)

E — Pour moi, je n'ai été qu'à . . . et je brûle de me revoir à Lesbos . . . O belle mer Égée . . . les îles éparses sur tes flots azurés comme les étoiles dans la nuit . . . Et toi, Lesbos, la plus belle de toutes . . .

Z — Et — Les sommets de Naxos bruyants de bacchanales?

H — Et Samos? et Junon? . . . etc . . . etc . . . et quoi! ma Délos sera-t-elle
la dernière . . . où il y a ceci . . . cela . . .

So they go on, and begin describing in more detail their home towns
or villages, to the point of quarrelling. Chénier was probably setting himself in the part of one of the sailors, the poorest of them all, who came
from Mykonos, the birthplace of Madame Chénier's grandmother:

Pour moi je ne veux point vanter ma patrie . . . Les Dieux ont peu fait
pour elle . . . Mycone n'a que des figues et des raisins . . . C'est un rocher
aride . . . Mais c'est ma patrie . . . C'est là que j'ai ouvert les yeux pour la
première fois . . . Là sont mes parents, ma famille . . . mes premiers amis
. . . Je m'y retrouverai avec joie, je n'en sortirai plus, et je le préférerai à
toutes les terres que j'ai vues, quoique plus belles. Mais voyez, la mer devient
houleuse . . . je crains bien un orage . . .

At this point a terrible storm blows up, and they all fear for their lives
and begin to make vows to propitiate the gods:

Le pilote. — Paix . . . quel bruit! on ne s'entend pas. Est-ce le temps de
disputer? Voici une tempête terrible. . . . Baisse la voile . . . prends ce câble
. . . Je crois que tous les démons sont à cheval sur cette vague . . . Quel
vent! Voilà la voile en pièces . . .

Les voyageurs pleurent et gémissent. . . . Ah, pourquoi ai-je quitté ma
famille, etc. . . . Ah, qu'avais-je à faire en tel lieu. . . . Ah, ne pouvais-je me
passer des richesses de telle ou telle contrée etc. . . . O Jupiter de tel lieu,
Neptune Ténien, Apollon Délien, Junon Samienne . . . (*chacun le Dieu
de son pays*).

Le pilote. — Paix donc!

Les voyageurs. — Cent moutons . . mille brebis . . . cent taureaux! O
Dieux! sauvez-nous!

So it goes on, full of piquant detail: when one of the men refuses to
work in the storm, saying 'Je suis un homme libre', the Pilot replies,
'Homme libre, travaille, de peur que dans peu ta liberté ne soit esclave
de Pluton.' In the end land is sighted, and the Pilot chaffingly reminds
the sailors and travellers of the generous gifts they had offered to make
to the gods:

Eh bien! vous qui faisiez des vœux . . . Vos cent brebis, cent bœufs, cent
moutons, voyons, donnez-nous-en un ou deux à compte sur le rivage, ça
nous refera un peu . . .

The height of comedy is reached when, one after the other, they find
various pretexts for forgetting the vows they had made. Chénier had
here contrived to write a new kind of fable, a straight short story, full

of characters and lively dialogue, ending with the moral which is pointed by the Pilot:

> Oui, le danger fini, les Dieux sont oubliés.
> Mais tout se paye enfin; patience, riez.
> Quelque jour, agités de nouvelles tempêtes,
> Les Dieux se souviendront quels débiteurs vous êtes.
> Vous leur promettrez tout; mais ils feront les sourds;
> Un habile pilote, on ne l'a pas toujours,
> Et vous irez là-bas dire aux noires peuplades
> Si les îles du Styx égalent les Cyclades.

Les Navigateurs, even in this draft form, shows Chénier at the height of his powers, and it also shows that his range was far wider than is commonly imagined. Few drafts throw more light than this on Chénier's cast of mind, with its dazzling changes of tone, vocabulary, emotions, and events, and above all its spice of generous humour. It also shows how he was developing in originality and could now turn his immense knowledge of the classical background towards sheer entertainment.

While there is a constant strain of melancholy running through the *Bucoliques* it is frequently offset by joy, humour, irony, and tenderness. The poems that Chénier wrote about lovers were not all sad, by any means. *La Jeune Locrienne* (folio 55) tells the story of a girl publicly rebuked by a Pythagorean for her easy morals, but a young Thurian comes to her rescue in a way that was natural to his indulgent tribe:

> Je crois qu'il la suivit et lui fit oublier
> Le grave Pythagore et son grave écolier.

The more we look at the *Bucoliques* from this point of view, the more Chénier emerges as the poet of childhood and youth. His stress on youthful emotions, pure and prompt, creates a direct link between these poems and his *Élégies*, though this is not easy to define. It comes out at some points where his editors have hesitated about the proper classification of his poems. For instance, Dimoff placed the poem 'Jeune fille, ton cœur avec nous veut se taire / Tu fuis, tu ne ris plus, rien ne saurait te plaire' among the *Élégies*, though in fact the prose draft of the poem is in the *Bucoliques* manuscripts and is clearly marked as such:

Une jeune fille travaillant près de sa mère devient distraite et, nerveuse, laisse tomber sa navette . . . sa mère la gronde de ce qu'elle ne travaille pas . . . elle répond (le fragment de Sappho).

This prose draft (folio 63) is printed among the *Bucoliques* by Dimoff, though its connexion with the piece he gives in the *Élégies* is quite obvious. Another bucolic poem which has made its way into the wrong collection is the following:

> Sous le roc sombre et frais d'une grotte ignorée
> D'où coule une onde pure aux Nymphes consacrée,
> Je suivais l'autre jour un doux et triste son
> Et d'un Faune plaintif j'ouïs cette chanson:
>
> 'Amour, aveugle enfant, quelle est ton injustice.
> Hélas! j'aime Naïs; je l'aime sans espoir.
> Comme elle me tourmente, Hylas fait son supplice,
> Écho plaît au berger; il vole pour la voir.
> Écho loin de mes pas suit les pas de Narcisse,
> Qui la fuit pour baiser un liquide miroir.'

It is obvious that though the manuscript bears the word *élégie* it was not intended for the modern elegies (Marie-Joseph was instinctively right in entitling *La Jeune Tarentine* 'Élégie dans le goût ancien'). Heredia printed it in the *Bucoliques* under the title *Le Faune*, concluding it with another fragment which runs:

> Quittant sa forme, hélas! non son âme première
> Le beau Narcisse en fleur aux rives des ruisseaux
> Aime encore à se voir dans le cristal des eaux.

It will be noted that, for once, Chénier broke his usual habit of versification, by writing the song (the second movement) not in couplets but in 'rimes croisées'.

Apart from the small group of narrative poems and the descriptive mythological pieces, most of the *Bucoliques* are really elegies in the usual sense of the term. Barthélemy in his *Voyage du Jeune Anacharsis* (1788) had argued that before drama was invented it was in the elegy that public or private disaster was celebrated: 'Leurs chants plaintifs, presque toujours accompagnés de la flûte, furent connus sous le nom d'Élégies ou lamentations.' This is an over-simplification, for, from the military elegies of Callinos of Ephesus and Tyrteus to the celebration of love by Mimnermus, the moral elegies of Theognis, to Catullus, Tibullus, Ovid, and others, the range of the elegy never ceased to widen. As the same thing happened to all the genres in their passage from Greek into Latin literature, and subsequently into Italian and French, the term 'bucolique' became just as elastic and is a blanket term for many genres. Thus in the *Bucoliques* of Chénier we find side by side narrative poems, items of pure description, elegies, idylls, and eclogues all merging one into the other. The personal elegy (as we find it in Chénier's modern *Elégies*) is a mode that had developed long before Chénier, and his only innovation, apart from making it more dramatic, was to enlarge this genre in the direction of comedy.[1] What most distinguishes his ancient from his modern elegies is that in the *Bucoliques* he never took the liberty of mentioning himself, and it is perhaps this tactfully oblique revelation of himself that makes the *Bucoliques* so distinguished, so superior to his directly personal work.

If there is a particular genre which ought to be more clearly marked off in the *Bucoliques*, it is the epigram, though not in the modern sense of a short, witty statement. The form began, in antiquity, with prose inscriptions on tombs or other objects, and it was not until about the sixth century B.C. that these works began to be written in verse, and no longer as inscriptions. These epigrams were short, self-contained poems, often impromptus to describe a beautiful woman or a landscape, or to enliven a banquet. Chénier imitated not only those of Anacreon but all those collected by Meleager and in the later expanded Anthology. This explains why many of the pieces in the *Bucoliques* which are commonly regarded as fragments are not fragments at all, but complete pieces. The first editor to recognize this was Heredia, who in his edition printed twenty poems under the title *Épigrammes*. G. Walter took this a little further and printed thirty-four items under this heading. While we can praise this aspect of their editions, it is clear on closer inspection that there are many more epigrams which are still being regarded as unfinished fragments. For instance, Heredia classified the exquisite *Leçon de flûte* under the vague heading 'Nymphes et Satyres', while Walter prints it with 'Fragments de Bucoliques', but it is obviously a complete and consummate epigram:

> Toujours ce souvenir m'attendrit et me touche,
> Quand lui-même appliquant la flûte sur ma bouche,
> Riant et m'asseyant sur lui, près de son cœur,
> M'appelait son rival et déjà son vainqueur.
> Il façonnait ma lèvre inhabile et peu sûre
> A souffler une haleine harmonieuse et pure.
> Et ses savantes mains prenaient mes jeunes doigts,
> Les levaient, les baissaient, recommençaient vingt fois,
> Leur enseignant ainsi, quoique faibles encore,
> A fermer tour à tour les trous du buis sonore.

[1] Ronsard also wrote some mock-elegies, viz. nos. I, II in the *Amours diverses* (Pl).

To return to our argument, there are also many pieces in the *Buco-liques* which were obviously destined for the *Élégies*. For instance, after *La Jeune Locrienne*, so obviously a classical poem, we find on folio 57 a free translation of a sonnet by Zappi. This poem has an unusually modern rhythm and it is not surprising that when Latouche published it some of the Romantics accused him of forgery. It begins:

> Près des bords de Venise et même de la mer
> Le gondolier nocturne au retour de Vesper
> D'un aviron léger bat la vague aplanie
> Chantant Renaud, Tancrède et la belle Erminie . . .

What has happened here is that folios 57 and 58, which consist of a large folded sheet, were mistakenly classified among the *Bucoliques* manuscripts. These two folios contain eleven pieces in all, which may be dated by reference to the second item, which is a dedication to Maria Cosway ('Docte et jeune Cosway, des neufs sœurs honorée . . .'). These folios show that Chénier worked simultaneously on his two collections, ancient and modern, for in the midst of a number of dedicatory pieces on folio 58 there is one piece marked *Βυκ* ('Un jeune berger dira — Ma Muse échevelée, amante des Naïades . . .') and the delightful epigram *Le Faune*, which perhaps inspired Mallarmé:

> Je sais, quand le midi leur fait désirer l'ombre,
> Entrer à pas muets sous le roc frais et sombre
> D'où, parmi le cresson et l'humide gravier
> La Naïade se fraye un oblique sentier.
> Là j'épie à loisir la Nymphe blanche et nue
> Sur un banc de gazon mollement étendue,
> Qui dort, et sur sa main, au murmure des eaux,
> Laisse tomber son front couronné de roseaux.

It is, of course, natural that a poet who was writing poems in two styles might confuse them in his manuscripts, but it is the sight of these docu-ments which helps us to realize how narrow the division sometimes was between the two groups of poems; for one of the unifying elements is that Chénier made almost as much use of classical sources, references, and reminiscences in his modern as in his ancient poems. Yet a further complication arises, however, when we consider that he himself classi-fied a translation from Shakespeare (*La Chanson des yeux*) among the *Bucoliques*, while there are other projects based on passages in *The Two Gentlemen of Verona* and *Hamlet*. Further, while he was in London he became increasingly interested in oriental literatures and there are projects marked Βουκ based on Persian and Chinese texts (folios 167, 96, &c.). After mentioning a song 'écrite sous le règne d'Yao' he added 'Je la traduirai in Βουκ'. It is obvious that Chénier, who greatly admired the *Che King*, considered the Chinese poets as being 'Ancients' just as much as the Greeks and Romans. This might have appeared a heresy for Boileau and most of the writers in the French classical tradition, though no one objected to La Fontaine's Aesop or his mysterious sage, Pilpay. All this shows that we cannot speculate far on how Chénier would, finally, have arranged his *Bucoliques*. If the collection was meant to range from Homer to adaptations of Shakespeare, Thomson, Young, Gessner, Richeri, and Zappi, it would certainly have had a different appearance from the entirely neo-classical image that Heredia gave to the world in his edition. The poems would certainly not have been classified according to their subject-matter, as in Dimoff's edition, either, but carefully sifted and presented according to their genres, while being placed as far as possible to pro-vide logical groupings while allowing for sharp contrasts. It is even possible that Chénier would have carefully separated poems of Greek or Latin inspiration, even going so far as to insist on some chronological scheme.

Folio 60 brings us back to Chénier's grand manner, with the text of his famous *Mort d'Hercule*. It contains no variants and is probably a fair copy: the title has been added by his editors.

> Œta, mont ennobli par cette nuit ardente,
> Quand l'infidèle époux d'une épouse imprudente
> Reçut de son amour un présent trop jaloux,
> Victime du Centaure immolé par ses coups.
> Il brise tes forêts. Ta cime épaisse et sombre
> En un bûcher immense amoncelle sans nombre
> Les sapins résineux que son bras a ployés.
> Il y porte la flamme. Il monte. Sous ses piés
> Étend du vieux lion la dépouille héroïque,
> Et l'œil au ciel, la main sur la massue antique,
> Attend sa récompense et l'heure d'être un Dieu.
> Le vent souffle et mugit. Le bûcher tout en feu
> Brille autour du héros; et la flamme rapide
> Porte aux palais divins l'âme du grand Alcide.

This poem, which was to become the model for the Parnassian style in French verse, is more than a rapid résumé of a long passage in Ovid (*Met.* IX), for it is based on an engraving by Antonio Tempesta, illustrating this incident in Chénier's own copy of the *Metamorphoses*, published in 1606. It combines all Chénier's plastic sense with his gift for conveying rapid movement and avoiding all superfluous comment. The dignity of the event is enhanced by this restraint, while the entire lack of expressed feeling leaves the reader to his own reactions. Almost too perfect in its severity of tone, it shows Chénier's narrative manner taken to its extreme limit, pointing back into itself, rather than outwards, and perhaps leaving the same sense of frustration, in the reader's mind, as Shelley's *Ozymandias*, while being superior in every way to it. Starting, as we have done, from the conviction that Chénier was a great poet, we pause for a moment to ask why what Heredia called 'ces magnifiques vers' are so highly rated. These fourteen lines, written in alexandrine couplets, while showing the alexandrine at its most powerful, produce the general effect of a fine sonnet, and make us regret that Chénier avoided that form. Of course, strength rather than sweetness is what Heredia and the Parnassians sought in poetry, and here there is strength, to the exclusion of all else. We might ask whether Chénier has not dehumanized his theme by overstressing Hercules' stoic acceptance of a horrible death. The classical poets did not always take heroism (in mortals) so far beyond the human level. It is true that Ovid, describing how Hercules spread out his lion-skin on the flames and lay down upon it, said that 'on his face [there was] an expression no different from that of some guest reclining among the wine-cups with garlands on his head'. But previously he had given a more human picture of his reactions: 'But now a new plague is on me, which no amount of courage can withstand, no weapons of war overcome. Consuming fire spreads into the depths of my lungs, feeding on all my limbs, and that while my enemy, King Eurystheus, is strong and well! And there are men who can believe in gods!' Chénier short-circuited all this feeling, as the Parnassians were to do in their turn. Is it possible that a narrative piece of so short a length cannot produce a complete poetic experience? Hercules, in Ovid's text, was a less monolithic figure, capable of self-pity, envy, irony, and blasphemy as well as heroism—but that is because there was room and time to convey all this in his text. In Chénier, it would be possible to say that the eighteenth-century notion of the Sublime had intervened—were there any signs of that Sublime in any other eighteenth-century poetry but his. No; the answer may be that he was wilfully correcting Ovid, in the direction of Greek heroism as he conceived it. It is the heroism of silence in the face of adversity, of destiny. Of course it is impossible

to know how Chénier would have used this passage, and whether it
needs a larger context is open to debate. As it stands it is a master's
demonstration of the epic style. We feel that it was a waste for Chénier
to have spent so long on *Hermès* and *L'Amérique*, when he alone could
have given the French language its perfect translation of Homer.
Again, we are set to reflect that perhaps the Centaurs episode would
have been less effective, were it not set in the rich human background
of *L'Aveugle*. Be that as it may, *La Mort d'Hercule* is a unique example,
in French, of the terse narrative style, throwing aside the French 'manie
de tout dire' (as Baudelaire put it), anticipating the 'hardness' of
Gautier, the directness of Baudelaire's *Don Juan aux Enfers*, the im-
passibility of Leconte de Lisle, the nervous power, like that of a coiled
spring, of some of the poems in Valéry's *Charmes*.

The manuscripts that we have so far considered already give a broad
idea of the great variety of themes, tones, and colours that make up the
Bucoliques. Without taking this survey much further, immediately after
La Mort d'Hercule we meet, in contrast, two delightful poems about
children, 'J'étais un faible enfant' and *Pannychis*. The poem about
Pannychis is set in the midst of a long prose draft which shows that
Chénier intended making a long work which would contain a number
of characters, mostly girls, who each in turn would have some kind of
song to sing. We begin to see, from this and the *Banquet des Satyres*
that Chénier's most obvious and favourite device would have been to
collect short poems into one longer piece by inventing characters to
speak them. This is, perhaps, another clue to the reason why so many
of his poems are already cast in the form of direct speech. Incidentally,
as part of the draft has a close relationship to one of Gessner's idylls,
we again see that modern sources could intrude even into a work based
on classical material. We must not overlook, either, the fact that what
Chénier saw around him in France could also find its way into the
Bucoliques. This is shown by a poem he wrote at the height of the
Revolution, the lovely 'Fille du vieux Pasteur' which bears the note
Bovк and 'Vu à Catillon, près Forges, le 4 août 1792 et écrit à Gournay
le lendemain' (folio 77). When he wrote it the *Journal de Paris* had
just been suppressed, and the poet was in danger. The manuscript that
has survived is obviously the first and probably the only draft, as the
first four lines on it were rewritten:

> Fille du vieux pasteur, qui d'une main agile
> Le soir emplis de lait trente vases d'argile,
> Crains la génisse pourpre au farouche regard

Qui marche toujours seule et qui paît à l'écart.
Libre, elle lutte et fuit, intraitable et rebelle;
Tu ne presseras point sa féconde mamelle
A moins qu'avec adresse un de ses pieds lié
Dans un cuir souple et lent ne demeure plié.

Without the poet's note it would be natural to regard it as a poem imitated from some ancient epigram, for in style and vision it is entirely classical. It shows the poet's eye so influenced by his classical background that he saw the modern rural scene, in 1792, much as he imagined the pastoral life of antiquity. At the same time we have to remember that in the eighteenth century France was still largely a pastoral community, and that Chénier and his friends spent as much time in the country as in the town. There was no such strangeness in the rural scene as there is for the modern poet or painter, but Chénier was sufficiently alert and detached to take note of a peculiar detail, the use of a leather thong to check the heifer's foot, which the average observer might then have taken for granted. The later Romantics had no such eye for detail, but in this respect Chénier's poem is Wordsworthian, though it is marked by conventional poetic diction. It shows the poet actively looking about him and not content to see nature only through books.

It would take a long time to enter, as we should wish to do, into the remaining manuscripts, and we must pass over *Clytie* (folio 94) and two good fragments on poetry ('Nymphe tendre et vermeille' and 'Vierge au visage blanc') which define the pastoral and heroic Muses of the *Bucoliques*. However, there are one or two items which must be considered before we leave this collection of manuscripts. One of them (folio 124, item 1) throws considerable light on Chénier's method of composition:

Personnifier avec des Épithètes et des attributs neufs et convenables: la jeunesse, la vieillesse, les Saisons, l'année, le temps, les heures, le jour, la nuit, l'aurore, le midi, le soir, la muse, la tristesse (in $\varDelta$ la pensée aux mille couleurs), la timidité, la pudeur, le baiser, le rire, la voix . . . sur des lèvres . . . l'inspiration poétique qui habite les lieux faits de telle ou telle manière (l'invoquer).

He was a more systematic person than the confused state of his papers might suggest, and he was more deliberate than most people expect a poet to be. It is this kind of groundwork, meditated in advance, which accounts for a poet's speed and spontaneity in writing: unless he has at least thought about such problems as those given above, informed spontaneity is impossible. Another note of this kind (folio 148) concerns flowers:

Il y faut parler d'un grand nombre d'arbres et de végétaux avec des circonstances, des peintures, des épithètes caractéristiques et brillantes.

That attempts were made to carry out his own instructions is shown by many isolated lines or expressions such as 'les myrtes embaumées', 'L'ombre pâle de la saule', 'La châtaigne épineuse et la pomme de Crète', and the synaesthetic image 'L'air trempé des parfums que respirent les fleurs', or 'les dédales de fleurs'. These all show that a deliberate programme did not stifle his inventiveness.

Another, more scholarly aspect of Chénier's craft is to be found in folios 35 and 36, on which he compiled a sort of dictionary of references, of which the following are specimens:

A *Diane*. Sappho, 2, p. 55. Mnasal. 2, p. 190; 5, p. 191. Léon. Tar. 2, 3, p. 220; 20, p. 225. Nicias, 2, p. 248. Pancrates, I, p. 259. Phaedimus, 3, p. 261. Callim. 29, p. 468; 33, p. 469. Antip. Sid. 19, vol. II, p. 10–23, p. 11; 36, p. 16; Damaget. I, 2, p. 38.

A *Bacchus*. Anac. 75 et 77, p. 117; 83, p. 119; Léon Tar. 15, p. 224; 18, p. 225; 30, p. 228; Theocr. ii, p. 379; Phalaecus, 3, p. 421.

A *Hercule*. Callim. 30, p. 468; Samius, 1, 2, p. 485; Antip. Sid. 13, vol. II, 8; 18, p. 10.

This kind of close work, which would enable him to look up his references quickly, was accompanied by massive annotations in his own fine library of classical texts, usually made on little slips of paper which he left in the books. He also wrote out close critical commentaries on classical philology and literature. Chénier's classical sources have been explored by Dimoff, who also gives a good description of the poet's library, most of which is still preserved at Carcassonne. The specimens given above show how Chénier's learning and manner of composition went together: it is also possible that the lists of references he was drawing up were a key to many of the 'plagiarisms' which he acknowledged openly in his *Épître sur ses ouvrages*. We thus see that nothing could have been more logical and systematic than Chénier's method of writing poetry. It was based on the habit of jotting down apt descriptions of nature or various types of experience; the compilation of references which would enable him to lay his hand quickly on the material he wanted to work into his poems; the aforehand translation of some of such passages, to have them ready for use; the scholarly habit of making short analyses of words or quotations;

the jotting down of *quadri* or drafts containing the outline or details of subjects and stories to be elaborated. It is his absorption in all these preliminaries which goes far to explain why so few of his major projects were completed.

There remain two *quadri* which are worth discussing as being possible epilogues to the *Bucoliques*. Whatever we think of their various stages of completion, it is interesting to see, from the inside, that Chénier himself was not dissatisfied with the state of his *Bucoliques*, and wrote about them as if they were complete enough. Folio 126 gives a long prose draft on this subject, which he transformed into verse on folio 58:

> Ma Muse est ambitieuse de faire entendre à la Seine de véritables bergers
> . . . Elle a parcouru tous les lieux célèbres par des chants bucoliques. Elle
> a visité les rives de Mincius, où Virgile . . . celles d'Aréthuse, où Théocrite
> et Moschus . . . celles d'Hermus, où Bion . . . et celles du beau lac de Zurich,
> où de nos jours le sage Gessner . . . Au bord de toutes ces belles et poétiques
> eaux elle a coupé des roseaux . . . (Puisse-t-elle avoir rencontré des mêmes
> qui jadis ont plu sur les lèvres de ces chantres de la nature.) De tous ces
> roseaux, elle a composé la flûte rustique avec laquelle elle chante ceci et
> cela . . .

This draft for a prologue could have been written at any time between 1785 and 1790, and is obviously a defence of the classical pastoral (to which he assimilated the work of Gessner) against the decadent pastoral tradition in France. It is a defence of his 'ancient' elegies, not the modern ones. Of course he had actually visited the haunts of Virgil and Gessner, but had (so far as is known) never been to Greece, where his 'Muse' had only travelled in the sense that Keats had travelled 'in the realms of gold'. But he makes it clear enough that his work would draw on both ancient and modern sources. It is curious to note that he made no mention of Homer and Ovid, on whom he relied so much, nor any mention of the heroic muse: this would bear out our view that *L'Aveugle* and other heroic pieces were not all early works. The poem he made from this draft is very beautiful in itself, ending:

> De ces roseaux liés par des nœuds de fougère
> Elle a su composer sa flûte bocagère,
> Qui, sous ses doigts légers exhalant de doux sons
> Chante Pomone et Pan, les ruisseaux, les moissons,
> Les vierges aux yeux doux, et les grottes muettes,
> Et de l'âge d'amour les chaleurs inquiètes.

Nature and love are the only subjects mentioned here, and it is with some mystification that we turn back to the draft for *L'Aveugle* and see that it is not marked *Buk*. This prologue, then, seems to refer to only a small part of the *Bucoliques* as we know them, and it must be concluded that it was an early poem. At the same time the various dedications he wrote, in presenting bucolic poems to his friends, show the same limitation. In a dedication to de Pange there is no mention of anything but idylls, though this little offering (folio 57) is important because it shows that he considered only Segrais[1] as a serious forerunner in France:

> Et sa flûte à la main, sa flûte qui s'apprête
> A défier un jour les pipeaux de Segrais,
> Seuls connus parmi nous aux Nymphes des forêts.

A dedicatory poem for the mysterious D.z.n (folio 171) again mentions nothing but pieces about nature:

> A toi, belle D.z.; pour toi mes mains rustiques
> Ont formé le tissu de ces fleurs bucoliques . . .

The same applies to a dedication to Maria Cosway ('Docte et jeune Cosway', &c., folio 57) and another 'A une Anglaise' on the same sheet. In other words, the dedicatory poems reveal no evidence concerning the heroic poems or such highly serious works as *La Liberté*.

It is in the draft for what was to be the definitive *Épilogue* that we see Chénier looking back on and interpreting this work. This draft (folio 125) is inscribed 'A la fin de toutes les Bucoliques' and runs as follows:

> Voilà ce que je chantais en voyageant . . . et ces chansons remplissaient mes voyages de délices. Mais ces Muses délicates et sensibles que tout occupe, qui rêvent sur tout, n'inspirent que la jeunesse . . . elles me quittent et des muses austères et guerrières . . . Adieu donc mes jeunes et rustiques chalumeaux avec qui j'ai célébré les champs . . . adieu, reposez-vous, passez en d'autres mains. Allez plaire sur d'autres lèvres . . . Les miennes ne sauraient plus animer en vous . . . Vous n'accompagnerez plus mes pas en de lointains pays. Assis sur une roche touffue au pied d'un chêne au bord de l'eau . . . je ne verrai plus à vos sons enchanteurs courir autour de vous les troupeaux et pasteurs. Les vallons du Languedoc, de la Provence et de l'Italie ne retentiront plus de vos douces chansons. Les abeilles de Sicile et d'Attique ne viendront plus bourdonner autour de vous. 'Des nymphes des vergers les amours

---

[1] Segrais (1624–1701) wrote many eclogues which were only collected in 1722. Boileau said of him, 'Que Segrais dans l'églogue en charme les forêts' (*Art poétique*, IV. 201).

innocentes' chantées par vous ne feront plus . . . les bois d'Olympie ou
d'Éphèse ou des sommets crétois. Et pour entendre vos soupirs les naïades
de tel et tel fleuve de Thessalie, de Phénicie . . . ne lèveront plus leur tête
humide au-dessus de leurs eaux.

This is followed by a draft of a few lines suggested by the prose:

> Des Nymphes, des bergers les amours innocentes.
> Et vous ne verrez plus les Naïades brillantes
> Que (tel fleuve) . . . les eaux,
> A vos soupirs . . . sortant de leurs roseaux,
> Tout à coup, au-dessus de leurs ondes limpides
> Lever leurs beaux cheveux et leurs têtes humides.

The draft appears to contain not only a farewell to pastoral poetry,
but also a farewell to the idea of travelling ('Vous n'accompagnerez
plus mes pas en de lointains pays'). This suggests that the draft must
have been written, not only after Chénier returned to Paris from
London in 1790, but after he had given up the idea of going back again,
that is to say in 1791. The reference to 'des muses austères et guerrières'
no doubt refers to his decision to enter the lists of political journalism,
and might also have something to do with his adoption of the Pindaric
Ode in writing his *Ode au Jeu de Paume* which occupied him in the
last months of 1790 and the first three months of 1791. The above
draft of an Epilogue therefore suggests that he was perhaps thinking
of publishing the *Bucoliques* in 1790 or 1791—but, as we know, he continued working on them and adding to them after that. There is, however, another fragment (the manuscript of which is lost, but which
was copied by Gabriel de Chénier on folio 115) which also contains a
reference to heroic poetry, or 'muses guerrières':

> Ma Muse fuit les champs abreuvés de carnage
> Et ses pieds innocents ne se poseront pas
> Où la cendre des morts gémirait sous ses pas.
> Elle pâlit d'entendre et le cri des batailles
> Et les assauts tonnants qui frappent les murailles;
> Et le sang qui jaillit sous les pointes d'airain
> Souillerait la blancheur de sa robe de lin.

This piece is very difficult to date. It could have been written very
early (1781 or 1782) when, in replying to Le Brun, he asserted that he
wanted to write only about love. It is likely that it was written long
before *L'Aveugle* (or at least the piece on the Centaurs), and probably
long before such aggressive poems as *La Liberté* and the *Hymne à la*

Justice. Following Chénier's drama from the inside, we can imagine him smiling ironically, during the Revolution, when he came across this piece at a time when he had begun to attack the Jacobins in his *Iambes.*

Chénier's *Bucoliques* have been an object of criticism of every kind since 1819, and much of what was written about them in the nineteenth century was expounded in detail by Paul Glachant in his *André Chénier critique et critiqué* in 1902. While there is little point in going over all that ground again, there are some tendencies that have to be noted. On the negative side there are those (L. Bertrand, Brunetière, Petit de Julleville, &c.) who, while treating Chénier with respect, argued that he was a poet of the decadence—'post-Pericles' or 'Alexandrian' or 'pseudo-classical'. Some went further than that: Béranger, in declaring stupidly that the *Bucoliques* were not written by Chénier, but forged by Latouche;[1] Frémy (1884), who suggested that Chénier was ignorant of Greek and borrowed details without understanding them;[2] Michiels (1862), who claimed that everything that Chénier stood for was already accomplished by such contemporaries as Delille and Le Brun and that he was in no sense an innovator.[3] He came down heavily on Chénier's poetic diction:

Veut-il nous décrire une fontaine? C'est Blandusie ou la nymphe Aréthuse. Un verger? Pomone en prend la place. Un troupeau? la fastidieuse Palès accourt. Un vallon? c'est celui de Tempé. Une montagne? c'est l'Hymette, l'Hélicon, l'Hémus ou le Rhodope.

As for Frémy, Sainte-Beuve wrote him a devastating reply in the same year ('Un Factum contre André Chénier'), but in spite of that it is still common to find sceptical readers. One of Chénier's scholarly admirers, J. Fabre, has suggested recently that 'son érudition reste cependant dans les limites de l'amateurisme et il ne prétendait pas à autre chose'.[4] This is no doubt a healthy reaction against the large claims made by Becq de Fouquières and Dimoff, but surely all scholarship in Chénier's time had this amateurish quality. His 'amateurism' was, in any case,

---

[1] Béranger (*Ma Biographie*, 1857, p. 195): 'Je l'ai souvent appelé [Latouche] l'inventeur d'André Chénier, dans les œuvres duquel il est au moins pour moitié; car j'ai entendu Marie-Joseph déplorer qu'il y eût si peu de morceaux publiables dans les manuscrits laissés par son frère.'

[2] G28.

[3] A. Michiels, *Hist. des idées littéraires en France*, 1862, t. ii, livre iii, ch. 1.

[4] F36, p. 54.

well on the way to solid scholarship in the modern sense, as we can see from the substantial draft of his *Essai*. The fact that he never mentioned certain Greek authors or took nothing from them does not mean that he had not read them. M. Fabre continues, 'Dans la littérature même, ne lui seront véritablement familiers que les textes à sa mesure.' Well, it would be possible to compile from his manuscripts, his library, and his printed articles a very formidable list of what were the 'textes à sa mesure'. It is certainly unfair for M. Fabre to pick out the *Voyage du jeune Anacharsis* as being 'un livre à sa mesure'. This was universally one of the best-sellers of the late eighteenth century, and Chénier was charmed by it as his contemporaries were. Nor did he rely blindly on Brunck's *Analecta*: as far as possible he went to the sources, and collected all he could of the best annotated editions of the classics that were published in England, Germany, Italy, and Spain. This hardly points to 'amateurism'. M. Fabre's remarks remind us of Mr. T. S. Eliot's suggestion that 'Blake did not know enough'; that Robert Burns was something of a muddy peasant, and that D. H. Lawrence was not sufficiently educated. A poet, in any case, does not need to be learned in the academic sense: what he needs to know is what is necessary for writing the kind of poetry he undertakes. It would, of course, be relevant to ask this question in the case of Keats; and one could answer that he could not follow Milton any further than he did, or finish *Hyperion*, because he was practically ignorant of the Greek which was the very basis of Milton's style and outlook. But all that is known about Chénier's background points to a very wide range of interests and great intellectual energy, as well as a knowledge of the sources on which he drew, which any young scholar today might envy. But such questions are really secondary, drawing the reader as well as the critic into side-issues.

Many critics and poets have looked at the *Bucoliques* with a very different eye. Lanson called them 'des œuvres absolument sans pareilles dans notre littérature'.[1] Sainte-Beuve went so far as to exaggerate his influence, though not perhaps his quality, in trying to create an 'école d'André Chénier'. Goethe affirmed that all modern elegiac poetry stemmed from Chénier. Villemain was on better ground than most university scholars in saying that Chénier had 'un *goût* singulier de l'antiquité' and 'une manière neuve de *la sentir et la rendre*'.[2] The notion of taste and sensibility is probably more important than an assessment

---

[1] Lanson, *Hist. de la litt. fr.*, 1898, p. 837.
[2] Villemain, *Tableau de la littérature au XVIIIe siècle*, t. iv, ch. 58.

of knowledge, in considering any poet's achievement. Victor Hugo instinctively thought in similar terms, attributing to Chénier 'la manière franche et large des Anciens; rarement de vaines antithèses, plus souvent des pensées nouvelles, des peintures vivantes, partout l'empreinte de cette sensibilité profonde sans laquelle il n'est point de génie, et qui est peut-être le génie même'.[1] Whatever the state of his knowledge might have been, and there is evidence that it was exceptional, Chénier's sensibility was a vital element through which the classical tradition was both prolonged and transformed. Le Brun, paying tribute to that sensibility, wrote, 'On est tenté d'être son ami, sa muse est pure et modeste, sa mélancolie douce et profonde.'[2] Nodier in 1823 found him 'le seul poète de ce temps dont l'âme tendre parut s'associer à l'immense tristesse de la société en deuil'.[3] Deschamps put his finger on the essential freshness and newness of the *Bucoliques*, saying, 'Dans ces sortes de composition, tout est *tableau* ou *dialogue*, et l'on évite aussi la narration, toujours si fatigante dans le grand vers français.'[4] All this genuine appreciation came from those Romantics who, none the less, did not manage to make a proper estimate of Chénier; yet Canat exaggerates in saying 'un helléniste peu dépisté, et quand il l'est, peu estimé; telle est en ces années l'histoire d'André Chénier'.[5] But it would be an error to think that the classical tradition broke down at that stage: it was merely transformed and re-directed. As Gautier put it, 'On peut dater d'André Chénier la poésie moderne. Ses vers, publiés par Latouche, furent une vraie révélation. Ce retour à l'antiquité, éternellement jeune, fit éclore un nouveau printemps.'[6] Gautier went on to show how Chénier had helped to modify the French alexandrine, with 'la césure mobile, les variétés des coupes, les suspensions, les rejets, toute cette secrète harmonie et ce rythme intérieur si heureusement retrouvé par le chantre du *Jeune Malade*, du *Mendiant* et de l'*Oaristys*'. While Gautier made a typically 'romantic' choice from the *Bucoliques* he began raising critical problems by dealing with poetry on its intrinsic qualities. Leconte de Lisle as early as 1840 called Chénier 'le régénérateur de la forme lyrique' and with terms like 'facture, pittoresque, mélodie, éclat' drew attention to those aspects of his work which were to obsess the Parnassians for many years to come.[7] It is likely that when Baudelaire asserted that 'André Chénier, avec sa molle antiquité à la Louis XVI, n'était pas un

[1] G40.   [2] *La Renommée*, 6 sept. 1816.   [3] See G13.
[4] In *La Muse Française*, 1823.   [5] G13, t. i.   [6] G31, p. 295.
[7] G49.

symptôme de rénovation assez vigoureuse', he was really replying to Leconte de Lisle rather than assessing Chénier.[1] There is much truth in Baudelaire's statement, however. While rejecting Baudelaire's emphasis on the purely period (Louis XVI) quality of Chénier's stock-in-trade, excessive imitation of the *Bucoliques*—accompanied by a complete failure on their part to grasp what was really original and modern in his style, that is to say its dramatic quality—led the Parnassians into a conception of poetry which rapidly became dull and academic. At the same time it has to be recalled that, in dismissing Chénier in this way as a formative influence, Baudelaire was biased owing to his hostility to what he called 'l'école païenne'—the poetry of Ménard, Banville, and Leconte de Lisle, while making an exception of their real leader, Gautier.

Passing over the tributes that were made to Chénier by Maurras, Brasillach, Claudel (who regarded him as one of the really great French poets), more recently Gaëtan Picon has described Chénier as the only great French poet between Racine and the Romantics. He remarks, 'Chénier noue entre eux certains vers, si bien qu'ils deviennent comme une longue phrase, toujours rompue et renaissante, première lueur de l'entrelacs mallarméen.' At the same time M. Picon, believing that it is 'moins une dramaturgie qu'une plastique qu'il puise dans l'antique', relates his work to sculpture.[2] But the evidence in this chapter surely points, not exactly the other way, but to both a dramatic and a plastic inspiration. However, M. Picon hastens to correct the impression of merely repeating Heredia, adding, 'C'est se méprendre que de le voir, comme Heredia, à travers ses descriptions de bas-reliefs. Ici règne une espèce de *lumière* où la légèreté s'unit à l'éclat, où toute image est d'une minceur transparente. Surface étincelante, brillant crystal continu, la poésie est miroir — non pas gouffre ou musée lapidaire. Pas d'image plus fréquente et plus révélatrice que celle du fleuve. Et le fleuve est ici, symbole visuel, surface réfléchissante.' He concludes, 'cette grâce, plus qu'à telle ou telle de ses époques, appartient à la poésie: aussi bien qu'à Virgile et à Racine, elle unit Chénier à Rimbaud.'

This brilliant comment relates Chénier firmly to both the past and the future of the European tradition. It is perhaps on the lines suggested by M. Picon that contemporary criticism must begin to revalue the essential and enduring qualities of Chénier's work. We have done our best to bring out the range and variety of the *Bucoliques* and to draw

---

[1] Baudelaire, *Œuvres* (Pléiade), t. ii, p. 55.
[2] In *Histoire des Littératures*, t. iii, Pléiade.

attention to their originality. The fact that this cannot be done without making comparisons, however inaccurate, with such poets as Wordsworth and Keats, La Fontaine, Racine, Baudelaire, Mallarmé, Rimbaud, Valéry, is perhaps enough to suggest that Chénier holds a necessary place in the French tradition.

PART III

POETRY AND ACTION, 1790–4

9

FIRST STEPS IN POLITICS

(1790–1)

THE last phase in Chénier's life is a story of increasingly strong commitment, during which a determined stand for moderation developed into a savage war against the Jacobins, followed by flight, intrigue, imprisonment, and his public execution. During the same period he found time, in occasional spells of relaxation, to continue work on his *Bucoliques* and his classical studies; to achieve a pure and disinterested love for Fanny Lecoulteux for whom he wrote his last lyrics; and to make his name as one of the greatest French satirical poets. But although, during this period, his poetic talents matured and were redirected, his production was so much bound up with his harassed daily life that we shall make no attempt to treat it in isolation from the events that are to be described; for it has to be shown that it was a poet, and not only a journalist, who went to the scaffold.

As we saw towards the end of the first part of this study, by the time Chénier returned to Paris in the summer of 1790, after many months of personal unhappiness in London, the Revolution had already gathered enough momentum to alarm him and his Moderate friends. François de Pange had already been active, publishing in September 1789 an article 'De la Sanction royale' in which he attacked the royal veto and asserted the principle of 'the sovereignty of the Nation'— a principle which was to be sorely abused in the years to follow. While believing that the King had an honest desire to serve the country as a constitutional monarch, he concluded, 'Las de dominer une troupe servile, un prince a voulu s'entourer d'hommes libres; il nous invite à le devenir, à dire ce qu'on usurpa sur nous et à le reprendre.'[1] There is something admirable but also pathetic in this use of the word 'nous', for the time was soon to be past when any citizen could use the word in the sense of the whole nation. The breach was already apparent in de Pange's second article, a brochure published in January 1790, his 'Réflexions sur la Délation et sur le Comité de Recherches', about a committee of inquiry of which Chénier's friend Lacretelle was a member. In this article, de Pange was one of the first theorists of the Revolution to denounce the practice of public informing, which had been used against Besenval and which was to undermine legal procedure for the duration of the Revolution. He also condemned the rough justice which allowed 'the people' to lynch their real or imaginary enemies, quoting the case of a baker who had been hanged in the street on the 20th of October. It is significant that the only attack on this enlightened article came from Brissot de Warville, a busybody who, while lacking political acumen or scruple, was to be entrusted for a time with the leadership of the Girondins and to steer them towards ruin. Rivarol wrote of Brissot, in his *Petit Dictionnaire des Grands Hommes de la Révolution* in 1790, 'Quand le peuple a besoin de quelque vengeance pour vivre, c'est à M. Brissot de Warville qu'il s'adresse.'

As we have seen (above, p. 87) Chénier completely approved of de Pange's call to order; but by the time he returned to Paris the situation had worsened. The real aims of the constitutionalists had been largely achieved as far back as August 1789, with the official abolition of Feudalism (4th of August) followed by the draft 'Déclaration des droits de l'Homme' and the setting up of the Constituent Assembly. But since then the royal family had been forcibly brought back to Paris from Versailles; church property had been confiscated in November; assignats had been issued in December, while pensions had been suspended and reduced—old Louis de Chénier's being cut in half in January 1790. In other words, changes and reforms of all kinds were being made too fast for those who had taken their stand to the Right or Centre. In this first year of the Revolution, not only the deputies but all ranks of society were jockeying for power or limelight, pushing others and themselves into such extremist positions that the atmosphere for all was one of exciting but disturbing insecurity, lit by the hope that the new Constitution and its acceptance by the Crown

[1] F76, p. 38.

would work a miracle. As happens at the beginning of the longest wars, calm and the return to normal law and order were expected to be reached within a year. But it was all very well for the intellectuals to pin their hopes on the Constitution. Political liberty is a mockery when it is not accompanied by economic emancipation. The masses needed bread, clothes, money, housing—none of which the Constitution could offer them. The Trudaines, de Pange, Chénier and his circle gave too little thought to this aspect of the social problem.

It has been mentioned that Chénier was a founder member of the 'Société de 1789', which had a 'ceiling' of 660 members and an inner circle of 89, of whom he was one. The membership cost three *louis* per annum. They issued a magazine at first called *Journal de la Société de 1789* which was edited by the philosopher Condorcet from June to September 1790, and later was renamed *Mémoires de la Société de 1789*. This was one of the few revolutionary clubs which attracted its membership from every political party, ranging from right-wing members, belonging also to the reactionary 'Club monarchique', to the extreme left, taking in a number of 'moderate' Jacobins such as David and Collot d'Herbois. Among the most prominent members of the Société were La Fayette, Mirabeau, Bailly, Roederer, Dupont de Nemours; the die-hard duc de Liancourt-La Rochefoucauld; the Jacobin Barère, and the whole Chénier circle including the Trudaines, the brothers de Pange, the Lecoulteux, Lacretelle, Pastoret, and Abel de Malartic (who also joined the right-wing 'Club monarchique' and 'Club Valois'). It is instructive to note that at first the Trudaines also belonged to the Valois, as did Turtot (brother-in-law of Fanny Lecoulteux), but at that time it was common to join several clubs, not always out of loyalty, but in order to know what was going on. The Valois, like the 'Société de 1789', later merged into the Feuillant party.

The 'Société de 1789' described itself modestly as 'ni une secte ni un parti, mais une compagnie d'amis des hommes et, pour ainsi dire, d'agents de commerce des vérités sociales'.[1] Condorcet, its first spokesman, described it as 'consacrée à la défense des principes d'une constitution libre, et à la perfection de l'art social'—meaning by 'art social' the art of government.

André Chénier was destined to be the most powerful spokesman of this Society, and to place it in peril by his writings, which had the effect of driving out all those—Condorcet, Brissot, Barère, and many

[1] F21, t. i, pp. 390–440.

others—who made up its left wing, and who were secretly in favour of republicanism even at the moment when a monarchical constitution was being drawn up. Not that Chénier's views had by any means hardened into bigoted royalism. The abbé Morellet relates in his memoirs how he met Chénier at that time. He had gone to stay with Madame Broutin, a worthy blue-stocking and a friend of Madame Helvétius, at Cernay, 'dans la vallée de Montmorency', in 1790, and found himself in a circle of young men:

Mais il y avait de plus une étrange analogie entre la retraite que je quittais — celle de Madame Helvétius — et celle que j'avais retrouvée; l'opinion des habitués y était presque la même. C'étaient Lacretelle, passant sa vie avec Madame Broutin; de Tracy, Desmeuniers, André Chénier et beaucoup d'autres députés du côté gauche de la première assemblée. Ils étaient du moins constitutionnels, et n'aspiraient qu'au bien de leur patrie. Mais, s'ils avaient voulu la cause, ils commençaient à craindre les effets.[1]

Morellet gives us some useful information here, as it shows that Chénier and Lacretelle were already friendly before they met at the Feuillants, and that the poet did not confine himself to the Trudaine–de Pange circles. Destutt de Tracy (1754–1836) was one of the leading 'idéologues': he wrote works on will, language, logic, and an appreciation of Montesquieu. Imprisoned during the Terror, he lived to become a senator under Napoleon and a peer under the Restoration. Desmeuniers (also spelt Démeunier, 1751–1814) had been secretary to the comte de Provence and was elected to the Tiers-État in 1789 and became its President. Desmeuniers played an important part in drawing up the Constitution, but in the process became an enemy of Pétion, who later replaced Bailly as Mayor of Paris. Escaping to America in July 1792, Desmeuniers did not return to France until 1796, when he became a member of the Directory. With his enlightened views on politics and his wide culture he was exactly the kind of friend we should expect Chénier to have: he wrote an 'Essai sur le génie original d'Homère' (1777), translated Gibbon into French, and also published a translation of Cicero's works. In any case it is interesting to note that Morellet did not regard Chénier as anti-revolutionary.

No sooner was Chénier back in France than he was asked by his friends to write for the *Journal de la Société de 1789*. His first essay, 'Avis au Peuple Français sur ses véritables ennemis', attracted wide attention. Incidentally, it has always been said that he wrote this at de Pange's house, but it is more likely that it was written at Madame

[1] F71, p. 399.

de Beaumont's (daughter of the statesman Montmorin) at Passy-sur-Yonne. Joubert's witness on this question is hardly to be disputed: 'Aussi Mme de Beaumont exerçait-elle sans y prétendre l'influence créatrice dont parlait le poète Le Brun. Chénier avait écrit, dans son cabinet même, les pages dignes de Tacite qu'il nous a léguées.'[1] Chénier's essay was printed with the statement 'Passy, 24 août 1790', though this does not figure on the manuscript. The Passy in question is not the present XVIth arrondissement in Paris, but the home of the Sérillys and Montmorins, the Château de Passy between Villeneuve and Sens. We begin to wonder whether the friendship between Chénier and Madame de Beaumont was not closer than his biographers have so far thought: it was she who obtained for him his post in London; who offered him a retreat where he could write, and she who, almost alone of her generation, helped to perpetuate his memory by showing his manuscripts to Chateaubriand. Is it possible that she was the mysterious D.z.n.? Is it not a coincidence that she fled to Rouen in September 1792, at the same time as Chénier went there?[2] She is said to have had many of Chénier's manuscripts, but when, at her death, she left her library to Chateaubriand, all the great René could find to do with it was to sell it.[3]

It is no easy matter to give a short account of Chénier's famous essay, which, so far from being the dispassionate call to order that he intended, offered a warm reprimand to all those whom he considered to be something of a nuisance. Though the essay is carefully reasoned, its leisurely pace and generalizations often recall Montaigne, and like Montaigne he turned round and round his subject, coming back to worry some part of it from time to time. There are one or two personal touches, such as

> J'avais résolu, dans le commencement, de ne point essayer de sortir de mon obscurité dans les conjonctures présentes, de ne point faire entendre ma voix inconnue au milieu de cette confusion de voix publiques et de cris particuliers, et d'attendre en silence la fin de l'ouvrage de nos législateurs, sans aller grossir la foule de ces écrivains morts-nés que notre révolution a fait éclore. . . .

It is plain that his manner was an irritable one, long before he fell foul of the Jacobins. The whole essay hesitates between humility and anger.

[1] F54, p. 35.
[2] F6(a), p. 205: 'Elle partit avec sa mère, sa sœur et son frère pour Rouen, où M. de Liancourt les recueillit.'   [3] Ibid., p. 81.

He began (as in his *Ode au Jeu de Paume*) by saluting the Revolution, which he called 'une insurrection juste et légitime' through which the nation 'rentre dans tous ses droits et renverse l'ordre des choses qui les violait tous'. It is in the use of this word 'insurrection' that we find the key to Chénier's view of the state of French society after 1789. Playing down the term 'Revolution' he affected to see only an 'insurrection', a mass-rising against previous authority, which should come to an end as soon as the country's rights were restored. It follows from this, that as soon as a new government was created and a Constitution made, the insurrection would no longer be legitimate, and must come to an end. Chénier was thus adopting a legalist position, properly based in political theory; but this is why his article was acceptable to the right wing and even to the exiles who refused to admit that a 'revolution' was taking place and must continue. We also note that the very title of Chénier's article was aggressive, like most of those that were being written at that time: it was the moment when Joubert could say 'Sois mon ami ou je te tue'; for the air was thick with threats as the parties were splintering and accusations were being hurled from side to side. After August 1789, when the 'Declaration of the Rights of Man' had been approved, the Revolution went on as though nobody took the trouble to read it again. Chénier's 'Avis' is for the most part, though he did not say so, a commentary on the Declaration in the light of a year's political acrivity. The Declaration had four main principles: natural rights such as personal liberty, equality with others, freedom to possess property and to resist oppression; the duty of the community as a whole to defend its rights as expressed in a Constitution; laws expressing the general will, placed in the hands of a recognized government, including the power to raise an army and impose taxes; measures to prevent the abuse of power against individuals. As J. M. Thompson has remarked, 'The general colour of the Declaration is that of middle-class individualism.'[1]

Having approved of the events which started the insurrection, Chénier went on to deplore the way in which everyone had become a 'politician', and he stressed that the kind of energy required for destroying one régime is not the kind required for setting up a new one: 'un si grand nombre de pieds retarde la marche; un si grand nombre de bras retarde l'action.' He objected particularly to the continued eruption of the masses, of 'cette dernière classe du peuple, qui, ne connaissant rien, n'ayant rien, ne prenant intérêt à rien, ne sait que se vendre à qui veut

[1] J. M. Thompson, *The French Revolution*, Oxford, Blackwell, 1944 (2nd ed.), p. 89.

le payer'. According to him 'la chose publique est dans un véritable danger': he then went on to seek out its real enemies.

The first enemies he named were the 'princes étrangers que notre révolution a pu blesser', and he named particularly Austria and England. At this point we are able to add a small contribution. In the printed text there are only a few words about England, as follows: 'ainsi ils dirigent nos inquiétudes, tantôt vers les Autrichiens . . . tantôt vers les Anglais, et cette nation, dont on parle tant à Paris, quoiqu'on l'y connaisse si mal, est en effet plus redoutable'.[1] But in the manuscript of the 'Avis' there is a longer statement about England, as follows:

D'autres appréhendent les Anglais; et l'avidité hardie et entreprenante de cette nation dont on parle tant à Paris et qu'on connaît si peu; le pouvoir qu'elle a de nous nuire avec ses immenses flottes, et le désir qu'elle en a toujours eu, sa haine éternelle contre nous, son infatigable ambition, la rendent en effet plus redoutable; quoiqu'une guerre déclarée ne lui soit pas nécessaire pour nous faire de grandes plaies dans cet instant.[2]

Chénier was absolutely right: there was little or no realization in France that Britain was then at the height of her power, and that at one stroke it would be possible to cut France off from her overseas possessions and world trade. Why, then, did Chénier not print these lines in his pamphlet? The reason is probably because he was still, technically, secretary to the Ambassador, and that he could not write in this way about Britain if he had any intention of returning to London. The manuscript also contains a much more forthright statement about the nature of his pamphlet than anything he printed in it; it continues: 'Plusieurs citent d'autres puissances encore. Mais quelques-uns ferment leurs yeux sur les autres nations, ne voyant d'autres ennemis que des Français même. Je suis de cet avis; et je pense que nos plus dangereux ennemis sont au milieu de nous.' This was a very bold statement to make, at a time when it was generally thought that the only enemies of France were the 'émigrés'.

In any case, there we have a plain statement of Chénier's intentions. He went on to study the question of the emigrant nobles, and refused to believe that they were a real source of danger, being for the most part idle and pusillanimous. All they really wanted was to return to France and settle down:

Qui peut les croire assez stupides pour préférer à la douceur de venir rétablir leur fortune, améliorer ce qui leur reste de biens, et achever de vivre

---

[1] D22, p. 202.   [2] BN, NAF 6852, folios 79–87.

PLATE 4

Chénier's last manuscript. *Coll. B.N.*
(actual size)

tranquillement avec leurs amis et leur famille sur le sol qui les a vus naître, l'ennui d'errer de contrée en contrée, pauvres, ne tenant à rien, *sans parents, sans amis*, seuls en butte à la fatigante curiosité ou à la pitié humiliante, ou même quelquefois à l'insulte et au mépris?

Chénier had seen the first wave of emigrants in London, and maybe he was right in his estimation of most of them. However, we can read into this passage the memory of his own exile—even to the echo of his poem 'Sans parents, sans amis, et sans concitoyens' which he had written by the Thames. He thought, in any case, that steps should be taken to make it possible for the emigrants to return unscathed. What was keeping them away was the collapse of law and order in France: he referred with distaste to the searches, spying, and opening of private letters which were a denial of personal freedom; that is to say, the violation of the first item in the Declaration.

Chénier's call to order involved a fairly close description of 'l'expérience d'une année', the year that had elapsed since the calling of the States General. He again attacked that section of 'the people' which was taking the law into its own hands, plundering and lynching: all he could see around him was a year of greed, tyranny, and contempt for liberty. Then he attacked certain writers whom he described as cunning knaves ('scélérats habiles'), whom he denounced as public enemies, preaching revolt and sedition at a time when calm and national unity were required. If the whole of the 'Avis' is full of references to journalists, demagogues, and scribblers (described also as 'bêtes féroces') it is because Chénier had, perhaps, an exaggerated idea of the part writers were playing, actually saying, 'Tout ce qui s'est fait de bien et de mal dans cette révolution est dû à des écrits: ce sera donc là peut-être aussi que nous trouverons la source des maux qui nous menacent.' But he went on to show, very cogently, how those who were working hardest for the national welfare, such as Bailly, La Fayette, Sieyès, and Condorcet, all of whom he named, were being denounced as traitors at a time when they were creating a new order. Their enemies 'hate the ancien régime, not because it was bad but because it was a régime'.

Chénier was right in pointing out that the National Assembly was the only legitimate power in France, and that the dispossession of the propertied classes and the idleness of the rest, together with the impossibility of raising public funds, were long-term dangers. But only at one moment, when he saw events in the light of history, do we begin to feel his powers as an orator:

Car, il ne faut point le perdre de vue, la France n'est point dans ce moment chargée de ses seuls intérêts: la cause de l'Europe entière est déposée dans ses mains. La révolution qui s'achève parmi nous est, pour ainsi dire, grosse des destinées du monde. Les nations qui nous environnent ont l'œil fixé sur nous et attendent l'événement de nos combats intérieurs avec une impatience intéressée et une curieuse inquiétude; et l'on peut dire que la race humaine est maintenant occupée à faire sur nos têtes une grande expérience. Si nous réussissons, le sort de l'Europe est changé: les hommes rentrent dans leurs droits; les peuples rentrent dans leur souveraineté usurpée; les rois, frappés du succès de nos travaux et séduits par l'exemple du roi des Français, transigeront peut-être avec les nations qu'ils sont appelés à gouverner; et peut-être, bien instruits par nous, des peuples plus heureux que nous parviendront à une constitution équitable et libre, sans passer par les troubles et les malheurs qui nous auront conduits à ce premier de tous les biens. Alors la liberté s'étend et se propage dans tous les sens, et le nom de la France est à jamais béni sur la terre.

Here Chénier was very close, in his noble diction, to what could have become the truth, and it is not surprising that Burke and others who read his article set their faces even more determinedly against events in France.

After insisting once more on the need for property and taxation, Chénier stressed the need for discipline in the army. He referred to the Swiss regiment (de Châteauvieux) which had turned on its officers and opposed the national guard, recalling the oath of the Fête de la Fédération in which the army had sworn obedience to the law, the nation, and the king. Chénier's stand against the Swiss culprits was to have repercussions for him four years later, when it became one of the charges against him before his execution. He then drew up a list of twelve principles of 'public weal' which are closely related to the seventeen points of the Declaration: he gave particular attention to freedom of thought and opinion. Then, after various savage thrusts at the trouble-makers—famished monsters as he called them—though without naming any of them, not even Marat, whom he detested—he summed up his case by saying, 'Il n'est point de bonheur, de bien-être, de contentement sur la terre sans l'amour de l'ordre et de la justice, sans l'obéissance aux lois, sans le respect pour les propriétés et pour tous les droits d'autrui.'

Who, then, were these trouble-makers whom Chénier claimed to be unmasking? One of them was Marat; then there was Hébert of *Le Père Duchêne*, and Camille Desmoulins who wrote in *Les Révolutions de Paris*, in defence of mob law, 'Lorsque vous immoliez les de Launay, les Flesselles, les Beaussets, les Voisin, vous usiez du droit de légitime défense, vous sauviez l'État.' Another paper hinted at was Fréron's *L'Orateur du Peuple*. But although Chénier's article was widely read, quoted from, and reproduced, only one journalist replied. This was Camille Desmoulins, who wrote in September 1790, 'Je me hâte de dénoncer ce n° 13; et qu'on ne me dise pas que c'est l'ouvrage de je ne sais quel André Chénier qui n'est pas le Chénier de *Charles IX*, et dont les opinions ne sont pas celles de la *Société*.'[1] Chénier, in a reply to Desmoulins which he did not publish, was content to remark that Desmoulins had publicly described himself as 'procureur-général de la lanterne', that is to say the public prosecutor of lynch law.[2]

If we have given so much attention to the 'Avis au peuple français sur ses véritables ennemis', though it was not his most important political work, it is because of its significance in Chénier's own life as well as in the political context of the time. It shows something of the reluctance with which he began to commit himself, and his desire to stand half-way between the extreme factions of right and left. It shows his capacity for powerful writing, both in the thorough and dignified handling of a case at its highest level, and in his capacity for shrewd and merciless thrusts at those whom he despised. It shows, also, a sound grasp of political principles, but without any indication of how they might be put into practice—here he is typical of his generation, who gave more attention to drawing up declarations than to practical measures. It shows, also, how at his very first blow he had become the natural enemy of the Jacobins. In spite of its fault of long-windedness, which came of a desire to be thorough, it was a prophetic work and has since been described as such by Michon in his history of the Feuillants:

C'est déjà l'essentiel du programme feuillant et, presque mot par mot, l'anathème que lancera Barnave du haut de la Tribune de l'Assemblée contre les libellistes en août 1791. Cet appel de Chénier est le premier cri de ralliement du conservatisme bourgeois et tout un plan de résistance sociale esquissé un an après les premières journées de la Révolution.[3]

Elsewhere, Michon points out that Chénier was the first to see the significance of the class struggle which was to crystallize only in the following year: 'Il s'agissait bien d'une lutte des classes, déjà signalée en 1790 par Chénier, qui se posait en 1791 dans toute son ampleur.'[4] One of the immediate consequences of the 'Avis' was that the poet received a gold medal from the King of Poland, who ordered the article to be

---

[1] For full text see E2, pp. 364–5.   [2] Ibid., p. 296.
[3] G. Michon, *Essai sur l'histoire du parti Feuillant*, 1924, p. 81.
[4] Ibid., pp. 222–3.

translated into Polish. The king wrote to Mazzei, his representative in France, 'Le livre de M. de Chénier m'a paru si modéré, si sage, si propre à calmer l'effervescence, et si applicable même à d'autres pays, que je le fais traduire. J'ai pensé que la médaille ci-jointe serait une marque convenable du cas que je fais de cette production et de l'opinion que j'ai de l'auteur.' However, the King of Poland was rather lavish with his medals: he sent one to Chénier's enemy, Barère, and another to Burke for his *Reflections on the French Revolution*. Chénier replied in a dignified letter in October 1790, in which he congratulated the monarch on his enlightened government.[1]

It was more important that his article appeared at a time when the editor of the *Journal*, Condorcet, was already beginning to fall out with the most influential members of the Society. Though Condorcet had printed in number 10 (7 August 1790) an article 'Aux amis de la Liberté, sur les moyens d'en assurer la durée', in which, like Chénier, he had insisted above all on obedience to the law, whatever it might be, he had destroyed its whole meaning by saying that the law should be obeyed 'sans professer à son égard un enthousiasme stupide' and 'sans superstition politique'. Whatever Condorcet's distinction as a philosopher, he had this habit of betting on all horses at once—for already he was a republican at heart, while ostensibly supporting constitutional monarchy—which in the end was to drive him to suicide in order to escape execution. Now such terms were unlikely to please either the extreme right or the moderate members of the Society, much less Chénier himself. Whether he wished it or not, Chénier's article appeared to come as a rebuke to Condorcet in this respect. But it would be going too far to suggest, as some critics have done, that Chénier's article was the cause of Condorcet's removal from his position as editor. He was already moving towards republicanism, while at the same time the *Journal* was running out of funds. None the less, Chénier's article must have made it clear how far Condorcet's views were from those of the Society he was supposed to represent.[2]

Another seven months were to elapse before Chénier returned to the fray, with a bitter attack on the Jacobins which was one of the turning-points of party history. In the meantime he was sincerely anxious to keep out of politics, partly because his health was not good, and perhaps also because he had not yet reached a definite decision concerning his post in London. The Ambassador was in failing health, and perhaps had no real need of his secretary at this time. Chénier

[1] See E2, p. 352.   [2] H. Delsaux, *Condorcet journaliste*, 1931, pp. 37–43.

spent this period working on his *Essai* and perhaps on his *Bucoliques*, but one of his occupations was the writing of a long political poem, an ode on *Le Serment du Jeu de Paume*. In June 1790 the Jacobins held a banquet, during which it was proposed that a subscription be raised to enable Chénier's friend, Louis David, to commemorate the Tennis-Court Oath by painting an enormous picture of the scene, in which all the deputies present on that historic occasion should be portrayed.

Thus the first poem that Chénier printed in his lifetime—and there were only two—was this little brochure containing *Le Jeu de Paume*, dedicated 'A Louis David, Peintre' and published 'Chez Bleuet, Libraire, rue Dauphine, de l'Imprimerie de Didot fils aîné'. Even the choice of bookseller is significant, for Bleuet was one of the centres of right-wing propaganda. It is a long poem of twenty-four pages, which no editor has printed exactly as it ought to be: for instance, none of the dozens of capital letters which figure in most editions—Poésie, Dieux, Égalité, Sénat, &c.—is to be seen in the original edition. We have a pleasant feeling, at this stage of Chénier's career, that what we might call the Chénier circle was still intact. He had not yet fallen out with his brother Marie-Joseph, or with David and Le Brun. As late as 1792, when Chénier was no longer on speaking terms with the painter, he wrote in an article on historical painting that David's *Jeu de Paume* was 'une des plus belles compositions qu'aient enfantées les arts modernes, dans laquelle une multitude de figures, animées du même sentiment, concourent à une même action, sans confusion et sans monotonie'. As for Le Brun, Chénier wrote to him on the 2nd of March 1791, sending him a copy of his poem with the words:

L'auteur de ce poème, en l'envoyant à M. Le Brun, n'est pas sans inquiétude pour son amour-propre. Il n'est pas assez sûr de lui-même pour se présenter le front levé devant un juge aussi éclairé, et qui a certes acquis le droit d'être difficile. Il espère cependant qu'il lira cet ouvrage avec quelque bienveillance. M. Le Brun y pourra remarquer, du moins, le désir de bien faire et de se rapprocher un peu de cette belle poésie grecque, que l'auteur a cherché à imiter même dans la forme des strophes. Il voudrait bien n'être pas resté entièrement au-dessous de ce noble genre lyrique, que M. Le Brun a fait revivre dans toute sa grandeur et sa majesté. Il n'oublie pas de compter, parmi les études qui lui ont été les plus utiles pour développer en lui le peu d'instinct poétique que la nature a pu lui donner, la lecture souvent répétée des odes et des autres sublimes poésies que M. Le Brun lui a communiquées autrefois, et dont le recueil, glorieux pour notre langue et pour notre siècle, est trop longtemps envié aux regards du public. Il le prie d'agréer ses très sincères compliments.

Although Chénier expressed gratitude and admiration, it is odd that
this letter should be written so stiffly and in the third person: it suggests
that although polite relations were maintained between the two poets
they were no longer the close friends they had been in the past. But
Le Brun, at a time when their political views had become diametri-
cally opposed, repaid the compliment most handsomely; for in the
following year he printed in the *Almanach des Muses*, for all to see,
the *Epistle* which he had written for André ten years earlier, in which
he had called him a genius.[1]

Few of Chénier's poems have been so consistently misunderstood
as this long ode. Admittedly, it has the disadvantage of being in the
so-called Pindaric style, brought into fashion by Le Brun. It has other
enormous defects: it is written in an unwieldy stanza of nineteen lines,
and there are too many—twenty-two—of them. Not only is the stanza
too long, but the poet has further complicated matters by occasionally
running over the meaning from one stanza to the next, resulting in
involved patterns of syntax and elephantine sentences.

The ode falls into two main parts. In the first, Chénier describes
enthusiastically the circumstances of the Tennis-Court oath and the
fall of the Bastille. The second half of the poem is a warning to 'the
people' against the abuse of power, as well as a warning to foreign
powers to take heed of the movement of liberty starting in France. Not
surprisingly, he begins by restating his theory that art can flourish only
in a free country and among free men:

> Reprends ta robe d'or, ceins ton riche bandeau,
> Jeune et divine poésie:
> Quoique ces temps d'orage éclipsent ton flambeau,
> Aux lèvres de David, roi du savant pinceau,
> Porte la coupe d'ambroisie.
> La patrie, à son art indiquant nos beaux jours
> A confirmé mes antiques discours:

[1] On some aspects of the relations between A.C. and Le Brun see my F87. That Le Brun
retained his affection for the younger poet is shown in an unpublished fragment of
an ode which he wrote in Chénier's honour after his death (BN, NAF 4182.18.29):
> Noble enfant de Byzance, espoir du docte empire,
> Chénier! toi qu'un Tyran précipite au tombeau,
> Jeune ami, ne crains pas que ta mémoire expire!
> Dans mes vers, dans mon cœur, survis à ton bourreau.
> 'Des Lois et non du Sang', dit ton généreux frère
> Qui défendait ta vie au péril de ses jours;
> Mais il fallait du sang à ces fils de Mégère,
> Et le Cygne expiré fut en proie aux vautours . . .

Quand je lui répétais que la liberté mâle
De l'art est le génie heureux;
Que nul talent n'est fils de la faveur royale;
Qu'un pays libre est leur terre natale.
Là, sous un soleil généreux,
Ces arts, fleurs de la vie, et délices du monde,
Forts, à leur croissance livrés,
Atteignent leur grandeur féconde.
La palette offre l'âme aux regards enivrés.
Les antres de Paros de dieux peuplent la terre.
L'airain coule et respire. En portiques sacrés
S'élancent le marbre et la pierre.

Then, after a rapid survey of David's work, including his *Socrate*, a reference to his painting of the oath of the Horaces serves as a neat introduction to the theme of the tennis-court oath. The meeting of the three Estates is described with proper dignity, but it is not surprising that critics have seized on Chénier's periphrases, which in those days were regarded as necessary to the 'noble style', in order to condemn the poem as a whole. For instance he described the tennis-court and the game played there in terms which are now laughable:

Au loin fut un ample manoir
Où le réseau noueux en élastique égide,
Arme d'un bras souple et nerveux,
Repoussant la balle rapide
Exerçait la jeunesse en de robustes jeux.

But such periphrases are few in the poem, which in any case has to be judged as a whole and not only for its weaknesses. That softness is quickly retrieved by an energetic description of the fall of the Bastille, an episode which overflows from strophe XI to the following one:

Déraciné dans ses entrailles,
L'enfer de la Bastille à tous les vents jeté
Vole, débris infâme, et cendre inanimée;
Et de ces grands tombeaux, la belle liberté
Altière, étincelante, armée,

Sort. Comme un triple foudre éclate au haut des cieux,
Trois couleurs dans sa main agile
Flottent en long drapeau. Son cri victorieux
Tonne. A sa voix, qui sait, comme la voix des dieux,
En homme transformer l'argile,

La terre tressaillit. Elle quitte son deuil.
Le genre humain d'espérance et d'orgueil
Sourit. . . .

We tend to forget that the Revolution produced a special kind of ephemeral poetry, a public poetry which was destined for formal declamation at official ceremonies. If we look at another specimen of this kind of verse, for instance Marie-Joseph Chénier's ode on the death of Mirabeau, we find such nonsense as this:

Beaux-arts qu'inventa le génie,
Unissez vos divins efforts;
Lugubre et touchante Harmonie,
Fais-nous entendre tes accords.
Marbre, obéis à Praxitèle . . ., etc.

It is no exaggeration to say that in spite of its faults André Chénier's *Jeu de Paume* is the only public ode of that period (apart, of course, from such songs as *La Marseillaise* and the *Chant du Départ*, which are in a different category) that is even worth looking at. Though this ode is the kind of composition in which we are no longer interested— I have called it elsewhere 'the last masterpiece of baroque rhetoric, ridiculously sublime'—it could have been declaimed with good effect, not by one voice but by a chorus of voices. The short specimen given above shows the rhetoric at its best, with all the emphasis laid on a series of verbs. It is at least alive. The excessive dislocation of the line is groping towards free verse. The immense variety in the rhythm-groups of the poem overcomes the oppressive length of the stanza. It has other qualities of organization. We have to note with what art a single verb—*descendre*—serves as a turning-point or hinge in the argument of the poem. The first half praised the energy and libera-tion of the people, but the second was a warning call to order. The change, falling on the verb *descendre*, is prepared for by a consummate orator, in a series of short, sharp sentences:

Vous avez tout dompté. Nul joug ne vous arrête.
Tout obstacle est mort sous vos coups.
Vous voilà montés sur le faîte.
Soyez prompts à fléchir sous vos devoirs jaloux.
Bienfaiteurs, il vous reste un grand compte à nous rendre.
Il vous reste à borner et les autres et vous:
Il vous reste à savoir descendre.

Here Chénier is far from Pindar, far from Le Brun. Nor could Voltaire or any eighteenth-century poet have inspired such a passage, whose strength comes of an absolute plainness of speech. We have to look back, oddly enough, to La Fontaine for such persuasive writing, such naturalness and logic in the placing of pauses, the preparation for that word *descendre* which it took a bold and courageous man to pronounce in 1791. While we do not look to poetry for close political reasoning (though we accept it, for instance, in some of Shakespeare's plays), it is still possible to admire the organization of much of the second part of this ode; for instance stanza xv:

> Vos cœurs sont citoyens. Je le veux. Toutefois
> Vous pouvez tout. Vous êtes hommes.
> Hommes, d'un homme libre écoutez donc la voix.
> Ne craignez plus que vous. Magistrats, peuples, rois,
> Citoyens, tant que nous sommes,
> Tout mortel dans son cœur cache, même à ses yeux,
> L'ambition, serpent insidieux,
> Arbre impur, que déguise une brillante écorce.
> L'empire, l'absolu pouvoir
> Ont, pour la vertu même, une mielleuse amorce;
> Trop de désirs naissent de trop de force.
> Qui peut tout, pourra trop vouloir.
> Il pourra négliger, sûr du commun suffrage,
> Et l'équitable humanité
> Et la décence au doux langage.
> L'obstacle nous fait grands. Par l'obstacle excité
> L'homme, heureux à poursuivre une pénible gloire,
> Va se perdre à l'écueil de sa prospérité,
> Vaincu par sa propre victoire.

This has much of the moral tone of La Fontaine, as well as his manner, containing every cunning trick of oratory: the thrice-repeated word *hommes* at the beginning; the overflow of the list (*magistrats*, &c.); the clever and successful mixed metaphor of the snake and the tree, and the numerous points at which the writing becomes epigrammatic. The whole movement has beneath it the qualities of good prose, but if political reasoning is to be versified (and here Chénier is versifying a paragraph of his 'Avis au Peuple français'), then it is hard to imagine a livelier way of doing it.

Substantially, the second half of the ode is a repetition of the warnings that Chénier had given in his 'Avis'. He appealed to the masses not to 'venger la raison par des crimes' and attacked the demagogues as 'orateurs bourreaux'. From a personal point of view stanzas XXI and XXII are interesting because they show (as already stanza XI suggested in describing the nobility as 'ces tyrans, valets sous le tyran suprême') that Chénier was still far from being a reactionary or a royalist. Now he threatened the remaining kings in Europe, those 'rois, colosses d'orgueil', with a vast, uncontrollable wave of liberty that would submerge them all if they did not take heed of events in France. Chénier, then, was still in an independent and anti-royalist position, though he was prepared to accept constitutional monarchy.

It is not to be pretended that the *Jeu de Paume* is a satisfactory work. For the first time, Chénier was consciously writing for publication, and this weighs the poem down with concessions to contemporary taste which we do not find so often in his other works. So far as we know, until then he had never written in any form but alexandrine couplets, yet now he set himself the problem of handling a nineteen-line stanza with variations on lines of eight, ten, and twelve 'feet' and highly complicated rhyme-schemes. All this had to be reconciled with a scrupulously careful statement of political doctrine. Obviously, Chénier set himself too many problems to be solved at once. Without making excessive claims for it, the poem is less bad than might be expected. Its subject-matter is certainly interesting enough to hold our attention, while no one interested in Chénier's life or politics can ignore it. It was Chénier's first step towards the new forms of odes and *Ïambes* that he was to chose for his expression a year later, and is thus a turning-point in his development as a poet. Faguet went much too far in condemning it outright, saying, '*Le Jeu de Paume* n'appartient pas à la troisième manière d'André Chénier, ni à aucune de ses manières.'[1] In the first place it is quite typical of Chénier's habit, already formed in *Hermès*, *L'Amérique*, and *Susanne*, of developing involved and tedious arguments in verse. Only the form was different. And there are certain moments in the *Jeu de Paume* which already announce the *Ïambes*—the occasional tendency to epigram, as well as the juxtaposition of alexandrine and octosyllabic, sometimes so successful that Chénier must have promised himself to take that combination further. The ode is fundamentally a didactic poem, linking the early didactic work to the *Ïambes* and other odes. It goes far beyond the conventional manner of the period in its syncopation, while taking us back to the movement of La Fontaine, though without its grace.

[1] G21, p. 12.

Chénier's second political article was the 'Réflexions sur l'esprit de parti', the manuscript of which is dated 3 mars 1791 and which appeared early in April of that year. In it there is a stiffening of his attitude towards both Right and Left. Beginning with a scornful slur on 'le patriotisme égaré de Mesdames de la Halle'—the stallkeepers and prostitutes of that quarter who were constantly jostling the Left into foolish and dangerous action—he admitted at first that 'l'établissement des clubs et de ces assemblées où l'on discute bien ou mal des principes de l'art social est très utile à la liberté'. But he regarded them as useful only so long as they were numerous, so long as they were easy of access and had a large membership. But by the time he was writing, the clubs and societies of the kind he was describing, in which men of all parties could meet together for discussion, were becoming increasingly sectarian, so that impartial debate was no longer possible in them.

He then passed on to denounce public informers and spies who came to stir up trouble in the clubs, supported by an idle populace itching to take the law into their own hands, for they confused violence with progress: 'la vraie populace, c'est-à-dire cette partie du peuple qui n'a ni propriété ni domicile, ni industrie, devient l'arme de qui veut s'en servir'. Here he was referring to the proletariat agitators who were being encouraged by the Jacobins with a view to exerting pressure on the Assembly.

Chénier's position looked more reactionary than it really was, because he proceeded to defend the king's aunts, Adélaïde and Victoire, who had set off for Rome on the 20th of February, where they became a centre of intrigue. He also condemned the law against the emigrants which he described as 'imprudente et vexatoire' and which had actually been rejected by the Assembly. His own view—sound enough in theory, but wrong in the context of the time—was that 'all good laws are laws against emigration', for 'if laws are just they will encourage all citizens to stay at home'.

If Chénier was wrong in both these cases—for the departure of the aunts involved the position of the royal family as a whole, while his defence of the emigrants underestimated the dangers from abroad— yet his liberalism restored the balance. After praising the *Déclaration des droits de l'homme* which remained always the sheet-anchor of his political theory, he condemned the royalist sections of the armed forces, 'armés pour le soutien du trône, qui certes n'a pas besoin d'eux, impudents et misérables parasites'. He rebuked those who objected to the limitation of the royal prerogative and who were distressed at seeing 'un prince réduit à être le premier citoyen d'une nation libre'—that is to say the 'old gang' intent on keeping as much of their old privileges as they could. Among these he condemned the higher clergy. While being careful to recognize the existence of good priests he denounced 'des prélats perdus de luxe et de dettes... des hommes sans vertu comme sans talent' who had disgraced the Church before the Revolution. He condemned the 'fureurs et extravagances des contre-révolution-naires'. His pamphlet ended with two important statements. One was an attack on Calonne's reactionary 'État de la France présent et à venir' which had recently been published in London, and the other was a scornful reply to Burke's *Reflections on the French Revolution.*

Chénier remarked, rightly, that Burke had done what he could to curb the authority of the Crown in England, yet would not tolerate the same policy abroad. He attacked also his snobbery and the treacherous argument by which he denied equality of rights by saying that such equality exists only when it is voted in law. Chénier in his impatience went to the extent of damning Burke's book as 'a grotesque mixture of clownish eccentricities and pedantic rubbish' which would be 'amusingly ridiculous were it not that his vulgar grossness and atrocious slanders provoke only nausea and indignation'.

It has to be admitted that Chénier's outburst against Burke, whom he described as barbarous in his callous treatment of George III during his mental illness, and as a 'rhéteur sans goût, sans jugement, sans aucune idée de critique', was not an entirely disinterested judgement. At the end of the article he confessed that his brother Marie-Joseph had been insulted by Burke's 'insolent imbecility'. In an interesting personal aside, Chénier added that during his 'three years in England' he had already been struck by Burke's 'intempérance désordonnée' and had heard Burke's friends trying to excuse his 'precocious senility'. Chénier was inexact in describing his stay in England. He went there in December 1787 and returned finally to France in the summer of 1790. As he had five months' leave in 1789 this reduces his exile to about two years. The evidence given by the poet himself when he was interrogated after his arrest in 1794 is conclusive on this point:

— A lui demandé quel son ses moyent de subsister.
— A lui repondu que depuis 1790 qu'il vie de que lui fait son père. [*sic*]

Chénier's article on 'L'esprit de parti' not only is a very important one-man survey of the political situation at that moment, but it really goes much further than appears on the surface. It was a moment when the Société des amis de la Constitution, the very matrix of all the most important revolutionary parties, was beginning to feel that strain which led to the break-off of the Feuillants two or three months later. Barnave, Adrien Duport, and the brothers Lameth, all known to Chénier, were already realizing that these private clubs should not try to act as undisciplined pressure-groups on the work of the Assembly. Just as Chénier had prophetically outlined the later programme and policy of the Feuillant party before it came into existence, in his 'Avis', so, in his second article, he was the first man to understand that the Société des amis de la Constitution had become too big, too powerful, and too divided to be useful. He sensed the great upheaval in the largest of all the clubs, that was now being prepared in silence. Is it possible that he had some inside knowledge of what was going on, and that he was not speaking only for himself?

It is thought to be in the same month, April 1791, that Chénier wrote one of his most admirable prose works, 'Les Autels de la Peur', a work of such power and modernity that it had the honour of being circulated by the Resistance during the 1939–45 war. For some reason he did not print it, but had he done so it would have brought him instant fame. I do not propose to analyse this work, which is a kind of prose poem in which he showed himself a master of irony, as well as, for once, defining that hidden cowardice which underlies so many of the most atrocious acts of the Revolution. It begins:

Des peuples anciens avaient élevé des temples et des autels à la Peur. Nous ne les avons pas encore précisément imités dans Paris, mais comme, de tous temps, les hommes profondément religieux ont observé que le cœur est le véritable autel où la Divinité se plaît d'être honorée, et que l'adoration interne vaut mieux mille fois plus que toutes les pompes d'un culte magnifique confié à un petit nombre de mains, et circonscrit dans certains lieux par une consécration expresse, nous pouvons dire que jamais la Peur n'eut plus de véritables autels qu'elle n'en a dans Paris; que jamais elle ne fut honorée d'un culte plus universel; que cette ville entière est son temple; que tous les gens de bien sont devenus ses pontifes, en lui faisant journellement le sacrifice de leur pensée et de leur conscience.

Describing some of the incidents of mob-rule which were then disturbing Paris, but against which nobody had the courage to protest, he then gave a particular example, trivial in itself but a symptom of worse to come:

Il y a quelques jours, une société de citoyens se rassemble pour se livrer, dans l'enceinte d'une maison privée, à des divertissements qui ne troublent en rien l'ordre public: une active et inquiète oisiveté attroupe autour de la porte de ce domicile une foule de curieux sans intentions, où se mêle, suivant l'usage, bon nombre de ces brouillons qui sont partout, à épier les occasions de mal faire. On crie, on menace d'enfoncer les portes; on menace de tuer. . . .

With his admirable devotion to Chénier's work, Becq de Fouquières followed up this incident and discovered that it was an event in which Madame de Bonneuil (Camille) was involved.[1] In an article in the *Journal général de France*, Thursday, 21 April 1791, is the account of how a musical recital was held in the hôtel d'Esclignac, which was let out for such occasions, in the rue du Faubourg Saint-Honoré. The tickets were twelve francs each and about 150 people were present. The idlers outside thought or were led by someone to think that a royalist meeting was in progress, and brought a 'prétendu commissaire' to investigate. All the names of those at the concert were taken, after which the mob ransacked the house from top to bottom, also over-turning a cart of hay in the courtyard to see whether it contained hidden arms: 'Enfin les dames et les hommes ont été vivement insultés: on les a retenus jusqu'à onze heures et demie du soir, et on les a laissés passer, après avoir pris leurs noms, au milieu d'une foule considérable.'[2]

This minor but symptomatic event had echoes elsewhere in the press. A brochure entitled 'Complot manqué d'aristocrates réunis' was published, while there were articles in *Le Journal du soir* (no. 100) and *Le Courrier français* (20 April), both of which mention Madame de Bonneuil. The *Journal des Lois* (19 April) gives fuller information:

On a fait la motion de conduire à la porte Saint-Honoré les voitures qui étaient à celles de l'hôtel, et de forcer les maîtres d'aller à pied, au milieu du peuple, chercher eux-mêmes leurs voitures. Cette motion a été arrêtée à l'unanimité, et les amateurs de musique, ou, si l'on veut, les contre-révolution-naires, ont été obligés de quitter la place et de traverser dans presque toute sa longueur la très grande rue du Faubourg Saint-Honoré au milieu des huées du peuple qui a ri beaucoup aux dépens de ces messieurs, qui étaient loin d'être aussi gais.

An abbé who protested at this treatment was molested by the crowd, 'on lui pressa un peu les côtes'; but there was no mention of other violence, though no doubt the 'counter-revolutionaries' were pelted with mud. Culture was suspect.

[1] E2, p. 72.   [2] Ibid.

Chénier's indignation at this occurrence, in which ordinary civil liberties were interfered with, resulted in this work, 'Les Autels de la Peur', which the bibliophile Jacob stated (in his edition of 1840) had been published at the time: 'Ce morceau, publié dans l'édition de 1819, avait paru dans un journal du temps, que nous n'avons pas su découvrir.' Oddly enough, Jacob was wrong in stating that 'Les Autels de la Peur' had appeared in the 1819 edition, while, as yet, it has not been traced in the newspapers published in 1791. The article ended with a protest which was to recur in the *Ïambes* and the *Ode à Charlotte Corday* and which reminds us of the eloquence of his enemy Marat:

Citoyens honnêtes et timides, les méchants veillent, et vous dormez. Les méchants sont unis et vous ne vous connaissez pas. Les méchants ont le courage de l'envie, le courage de la haine; et les bons n'ont que l'innocence et n'ont pas le courage de la vertu.

J'ai indiqué un bien petit nombre des sacrifices que chaque jour reçoit la *Peur*; je lui en ai peut-être fait plus d'un moi-même; je ne lui ferai pas celui de dissimuler le nom de l'auteur qui vient de chanter cet hymne à sa louange.

It is quite possible that, by another twist of irony, Chénier was unable to find a journal with sufficient courage to print this diatribe against Fear.

10

CHÉNIER AND THE FEUILLANTS

IT is obvious that a man who felt so strongly about public events could not remain long uncommitted, even though his deepest desire was to give his time to study and poetry. Thus it is not surprising that in June 1791 Chénier took another step into the political arena by having himself admitted to the polling list and to eligibility as a deputy. This was not so easy as it might appear. Owing to his birth in Constantinople and his service with the Foreign Office under the old régime, he was obliged to produce proper evidence of his citizenship. He was now living with his father at 24 rue du Sentier: the house did not belong to his father but to a Monsieur de Presles.[1] Chénier had himself made an elector and perhaps an 'éligible' for the Section de la Fontaine de Montmorency. This document, which is now at Carcassonne, is a 'Certificat pour être admis à l'assemblée primaire, 15 juin 1791, pour procéder aux élections de l'assemblée législative'. It testifies to his identity and is signed by 'Ruffineau Delile, notaire'.[2] At the very least, this eligibility gave Chénier that status as a citizen which enabled him to write and speak with confidence about political questions and at the same time to attend meetings at which candidates were nominated for election. This in itself points to all sorts of social and public activities which would go far towards forming or modifying his political views.

---

[1] This is a complicated matter. G. de Chénier (D7, p. lxiv) affirms that at that time 'Son père, chez qui il demeura toujours, habitait alors une maison rue du Sentier, appartenant à M. de Presle [sic]'. This is borne out by the fact that André gave the address 24 rue du Sentier, between July and October 1791, when enrolled as a Feuillant. However, Mlle Balayé (H1, p. 19) has recently produced a document from the Archives Nationales, showing that Louis Chénier leased a house in the rue de Cléry on 6 Sept. 1790: André gave his address as rue de Cléry in 1794. On the other hand it is true that M. de Presles owned nos. 22–24 rue du Sentier, which had originally been all one house. Hillairet (*Évocation du Vieux Paris*, t. ii, pp. 141–2) points out that the street was successively called rue du Chantier, du Centier, Centière, Sentier. Jeanne Poisson (Mme de Pompadour) lived at nos. 22–24 until her separation from d'Étioles in 1745. Harenc de Presles took over no. 24 (separated from the rest by a low wall) in 1787. According to Hillairet, no. 24 was taken over some time in 1791 by Sophie Michault de Lavalette and Gaspard Liottier: maybe the Chéniers used the house in the interval, or part of it was sub-let to them?   [2] BMC 11815.

It is not at all certain whether at this stage Chénier actually tried to have himself nominated for election to the new 'Assemblée législative'. He was certainly in quite a good position to do so if he wished, for influence was not lacking. Jacob, in his notice on Chénier's life, asserted that he did: 'Interrompant ses études . . . il se mit sur le rang des candidats qui se présentèrent aux élections de 1791; mais il ne put réunir le nombre de voix nécessaires pour être envoyé comme député de Paris, à la nouvelle Assemblée législative.'[1] But there can be no certainty on this question. Charles Labitte, in his article on Marie-Joseph in 1844 (in the *Revue des Deux Mondes*), further developed this view, that Chénier had tried to have himself elected. Gabriel de Chénier, his nephew, stated that 'André se borna à se proposer pour député; il ne fit aucune démarche active pour réussir'.[2] On the other hand his brother Marie-Joseph insinuated that André had tried to be elected but had failed.[3] The most likely possibility is (in view of the fact that no known list of candidates carries André Chénier's name) that the poet went no further than trying to have himself *nominated*: these nominations were frequently made in the clubs (such as the Club de la Sainte-Chapelle, of which he was a member), where stormy meetings were held before the 1791 elections, to discuss the merits of potential candidates.

Meanwhile, Chénier was taking a more direct interest in politics, no longer writing in a general way and from the outside, but as one who was following every detail of the game. On the 1st of June he wrote an open letter to the Abbé Raynal, which appeared in *Le Moniteur* on the 5th. The historian Raynal had been one of the victims of the old régime and was universally respected as such. When he sent an address to the Assembly, everyone was astonished that he now appeared to condemn all the reforms that he had previously advocated. It was rumoured that the letter was forged by Malouet and

[1] E1, p. xiii.

[2] D7, t. i, p. lxiv: 'Quand André se fit inscrire en qualité d'électeur, il se présenta comme *éligible*.'

[3] In a letter to *Le Moniteur* dated 20 mai 1792 Marie-Joseph replied to attacks that had been made on him in the *Journal de Paris*. André had referred to 'ces succès littéraires dont la nature est d'avoir les applaudissements de la multitude', meaning Marie-Joseph's demagogic plays. Marie-Joseph replied that if he had written 'pour un Journal, quelques pamphlets *modérés*, j'aurais trouvé un grand nombre de *prôneurs puissants et actifs*, et peut-être . . . ils m'auraient consolé de n'avoir pu, en 1791, *me glisser* dans la foule des députés de Paris, et siéger à l'Assemblée nationale entre M. Robin-Léonard et M. Thorillon'. Becq de Fouquières (E2, p. xxix) wrongly maintained that Marie-Joseph was referring to himself. It is clear that his words were entirely ironical and that he was implying that André had tried to get into the Assembly 'by the back door' in 1791.

Clermont-Tonnerre, or that they had some hand in it. Chénier's letter was a clear and dignified call for more liberal views, with significant references to the 'Déclaration des droits de l'homme' and Paine's *Common Sense*. Though Chénier's letter to Raynal is not an important work in itself, it is a useful pointer to his ambiguous political position. Raynal's address, whether forged or not, angered the Left factions and delighted the die-hard royalists. Chénier's reply did not suit the die-hards at all. The *Journal général de France* attacked him two days later, as follows:

Et M. Chénier, qui se mêle ainsi de se mesurer avec M. l'abbé Raynal! Oh, c'est bien le coup de l'âne, il faut en convenir; André Chénier répond à ce grand homme, comme M. Robespierre, dans une longue lettre qui ne finit pas. André Chénier dit que l'abbé Raynal a fait amende honorable d'avoir été prêtre: quand André Chénier fera-t-il amende honorable d'avoir voulu être poète?

Although, as is shown by a further attack on him in the same paper a week later, there was some confusion between him and his brother Marie-Joseph—for though his name is given as André he is also described as 'l'auteur de *Charles IX*' (which means that it was Marie-Joseph's claims to being a poet that were in question)—it was certainly his article that was under fire. The fact that his name is coupled with Robespierre's arises from some personal remarks at the end of his letter to Raynal:

Je ne vous ai point parlé un langage de parti: le peu de personnes qui me connaissent savent que je n'ai jamais été attaché à aucun parti, que je n'ai jamais rien fait pour plaire à aucun, que je n'en servirai aveuglément aucun, et qu'un ardent désir du bonheur des hommes est la seule passion que je porte dans les discussions politiques.

This is a rather surprising statement for a man whose membership of the 'Société de 1789' was well known, and who had published works in its journal: however, it shows that Chénier did not regard the Société as a political party but only as a club. As we have seen in the 'Réflexions sur l'Esprit de parti', he had been dealing blows to both Left and Right, so that it is hardly surprising that he was unable to have himself elected. The time had passed when deputies could remain independent—though perhaps he did not yet realize this—and his reluctance to commit himself one way or the other was enough to cut him off from a parliamentary career.

In the following month occurred one of the most important events of the Revolution. This was the splitting of what in 1789 had been known as the Club Breton, and which in February 1790 had changed its name to 'Société des Amis de la Constitution (séant aux Jacobins)'. After heated discussions during June over the re-eligibility of deputies for the new Assembly, this great society split into Jacobins and Feuillants. The position was that the Left, headed by Robespierre, Buzot, and Pétion, opposed the re-election of deputies. Lameth, Duport, and Barnave argued (rightly, in our opinion) that this would destroy all continuity of government between the Constituent and Legislative assemblies. Tension reached its height between the two groups after the King's flight to Varennes and his return to Paris (20–25 June).

This great schism, the forerunner of many others, occurred on the 15th of July 1791. A large number of deputies marched out of the Jacobins and held an emergency meeting in the building on the Terrasse des Feuillants, which was later destroyed by Napoleon. Within two days the 'Club des Feuillants' was founded. Its strength may be judged by the fact that at first it had 264 deputies among its members, quite apart from its general membership. By the following year (10 August 1792) this number had shrunk to fifty-six. The Feuillants received such nicknames as 'Monarchistes', 'Moyennistes', and 'Constitutionnaires'.[1] The first list of Feuillants, drawn up on 16–18 July, contains 365 names,[2] including those of La Fayette, Talleyrand, Sieyès, Barnave, Duport, Chapelier, Lecoulteux, and Duquesnoy. It was Charles de Lacretelle, Chénier's friend, who proposed their famous motto 'La Constitution, toute la Constitution, rien que la Constitution'.[3] If the Feuillants, in their struggle with the Jacobins, finally failed to impose this view, it was because once the Constitution was adopted on the 14th of September 1791 they had no idea that it might evolve, but clung to it as it stood, rather than move with the times. However, they were instrumental in saving the King after Varennes, and without them the Constitution might never have been adopted in its particular form.

We have just mentioned Lacretelle, and it is he who left evidence that Chénier was one of the moving spirits in the Club des Feuillants. Lacretelle as a young man had helped with some of the articles on moral philosophy in the second *Encyclopédie*, and this had brought him into contact with the statesman Malesherbes. He was friendly with Target, Camille Desmoulins, and Barère, of whom he said that he was

[1] See F21.   [2] BN, Lb 40. 3284.   [3] See below, Appendix C.

not fundamentally an evil man but that 'son malheur fut d'avoir été le compagnon de collège et l'ami de Robespierre'.[1] He relates in his memoirs how the approach to the Feuillant meetings was made by entering through the church cloisters, and how members had to go at midnight the day before, to retain seats for the next day, so great was the crush.

In his pages consecrated to the Chénier circle, which were published only fifty years later, in 1842, Lacretelle drew one of the most vivid pictures of Chénier that might be hoped for. One might wonder, impatiently, why so few testimonies of this kind have come down to us. The answer is not far to seek. Of Chénier's intimate friends, the Trudaines were put to death the day after him; de Pange was obliged to hide or destroy many of his private papers, and himself died only two years after the poet. Very little of Le Brun's correspondence has survived. As the poet fell out with David, it is not surprising that the painter did not keep his letters. As for his political and journalistic associates, the intervention of the Consulate and Empire is enough to explain why most of them did not publish memoirs at that time, when most people were anxious to efface or forget the part they had played in the Revolution. Lacretelle, turned historian, had a sufficiently long life to go back over those early years of his career. He began by describing Chénier's participation in the meetings of the Feuillants:

J'avais fait mes premières armes au Club des Feuillants, avec plusieurs des députés; j'assistais souvent à leurs réunions qui n'étaient plus alors que des cercles assez étroits et surveillés par la police jacobine.

This places the events towards the end of 1791, as we shall see, or the beginning of 1792; for Lacretelle was absent from Paris for some five or six months after the founding of the Feuillants. He continues:

C'était prendre rang parmi les conspirateurs que de parler du maintien des lois. Un homme y attira fortement mon attention par la double amorce d'un grand talent et d'un grand caractère: c'était André Chénier. Frère d'un poète dont la muse tragique avait voulu traduire sur la scène les principes de la Révolution, et qui déjà s'engageait trop dans les voies républicaines, il n'avait point voulu sacrifier à l'amitié la plus sincère des principes plus nobles, mieux médités, qui pouvaient conserver ou plutôt rendre à la Révolution un caractère plus digne à la fois de la liberté antique et de la philosophie du XVIIIe siècle.

In his assertion that Chénier refused to sacrifice his principles to his

[1] For this and subsequent references see F57.

friendship, Lacretelle was no doubt referring to the poet's unyielding attitude towards his brother Marie-Joseph as well as towards David.

Lacretelle now gives us an unexpected portrait of Chénier in action:

L'avis le plus énergique et le plus éloquemment exprimé partait toujours de sa bouche. Ses traits fortement prononcés, sa taille athlétique sans être haute, son teint basané, ses yeux ardents fortifiaient, illuminaient sa parole. Né a Constantinople, il communiquait avec les Grecs par sa mère, qui était de cette nation. Leur langue, leur haute littérature lui étaient familières. Frondeur du goût efféminé qui lui paraissait dominer notre poésie devenue froidement coquette, il voulait la ramener aux beautés fortes et sévères qu'il avait profondément étudiées dans leur source primitive.

Démosthène n'avait pas été moins que Pindare l'objet de ses études. Le fond de son âme se révélait par sa vive amitié pour les frères Trudaine, modèle de tendresse fraternelle, après l'avoir été de piété fidèle pour un père l'un des plus dignes amis et des collaborateurs les plus distingués de Turgot. Ces trois amis étaient inséparables. Même toit, même table, mêmes goûts, même ardeur pour le bien. 'L'un ne possédait rien qui n'appartînt à l'autre.' André Chénier était riche de la richesse de ses amis, et s'en faisait gloire.

Chacun de nous regrettait que ce talent plein de force et d'éclat, échauffé par une âme intrépide, ne fût pas encore appelé à la tribune. Lui seul eût pu disputer la palme d'éloquence à Vergniaud.

It is clearly established, then, that Chénier spoke at the Feuillants, and that his ability as an orator was more than appreciated: no greater compliment could be paid to him in this respect than the comparison with Vergniaud, who was one of the most brilliant speakers of his generation, described more than once as a French Cicero. One of the leaders of the Girondins, he perished under the guillotine in October 1793. But to return to Lacretelle: he made a suggestion of the utmost importance for any interpretation of Chénier's activities as a journalist:

Cet honorable et malheureux parti [les Feuillants] était très faiblement défendu par la presse périodique . . . *André Chénier s'offrit pour ce genre de combat.*[1] Suard lui ouvrit le *Journal de Paris.* Le poète Roucher, un jeune noble, de Pange, qui joignait un esprit fin à une âme chaude et droite, François Chéron et moi, nous nous associâmes à cette entreprise. Je l'ai dit: c'est un souvenir que j'aime. Le grand succès des articles d'André Chénier rejaillit sur nous, mais d'une manière fatale pour Roucher, qui, deux ans après, accompagna à l'échafaud André Chénier et les deux frères Trudaine. Chacun de nous fut également poursuivi, mais il nous était plus facile de nous perdre dans la foule des proscrits . . . Moins il y avait de chances pour le succès du combat, plus il était honorable de le tenter.

[1] My italics.

If we have given so much place to Lacretelle's testimony, it is because there are some contradictions in Chénier's own account of his position during the period 1791–2, and because his enemies never hesitated to say that he was in the pay of the court, or of Montmorin, for the use of his pen. As late as May 1792 Chénier maintained in his article 'Des manœuvres des Jacobins' that 'Je sais que la plupart des hommes ne sauraient comprendre qu'on ne tienne à aucun parti, à aucune secte, et qu'on ose penser seul'. The 'on', of course, refers to himself. On the 4th of March in the same year he wrote in the *Journal de Paris*:

Mais je veux faire savoir à tous les lecteurs qui ne sont pas aveuglés par leurs passions ou par celles d'autrui, que je n'ai et que je n'eus jamais aucun rapport politique direct ou indirect avec aucun ministère, que je n'en connais particulièrement aucun; que je ne vais à aucun club; que je n'appartiens à aucune Société, à aucune personne, à aucun parti.

Admiration for Chénier cannot prevent us from proving that almost every circumstance in this statement is untrue. The only exception is in the word 'personne', for obviously he was in nobody's clutches. We shall prove shortly (see p. 252) that Chénier had on at least one occasion written to a Minister, and perhaps been received by him. We know already that he had been a member of the 'Société de 1789' which in spite of its protestations was a club indistinguishable from the other revolutionary clubs, and which rapidly turned into a party, bringing most of its members to join the Feuillants. We have just given undeniable evidence from Lacretelle that Chénier went to the Feuillants and was perhaps the club's most outstanding orator. Lacretelle has even added that Chénier's contributions to the *Journal de Paris* were Feuillant propaganda. As it was only in September 1791 that the Jacobins forbade their members to remain in the Feuillants' club, it is clear that Lacretelle was referring to a period later than that, and in view of his own absence from Paris, it is clear that he must be referring to some time after December 1791.

Chénier's biographers have either discreetly avoided this issue, or taken it for granted that Chénier had no political affiliations, or equally for granted that he was in the pay of the Feuillants. G. Walter, while believing that the *Journal de Paris* was never the official organ of the Feuillants, and generously setting aside the idea that Chénier was a hired journalist, does make it clear that the poet's financial sponsor was the elder Trudaine, and that behind Trudaine was Montmorin,

Mme de Beaumont's father, who had large funds at his disposal.[1] The implication is, thus, that it was ultimately Montmorin who paid for the printing of Chénier's 'supplements' in the *Journal de Paris*. If we accept Walter's statement that Lacretelle's testimony was 'le témoignage unique parvenu jusqu'à nous sur cette étape si importante de sa carrière politique', some doubt might remain; but it would leave Chénier in a very ambiguous position. But if Walter is wrong, if there is some other evidence available, the whole problem is changed.

Other evidence does exist that Chénier supported the Feuillants because he was one of them himself. Though Chénier's name does not figure on the first list of Feuillants, it is to be found on the second. This second list, issued with a supplementary detail of new members dated 4 October 1791, must have been drawn up at some time between the first list (18 July) and the 4th of October. It contains, in all, 798 names, among which are not only those of his friends Destutt de Tracy, François de Pange, Montmorin, Ginguené, Joubert, and Lacretelle, but that of 'Chesnier, André, rue du Chantier 24'.[2] Here, then, is a clear proof in support of Lacretelle's statement that Chénier was a Feuillant. If this evidence has been neglected it is because of the peculiar circumstances in which the nominal roll was taken. Those who became members did not sign, but spoke out their names and addresses, many of which were mutilated in the process. Thus Montmorin became *Montmoran*, Lecoulteux became *Lecouteux, Le Couteul*; and Gouy d'Arcy became Gouy *D'Acis. Chesnier* is obviously Chénier, and the rue du Chantier, the rue du Sentier where he was then living.[3] It is interesting to find, also, on this list, the names of the poet Roucher, Boissy d'Anglas (who later wrote an interesting commentary on Chénier), Trudaine, and the husband of Fanny Lecoulteux.[3] It is probable that Chénier became a member before the supplementary list (attached to the second) was drawn up, since the supplement names only those who were Deputies.

The Feuillants admitted only 'citoyens actifs', which means, presumably, only those who paid direct taxes. It is hard to see on what income Chénier was paying taxes, but he might have been admitted on the grounds of having been certified 'éligible'. The result of this clause, of course, was that the Jacobins, who opened their club to all and sundry, were able as early as August 1791 to accuse the Feuillants of excluding 'les pauvres'. A further reason for the final split between Feuillants and Jacobins in September was that the Feuillants are said

[1] F101, p. 207.　　　[2] BN, Lb 40. 805.　　　[3] See note 1 to p. 240 above.

to have drawn up Louis XVI's message to the Assembly, dated 13 September, in which he accepted the new Constitution. But the club was vulnerable for other reasons: it held its meetings on public premises (their hall was next door to the Assembly), from which the Jacobins soon manœuvred to have them expelled, having on their side the Jacobin Mayor of Paris, Pétion. Further, the club insisted on holding its meetings in private (we have seen that seats had to be retained as long as twelve hours before meetings, in order to get in) and the Jacobins were thus able to denounce it as a 'secret society', especially as it refused to publish its minutes. Disturbances were systematically created, resulting in a violent scene on 21 December 1791, after which the Feuillants were forced to make their meetings public. The document 'Grand détail de ce qui s'est passé hier aux Feuillants, au sujet d'une insulte faite aux Citoyens qui assistaient à la Séance de cette Société' describes this 'grand combat dans lequel les Aristocrates ont été chassés et poursuivis à coups de pied et à coup de poing'.[1] This, of course, was another of those fishwives' brawls which the Jacobins were so clever at organizing, and to which Pétion closed his eyes. The document relates how the Citizens, after breaking into the meeting by force, demanded that the proceedings be held in public. The Feuillants, according to this version, then pretended to agree, but continued with mock meetings during which they pretended to hold the very opposite opinions to what were really theirs, while raising funds with which to pay 'tous les espions que soudoyait M. Bailly'. A 'bon citoyen' stood up and demanded the expulsion of Barnave, and this was refused by the chairman (Chénier's friend François Chéron). As the 'bon citoyen' was not a member of the club, and Barnave was one of its founders, the ruling is understandable. The next step was that the 'bons citoyens' smashed up the furniture and attacked the members with 'quelques coups de pied et de poing'.

This, then, is what the only remaining Moderate party was up against at that time, but it did not prevent it from carrying on its struggle for another nine months, during which other parties— Girondins, Hébertistes, and the like—emerged.

In the meantime Chénier had produced several more articles, four of which were printed in Le Moniteur. After his open letter to Raynal came his 'Observations sur l'Acte constitutionnel', written on the 7th and printed in Le Moniteur on the 9th of August. In it he once more defended the 'Déclaration des droits de l'Homme' of 1789, while

[1] See BN, Lb 39.5628.

criticizing the new version of it. At this stage he parted company with Montesquieu, by disapproving of the separation of powers. At the same time he condemned colonialism and suggested that the benefits of the new Constitution should be extended to French overseas possessions—perhaps the most short-sighted article in the Constitution, as he saw, being the stipulation 'Les colonies et possessions françaises dans l'Asie, l'Afrique et l'Amérique ne sont pas comprises dans la présente constitution'.

His next article was a letter to *Le Moniteur* (4 September 1791) 'Sur le choix des Députés à la prochaine législature'. The Paris electoral assembly had been convoked since the 25th of August and was now electing the deputies who were to replace the old Constituent Assembly on the 1st of October. Chénier had little to say on the subject, except to draw a portrait of his ideal deputy—an incorrigible, impartial idealist, governed entirely by Reason. Like his contemporaries, he was looking forward to a House full of gods, not men. He could never accept the realities of party government, or any of those shifts and compromises which make democracy possible. The only thing that distinguishes his article from many others that appeared on the subject at that time was his premonition of war: '. . . supporter peut-être une guerre, et avoir à contenir une grande nation dans ses succès ou à l'encourager contre des revers'—a thought which was far from most people's minds at a time when everyone was passionately engrossed in the elections.

More important was the wise and penetrating article he published on the 19th of October, 'Sur les Dissensions des Prêtres'. It will be recalled that the Civil Constitution of the Clergy had been proclaimed as long before as July 1790. This Civil Constitution was condemned by Rome in March 1791, and one of the causes of the King's flight was the scandal arising from his insistence on confessing only to an orthodox Catholic priest. In the meantime, while many priests accepted their new civil status which, among other things, detached them from Rome and allowed them to marry, trouble was arising all over France because there were now two kinds of clergy. This was causing confusion not only among the priests but among the laity, who were perplexed when it came to the matter of obtaining documents signed by a priest, if not for other reasons. It was François Chéron, chairman of the Feuillants and a friend of Chénier's, who was responsible for offering a Moderate solution to the Assembly in November. The Jacobin, Couthon, had introduced a plan for severe measures against the 'refractory priests' who refused to submit to the civil constitution, early in October. Subsequently (29 November) the Assembly passed a Decree against the refractory priests, which led to the King's making use of his power of veto.

The fact that Chénier produced such an animated and cogent article on this unlikely subject suggests that it might well have been one of the themes on which he spoke at the Feuillants. He so clearly outlined the Feuillant policy on this matter, a month before it was put to the Assembly, that there is little doubt that Chénier's article was the basis of Chéron's case. Chénier put his finger on the paradox whereby, after effectively ousting the clergy from its ancient stronghold, the Civil Constitution had immediately re-created it in another form, equally disastrous. To proscribe 'refractory' priests was, in his view, against all reason and justice, so long as they were not engaged in or convicted of active sedition. He pointed out that dissidence itself is not a crime, and that other citizens were not obliged to take oaths in order to carry on with their work. Priests active against the State should be brought to trial like anyone else, but not massacred out of hand. As usual, Chénier was arguing from the 'Déclaration des droits de l'Homme' which formally recognized the liberty of all sects and religions. Cleverly he argued 'et faut-il laisser dire aux malveillants *qu'en France toutes les religions sont permises, sauf une?*' Neither Jews nor Muslims were molested: only Catholics. His interpretation was that the priests who had taken the civil oath represented one form of new religion— a new one, indeed—while those who refused the oath represented another which had an equal right to be respected. He went on to show that it was not the Assembly's job to try to unite the Churches. His own solution (at a time when, in spite of the Civil Constitution, believers and unbelievers flocked to the refractory clergy for 'tous les actes civils auxquels le ministère ecclésiastique est nécessaire') would be to deprive all clergy, both civil and refractory, of civic duties: 'Il est urgent de faire une loi par laquelle aucun acte civil n'ait rien de commun avec le ministère ecclésiastique.' Never, in modern times, has a layman succeeded better, on the plane of everyday affairs, in interpreting what should be left to Caesar, and what to the priesthood. Had Chénier's wise advice been followed, thousands of lives would have been saved and the whole course of the Revolution, including the religious war of the Chouans, would have taken a different complexion. In a man who had no personal religious position, this spirit of understanding and tolerance must compel admiration.

At about this time the poet must have been casting round to find himself some official post, as he now knew that there was no immediate hope of being elected to the Assembly. A few months later there appeared in the *Annales politiques et littéraires en France* the following statement about this matter: 'André Chénier désirait beaucoup, l'année dernière, d'être envoyé Ambassadeur en Suisse. Il est l'ami des Trudaine, ceux-ci le sont de Montmorin, et les Montmorin le sont de la Reine.'[1] As this notice was printed as late as May 1792, it could only have been designed maliciously, to harm Chénier during his struggle against the Jacobins. However, it was very likely true, and gives some idea of his personal preoccupations in the autumn and early winter of 1791. La Luzerne, his former employer, had died in September after a long period of failing health, so there was no prospect of Chénier's returning to London. In any case he had already written to the Minister at the embassy in London, his friend Barthélemy, asking him to have his books and personal effects sent back to France—further evidence that he must have been on leave of absence until about that time, that is to say for a whole year. After La Luzerne's death, Barthélemy, who for some months had been charged with the Ambassador's work, was naturally hoping to succeed him, but the appointment was first offered to de Chauvelin, and finally accepted by Choiseul-Gouffier in December. Meanwhile the post of diplomatic representative to the Swiss republics had fallen vacant, and Chénier, though he was only twenty-nine, must have applied for it, hoping no doubt to have the support of such Feuillant Ministers as Montmorin, Duport-Dutertre, and Cahier de Gerville. What happened was that Barthélemy, with his much greater diplomatic experience, was ultimately appointed to Basel. This announcement was made in the *Journal de Paris* (17 December 1791) as follows: 'M. Barthélemy, Ministre du Roi à la Cour de Londres, vient d'être nommé Ambassadeur en Suisse. Cette Ambassade est très-importante dans ce moment-ci, où il s'agit de renouveler la capitulation des Suisses avec la France.'

It must have been during this same period, towards the end of 1791 or the beginning of 1792, that another mysterious event occurred in Chénier's career. We have already quoted his statement (p. 246, above) in which he said that he had never been in contact with any Ministry. However, in the family papers at Carcassonne there is a document (which I have expounded fully elsewhere[2]) addressed to the poet, and which runs as follows:

[1] E2, p. xxvi.   [2] F88, pp. 287–94.

Le Ministre de la Justice est désolé de n'avoir pu répondre sur le champ, à la lettre que Monsieur André Chénier lui a fait l'honneur de lui écrire. Mais il ne l'a ouverte que chez le Roi, et n'y a trouvé aucune adresse à laquelle il pût faire venir sa réponse.

Il est infiniment sensible à l'empressement que Monsieur André Chénier a mis à se rendre à Paris. C'est une nouvelle preuve de son civisme, qui a déjà été utile à la chose publique, ne fût-ce qu'en montrant qu'il existait encore en France des hommes dont l'intérêt n'avait pu fléchir la vertu, que le torrent de l'opinion générale n'avait pu faire dévier des principes et qui avaient assez de lumières pour connaître encore la vérité, et de courage pour le dire.

Les circonstances actuelles exigent pour la défense de la constitution et de la justice la réunion des vertus et des talents. C'est pour cela que le Ministre de la Justice désire vivement de causer avec Monsieur André Chénier. Il sera chez lui toute la journée, à moins de quelque affaire qu'il ne peut prévoir, et sera enchanté de le recevoir à l'heure qui lui conviendra le mieux. Il a l'honneur d'assurer Monsieur André Chénier que celles qu'il voudra bien lui donner lui seront toujours très agréables.   Ce Jeudi, 2. 1/2.[1]

In discussing this letter I have already shown that, if it is not the original holograph, it must be one of those copies of official documents concerning his uncle which Gabriel de Chénier obtained from government archives during the period when he was collecting material for the biographical notice to his collected edition of the poems, published in 1874. Reasons why Gabriel did not reproduce the letter are that it is unsigned and undated, and its gist destroys the legend, created by the poet himself, that he had no commerce with the ministries. But the letter is not so difficult to date: since the Constitution is mentioned, it must have been written after September 1791, and the reference to the King means that it must have been written before his imprisonment in August 1792. As Chénier was hostile to the Rolandist government and all its successors, the only possible Minister for Justice in question must be Duport-Dutertre, a Feuillant, who held that office without interruption from November 1790 until 23 March 1792, when he was succeeded by Roland himself.[2] It would be natural to suppose that Chénier might have wished to contact the Minister in the autumn of 1791, when he was seeking to be appointed envoy to Switzerland, or else when he was trying to establish his claim to eligibility. However, the reference

[1] BMC 11814.3.
[2] The Ministers for Justice between Nov. 1790 and Mar. 1793 were: Duport-Dutertre, 21 Nov. 1790; Roland, 23 Mar. 1792; Duranthon, 13 Apr. 1792; Dejoly, 3 July 1792; Danton, 12 Aug. 1792; Garat, 19 Oct. 1792; Gohier, 20 Mar. 1793.

to the threatened constitution hardly points to personal business of that kind. We can possibly rule out Danton, who was Minister for Justice from 12 August to 19 October 1792, as in any case Chénier fled from Paris after the events of 10 August. Nor is it likely that the Minister was Garat (19 October 1792 to 20 March 1793), for even if Chénier's approach was on the occasion of offering his services in the King's defence Garat could not have replied in such flattering terms at that date. The two most likely moments for Chénier to write to Duport-Dutertre were, first, in January 1792, when the Feuillants were drawing up their manifesto in favour of the Constitution, and, second, in the same month, when Chénier was appointed a Juror. The importance of the letter lies not so much in what it says or what it might have arisen from as in the very fact that, in spite of his denials, it shows that on at least one occasion Chénier had been in direct contact, and on his own initiative, with a Minister who obviously approved of his political views and who, therefore, could only have been a Feuillant.

With his hopes of the official appointment to Switzerland dashed, Chénier, while collaborating with the Feuillants, now threw himself entirely into political journalism for several months. Between November 1791 and the end of July 1792 he published a letter, a political poem (the 'Hymne aux Suisses de Châteauvieux'), and twenty-one articles in the *Journal de Paris*, and would no doubt have contributed more if they had been accepted; for he left numerous posthumous fragments about political questions. It has been said that he withdrew from *Le Moniteur* after the rejection of an article, which was an address to the new members of the Legislative Assembly in October 1791.

Chénier's articles in the *Journal de Paris* were of a special kind. Although he signed them, they were not usually printed in the main body of the paper but were added as 'Supplements'. One suspicious circumstance which has disturbed his biographers is that those who inserted supplements had to pay for them. Where could Chénier find the money? He is said to have come into possession of a fairly large sum towards the end of 1790, when he paid off some debts, and this might well have been a gift from his former patron and employer, La Luzerne.[1] The cost of an article of this kind was 36 *livres* for a column of 52 lines; 21 *livres* for half a column; 12 *livres* for a quarter-column, and 9 *livres* for less than a quarter. Chénier's own brother, Marie-Joseph, did not scruple to attack him publicly on this account,

---

[1] See F101, p. 177. It is not unlikely that, in addition, Chénier might have received a legacy from La Luzerne in 1791.

writing in a letter to *Le Moniteur* (1 June 1792), 'J'avais bien la res-
source d'un *supplément*, mais un *supplément* coûte fort cher, et ma
fortune ne me permet pas de faire cette dépense.' There are many
possible replies to this insinuation. Of his twenty-one articles, eleven
were printed as supplements and the normal cost would have been
about 3,000 *livres*. It is often assumed that Trudaine—if not the
Feuillants or even the *liste civile* or secret funds—must have paid for
the insertions; but there is no evidence of this. Chénier had already
been friendly with Suard years before the latter became editor of the
Journal de Paris in November 1791, and that might explain why the
poet moved away from *Le Moniteur*. Quite a number of his friends—
all, admittedly, Feuillants—wrote for it, such as Roucher, de Pange,
Chéron, Lacretelle, Pitra, and Regnault de Saint-Jean-d'Angély. The
paper was in a sound financial position and it is quite possible that
Chénier's articles were issued as supplements because there was no
other room for them; or because the violence of his expression made
this necessary in order to safeguard the editors from responsibility; or,
even more likely, because the articles were recognized as an asset to the
paper and were therefore printed free of charge or were even paid for
though under the guise of supplements. Perhaps it was an error on the
part of the management—or of the Feuillants, or both—not to have
made Chénier political editor in the first place. It is also interesting to
note that three of his articles were reprinted in another journal, *L'Ami
des Patriotes*, which was run by Saint-Jean-d'Angély. This paper paid
him the following tribute in its twenty-fourth number:

Si douze citoyens du mérite et du courage de M. André Chénier se
réunissaient pour combattre les anarchistes dans un journal quotidien, ils
réussiraient à discréditer les charlatans, donneraient plus de confiance à la
saine majorité de l'Assemblée, et rallieraient autour d'eux les vrais amis du
peuple, de la raison et de la liberté.[1]

Chénier began his collaboration with the *Journal de Paris* with
a letter 'Sur la candidature de Lafayette' on the 12th of November
1791, that is to say the day after Condorcet gave up the political
editorship to be replaced by Chéron. When Bailly resigned from being
Mayor of Paris in September, he continued in office until a new Mayor
was elected. This was one of the moments in the Revolution when the
split between the main parties became more clearly defined. The

---

[1] Arnault, in his *Fables et poésies diverses*, 1825, p. 305, stated that Chénier also wrote
for *L'Ami des Patriotes* together with Duquesnoy, Regnault, and Chéron.

candidates against La Fayette included another Feuillant, d'André, who is said to have had the backing of the Court. Among the other candidates were the die-hard de Liancourt, Pétion, Condorcet, and Robespierre himself. Although Robespierre had the Jacobins behind him, he had not the support of the middle class and received only 100 votes. Pétion (an ambiguous person, toadying to several parties at that time) was supported by Brissot (editor of *Le Patriote français*) and his Girondin friends and was elected with 6,708 votes. La Fayette only polled 3,123. This event helped to shape the Girondin party, who began to draw members away from the Feuillants. More important, Pétion, after being opposed by the Feuillants, bore them a grudge and supported the mob against them, having them driven out of their premises.[1] Chénier was, of course, backing the wrong man in La Fayette, but did so because he was one of the leaders of the moderate group in the Feuillants. In spite of his record in America and at the outbreak of the Revolution, La Fayette was not a strong character and lacked political insight. Chénier's recommendation of him to the readers of the *Journal de Paris* lacked conviction: 'Ce passage des emplois militaires aux emplois civils est une des choses qui caractérisent le mieux un gouvernement populaire, ennemi de tout esprit de corps; et un peuple libre n'a pas de plus beau moyen pour récompenser un citoyen qui a bien servi sa patrie, que de lui donner une occasion de la servir encore.' (It has to be pointed out that the term 'esprit de corps' has a pejorative sense in French, meaning a clique.)

Chénier's next article, 'Sur l'éditeur des Lettres de Mirabeau' (12 February 1792), was innocent enough in appearance, but it was his first open attack on a Jacobin personality. Manuel, who had published Mirabeau's letters without authority, was not only 'procureur de la Commune' but also one of the most powerful Jacobins. At the same time, by defending Mirabeau Chénier appeared to ally himself with the right wing, since Mirabeau had long been suspected of double-dealing between the Court and Assembly. The Jacobins were later to have Mirabeau's body removed from the Panthéon and thrown into a pig-sty.

In the meantime some important events had happened. After the stormy scenes at the Feuillants in December, they were obliged to move from their premises, thus losing more of their members. Though

---

[1] After leaving the premises on the Terrasse des Feuillants, the Club moved to the Hôtel de Lusignan, then to the Hôtel de Richelieu, and finally to the Cloître Saint-Honoré where they continued meeting until 10 Aug. 1792.

their influence at the head of public affairs was still strong, as there were a number of Feuillant Ministers, they were a disorganized body from now on. However, on 6 January they issued an important manifesto entitled 'Déclaration des Amis de la Constitution, ci-devant réunis aux Feuillants'. As Chénier probably had a hand in drawing up this Declaration it is given as an appendix to this book.[1] The Manifesto made it plain that the Feuillants did not regard themselves as a political party, and this explains why, instead of creating a third or fourth party in the Assembly, as they ought to have done, they had links with both right and left which they were anxious to preserve. They hoped in this way to hold the balance between all shades of opinion. However, the challenge they now threw out to both Jacobins and Girondins—both of which parties were now becoming more openly republican—was made in no uncertain terms:

L'exposition de leurs principes est toute entière dans la devise simple et précise qu'ils ont choisie, et dont ils font leur règle unique; ils ne prétendent pas se la réserver, mais la rendre commune à tous les Français. Cette devise est *La Constitution, toute la Constitution, rien que la Constitution.*

The pamphlet went on to say that they would defend 'l'inaltérable souveraineté du peuple, la libre action des pouvoirs séparés, dont il a délégué l'exercice, et le respect des autorités constituées'. The manifesto was a declaration of war not only on the unruly Jacobins but on the royalist *émigrés* as well:

La Société tient pour ses ennemis, tous les ennemis de la Constitution, sous quelque bannière qu'ils se rangent, sous quelque forme qu'ils se cachent, et les parricides armés contre leur patrie.

At the same time they announced a purge, in their own ranks, of all those who did not hold with this declaration. The only surprising omission is any direct reference to the Throne; but the word 'constitution', as used by the Feuillants, naturally refers to the constitutional monarchy as it then was.

It was at this time that attention was drawn to Chénier, in various ways. The first was the surprising gesture of Le Brun, who in January 1792 published in the *Almanach des Muses* the flattering ode he had written for him ten years earlier. Le Brun was later, to save his skin, to write venomous attacks on the monarchy, clamouring for the execution of Louis XVI, from whom he had previously accepted a pension. Maybe the gesture of publishing this ode was an attempt to show that

[1] Appendix C, below, p. 373.

their friendship might continue, in spite of their opposite political views.[1]

Another event was the only public recognition that Chénier was ever to receive from the Government, when towards the end of January 1792 he was appointed a juror. This was, at the time, the kind of privilege which might have led to minor forms of office. For Chénier, it was perhaps a factor which protected him during the next few months, and also gave him some status in the Brutus Section or ward in which he was living. There is no evidence as to how or when he exercised his functions as a juror, to which he was appointed by the Feuillant, Roederer, who was then 'procureur-syndic'. Though the poet later wrote an unpublished note against Roederer, accusing him of cowardice, Roederer was one of those who tried to save Louis XVI in the summer of 1792. He was to live to hold high office under the Directory and under Napoleon.

[1] See above, p. 230 n. 1.

11

THE ANTI-JACOBIN

THE Feuillant manifesto was a signal for Chénier to enter into the fray against the Jacobins, and against all those whom he regarded as enemies of the Constitution. As the Feuillants had, as we might think, rather disingenuously announced that they were not a political party, though they had at least three Ministers in the Cabinet, Chénier was able to persuade himself that he was an independent and impartial voice, standing above the mêlée and castigating the enemies of the public weal. Whatever course the Revolution had subsequently taken, ending in a triumph for the Jacobins, or the Cordeliers, or the Girondins, or indeed anyone but the diminishing Feuillants, in this battle which was to last seven months and more he clearly marked himself for the guillotine; for he not only attacked the policies he disliked, but made bitter enemies by his contempt for persons.

After firing the first volley, against Manuel, Chénier issued one of his most powerful articles, 'De la cause des désordres qui troublent la France', in the *Journal de Paris* on the 26th of February. It caused such a stir that it was subsequently reprinted and distributed—at whose expense, this time?—as a separate pamphlet, while a number of papers including *La Gazette universelle* and *L'Ami des Patriotes* went so far as to reproduce the whole of it in their columns; thus, no doubt, earning its author a little pocket-money. The *Spectateur et Modérateur* wrote of it in an editorial, 'Nous ne connaissons point d'écrit où l'influence des sociétés jacobines soit mieux démontrée que dans un morceau très-bien fait de M. André Chénier, qui est imprimé à part et que plusieurs papiers ont répandu.'[1]

The poet began by describing the Club des Jacobins and the support it had from the Paris hooligans and fishwives who had the effrontery to regard themselves as 'le peuple', then, more important, drew a vivid picture of the whole complicated provincial organization of the Jacobin groups which were paralysing freedom of thought in France: in a powerful image he said that 'Ces Sociétés, se tenant par la main,

---

[1] *Le Spectateur et Modérateur*, 6 mars 1792.

forment une espèce de *chaîne électrique* autour de la France'. He was in a good position to know how the provincial network was manipulated from Paris, for only a few months earlier the Feuillants had attempted to influence the provincial cells by issuing bulletins, and while many of the groups far away from Paris were in enthusiastic support, they had been called to order by the Jacobins. Perhaps it was this failure to build up a parallel organization in the provinces that accounts for the ultimate defeat of the Feuillants.

He then came into the open about Jacobin personalities by pointing out that the 'Avignon monsters' were not only Jacobins but had their approval: 'les monstres d'Avignon ont trouvé là des amis, des défenseurs, des jaloux.' This was an attack on Jourdan, nicknamed 'coupe-tête', who had conducted a wholesale massacre of 'suspects' in the Avignon region in October 1791. Without going into a complete résumé of it, it has to be mentioned that G. Walter, in his sympathy for the Jacobins, failed in his study of Chénier to mention the central point in this article.[1] It is, that Chénier saw in the manner in which the Jacobins conducted their activities in Paris a way of side-tracking the government and acting as if the Jacobin Club were itself a parliament. This is surely the most significant and best-founded statement in Chénier's essay:

Ils reçoivent, à la face de la France entière, des députations qui, comme s'il n'existait ni Assemblée législative, ni tribunaux, ni pouvoir exécutif, s'adressent à eux pour obtenir une loi, ou la réparation de quelque tort, ou un changement d'officiers publics.

Chénier was the first to see, or to state so boldly, that the Jacobins' methods could result only in the breakdown of the Constitution, and a dictatorship. He pointed out that it was with the Jacobins' support that the 'people' were now arming themselves and running about Paris with pikes: this had become so serious that the municipality was trying to transform this undisciplined mob into a kind of branch of the national guard (11 February), yet at the same time the Jacobins 'ont osé de promettre, d'une ville à l'autre, l'appui d'une force armée'. Nobody reading this today can fail to wonder at such developments, which in our time had their parallel in Hitler's brown-shirts. Chénier's next onslaught was directed against the Mayor, Pétion, who on the 6th of February had published a letter in which he asserted that

[1] F101, p. 212: 'Il est certain qu'il exagère manifestement le "radicalisme" des Jacobins de l'hiver 1791–1792', &c.

'la bourgeoisie n'est plus aussi attachée à la révolution'. This letter was
one of the major symptoms of the class-war which was now developing. It is interesting to see that Chénier's standpoint on this matter
came very close to English political theory since Walpole: he replied
to Pétion that the *bourgeoisie* stood half-way between the extremes of
wealth and poverty, and therefore 'fait essentiellement la masse du
vrai *peuple*', and that 'lorsque cette classe entière est mécontente, il en
faut accuser quelque vice secret dans les lois ou dans le gouvernement'.
To him, it was logical to attribute the public lack of confidence, and
fear for the future, to the machinations of such pressure-groups as the
Jacobins, who claimed to represent the nation but stood for only a small
part of it. His conclusion was 'que leur destruction est le seul remède
aux maux de la France, et que le jour de leur mort sera un jour de fête
et d'allégresse publique. Ils crient partout que la patrie est en danger;
cela est malheureusement bien vrai; et cela sera vrai tant qu'ils existe-
ront'. The reference to France's danger is quite clear, for already the
Jacobins were beginning to demand what they called 'a people's war'.
Nothing but this threat of war could have driven Chénier to write
what was, in the whole of the Revolution, the most direct and courageous attack on the Jacobins all over France. At the same time, in his
defence of the *bourgeoisie* and his contempt for what he regarded as
the rabble, he failed to understand that in spite of over two years of
revolution the lot of the poor was no better than it had been before,
and though the methods of the Jacobins were as dangerous and un-
constitutional as he portrayed them, yet they were the only party that
was alive to this injustice—while doing nothing to remedy it when they
came to power.

Chénier added a postscript to this article, which was nothing less
than a declaration of war on the Jacobins. After admitting that he was
the author of the attack on Manuel, he said:

J'ajouterai que j'ai dessein de vous adresser de temps en temps quelques
articles que je signerai, dans lesquels, me présentant sans ménagement et
sans crainte à l'honorable inimitié des brigands à talons rouges et des brigands
à piques, je tâcherai, autant qu'il sera en moi, de venger la justice, l'humanité,
l'honnêteté publique, des outrages journaliers qu'elles reçoivent de cet
abominable amas de brouillons qui vivent de la liberté, comme les chenilles
vivent des arbres fruitiers qu'elles tuent, et de cet amas d'écrivains et de
parleurs ignominieux pour qui la liberté n'est autre chose que ce qu'était un
bon festin pour les harpies qui ne savaient que le couvrir d'ordures.

To put this violent article into its perspective: it came at a moment

when the Jacobins themselves were perplexed as to how to deal with
the mob who so frequently interrupted their sittings. After a long
debate in which Danton found a solution, they allowed the mob to
come into the meetings with their pikestaffs, lances, swords, daggers,
and bludgeons, so long as these were draped in a flag. It was now that
the Jacobins, in a further sacrifice to this bloodthirsty section of the
community, began to wear the *bonnet rouge* even at their most formal
meetings. Robespierre was one of the few who refused to wear it in
public. If there was any doubt that the Jacobins were undermining the
constitution and public order just as much as the 'brigands à talons
rouges' (i.e. the nobles), whom Chénier had also attacked, the reader
need only refer to G. Walter's account of their meetings.[1]

Chénier's article caused an uproar, but the most painful aspect of it
was that his brother Marie-Joseph was tempted to reply to it on behalf
of the Jacobins. Marie-Joseph felt himself to be personally involved because André had mentioned how the mob, supported by the Jacobins,
had invaded a theatre and prevented a play from going on: the play in
question was a skit against Marie-Joseph, called 'L'Auteur du Moment',
which had been shown at the Vaudeville. Without going further
into the unfortunate public exchanges between the two brothers, their
private war became one of the scandals of the Revolution, while perfectly illustrating the 'classical' spirit in which they each imagined they
were acting with the impartiality of a Brutus.

One of the consequences of his article was that Chénier was publicly
accused of being in the hire of the government, while Roederer came
in for abuse for having appointed him as one of the hundred 'jurés'.
Chénier replied on the 4th of March that Roederer was innocent, as he
had appointed him before the attack on the Jacobins was published.
He was indignant at being accused of receiving payment from the civil
list. At the end of his reply he disdained to defend himself against this
accusation, and gave the disclaimer (quoted above, p. 246) concerning
his relationship to the government or political parties or clubs. Maybe
he had, by now, ceased attending the Feuillant meetings, but in view
of what had gone before he was obviously protesting too much.

Shortly after all this the *Journal de Paris*, led this time by Morellet
and François de Pange, began to attack Brissot, the editor of *Le
Patriote français*. Brissot was a harmless enough person, though always involved in some intrigue or other, making more noise than his
intelligence justified—for instance, in loudly demanding the King's

[1] F102, chapters xvii–xix.

deposition in July 1791. From his entertaining memoirs it emerges that he had been in the pay of the duc d'Orléans, so maybe his eagerness to see the end of Louis XVI was not entirely disinterested. It is hard to understand how such a superficial demagogue ever became leader of any group inside or outside the Assembly: he enjoyed coining such puerile definitions as the following, which he offered in all seriousness:

> Patriote: ami du peuple, ami de la constitution.
> Modéré: faux ami de la constitution, ennemi du peuple.
> Enragé: faux ami du peuple, ennemi de la constitution.[1]

The reason why Brissot now became the butt of the Chénier circle is that he and the Girondins were agitating for war at any price. The so-called 'Brissotin Ministry' came into power on 10 March 1792, bringing about the fall of Duport-Dutertre, Delessart, Cahier de Gerville, and Narbonne, all of whom were or had been Feuillants. What Morellet and his friends set out to do was to discredit Brissot, raking up some of his early works such as his simple-minded *Théorie des lois criminelles* and *Sur le vol et la propriété*. Although Brissot had been involved in many dubious transactions during his exile in London in the 1780's it was probably unjust to accuse him, as Morellet and de Pange did, of being in the pay of the police during the old régime. He had actually been imprisoned in the Bastille in 1784. However, his own memoirs show that he resorted to every shift for money after that: he was one of those for whom the outbreak of the Revolution was a heaven-sent way out of their troubles. Anyway, Brissot replied that these accusations 'made his blood boil' and said that his work and his past were being subjected to what he called 'dissections ministérielles', that is to say that Morellet and his friends were following government instructions in attacking him. Chénier's answer was to denounce him as a liar, in capital letters, in an article on Brissot dated 16 March.

When Brissot, cast into prison by the Jacobins and awaiting his trial and death in 1793, began writing his memoirs, which were to form part of his defence, he wrote about this episode:

> Cette dissertation [*Sur le vol et la propriété*] a été une source de calomnie contre moi. Elle fut déterrée lors de l'assemblée législative, par un petit club secret, soudoyé par la cour, pour diriger l'opinion publique en faveur du feuillantisme, Club dont étaient membres Pange, Morellet, Suard, André Chénier, Ramond etc. Ils me traduisirent en public comme un apologiste du

---

[1] F19, t. iii, p. 332.

vol et de l'anthropophagisme. Au fond, cette brochure n'était qu'une amplification d'écolier.[1]

Brissot might have been wiser to have laughed the whole thing off,
and to have admitted (as he did, in his memoirs) that he had argued as
a young man that property had no basis in nature, that there was no
such thing as theft, and that in the natural state cannibalism was not
a crime. Such arguments were typical of this charming but irresponsi-
ble man all his life: in 1792 he could find no better argument in favour
of war than 'The force of Reason and of facts has persuaded me that
a people which, after a thousand years of slavery, has achieved liberty,
needs war. It needs war to consolidate its freedom'.

It was at this stage, when the Feuillants had successfully alienated
the other parties, while remaining representative of a large section of
inarticulate moderate opinion among the middle class, that one of
those apparently minor events occurred which had a significance that
was not fully understood either then or now. This was the 'Fête des
Suisses de Châteauvieux'. Critics have wondered why Chénier and his
friends made such a 'song and dance' about it, and why he wrote four
articles and a poem about the event.

In August 1790 the Swiss mercenaries in the Châteauvieux regiment
revolted near Nancy. They held their officers to ransom, stole the regi-
mental funds, fired on the national guard, and were finally brought to
trial. In the process a young officer, Desilles, had tried to avoid bloodshed but was massacred by the Swiss for his pains. The culprits were
harshly dealt with, twenty-three being executed and forty-one sent to
the galleys, though according to martial law at that time they could
have all suffered the extreme penalty. At the time there was a debate in
the Assembly on the matter: a pension (which was never paid) was
awarded to Desilles's mother and a bust was made of him. Those who
were toiling in the galleys were amnestied in December 1791 and finally
freed in February 1792. They then held together in a band, were fêted
by the patriots at Brest, then set out to march on Paris, being drunk
all the way.

The Jacobins saw that political capital could be made out of this
gang by glorifying them as martyrs. Collot d'Herbois, Marie-Joseph
Chénier, Madame Théroigne, and David were foremost in insisting that
they should receive public honours, and preparations were made for
building a cardboard galley in which they were to be paraded through
Paris.

[1] F19, t. i, p. 88.

Chénier had already mentioned the Swiss mercenaries and the danger of disorder in the armed forces, in his 'Avis' of August 1790. But to understand why he now entered the fray with such energy against the fête, we have to look behind the scenes. Nobody except Chénier, at that time, saw the situation as clearly as Earl Gower, who was then British Ambassador to Paris. He wrote as early as 6 January 1792:

> The release of the soldiers of the Swiss Regiment of Châteauvieux, who were confined at Brest, *by which they have certainly infringed their last treaty with the Swiss cantons*, will hasten M. Barthélemy's departure from thence.[1]

Gower here puts us on several tracks at once. It would certainly not occur to such men as David and Marie-Joseph Chénier that public recognition of the Swiss rebels had more than local significance. But Gower's dispatches, Barthélemy's memoirs, and the dossier on the Châteauvieux affair which can be consulted at Nancy,[2] all show that the Swiss were very sensitive about the whole affair. If Barthélemy did his best to stop the ceremony, it was not for internal, party reasons but in order to protect part of France's frontier by maintaining relations with Switzerland. It has to be remembered that the fête for the Swiss was held on Sunday the 15th of April, and that the French declared war on Austria on the 20th.

The mention of Barthélemy's name suggests that, back in Paris, Chénier was campaigning not only for the principles he put forward with such energy but in order to help his friend, who himself went to the length of writing to Pétion, the Mayor of Paris. Let us, for the moment, follow the story as given in Gower's papers:

Feb. 24. 1792. Mr Barthélemy's cool reception at Saleure does not give him reason to hope that his negotiations with the Swiss cantons will have a speedy and successful termination.

March 23rd. The soldiers of Châteauvieux, who are coming from Brest, are to be received here with patriotic honours and a fête, in order, I suppose, to encourage insubordination.

March 30. The administration of the Department of Paris are endeavouring to prevent the intended fête for the 40 soldiers of Châteauvieux, in honour of their having disobeyed orders, but the municipality is desirous that it should take place and it will probably prevail. They are expected tomorrow

---

[1] My italics. F49, p. 146. Subsequent references to Gower are taken from the same source.

[2] BMC: No. 852, Affaire de Nancy, 105 pièces; also 453, 18ᵉ siècle, catalogue Noël, 1193–1296.

at Versailles. They seem to be playing the game of the Spanish negotiator who is arrived in Switzerland.

April 6th, 1792. The Fête civique intended to be given to the soldiers of Châteauvieux *will be a good criterion of the strength of the Jacobin party in the Metropolis.* If that should take place without disturbance their preponderance will be undoubted.

April 11th. The soldiers of Châteauvieux had the *honneurs de la Séance* in the Assembly last Monday. Their fête will take place on Sunday next.

April 13th. The majority of the National Guard, especially those who are attached to M. de La Fayette, murmur at the indecency and impropriety of leading, as it were in triumph, these soldiers of Châteauvieux, whose sole merit consists in having disobeyed orders, *but who are now used as tools to render M. de La Fayette unpopular.*

April 20th. Owing to the moderation and proper behaviour of the National Guard, the absurd Fête of last Sunday concluded without any disturbance: upon the whole it has tended more to affect the popularity of the promoters than those against whom it was aimed.

Let us now turn to Barthélemy's papers on the subject:[1]

La pièce publiée dans le *Patriote français* [Brissot's paper] du 17 mars, et la Fête préparée en honneur des soldats de Châteauvieux, ont fait un mal horrible.

Lettre de Barthélemy à Pétion [*maire de Paris*] — Conséquences fâcheuses que pourrait avoir la fête qui se prépare en l'honneur des soldats de Châteauvieux.

Dumouriez à Barthélemy, avril 1792: Je souhaite très fort que l'enthousiasme public se refroidisse en France et que la fête projetée à Paris pour la réception de ces galériens n'ait pas lieu.

Barthélemy à Dumouriez, 14 avril 1792: La protestation de Lucerne sur Châteauvieux ne signifie absolument rien. Cet État le sait bien. Mais si la Fête qu'on préparait à Paris a eu lieu, soyez assuré que nous allons réveiller bien des douleurs et nuire à nos propres intérêts.

Barthélemy à Dumouriez: Au reste, les détails de la réception qui a été faite par une partie du peuple aux galériens de Châteauvieux ne présentent rien de fâcheux; il n'en est pas de même de leur admission à l'Assemblée nationale, qui a fait le plus mauvais effet dans toute la Suisse.

André Chénier's violent onslaught on the proposed fête came at a time when his brother Marie-Joseph was attacking him in public, and this source of difference did not help matters. Perhaps the article he published on 'La Peinture d'Histoire' on the 20th of March, in

[1] F9: the references are, in order, to t. i, pp. 63, 66, 77, 89.

which he praised the genius of David, was intended to show that he could forgive a Jacobin and pass over political differences, but Marie-Joseph did not take the hint. André's first article on the Swiss mercenaries was heavily ironic. He said that it was the custom to make an official citation, when commemorating heroes, and that in this case it should state that they were being honoured for armed mutiny; for having been condemned by the National Assembly for treason against the nation; for having robbed the till; for having said 'We are not French, but Swiss, and we need money', and for having fired on the National Guard. He did not object to their being amnestied, pointing out that the word 'amnistie signifie *oubli*', but suggested that the whole affair would be best forgotten. Apart from the national hero, Desilles, no names were mentioned in this article, in which the whole emphasis was on the national honour. Without naming the Jacobins, it was they whom he designated as 'despotes insolents qui tyrannisent la liberté' and 'brouillons tout-puissants, ivres d'avarice et d'orgueil' and 'factieux avides et injustes'. This article appeared on the 27th of March. Incidentally, he pointed out in the same article that if General Bouillé (who had been responsible for bringing the Swiss to order) had since become a traitor to the country, that did not mean that he was one at that time, or that the Swiss were martyrs.

Meanwhile, the whole of Paris had been in ferment over this question, and was to remain so for another fortnight. Already, before publishing his first article, he had been approached by a battalion of the National Guard (the section of the Capucins–Saint-Honoré, commanded by Trudaine) to draw up a statement on their behalf to be presented to the 'directoire du département de Paris', or County Council.[1] His draft is dated 23 March, that is to say as soon as the news of the projected fête was available. This battalion was involved, as the procession would have to halt on its way to the Champ de Mars for a short ceremony at the Place Vendôme, which the Guard of that section would have to attend. Chénier's plea was a dignified statement of the facts, pointing out that the National Guard should not be called on to honour a group of foreigners who had taken arms against them.[2] The next event was that Tallien (as we learn from the correspondence of Palloy, who was in charge of the practical organization of the

---

[1] The fact that Trudaine was in command detracts nothing from Chénier's contribution. The point is that the majority of the Sections of the National Guard in Paris were now solidly behind the Feuillants, though powerless to help them unless they mutinied. Had they done so at this moment, the King might never have been deposed.

[2] 'Adresse au Directoire du Département de Paris', in E2, pp. 140–3.

event), after being asked to draw up the plans for the procession, resigned owing to what he called 'les clameurs insultantes de quelques mauvaises têtes contre les Suisses de Châteauvieux'.[1] The truth is that Tallien did not approve of the ceremony himself. Then, on 28 March, the day after André's first article appeared, Marie-Joseph, Théroigne, David, and Hion went to the Hôtel de Ville and presented to the Mayor and corporation a petition that the fête should be held. They did not mention, in this document, that they had been sent by the Jacobins, but said merely, 'De nombreux citoyens nous ont chargés auprès de vous d'une mission que nous remplissons avec confiance et avec joie . . .'.[2] The truth is that they had proposed the fête themselves and only afterwards contrived to have themselves pushed forward as representatives of the 'people'. Their petition contained an extraordinary travesty of the facts, only too typical of the bad faith which was characteristic of Marie-Joseph all his life; for, without being deliberately dishonest, he was generally incapable of distinguishing the truth from his own imaginings: 'Bientôt ces *soldats généreux* reverront le Champ de Mars, où leur résistance au despotisme a préparé le règne de la loi; bientôt ils embrasseront *leurs frères d'armes, ces braves gardes françaises,* dont ils ont partagé la *désobéissance héroïque.*' The fact that these 'frères d'armes', the National Guard, were all over Paris in a state approaching revolt at the prospect of 'embracing' the Swiss mercenaries, meant nothing to Marie-Joseph, whose only desire was to be in the limelight. As Pétion, the Mayor, had already authorized the fête four days ago, their pompous visit was really unnecessary. But they must have known that Acloque, head of the National Guard in Paris, had protested strongly against the participation of the Guard in the ceremony, and that numerous petitions were coming in against it from all parts of Paris, including one which was signed by seventy-one citizens of the Île Saint-Louis.[3]

André Chénier's second article appeared in the *Journal de Paris* on the 2nd of April. In measured terms he said that, far from their being any public enthusiasm for the fête, all the evidence was to the contrary. He went over the circumstances of the revolt during which the Swiss

---

[1] For the inner story of the organization of the fête, see the Palloy MSS. in the B.N. and especially NAF 308.3071.

[2] 'Pétition au Conseil Général de la Commune de Paris', in E2, pp. 371–2.

[3] For Acloque, see BN, NAF 308.3071, 63–64. The Île Saint-Louis petition (NAF 308.307, f. 99) asserts 'que les mânes des Gardes nationales immolées par les Suisses de Châteauvieux seraient insultées, que leurs veuves, que leurs enfans verraient renouveler l'amertume de leurs pertes par le triomphe de leurs Assassins'.

had attacked the National Guard at Metz. Far from dressing the public monuments on this occasion, it would be more proper for the Guard to parade in mourning. He pointed out that another Swiss regiment, 'les soldats d'Ernest', had laid down their arms at Aix rather than fire on the French.[1] The only name mentioned in the article was that of Brissot, whom he accused of rousing the mob in July 1791, as he had done. The essay ends with one of those proud personal statements, with which we are becoming familiar, in which Chénier liked to define his own independent position while pouring contempt on his opponents:

En lisant et en écoutant quelques-unes des apologies de cette fête, je n'ai pu m'empêcher de plaindre leurs auteurs et de me dire à moi-même: heureux l'homme droit et sage qui, méprisant tout esprit de corps, repoussant toute association à un parti quelconque, ne connaît d'autre lien parmi les hommes que la justice et les lois! Ne voulant arriver aux emplois et aux honneurs que par l'étude et la vertu, il n'aura jamais à servir l'ambition de personne pour satisfaire la sienne. La reconnaissance ou l'espoir ne lui imposeront jamais le sacrifice de sa conscience et la nécessité de soutenir des absurdités par des mensonges, et des turpitudes par des sophismes.

Meanwhile, other letters and articles in the *Journal de Paris* were supporting Chénier's stand, in particular one from the poet Roucher, on the 1st of April, announcing that he had refused to be the delegate of his Section, or ward, at the fête. They were attacked by Marat in *L'Ami du Peuple*, by Hébert in the *Lettres patriotiques du Père Duchesne*, and by Carra in the *Annales patriotiques*. Preparations for the ceremony were well in hand, with David making the decorations, Marie-Joseph the songs and dances, Gossec the music, Palloy the arrangements for processions and refreshments. Then Collot d'Herbois, a former 'ham' actor and friend of Marie-Joseph, and now one of the most powerful of the Jacobins, denounced Chénier and Roucher at a session of the Jacobins on the 4th of April, in a speech subsequently printed with the fiery title 'Réponse de Collot d'Herbois à des notes barbares envoyées à divers journaux contre les Suisses de Châteauvieux, et notamment à celles envoyées par MM. Roucher et André Chénier au *Journal de Paris*'. He described the two poets as 'mouchards' (police spies) and sycophants, and ironically as 'gens de bien', then 'écrivains perfides et

---

[1] This occurred in February 1792, when the 'Ernest' battalion of Swiss mercenaries (the oldest in France) almost clashed with some 4,000 armed rioters from Marseilles. The protest of the Berne Council over this is closely related to the Châteauvieux affair and explains Gower's and Barthélemy's anxiety.

allacieux' and 'rhéteurs glacés'. In spite of all this it is remarkable that he arch-Jacobin left a loophole for André Chénier, concluding:

> Rhéteurs glacés! Vous faites mine d'être moralistes et sages. Votre sagesse st celle des eunuques. Mais au moins *André Chénier*, prosateur stérile, especte le peuple producteur et abondant. . . . Va, le peuple est plus sage que toi; il te méprise . . . et te pardonne.

The fact that Collot was a friend of Marie-Joseph is not a sufficient eason why he should express forgiveness for André Chénier. While calling him a sterile prose-writer, he admits that Chénier had some espect for the people. He could hardly have found this evidence in any of the prose writings, in which Chénier had been at pains to show that he 'people' was not the mob but the laborious *bourgeoisie*, except in his first article, the 'Avis'. But it is just as likely that Collot had been impressed by Chénier's generous praise of 'le peuple souverain' in his *Ode au Jeu de Paume*. Is it possible that some Jacobins still thought Chénier's pen could be won over to their cause?

Collot's diatribe was followed by a public letter from Pétion, the Mayor, who by now must have replied to Barthélemy. He protested hat the reception of the Swiss would have passed almost unnoticed had it not been for a few writers who 'ont soufflé sur le feu de la discorde'. Without denying that the fête was to be paid for out of public funds—one of Chénier's accusations—he pretended that it was not a 'public event'.[1]

Collot d'Herbois was sadly mistaken if he thought that the overture at the end of his pamphlet, coming as it did after a series of insults, was likely to pacify Chénier in any way. The poet replied on the 10th of April, in the most contemptuous terms, to Collot's threat to 'm'attaquer devant les tribunes comme un lâche calomniateur':

> On verra de quelles *calomnies* il me prouvera capable; et l'on verra si je serai regardé comme un *lâche* pour avoir, seul et sans soutien, démasqué et dénoncé à la France entière une poignée d'effrontés saltimbanques qui envahissent l'empire au nom de la liberté, et qui osent décorer du nom de *vœu du peuple* leurs insolents caprices et leurs fantaisies tyranniques.

Chénier again returned to the accusation of being a hired journalist, saying:

> Il dit que je suis un hypocrite qui ne pense pas un mot de ce qu'il dit; que j'appartiens à un parti; que je suis l'agent et l'instrument d'intrigues et de

---

[1] For full text see E2, pp. 376–8.

manœuvres etc. Toutes ces imputations n'admettent d'autre réponse que
celle-ci: M. COLLOT D'HERBOIS A MENTI.

On the previous day Chénier had also replied to the Mayor, in his
'Réflexions sur la lettre du Maire de Paris à ses concitoyens'. By now
Chénier had purified his style to a degree that made his pen the most
formidable weapon wielded during the Revolution, with the possible
exception of Marat's. He had cut out the flowers of rhetoric which
decorated his early, more leisurely articles, while broadening his
vocabulary to match the coarseness of his opponents—a development
which was to give edge, later, to his *Iambes*, which are such a curious
mixture of noble and vulgar images and vocabulary. In his reply to
Pétion, Chénier showed himself to be the only person in France, at that
moment, to realize that what was at stake in this affair was the relationship between three powers: the Assembly, which was a national body;
the municipality of Paris, which was a purely local body but affecting
national policy by infringing the powers of the Assembly; and the
Jacobin Club, which, by using the Mayor and the municipality as
a tool, was undermining the Assembly's authority. The Jacobins had
succeeded in inflicting their will on the Assembly, the Municipality of
Paris, and the Department or County Council of Paris.

By now it was too late to stop the fête, but Chénier must have received some consolation from the number of voices that came to his
support, including that of the intrepid Bayard, who commanded one
of the battalions of the National Guard and who was later to have
a brilliant military career. On the 12th of April the *Journal de Paris*
published a letter from Bayard in which he said:

C'est vous, éloquent Chénier, c'est vous, Éleuthère [a grenadier who had
written to the *Journal* on 7th April], vous, Naudeville [one of those who
replied to Pétion], qui les premiers avez provoqué la sainte insurrection de la
loi! vous avez ouvert à vos concitoyens les pages à demi effacées de notre
constitution; vous avez proclamé ces paroles sacrées, l'exorcisme, pour ainsi
dire, des factieux: '*Le Corps législatif a seul le droit de décerner des honneurs
publics.*'

Éloquent Chénier, à qui l'histoire a remis les pinceaux de Tacite pour
peindre un jour nos nouveaux Domitiens, je n'ai pas tes talents, mais j'ai
ton âme et ton courage; je me voue, comme vous, à la proscription qui attend
les bons citoyens.

Chénier, in disgust, went to spend the week-end of the fête, which
was celebrated on the 15th of April, with his friends the Trudaines.
But on the same day he published in the *Journal de Paris* his last word

on the subject. This was the first of his famous *ïambes*, the *Hymne aux Suisses de Châteauvieux*, a remarkable parody of the ceremonial odes and hymns which accompanied all such gaudy manifestations during the Revolution. This poem is of the greatest importance, not only as being the first *ïambe*, but because, as one historian put it, with this poem Chénier signed his own death-warrant.[1] This intensely ironical work surprised both his friends and his enemies, who had not expected anything like it from this 'prosateur stérile'. In a new verse-form, created for the occasion, consisting of alternate alexandrines and octosyllabics, not disposed in quatrains as J.-B. Rousseau had used them, but linked and flowing so easily that one might imagine Chénier was using his natural medium rather than something newly found, the poet affected to set this event high above the solemn occasions when Mirabeau and Voltaire had been honoured by burial in the Panthéon. It starts straight away with intensely biting irony:

> Salut, divin Triomphe! entre dans nos murailles!
> Rends-nous ces guerriers illustrés
> Par le sang de Désille, et par les funérailles
> De tant de Français massacrés ...

It has all the wit and fire which had been lacking in the *Jeu de Paume* ode:

> Tandis que parmi nous quel orgueil, quelle joie
> Pour les amis de la vertu,
> Pour nous tous, ô mortels, qui rougissez encore
> Et qui savez baisser les yeux,
> De voir des échevins, que la Râpée honore,
> Asseoir sur un char radieux
> Ces héros, que jadis sur les bancs des galères
> Assit un arrêt outrageant,
> *Et qui n'ont égorgé que très peu de nos frères,*
> *Et volé que très peu d'argent ...*[2]

The 'échevins' or scriveners were the Jacobin leaders, most of them lawyers, who were said to indulge in orgies at the *La Râpée* restaurant. The last two lines recall the wit of La Fontaine. But Chénier went further, actually naming two of these leaders:

[1] F101, p. 233. 'Les milieux patriotes se sentirent profondément offensés par ses invectives furieuses. On ne les oubliera pas et il est certain que ce jour-là, d'ores et déjà André Chénier avait signé lui-même son propre arrêt de mort.' As we have already remarked on M. Walter's prejudice against Chénier and his (Marxist) bias in favour of the Jacobins, we note his characteristic begging of the question by describing the Jacobins as 'les milieux patriotes'.   [2] My italics.

> Quarante meurtriers, *chéris de Robespierre,*
> Vont s'élever sur nos autels.
> Beaux-arts, qui faites vivre et la toile et la pierre,
> Hâtez-vous, rendez immortels
> *Le grand Collot d'Herbois,* ses clients helvétiques,
> Ce front qui donne à des héros
> La vertu, la taverne, et le secours des piques,
> Peuplez le ciel d'astres nouveaux,
> O vous, enfants d'Eudoxe et d'Hipparque et d'Euclide . . .

Here he was gibing as much at David, Marie-Joseph, and Gossec, responsible for the 'artistic' arrangements, as at Robespierre and Collot. In actual fact Robespierre kept strangely silent about the whole Swiss affair: in 1790 he had raised his voice on behalf of two of the culprits, but at the present time he did not entirely approve of according them honours: Chénier was attacking him as having been their first defender. Poor Collot had no defence against Chénier's irony, when he suggested that, like Orpheus or Berenice's golden hair, the galley-birds would surely have a new constellation in the heavens:

> Que la Nuit de leurs noms embellisse ses voiles,
> Et que le nocher aux abois
> Invoque en leur Galère, ornement des étoiles,
> Les Suisses de Collot d'Herbois.

Some critics have regarded this as a laboured and pedantic ending, but it is far from being so: the double meaning of the word *Nuit*, meaning not only darkness but oblivion, is quite an accessible joke.

If so much attention has been given to the Swiss affair it is because, though it is usually glossed over quickly by historians, it was a really important event at this stage of the Revolution. We have seen how Barthélemy saw in it a menace to French relations with Switzerland, and how Gower read into it a turning-point in the rise of Jacobinism. In addition, it undermined the authority of the Assembly and was a test case in the relations between the Jacobins and the municipality as opposed to the government. It showed, also, that the Moderates or constitutionalists as well as the Right were powerless to check the Jacobins, and that the Girondins, not seeing which side their bread was buttered, played into the Jacobins' hands by supporting them against the Feuillants. The consequences for public safety were even more alarming. The Swiss affair explains the decline of the National Guard in the coming months, for it left such a distaste that there were wholesale resignations. At the same time, as Chénier had predicted, the effect on army morale was disastrous, as events were soon to demonstrate. Within not more than fifteen days the effects of demagogy on the army were plain for all to see, when it crumbled under the first half-hearted attacks it had to face in Belgium. General Dillon was murdered in the field by his own troops as they fled. Those under Biron stopped to take a vote on the order to attack, and he had to withdraw his instructions. The monarchy was shaken to its foundations. Dumouriez (who, as we have seen, had been in anxious correspondence with Barthélemy during the affair, for he was then Minister for Foreign Affairs) was discredited and was soon to be denounced as a traitor for his lack of success. Last but not least, the Swiss affair shook the Rolandist government as well as the monarchy.

Chénier, who saw all this as clearly as it could be seen at that time, was not slow to return to the charge. On the 29th of April, a week after the declaration of war on Austria, he published his article on 'Les Sociétés patriotiques', an ironical title, for he was to survey the disorders all over France. He showed how in the various provinces the French were at grips with each other, although there was a war on; how the ports were in a state of turmoil; how members of the Assembly such as Dupont de Nemours (also defended by Roucher), and even magistrates like Roederer who were supposed to be immune from political attack, were being denounced as 'public enemies' in the Jacobin Club—Dupont's crime being that he had written a letter to the Mayor; and Roederer's, that Collot had spied on him through a window when he was alleged to be dining with other 'public enemies'— to wit, Ramond and Lacretelle.[1] Chénier referred to Robespierre scornfully as 'un parleur'—a windbag—and argued that in a time of national crisis the time was past for listening to a few extremists.

His next article, 'De l'indiscipline des armées' (3 May 1792), recalled how he and others had been insisting, during the Swiss affair, on the need for discipline in the armed forces. He squarely put the blame for the events in Belgium and Lille, on the Jacobins. It has to be recalled that the Jacobins, far from being chastened by these catastrophes, had laid the blame on the generals (1 May), accusing them of treason because their troops would not fight. No evidence has ever been given to prove that the honourable Dillon was a traitor of any kind: indeed the drop

---

[1] 'Séance extraordinaire des Jacobins, 17 avril', in the *Journal des Jacobins*, 19 avril 1792. 'Hier, je passais dans la rue du Théâtre Français: j'aperçois à une fenêtre M. Roederer, à côté de MM. Ramond et Lacretelle. Je m'informe et on me dit qu'ils sont chez M. de Jaucourt. . . .'

in the prestige of the monarchy owing to failure in the field was what the generals were most anxious to avoid. Chénier's eloquent article reads more like a speech than most of the others: it is a glowing appeal for patriotism and national unity, overriding party politics: 'La perte d'un poste est peu de chose; mais l'honneur de la France a été plus compromis par de détestables actions qu'il ne l'avait été depuis des siècles.'

By now Chénier was frequently receiving letters or what we call 'fan-mail' from all over France. In his violent attack called 'Le Parti des Jacobins', dated 8 May, he quoted a letter from a citizen of Lille, asking all those who believed in the Constitution to regard the Jacobins as public enemies. Chénier, again denouncing anarchy, mentioned that people had not only been violated and assassinated in the provinces but had even been eaten at Avignon and Polémieux. Meanwhile Carra, a Jacobin, had proposed at a Jacobin meeting that Louis XVI should be replaced by a prince from the English royal family. This was a treasonable statement, made in public, which shows how much regard the Jacobins then had for the constitution. Chénier said that the Jacobins should now drop their title of 'Amis de la Constitution', since they were out to destroy it. Some months later they were to take his advice, changing their title to 'Amis de la République'.

His next and very long article dated 12 May was a reply to his brother Marie-Joseph, who had come forward as official defender of the Jacobins. Chénier went thoroughly into his own political position and his reasons for attacking the Jacobins. In passing he mentioned that in London he had known Dr. Priestley, and expressed admiration for Fox and Wilberforce. Completing the self-portrait to which he returned from time to time in his journalism, he added:

Et quel intérêt particulier puis-je avoir à cette haine qu'on me reproche? Ai-je trouvé quelque part sur mon chemin les hommes dont il s'agit? Ai-je demandé, désiré, cherché quelque poste, quelque emploi? Ai-je été leur rival à quelque tribune, dans quelque société primaire ou électorale, dans quelque cabinet ministériel? Je n'ai paru même à ma Section que lorsque des affaires vraiment publiques et ma qualité de citoyen exigeaient de moi un vœu. Inconnu et pauvre et content de l'être, je vivais dans la retraite, dans l'étude et dans l'amitié. La seule vue des maux dont ces corporations sont la cause, et le silence de beaucoup d'hommes, trop timides, qui le voyaient et qui n'osaient le dire, m'a pu faire renoncer sitôt à ma pénible obscurité.

As if to answer his remark about seeking a post, it was only three days later that a Swiss paper reported that he had tried to be appointed

Ambassador a few months earlier, while Marie-Joseph was to insinuate that he had tried to become a deputy.[1] For the rest, Chénier's only regrettable lapse in his reply to Marie-Joseph was to suggest that he was too fond of being in the limelight, saying that the Jacobins had more fingers in the pie than anyone else, intriguing on behalf of 'cette partie des succès littéraires dont la nature est d'avoir besoin des applaudissements de la multitude'. He was referring to the Jacobin *claque* which ensured the success of Marie-Joseph's plays. After this personal thrust it is difficult to believe that the two brothers were ever reconciled.

Chénier never approved of the policy of war which had led France into hostilities on the 20th of April. He had already expressed his distrust of Britain in 'L'Avis au Peuple français' of 1790. Now, on the 29th, he warned those who imagined that Britain might become France's ally, describing Britain as 'une nation avide, entreprenante, calculatrice et constante dans ses projets, qui n'a jamais fait un pas que vers l'empire absolu de la mer, dont toute la prospérité est fondée sur le commerce, qui n'a jamais vu qu'avec un œil avide celui que nous faisons dans les deux mondes'. Once again his insight took him far ahead, not only of the Jacobins but of all the parties in France at that moment. It was this opposition to war, which he regarded in any case as barbarous, that had led him to oppose the new government under Roland, which came to power on the 10th of March 1792. It was not bigotry or devotion to the Feuillants that led him into what some critics have interpreted as foolish hostility to the Rolandists, who in everything but their war policy might be regarded as liberals, like himself. His article 'Sur les conséquences du 10 mars' is, in part, a defence of the ex-minister Delessart, a Feuillant who had been impeached by the Girondins. An unpublished fragment also shows that, in his view, the new government had been brought to power by a few 'catins' or harlots, namely Mme Tallien, Mme Roland, and Mme de Staël.[2]

In 'Des manœuvres des Jacobins' (10 May 1792) he was answering an article by his former friend, Condorcet. Chénier was outraged by Gensonné's proposal that all municipalities, districts, and departments should have full powers to investigate, accuse, and try anyone suspected of subversive activities. Offences against the realm are obviously not matters for local government to deal with. We can see today that

---

[1] See above, p. 251 and p. 241 n. 3.
[2] D22, p. 738, 'comme autrefois, le gouvernement est entre les mains des femmes, etc. . . .'

such proposals were laying the foundations of the Terror which was to begin a few months later. At the same time he attacked Servan's proposal to station a 'federal' army of some 200,000 volunteers near Paris, in order to 'keep the peace'. This would be the death-knell of the already weakened National Guard, which so far had tried to hold the balance between the different factions, even swallowing its pride over the Châteauvieux affair. Though it was only the call to arms of the French masses that later saved France, this was different; for Servan's proposal amounted to a kind of military dictatorship over Paris, against which the National Guard would be powerless.

For once, Chénier was in agreement with Robespierre, who denounced Servan's plan at a meeting of the Jacobins. But Chénier was dealing out his blows on either side, describing the Jacobins as 'lâches et cruels imposteurs, bourreaux de votre patrie' and pouring scorn on Brissot in the same breath as Collot. The essay ends with a statement which we can only consider disingenuous, saying that he was writing independently:

Je les prie de se souvenir que je ne suis point rédacteur de ce Journal; que je n'en connais même point; que plusieurs des personnes qui insèrent, comme moi, des articles dans le supplément me sont pareillement inconnus; que chacun est maître d'y publier ses réflexions, à ses frais; que chacun ne doit répondre que de son ouvrage, et que nul n'y est solidaire pour la louange ou pour le blâme d'autrui. Je sais que la plupart des hommes ne sauraient comprendre qu'on ne tienne à aucun parti, à aucune secte, et qu'on ose penser tout seul. . . .[1]

The truth is that Chénier did know Suard; he knew intimately the political editor, Chéron; he knew Regnault, de Pange, Roucher, Morellet, Lacretelle, and most of those whose articles appeared in the *Journal de Paris*. And he forgot to mention those articles of his, and the poem on the Swiss, which had not appeared in the Supplements but in the body of the paper itself. And how could he pay for his supplements, when he was earning nothing? The only thing that is true in his statement is that he wrote what he thought, himself. His denial shows him using the same evasive methods as his enemies, Marat, Hébert, Collot, and Brissot. The most that can be said in his favour is that he was lying to defend the paper and his friends.

So far, in all his articles, Chénier had had little or nothing to say

[1] D22, p. 340.

about the monarchy, to which he was indifferent except in its function as part of the Constitution. He was less of a royalist than de Pange or the Trudaines. But in June 1792 for the first time he came to the King's defence, in his article 'La Journée du 20 juin' which appeared in the *Journal de Paris* a week later. On the 20th of June some eight thousand people from the different Sections formed a procession, led by the brewer Santerre, with the object of planting a 'tree of liberty' on the terrace of the Feuillants. They entered the Assembly and made threatening speeches. Then they forced their way into the Tuileries, where Santerre had guns trained on the royal entrance. The Guards stood by, powerless, as the King was anxious to avoid bloodshed. When the mob swarmed into the Louvre, Louis XVI acted with great calm and courage, even allowing the red bonnet to be placed on his head and drinking a glass to the health of the nation. Meanwhile the Mayor, Pétion, had turned a blind eye to these frolics, though he had been informed in advance. He now arrived at the palace and dispersed the mob by flattery, telling them that they had behaved 'avec la fierté et la dignité d'hommes libres'. Chénier's article attacked Pétion and the demonstrators and defended the monarchy's constitutional rights. This time he did not hesitate to praise Louis XVI:

Pour moi, citoyen obscur, mais intègre et fidèle aux lois, j'élèverai la voix en leur nom et au nom de la patrie, et je remercierai le roi du service signalé qu'il vient de leur rendre. Je le remercierai d'avoir fait un usage prudent et judicieux du pouvoir que la constitution lui donne, et de n'avoir point cédé cette partie de la constitution, par conséquent la constitution entière et le salut de l'empire, à des menaces sanguinaires, à des clameurs et à des intrigues puissantes.

In the meantime Roland's government had been overthrown and on the 18th of June the King had appointed a new one largely composed of Feuillants (Beaulieu, Chambonas, Monciel, and Duranthon) who were powerless to stem the unrest that was spreading all over France, through the state of emergency arising from the army's reverses. It was naïve to think that by changing the ministers without new elections, or without suppressing the Clubs, the situation would improve. The Feuillants achieved power too late, and their government lasted only about three weeks.

Chénier was now fighting a losing battle and must have known it. His last articles followed in rapid succession: 'De la nécessité de l'union' (5 July 1792) called on all Frenchmen to sink their differences and unite in supporting La Fayette against the foreign enemy. 'De l'aveuglement de l'Assemblée nationale' (10 July) was directed against Torné and others who wished to suspend the Constitution and have a kind of dictatorship over the Assembly, supported by the Federal troops to be stationed near Paris, doing nothing when they were needed at the front. Chénier lost his faith in the monarchy before it fell, and went so far as to publish an open letter to Louis XVI on 19 July, deriding his new choice of ministers:

AU ROI

On prétend, mais cela n'est pas possible, que le ministère va de nouveau être abandonné à Roland, Clavière et Servan.

Ah! Sire, voudriez-vous gâter le 20 juin?

André Chénier.

He had at last realized that Louis XVI's vacillating policy, his unwillingness ever to trust a strong man at the head of affairs, his toadying to public opinion and to his enemies, could only result in the collapse of the constitution and of the monarchy itself. He was right: what would Chénier have written had he known the King's real thoughts on the matter? Brissot quotes in his memoirs a letter by Louis XVI, dated 27 July 1792, not many days before his downfall. Vergniaud had made overtures to the Court and was rebuffed, as other politicians had been before him; according to Brissot, Louis XVI wrote:

Il [Vergniaud] est venu me présenter une déclaration qu'il dit être franche et loyale. Ces gens-là, qui ne peuvent croire à la loyauté, à la franchise d'un Roi, font toujours des propositions de ce genre.

Les *Girondins* et les *Feuillants* ne songent qu'à eux, ils oublient les Français, leur patrie, les exilés; leurs propositions ne seront pas accueillies.[1]

Obviously, Louis XVI did not read the *Journal de Paris*. He was so stupid or ill-informed that he could not realize that while the Girondins, for all their republicanism, were to go to the scaffold because they tried to save his life, and should have been used as a buffer against the Jacobins, the Feuillants were the only group, apart from some royalists, who seriously believed in constitutional monarchy, and were practically his only genuine supporters. Chénier's last article in the *Journal de Paris* (27 July) was a personal one. It was a furious reply to Brissot, who had referred to him in *Le Patriote français* as a foreigner, writing, 'Un étranger, tant soit peu autrichien, barbouille huit colonnes dans le *Journal de Paris*, à raison de deux-cent-seize livres.' Chénier's violent reply ended on a prophetic note in which he foretold his own doom:

. . . Je veux qu'il sache que, parmi les auteurs des Suppléments, il en est

[1] F19, t. iv, p. 206.

sans doute plusieurs, mais au moins un, dont les méchants, heureux, n'intimideront jamais ni le cœur ni la bouche; qui, dans les cachots et sous le fer des bourreaux, ne cesserait pas d'en appeler aux lois, aux autorités légitimes, à la justice, à l'humanité, et de dévouer à l'exécration publique les tyrans déguisés sous le nom de patriotes; qui est prêt à mourir pour cette doctrine, impudemment traitée [par Brissot] de *parricide*; et qui mourra content de n'avoir plus sous les yeux l'avilissement d'une grande nation, réduite par ses fautes à choisir entre Coblentz et les Jacobins, entre les Autrichiens et Brissot.

After this, events moved so fast that there was little that Chénier or any journalist could do. He drew up a petition dated 31 July for a battalion of the National Guard, entitled 'Adresse à l'Assemblée nationale'. The Guards had been molested by the Marseillais on their arrival in Paris, one of them being killed and several wounded. They sent their deputation to the Assembly on the 31st, but Chénier's petition was probably written too late to be used. He was again in ill health and went for a few days to take the waters at Forges-les-Eaux. It was then that he wrote the beautiful poem 'Fille du vieux pasteur', one of his *Bucoliques*, which we have already discussed (above, pp. 207–8). It is a relief to see that his poetic gifts had not been affected by six months of vituperation. He returned to Paris on the 6th of August in time to witness the end of the monarchy and of the Legislative Assembly. As if to illustrate the influence of the municipality on the national government, on the 3rd of August Pétion handed the Assembly a petition from the Paris sections, calling for the king's 'déchéance' or dethronement. This was put down for debate for the 9th of August. On the 8th, defying popular opinion, the Assembly rejected a demand for La Fayette's impeachment. During the night of the 9th the Sections, prompted by Pétion and the Jacobins, formed an 'Insurrectional Commune' which organized the rising the next day. It was on the 9th, probably, that Chénier drew up his 'Projet d'un Discours du Roi à l'Assemblée Nationale', which was not used. The Tuileries and palace were invaded on the 10th of August and the royal family took refuge with the Assembly, who discussed their fate before their imprisonment in the Temple. Pétion, after spending some time in the Louvre, falsely promising the King his protection, had slipped away, while Chénier's former friend Roederer, perhaps mistakenly, advised him not to defend the palace, with the result that 600 out of 900 Swiss guards were massacred after laying down their arms. The National Guard went over to the 'people'.

The *Journal de Paris* was one of the few papers that dared to appear on that day, and its premises were sacked two days later, while a number of journalists were hacked to death all over Paris. Chénier's name had already been published on a 'liste de proscription': he was outlawed in the company of Regnault de Saint-Jean-d'Angély, Roucher, and Dupont de Nemours. Thus ended their campaign against the Jacobins as well as the Mayor, the Girondins, the 'brigands à piques', and the 'brigands à talons rouges'.

12

THE SUSPECT

THERE now began a mysterious phase in the poet's life, when at any moment he was in danger of being denounced for his past activities and executed as a public enemy. He went into hiding all that summer, and it is said that he spent part of the time at Marly, where the Trudaines hastily acquired a new house as well as obtaining another hideout at Rouen. Chafing in captivity, Chénier must have witnessed with anger the return to a semblance of power of Roland and his group, together with the promotion of Danton as Minister of Justice, while in fact the Assembly was, for a time, little more than the tool of the Insurrectional Commune. A second Revolution had taken place, in which the Declaration of the Rights of Man and most of the Constitution had been quietly buried. By the end of August the prisons were packed with close on three thousand untried prisoners, awaiting execution or massacre. Jeremy Bentham offered his services to create a more humane and efficient prison system, and even proposed himself as Governor, but the offer was refused. Special courts were set up in August, and slowly, too slowly for the mob, the executions began.

If he ever returned to Paris, Chénier could count on the protection of his father, who was a highly respected representative of his Section. He might also have counted on the support of Marie-Joseph, for what that was worth, and one or two deputies who were still in sympathy with his ideas. Apart from his stay at Marly, he must also, at this time, have spent some time with Mme Lecoulteux at Louveciennes (also spelt Lucienne or Luciennes) as well as with friends at Saint-Germain-en-Laye. He must have been at the Château de Voisins at Louveciennes in early September, where he heard of the terrible massacres that broke out at Versailles and in Paris, for he wrote from Rouen on the 15th of September (not the 22nd, as stated by G. Walter), 'Je savais, avant d'arriver ici, ce qui s'est passé à Versailles. Je l'appris le jour même et le lendemain, à Lucienne et à Saint-Germain.' He was later to refer to the Versailles massacre in the finest of his odes, the *Ode à Versailles*. It was on the 2nd of September that old M. Montmorin, father of Madame de Beaumont, after clearing himself of accusations against him (one of the pieces of evidence having been forged by Brissot), was murdered by the mob waiting at the door, and his body impaled and paraded in triumph. A few days later Chénier passed through Paris again and spent a night at Forges, followed by ten days at Rouen before going to Le Havre.

What was Chénier doing at Le Havre in the autumn of 1792? G. Walter has suggested that he was making plans to escape from France with his father; but there is no sign that Louis de Chénier made any preparations for leaving Paris. With whom did he stay? The Trudaines took a house at Rouen at this time, and he might have been with them. However, at the same time his brother Constantin was making arrangements to sail for Alicante, to which he had been posted as Consul. A letter written by Constantin some years later (An 6) and addressed to 'Lecoulteux et Cie, Négociants à Rouen' begins: 'Citoyens: les politesses que j'ai reçues en votre maison lorsque je passai par Rouen à la fin de 1792, allant au Havre m'embarquer pour Alicant, ne sont pas les seuls droits que vous avez à ma connaissance.'[1] He was grateful also for their sheltering André. That he was not only referring to business matters, but also to a social relationship, is shown by his last sentence, 'Permettez que je présente mes respects aux dames que j'ai eu l'honneur de voir.' It is known that André Chénier went to stay, before his brother, with the important banker and merchant Lecoulteux (or Lecouteulx) who was related to his close friend, Fanny Lecoulteux, of Louveciennes. He might also have paid his visit to Le Havre in order to make advance arrangements for his brother Constantin. More interesting, in view of what we have already seen of his relations with Mme de Beaumont, is the fact that Pauline fled to Rouen after her father's murder: is it possible that he accompanied her, or went there in order to see her?[2]

But to take such a mild view of his activities would be to forget Chénier's intrepid character and his political fanaticism. Rouen had become one of the main centres to which moderates, royalists, and independents were flocking in order to escape from the massacres and to prepare for further action. A large number of the remaining Feuillants were already there. Chénier wrote the following letter to his father from Rouen on the 13th of September 1792:

---

[1] BMC 11798/420/320.

[2] F6(a), p. 205. Mme de Beaumont stayed with the duc de Liancourt. Chénier might also have gone to Le Havre in order to settle the estate of her uncle, the Marquis de Montmorin, who had been assassinated on the same day as her father.

J'arrivai hier ici, mon très cher père, après avoir passé vingt-quatre heures à Forges. Je trouve ici votre lettre avec le papier qu'elle renfermait. Cette ville me paraît fort tranquille. L'affluence de Paris y est grande et il est à craindre que cette cause n'en trouble la tranquillité.

J'ai ici beaucoup d'amis qui ont le dessein d'y passer l'hiver. Ils me pressent fort d'y rester avec eux. Je ne puis leur répondre rien de décisif encore, car, pour vous et pour moi, je suis obligé de ne point perdre de vue le projet que vous savez. Cependant je passerai ici quelques jours, pour voir si les choses s'acheminent vers une décision prompte.

Mon départ, qui vous afflige, m'a vivement affligé aussi. Mais il le fallait. Au reste, si quelques circonstances me faisaient rester ici, ce qui ne pourrait être que dans le cas où je serais entièrement rassuré sur les dangers qui menacent notre fortune, je pourrais aller vous voir de temps en temps à Paris. Je vous écrirai sous peu de jours. Vous pouvez m'écrire ici sous mon nom, avec une enveloppe à l'adresse que je vous ai laissée. Adieu. Je vous embrasse aussi tendrement que je vous aime et respecte.

In spite of the affection it shows, the letter was not signed: the situation was too dangerous for that. When we look closely at the letter it is true that the words 'pour vous et pour moi' in the second paragraph suggest some common plan affecting both father and son, as do the words 'les dangers qui menacent notre fortune' in the third. They could, perhaps, suggest a plan of escape such as accompanying Constantin to Alicante. However, the speculations about staying the winter in Rouen, especially in the third paragraph, suggest that if Chénier had plans for escape he did not regard them as very urgent. There are other possibilities behind the words 'ce projet que vous savez'.

There were, at the time, two important plots in progress in Normandy, both of which had their centre in Rouen and Le Havre. The first was concocted by the reactionary duc de Liancourt who, while being a member of the most diehard royalist clubs, had also been a Feuillant. He was busy raising and distributing funds and bribing people in Paris, with the object of enabling the royal family to escape from the Temple to England through Le Havre. When de Liancourt had to flee from Rouen it was Chénier's friend Lacretelle who took over his affairs.[1] De Liancourt had managed to bribe the *Journal de Rouen*, which in any case was favourable to the monarchy, and Lacretelle relates how 'J'y insérai, et sous mon nom, une suite d'articles destinés à chauffer l'esprit un peu froid des Rouennais'.[2] De Liancourt was received by a Mme de Boulogne and remained in secret correspondence with the

---

[1] F57, p. 93.   [2] Ibid., p. 96.

King during his imprisonment: as he was still military governor of the Normandy ports, the only real problem was to get the King out of prison. Incidentally, Lacretelle mentions that Chénier's friend Desmeuniers (see above, p. 221) was also in Rouen at that time, and so was Chéron, one of his collaborators on the *Journal de Paris*.

The second plot was one which involved Chénier's other set of friends, the Lecoulteux. The Spanish envoy, Ocariz, had two million *livres* at his disposal—part of which is said to have gone to Danton—and was trying to persuade the British government to double that amount. Among the Feuillants who had fled to Rouen were the Feuillant leaders, Charles and Théodore de Lameth and Adrien Duport. The Lameths were concerned in both plots. Théodore relates in his memoirs: 'Le chevalier d'Ocariz, ambassadeur d'Espagne, fit tout ce qui était possible pour sauver le Roi. Il avait deux millions à sa disposition. Cependant cette somme se trouvait insuffisante et le temps lui manquant pour faire compléter par l'Espagne ce qui était nécessaire, il s'adressa au gouvernement anglais, mais vainement, malgré les plus vives prières.'[1] According to Lameth it was Danton who insisted on obtaining a further two millions, which Pitt refused to find. He mentions the other plot elsewhere,[2] saying that de Liancourt was commanding a division in Normandy and preparing the king's escape.

While it is possible that Lacretelle might have interested Chénier in de Liancourt's plot and that this took him to Le Havre, there is direct evidence that he was in some way concerned with that of Ocariz. His distant patron, Montmorin, had formerly been ambassador to Spain, and Chénier had learnt some Spanish while he was in London with the idea of writing some Spanish elegies. One of the charges raised against Chénier while he was in prison at Saint-Lazare was as follows:

André Chénier: avoir recélé les papiers de l'ambassadeur d'Espagne et les avoir soustraits aux recherches du Comité de Sûreté générale, depuis qu'il était à la maison Lazare.[3]

In the autumn of 1792 Ocariz was negotiating with the banker, Lecoulteux, in Rouen. In December and January he came into the open with two appeals to the Convention which were dismissed.

On the 15th of September Chénier wrote to his father a letter, from Rouen, which contains the following information:

. . . Il y a ici des commissaires de l'Assemblée nationale et d'autres du

---

[1] F62, p. 147.   [2] Ibid., p. 178.   [3] E3, p. xl.

pouvoir exécutif, qui font tous leurs efforts pour réchauffer le patriotisme, mais malgré cela, il paraît que même le petit peuple demeure fort tiède.

Je suis obligé pour des raisons particulieres d'aller au Havre. Je pars après-demain lundi soir, j'y resterai six ou sept jours; après quoi je reviendrai probablement trouver mes amis ici; car, depuis mon départ, il a été fait des choses que vous devinez bien devoir changer ou suspendre mes premiers projets. Vous aviez prévu cela, moi je ne le croyais pas possible. Il ne faut plus m'écrire ici, mais au Havre: à Monsieur Ant. Caun, poste-restante. Je vous ai mandé différemment par ma dernière lettre qui vous est parvenue maintenant, j'espère. . . .

It seems clear from this that if Chénier had ever thought of going abroad he had already changed his mind before going to Le Havre, so that he was not going there just to arrange a passage. Biographers have, for some reason, not noticed that he was travelling under a false name, *Antoine Caun*: this means that he must have had false papers of identity in this name. As he added 'dorénavant il faut s'en tenir à cette dernière manière' it is likely that he maintained this pseudonym for some time. This was a wise precaution, for in the only letter that has survived from his stay at Le Havre, dated 24 September, he told his father that he had received a letter from him but 'En l'ouvrant, je me suis aperçu que le cachet n'était pas intact, et que probablement je n'étais pas le premier à l'ouvrir'. He went on to warn his father against the lack of discretion with which he wrote.[1]

Back in Rouen on 26 September he wrote to his father on the 29th to say that his brother Constantin had joined him. As for his stay at Le Havre, he wrote:

J'ai été au Havre chez le bon vieux excellent homme à qui vous m'aviez adressé. Dès que je vous ai nommé, il m'a reçu avec une politesse amicale et une bonhomie extrême. Il m'a invité à dîner, et à un dîner dont il a arrangé les convives exprès pour moi. Il s'est prêté à tout ce que j'ai voulu. Il m'a parlé de vous quand nous avons été seuls avec beaucoup d'effusion de cœur.[2]

The fact that there were guests at this dinner, specially invited to suit Chénier's purposes, suggests that he was there on some business which was probably of a political nature. At the end of his letter Chénier told his father that if he was in danger he should come to Rouen, adding, 'Je vous recommande aussi tous les écrits et ouvrages et papiers que

---

[1] G. Walter (D22, p. 797) states that the manuscript of this letter is at Carcassonne: the present writer noted its absence from the collection in 1956.

[2] D22, p. 797.

vous savez. S'ils se perdaient, tous les plaisirs, les études, les amusements d'une vie entière seraient perdus. Adieu, je vous embrasse de tout mon cœur.' This letter, like the others, was unsigned.

The next letter from Rouen was dated 2 October and said that Constantin had left on the previous day for Le Havre. He said that the commissars were suspicious of the two or three thousand visitors from Paris and that steps were being taken to check their identity, but that he did not expect to be molested. He added, 'J'ai envie d'aller voir Nantes; car, dans les inquiétudes où l'on est pour plusieurs personnes chères, je ne vois d'autres distractions que de courir et changer de lieu.' Rouen, Le Havre, and now Nantes: it is plain that if he was not anxious about himself, Chénier was trying to get someone else away through one of these ports, and perhaps the 'personnes chères' were none other than the royal family. He continued, 'Cependant je reste ici, et ne suis point déterminé à faire ce voyage. Vous pouvez m'écrire comme à l'ordinaire chez *MM Le C. et comp.*'[1] Much of this is a blind, and it would hardly be surprising if he did visit Nantes between this letter and the next, dated 10 October, a week later. In this letter he showed his anxiety at not having heard from his father for fifteen days, adding, 'Vous jugez bien, combien l'idée de Paris est accompagnée de craintes et d'alarmes; et vous êtes maintenant la seule personne qui y réside à laquelle je prenne un si vif intérêt.' This letter, also, was unsigned.

At this point the correspondence breaks off, and the next evidence we have of his movements is a letter written from Paris on the 28th of October 1792, which shows that he had decided to cut short his visit to Rouen. This is hardly surprising, as the political 'commissars' had done their work thoroughly in Rouen: among those captured and later executed was one of the Lameth brothers. Chénier's letter of 28 October was addressed to a M. Brodelet, who had written to him on the 28th of September on behalf of the German poet Wieland, who had been inquiring about him. Chénier was no doubt flattered

[1] My italics. D22, pp. 798–9. This (Pléiade) edition gives a faulty text of most of the letters, but is quoted as being the most complete. The manuscript in this case ends as follows, the words in italics being omitted by Walter:

'Je me dis souvent que dans l'état et dans la maison où vous êtes, respecté de tous, *excellent citoyen dans toute la force du terme*, vous n'avez rien à redouter, et cependant je ne puis me défaire des inquiétudes que je vous ai déjà témoignées sur votre séjour à Paris. *Je vous prie de donner à Claster le billet ci-joint et de lui dire de vous remettre ce qu'il aura à me répondre, s'il a quelque chose à me répondre.*'

The note to Claster was (ostensibly) an order for some hand-made boots, but might have been a message in code. In addition the manuscript bears the note 'reçu le 9 oct.'—that is, a whole week later.

at this anxiety on the part of 'l'illustre Wieland, dont je ne connais que le nom et la célébrité'. To his question, 'si je suis encore en vie', he replied, 'Je suis encore en vie. Je pourrais ajouter qu'ayant fait du bien à plus d'un homme et n'ayant jamais fait de mal à qui que ce soit, je ne dois avoir couru aucun risque ni avoir eu rien à craindre.' To the second question, 'ce que je fais dans la Révolution?', he replied at more length. Saying that he had published 'reflections' on events from time to time and that he had thus made many enemies, he added that he had now given up politics:

. . . Aussi suis-je bien déterminé à me tenir toujours à l'écart, ne prenant aucune part aux affaires publiques, et me bornant dans la solitude à faire, pour la liberté, la tranquillité et le bonheur de la république, des vœux qui, à dire vrai, surpassent de beaucoup mes espérances.

There was a third question, 'ce que je fais dans le monde?' To this he answered—*rien*, then, relenting:

. . . me livrant tout entier aux goûts que j'ai toujours eus, je m'attache, dans la retraite, à une étude approfondie des lettres et des langues antiques, et je consacre ce qui me reste de jeunesse à me mettre en état de suivre un jour ses traces; heureux si je puis, comme lui, faire quelque honneur à ma langue et à mon pays et à moi-même.

Chénier asked Wieland to pay his respects to the 'savant et judicieux M. Heyne', the classical scholar who was a professor at Göttingen, and described himself as 'un homme qui, sans l'avoir jamais vu, oserait presque se dire un de ses disciples'. This letter is, in its way, a valuable contribution to our knowledge of Chénier's state of mind at that time: it shows that he had now decided to abandon politics and journalism, and that he was trying to resign himself to the Republic which had been declared on the 21st of September. More important, we see that he was turning back to poetry as well as learning, while his tribute to Heyne suggests that he intended producing a work of scholarship.

But if Chénier honestly thought he had finished with the turmoil of politics, it had not yet finished with him. He had yet one more supreme effort to make before he could enjoy a few months of relative calm. During October and November the Convention was debating whether the King should be brought to trial. Royalty was abolished on the 21st of September, a new Constitution was being made, and the French armies under Dumouriez successfully invaded Belgium and Savoy. But it was only a week after Chénier's statement to Wieland, saying that he had retired to a quiet life, that discussion of the King's trial came to a head.

It is commonly held for a fact—first mentioned by Chateaubriand in 1802—that Chénier volunteered to act as secretary or assistant to Malesherbes in preparing the King's defence.[1] It was only on the 11th of December 1792 that the King was allowed to choose lawyers for his defence. At first he chose Target and Tronchet. Target declined and was thereafter branded a coward, even by the King's enemies. Malesherbes came forward and prepared the defence with de Sèze.[2] If Chénier did help, it must have been in a private capacity, probably in preparing documents at Malesherbes's house, for there is no mention of his share in these events in the *acte d'accusation* drawn up against him at Saint-Lazare. Also, it is not necessary to think that Chénier volunteered for this task, and it is just as likely that his nephew was right in stating that it was Malesherbes who invited him to give his services.[3] Lamoignon de Malesherbes, despite his age—he was now 71 years old, and was decapitated in 1794 at the age of 73—had hastened from Lausanne to come to the King's help. That Chénier's participation in the trial, if only behind the scenes, was more than a family tradition, is shown by all those who first took up the story of his life—Latouche, Jacob, Labitte, Sainte-Beuve, and others. Gabriel de Chénier pointed out that 'Il [Malesherbes] avait, d'ailleurs, un motif particulier pour avoir un entretien avec André. Il était l'oncle de M. de La Luzerne, l'ambassadeur en Angleterre . . . il le connaissait déjà; il l'avait souvent vu dans la maison Trudaine.'[4] If there was such an invitation, it was not one that Chénier could refuse; for, we remember, he had praised Malesherbes as one of the saviours of France, along with Turgot, in his *Hymne à la Justice* of 1787.

According to the bibliophile Jacob (1840), in the short period before the King's death Chénier published a number of anonymous articles

[1] Chateaubriand: *Le Génie du Christianisme*, 2ᵉ partie, livre iii, ch. vi (Éclaircissements, note 15), '. . . son courage, *sa noble proposition à M. de Malesherbes* . . .'. I have been unable to find any earlier statement of this kind; but the fact that Chateaubriand's brother had married into the Malesherbes family suggests that he might have had inside information.

[2] Malesherbes's letter to the President of the Convention, dated 11 décembre 1792, was written before the official decision to allow a defence was known, since it begins, 'J'ignore si la Convention nationale donnera à Louis XVI un conseil pour le défendre, et si elle lui en laissera le choix.'   [3] D7, t. i, pp. xcii–xcviii.

[4] Ibid., p. xcvii. Of course there will always remain some doubt whether the letter from the Minister of Justice (see above, p. 252) was not a reply to an offer from A.C. to help in the trial. But it does seem unlikely that he would have volunteered, having no legal training.

n his defence, as well as 'placards' or posters which were put up all
)ver Paris.[1] Two of the articles attributed to him appeared in the
Mercure Français and their authenticity has not been contested. If
here were any doubt that Chénier, in spite of his vows, had again
:ntered the arena, this is dispelled by a number of fragments which are
o be found among his papers. The first of these begins with a plea for
lumane treatment of the royal family while in prison and refers to
l debate on the trial, held in the Assembly on the 3rd of December.[2]
Iere he argued that if Louis were not tried, then the whole of the Con-
/ention must be: 'Tous avouent donc . . . et c'est ce qu'avouent plus
jue les autres ceux qui prétendent qu'il faut ou faire périr le Roi, ou
áire le procès à la Convention ou au 10 août.' This was a very dangerous
argument. The second manuscript is an address 'A tous les citoyens
rançais', in which Chénier, who must have been one of those who were
)ressing for a referendum, drew up a detailed and carefully reasoned
:tatement of how the referendum could be carried out. The third,
:ast in the form of a speech, set out the procedure for voting for or
against the death penalty.

The remaining manuscript (first published by Latouche in 1819) was
l most dignified appeal to be made by the King to the Convention,
l 'Lettre de Louis XVI aux Députés de la Convention'. This was
lated 17 January 1793. Boissy d'Anglas, in his life of Malesherbes, does
lot mention Chénier's activity at this stage, but elsewhere he wrote:

Par exemple, il n'est pas exact de dire qu'André Chénier fut le rédacteur
l'une lettre de Louis XVI à la Convention, pour interjecter, après sa con-
lamnation, un appel à la nation elle-même, et que cette lettre fut signée dans
a nuit du 17 ou 18 janvier. Je ne sais pas si elle fut signée, mais, hélas! ce que
e sais trop bien, c'est que les trois défenseurs de cet infortuné prince, vinrent à la vérité lire de sa part une note dans cette intention, mais qu'elle
l'avait rien de commun avec la prétendue lettre attribuée à André Chénier,
:t imprimée à la fin de ses œuvres; la noble brièveté de cette note la rendait
)ien plus convenable que la lettre dont il s'agit, quelque pathétique et quel-
jue éloquente qu'elle puisse paraître à ses lecteurs.[3]

[1] E1, p. xxxiv. See also Labitte, F56: 'André, plein de dédain pour ces "grands pa-
riotes", continua sa tâche périlleuse . . . adresses, articles, *placards*, correspondance, rien
le fatiga son courage.'

[2] E1, p. 211. In his article of 25 Dec., Chénier gave a harsh enough picture of Louis
XVI, whom he described as 'Louis le Dernier' at the same time as he pleaded in his favour.

[3] F14, t. ii, p. 100. Whether Boissy was right or not, the real reasons for the obscurity
hat surrounds Chénier's contribution to Malesherbes's work are, first, that it was de Sèze
vho had the last word as to what documents would be used, and, second, that after the
:rial Malesherbes was forced to destroy all the papers in his possession.

Boissy d'Anglas was a warm friend of Chénier's but his testimony here is not conclusive. As for the 'prétendue lettre' it certainly exists in Chénier's papers. Whether it was used or not is another question: it is not unlikely that it was both considered and rejected, for Louis XVI set his face against any emotional appeal and suppressed the most sensitive passages from de Sèze's defence.

As for Chénier's articles in the *Mercure Français*, these appeared on the 25th and 29th of December 1792. They were written with great detachment, though his customary bitterness broke out in a reference to the Jacobins as 'un parti qui a affiché d'une manière ouverte l'esprit d'anarchie et de désorganisation et qui s'est fait un système d'avilir et de perdre la Convention'. It is hard to imagine anyone but Chénier having the audacity to write about them in this way at such a time.

When we remember that until the last moment Ocariz and Lecoulteux were trying to buy off the king's enemies, and that Chénier was not only helping Malesherbes but feverishly writing and circulating anonymous articles, we can see that he must have passed a month of feverish activity. In all this there was no sign that he was thinking as a 'royalist'. He shared the same qualms, now, as the Girondins, who at first hesitated over the competence of the Convention to try the monarch, then pinned their hopes on a referendum, and finally on an appeal for clemency. While he was doing this, Louis XVI was being tried under the chairmanship of Barère, whom Chénier was to attack violently in his *Ïambes*. Marie-Joseph took the plunge in the opposite direction to his brother. Anxious to keep in with the Jacobins, for he had been elected deputy for the Seine-et-Oise only in September, he did not dare to qualify his vote, as some did, but wrote out a little speech, as follows:

J'aurais vraiment désiré, je l'avoue, de ne prononcer jamais la mort de mon semblable; et si je pouvais m'isoler un moment du devoir pénible qui m'est imposé, je voterais pour la loi la moins sévère. Mais la justice, qui est la raison d'État, l'intérêt du peuple me prescrivent de vaincre mon extrême répugnance. Je prononce la peine qu'a prononcée avant moi le code pénal. Je vote pour la mort.

It seems impossible that André Chénier should ever have accepted help from Marie-Joseph, after this.

The King was declared guilty by 683 votes and the referendum ('appel au peuple') was rejected by 424. When it came to voting on the penalty there were 721 voters in the Assembly, of whom 361 voted for death and 360 against. By the simple process of subtracting from the second figure and adding to the first all those who had voted for death 'with certain reservations', 26 were added to the first group, resulting in a vote of 387 against 334. The Girondins made a final effort on the next day (17 January 1793) and had a vote taken on the question of a reprieve: this was rejected by 380 to 310. The King's execution took place on the 21st of January, to be followed in due course by other members of the royal family, after whom came the Girondins, the Dantonists, the Hébertists, and so on, until Robespierre was guillotined in 1794. Chénier, whose life was now more in danger than before, obtained a medical certificate stating that his health required him to live in the country, and retired to Versailles.

Apart from the occasions when Chénier had to come to Paris in order to register at his Section, and perhaps spend a few days with his father, he seems to have spent the rest of his spell of liberty, until his arrest in 1794, at Versailles. There he took a little house, which was then the last but one in the rue de Satory, just beside the Porte de Satory, on the outskirts of the town. It was a self-contained house with a little orchard round it, and a view across the palace grounds.[1] Though his health was in a very poor state, so that his request for a medical certificate served a double purpose, this seems to have been one of the happiest periods in the poet's life. He had, at last, a place of his own, and enjoyed his garden and even his solitude. Offering Fanny Lecoulteux a basket of fruit which he described as 'the first fruits of his orchard' he said that he also had a little glass-house of his own:

> Précurseurs de l'automne, ô fruits nés d'une terre
> Où l'art industrieux, sous ses maisons de verre
> Des soleils du midi sait feindre les chaleurs,
> Allez trouver Fanny, cette mère craintive.
> A sa fille aux doux yeux, fleur débile et tardive,
> Rendez la force et les couleurs . . .

He referred to his house, also, in his *Ode à Versailles*:

> Paris me semble un autre empire,
> Dès que chez toi je vois sourire
> Mes pénates secrets couronnés de rameaux;
> D'où souvent les monts et les plaines
> Vont dirigeant mes pas aux campagnes prochaines,
> Sous de triples cintres d'ormeaux . . .

[1] Then no. 69 rue de Satory, now rue du Maréchal Joffre, it was not, as stated in H1, p. 26, the present no. 35, but the very small house before the church, now containing a café on the ground floor and one story above.

The country walk he referred to would take him about an hour. The supreme consolation of these last months was his platonic friendship with Madame Laurent (Fanny) Lecoulteux, at Louveciennes. A fine road, specially constructed for Madame du Barry who had had a country house there, and planted with elms, led to Louveciennes through the Chesnaye valley. The Lecoulteux had taken the Château de Voisins as long ago as 1787, and as yet had remained unmolested. Françoise Lecoulteux was the daughter of Madame Pourrat, a well-known beauty and wit in her day, who had kept a literary salon and known Voltaire.[1] Born in 1767, Françoise was only about eighteen when in 1785 she married Laurent Lecoulteux de la Noraye, whose name we have already noted as being on the list of members of the Feuillants. The Lecoulteux held a strong position behind the scenes, having through their banking-house some control over public finance. They enjoyed all those amenities which enabled them, at the same time, to lead a rich intellectual life and, as patrons of the arts, to surround themselves with a select company of minds. Chénier is said to have known Françoise before her marriage, through Trudaine and Madame de Beaumont, if not through Suard.

Fanny Lecoulteux had her portrait painted by David, but while she had what Becq de Fouquières described as 'un profil aux traits nobles et purs' she appears to have attracted people more through her fragility and refinement than by her beauty. She had not the energy or wit of her mother, or of her sister the comtesse d'Hocquart de Turtot. Lacretelle reports her as giving an amusing retort to Condorcet's materialism. Condorcet was at Suard's house at Fontenay-aux-Roses in 1789, animatedly talking about the possibility of man's achieving 'immortality on earth' thanks to Reason, Virtue, and Science. He said that in heaven, the angels were more likely to favour young beauties than old dowagers. To this Fanny replied, 'Je ne sais de quel prix seront ces pauvres charmes formés du limon de la terre, aux yeux des anges et des saints; mais je crois que la puissance divine saura mieux réparer les outrages du temps, s'il en est bien dans un tel séjour, que votre Physique et votre Chimie ne pourront y parvenir sur cette terre. Il me semble que tout s'embellit avec une auréole céleste.'[2] Behind this light reply there is evidence of some religious conviction which, as well as her failing health and married state, helped to purify Chénier's attachment to her.

Chénier's first poem for Fanny Lecoulteux had been written before

<hr>

[1] See F75.   [2] F58, t. i, p. 355.

he left London in 1790: for him, one of the pleasures of returning to
France was to go and see her with her child:

> Allons, douce Élégie, à qui dans mes beaux jours
> J'ai tant fait soupirer d'inquiètes amours,
> Ta voix n'est pas toujours à gémir destinée.
> Près d'un lit maternel viens bénir l'hyménée . . .

But this child died in 1792, when Chénier, in the midst of his political
activities, wrote a tender elegy 'Sur la mort d'un enfant' which ended
with the touching words,

> Adieu, dans la demeure où nous vous suivrons tous,
> Où ta mère déjà tourne ses yeux jaloux.

Now she was in fear of losing her second child. Her father was to be
executed a fortnight before Chénier, and she survived the poet by only
eighteen months.

   At last Chénier had found a pure and profound affection, which he
took with him to the grave. In the past, however, his loves had all
been so full of violence, doubt, jealousy, and despair that he now
found it hard to resign himself to the platonic affection which is described in the odes of this period. He sent her fruits, flowers, poems,
accompanied her on walks in the woods, sat with her at the bedside of
her ailing child, and even suggested, in 'Aux premiers fruits de mon
verger', that he would gladly die to preserve her child, if, in exchange,
he could be sure of the mother's love. This poem (a manuscript of
which has recently been discovered in Dublin by H. Shields) ends as
follows:

> Sur ses pieds délicats ma bouche défaillante
> Savourerait la mort; et mon âme expirante
> Du bonheur d'une mère irait payer les Dieux.
> Je voudrais seulement que du moins sur la terre
> Où dormiraient mes os, s'élevât une pierre
>   Qui fût voisine de ses yeux.
>
> Mon nom, à cet aspect, troublerait sa pensée.
> Quelque jour, à sa fille entre ses bras pressée,
> L'œil humide peut-être en passant près de moi:
> 'Celui-ci, dirait-elle, à qui je fus bien chère,
> Fut content de mourir, en songeant que ta mère
>   N'aurait point à pleurer sur toi.'

(H4)

This, of course, was little more than emotional blackmail, but of a tender kind. Biographers have naturally speculated on the exact relationship between the two; all that can be gathered from the poems he wrote about her is that it was unlike any experience he had known with other women. He yielded sometimes to feelings of frustration and jealousy, but now it was with shame: in one of the uncompleted odes he wrote:

> J'ai vu sur d'autres yeux, qu'Amour faisait sourire,
> Ses doux regards s'attendrir et pleurer,
> Et du miel le plus doux que sa bouche respire
> Une autre bouche s'enivrer.
>
> Et quand sur mon visage inquiet, tourmenté,
> Une sueur involontaire
> Exprimait le dépit de mon cœur agité,
> Un coup d'œil caressant furtivement jeté
> Tempérait dans mon sein cette souffrance amère.

Another ode just as violently thrust away these tortured and unworthy feelings. The ode beginning 'Non, de tous les amants les regards, les soupirs / Ne sont pas des pièges perfides' is a most unusual analysis of such a situation. Almost entirely written in a series of negatives, it dismisses the idea that either he or Fanny could be treacherous. Yet it is plain that he suffered more deeply from her extreme sensitiveness than he had done from the inconstancy of those whom he had loved before:

> Des lèvres d'une belle un seul mot échappé
> Blesse d'une trace profonde
> Le cœur d'un malheureux qui ne voit qu'elle au monde . . .
> Son cœur pleure en secret frappé
> Quand sa bouche feint de sourire . . .

The poem ends with the extraordinary question, 'Crois-tu qu'il soit des cœurs sincères?' It is obvious that Chénier was having a hard apprenticeship to virtue, and that he loved her more than she loved him. We can see her as the poet saw her, through Palewski's excellent description:

Fanny a les lignes du visage pures, le nez mince et droit, la bouche petite, le menton haut, le col très-haut. Les cheveux châtains, frisés à la diable, suivant la mode de l'époque, descendent en désordre sur le front, cachent ses oreilles, s'avancent en mèches sur ses joues et se relèvent par derrière en lourd chignon. Elle a la poitrine bien faite, la ligne de la nuque nettement

dessinée. Elle est belle, mais sans éclat, son regard est doux, timide, vertueux.
Elle écoute, parle peu, prodigue les consolations, compatit aux douleurs.
Elle répand le charme de ses sourires, de son innocence; elle est instruite et
se tait, de crainte d'être pédante.[1]

Chénier sometimes accompanied her when she went to visit the sick,
and envied them her tenderness:

> Le ciel t'a vue en tes prairies
> Oublier tes loisirs, tes lentes rêveries;
> Et tes dons et tes soins chercher les malheureux;
> Tes délicates mains à leurs lèvres amères
> Présenter des sucs salutaires,
> Ou presser d'un lin pur leurs membres douloureux,
>
> Souffrances que je leur envie . . .

The odes he wrote for Fanny are thus a curious mixture of conflicting
and almost irreconcilable elements, as were the early elegies. But their
interest and novelty does not lie only in the extremes between patience
and impatience, jealousy and shame, humility and pride: we witness
the poet sounding a new instrument as well as exploring new regions of
his sensibility. There are no odes to compare with these, either for
sincerity or craftsmanship, in the eighteenth century. They are constructed in a wide variety of verse-forms which strike an entirely new
note in his work. He was developing new stanza-forms of six or seven
lines, learning to place the shorter line with a cunning that prepared the
way for the *Ïambes*. Though 'Fanny, l'heureux mortel' after it was set
to music became one of the most hackneyed drawing-room pieces in
the nineteenth century and has moments of slick writing and imprecise
generalization, it contains some passages which can never lose their
charm:

> Je pense: Elle était là. Tous disaient: 'Qu'elle est belle!'
> Tels furent ses regards, sa démarche fut telle,
> Et tels ses vêtements, sa voix et son discours.
> Sur ce gazon assis, et dominant la plaine,
> Des méandres de Seine,
> Rêveuse, elle suivait les obliques détours.

The same ode ends with a finely-expressed baroque conceit:

> Ainsi dans les forêts j'erre avec ton image:
> Ainsi le jeune faon, dans son désert sauvage,

[1] F75. David's portrait of Fanny Lecoulteux is reproduced in D6, edition of 1884. All
that is to be added to Palewski's description is that she looks highly intelligent and that
her eyes are not only 'doux, timides' &c. but suggest a shrewd wit.

> D'un plomb volant percé, précipite ses pas.
> Il emporte en fuyant sa mortelle blessure;
> Couché près d'une eau pure,
> Palpitant, hors d'haleine, il attend le trépas.[1]

It is interesting to notice that Chénier had already used the same image of the wounded fawn in one of the elegies he wrote for the mysterious D.z.n:

> Tel que le faon blessé fuit, court, mais dans son flanc
> Traîne le plomb mortel qui fait couler son sang,
> Ainsi là, dans mon cœur, errant à l'aventure,
> Je porte cette belle, auteur de ma blessure.

A comparison of the two passages shows very well how Chénier had matured as a poet. The stanza in the ode is not only more fluid and harmonious, beautifully imitating the movement of what is described: Chénier has also learnt how to develop an image to the full, instead of throwing it out, one of many, without exploring the feeling it implies. In both cases the image is probably based on Virgil (*Aen.* iv. 89) and also recalls Racine's lines in *Phèdre*, 'Depuis près de six mois, honteux, désespéré / Portant partout le trait dont je suis déchiré'. But in this ode Chénier found not only a rhythm that was all his own, but an absolute delicacy of expression that was sometimes lacking in the earlier poems.

One of the most famous odes of this period is the one beginning:

> Mai de moins de roses, l'automne
> De moins de pampres se couronne,
> Moins d'épis flottent en moissons,
> Que sur ma lèvre, sur ma lyre,
> Fanny, tes regards, ton sourire
> Ne font éclore de chansons . . .

Opinions are divided about this poem, which was first published by Sainte-Beuve in 1839. It is a poem in which fancy has overruled imagination, for it proceeds from one conceit to another, most of them conventional images which only the pleasing rhythm redeems. The poem ends with an unfinished conceit:

> Les perles de la poésie
> Forment, sous leurs doigts d'ambroisie
> D'un collier le brillant contour.

---

[1] Perhaps there is a reminiscence of it in Baudelaire's *Le Cygne*, 'Ainsi dans la forêt où mon esprit s'exile'.

> Viens, Fanny: que ma main suspende
> Sur ton sein cette noble offrande,
> . . . . . .

Sainte-Beuve, not with the best of taste, suggested that the last line
should be something like 'Tes bras sont le collier d'amour' or 'Ton
sein est le trône d'amour'.[1] He did not appear to see that the first would
mean repeating the word *collier*, the second, the word *sein*. His second
suggestion, with its 'throne', is in any case ridiculous, while both suggestions are banal and merely sensual, out of keeping with the tone
of the odes. We have to look for a line which Chénier had certainly
written but suppressed out of delicacy for a married woman; probably
something like 'Le poème de mon amour' which would complete the
thought in the first three lines. There could have been no easier task
for Chénier than to find a line of eight syllables rhyming with 'contour'.
It is perhaps the shallowest poem he wrote for Fanny, and the least
worthy of her, though there is a fault of taste, also, in 'A Fanny,
malade', with its last two lines,

> Vivre est te regarder, et t'aimer, te le dire;
> Et quand tu daignes me sourire,
> Le lit de Vénus même est sans prix à mes yeux.

The odes for Fanny Lecoulteux have certain imperfections, but they
are of the kind that arise from an uncertainty in the emotions; one
might say that trembling of heart and will which results from a conflict
of too varied emotions. This weakness sometimes overflows into the
expression itself, even though the poet has invented forms of which he
is perfectly sure. The outcome of this is to direct the reader's attention
more to the poet's predicament than to his poetic achievement. In this
case the achievement is indeed hard to appreciate. We have the impression that in spite of the destructive influence of his journalism
and polemics the poet's sensibility had emerged unspoilt, and yet at the
same time he appears, himself, to be surprised by this access of tenderness. His anxious eye for jealousy or treason reflects his need to seek
an opponent, even in love. These odes give the impression of a tiger
submitting to the yoke, and to that extent are not the poems of fulfilment that critics have taken them to be. Remembering the poet's
own poor health, we are less surprised, perhaps, to find in them some
of the exasperation and plaintiveness of Baudelaire, for instance in such
outbursts as 'Crois-tu qu'il soit des cœurs sincères?' The induced

[1] G68, p. 142.

torment of the earlier elegies has become a real torment, though for the most part disguised with social refinements, in these odes. None the less this last love, and this last attempt at disciplining his pen to gentleness, is all the more poignant when we recall the end that was awaiting him, and the purely masculine fulfilment in which he was to delight in his *Íambes*. We cannot grudge the poet this interlude of sisterly affection, nor those baffled feelings which led him to write a series of odes which, on the whole, strike us as exercises in prosody as much as exercises in suffering.

After the poet's death the following unsigned and undated letter (hitherto unpublished) was found in his wallet, and it is possible that he had it with him while he was at Saint-Lazare.[1] It is given here with the spelling and punctuation unchanged:

Je vous rends mille grâces Monsieur de la nouvelle que vous avez bien voulu me donner. j'avais emporté jeudi soir quelques consolations, mais je n'étais pas encore entierement rassurée, vous m'avez fait trouver mon ennuyeux diner de nopce charmant, ce miracle vous était réservé. si j'avais pu m'échaper un instant, vous auriez reçu mes remerciements ce soir, j'espere qu'ils arriveront assez à temps pour vous convaincre de toute ma reconnaissance. Maman et ma sœur me chargent de vous remercier de la bonne journée que vous leur avez fait passer, elles sont ainsi que moi bien fachées de rompre pour quelque tems la douce habitude de vous voir, nous seront toutes les trois bien enchantées de la reprendre à votre retour. je vous prie Monsieur de recevoir mes complimens et mes adieux.

                                                    Luciene ce vendredi soir

Though this letter has no signature or date it tells us a little about itself: it was written from Louveciennes by a person who had her mother and sister living with her, and as it is unlikely that Chénier received letters from the comtesse Hocquart, it is more probably from Fanny Lecoulteux. The dinner she mentions suggests some formal celebration at which she had to be present. The poet had brought good news and spent a cheerful day with the family, while announcing that he was going away for a while. The poet moved about so frequently that it is difficult to follow that line of investigation. However, it is probable that the letter was written before August 1793, when MM. Pourrat and Lecoulteux were both placed under house arrest. It could have been written in 1792 before Chénier went off to Rouen. In any case the letter

[1] Given in my edition, D25. H1, p. 26, item 125, suggests that it was written by her sister, Mme Hocquart de Turtot. The manuscript is in BMC 11814, no. 10. H1 also gives a letter by Fanny dated from Dieppe, 5 Fructidor, an II.

is written with such naturalness and friendliness as to give an adequate impression of the relationship between these two young people.

Of all the odes that Chénier wrote during this period, the finest is his *Ode à Versailles*, which is in all respects one of his most perfect works. Sainte-Beuve called it 'la plus belle, la plus complète des pièces d'André Chénier . . . il y a là élégie royale dans toute sa gloire'.[1] After a first movement of three stanzas in which he evokes the present calm of Versailles, abandoned by the court, the poem becomes more personal, yet without any loss of dignity:

> Ah! malheureux! à ma jeunesse
> Une oisive et morne paresse
> Ne laisse plus goûter les studieux loisirs,
> Mon âme, d'ennui consumée,
> S'endort dans les langueurs. Louange et renommée
> N'inquiètent plus mes désirs.
>
> L'abandon, l'obscurité, l'ombre,
> Une paix taciturne et sombre,
> Voilà tous mes souhaits. Cache mes tristes jours,
> Et nourris, s'il faut que je vive,
> De mon pâle flambeau la clarté fugitive,
> Aux douces chimères d'amours.
>
> L'âme n'est point encore flétrie,
> La vie encor n'est point ravie,
> Quand un regard nous trouble et le cœur et la voix.
> Qui cherche les pas d'une belle,
> Qui peut ou s'égayer ou gémir auprès d'elle,
> De ses jours peut porter le poids.

He goes on to celebrate his love for Fanny Lecoulteux:

> J'aime; je vis. Heureux rivage!
> Tu conserves sa noble image,
> Son nom, qu'à tes forêts j'ose apprendre le soir;
> Quand, l'âme doucement émue,
> J'y reviens méditer l'instant où je l'ai vue,
> Et l'instant où je dois la voir.
>
> Pour elle seule encore abonde
> Cette source, jadis féconde,
> Qui coulait de ma bouche en sons harmonieux.
> Sur mes lèvres tes bosquets sombres
> Forment pour elle encor ces poétiques nombres,
> Langage d'amour et des Dieux.

[1] F86.

These personal statements have an Augustan expression which is far from the excited gush of Chénier's Romantic successors, though in his case there was cause enough for melancholy: not only was he a suspect, living as a fugitive, expecting at any time to be caught and thrown into prison, but he was really ill. A Latin note among his papers, written towards the end of the year, reads, 'Scribebam Versiliae, animo et corpore aeger, morens, dolens, die novembris undecima 1793, Andreas C. Byzantinus'. But it is not this autobiographical aspect of the ode that makes it a satisfactory work. It would not be the great poem that it is without the evocation of Versailles with which it begins ('O Versailles, ô bois, ô portiques'), and·which is taken up again at the end:

> Ah! témoin des succès du crime,
> Si l'homme juste et magnanime
> Pouvait ouvrir son cœur à la félicité,
> Versailles, tes routes fleuries,
> Ton silence, fertile en belles rêveries,
> N'auraient que joie et volupté.
>
> Mais souvent tes vallons tranquilles,
> Tes sommets verts, tes frais asiles,
> Tout à coup à mes yeux s'enveloppent de deuil.
> J'y vois errer l'ombre livide
> D'un peuple d'innocents, qu'un tribunal perfide
> Précipite dans le cercueil.

Thus an ode written out of love is at the same time a political poem, with those impersonal overtones that we find in Coleridge's 'Ode to Dejection'. What is pleasing in Chénier's ode is its natural but proud slow movement, the unusual ease with which its transitions are made: he had learnt his lesson from Malherbe and it is, in his own words, 'plein de choses'. J. Fabre has remarked of this poem, 'Dans cette ode intime et grandiose, pompeuse et familière, poignante mais sereine, une âme rassemble ses forces et ses rêves, un art tous ses prestiges, dans une totale harmonie.'[1] It has the qualities of a fugue, with its themes intermingled without the slightest dissonance. It is modern in the way private and public life are brought together, as in Arnold's 'Dover Beach' or Auden's 'Lay your sleeping head, my love', in which the personal predicament is enlarged and ennobled by its greater context.

We do not know whether this ode was written before or after that which celebrated the heroism of Charlotte Corday in July 1793. If it

[1] F36, p. 220.

was written before, then events in the family of Fanny Lecoulteux were soon to show that the sombre vision at the end of the poem was prophetic as well as referring back to the September massacres. Her father and husband were placed under house arrest in August, then removed to prison—the one to the Luxembourg and the other to the Évêché—in December. Our own view is that it was probably written after August. After that date, also, one of Chénier's objects in visiting Paris would no doubt be to help by obtaining news of the two prisoners, or taking them letters and comforts from their family, until his own arrest in the following March.

Meanwhile, Chénier had written one of the most interesting political odes in the French language, celebrating an important public event and an act of unusual courage on the part of a woman. Charlotte Corday was an unusual person, belonging to the family of the great Corneille. On the 9th of July she left her home at Caen. Arriving in Paris on the 11th, she spent a night at the Hôtel de la Providence in the rue des Vieux-Augustins (now rue Hérold). She spent the day of the 12th in trying to enter the Assembly in order to see Marat. On the morning of the 13th she bought a long kitchen-knife, was not admitted to Marat's house in the rue des Cordeliers, but left a letter for him. In the evening she returned, was admitted while he was sleeping in his bath, and assassinated him. Marat had recently been accused of unpatriotic conduct, and was acquitted on the 24th of April by a court under the public prosecutor, Fouquier-Tinville, after describing himself as 'l'apôtre et le martyr de la liberté'. The girl who had taken the law into her own hands was tried and executed on the 17th of July after a most dignified defence. She was the only person in France to lay down her life to defend the Girondin leaders who had been expelled from the Convention in June; but Marat's assassination was a signal for their wholesale extermination. By the end of October many of Chénier's former enemies—Pétion, Brissot—had met a ghastly end. Resulting in a final extinction of the rights of the citizen, and of deputies, Charlotte Corday's action was not the unmitigated blessing that Chénier supposed, though that does not reduce the mystery of her sensational courage.

Chénier's *Ode à Marie-Anne-Charlotte Corday* may be dated, from internal evidence, as being written between 26 and 28 July 1793, for in the first stanza he referred to an 'impudent reptile' who had written an 'infamous hymn' in honour of Marat. This was probably a reference to a poem published by the Jacobin Audouin on the 21st of July. Line 38,

'C'est au monstre égorgé qu'on *prépare* une fête', refers to a ceremony which was voted in honour of Marat by the Paris Commune on the 26th of July and carried out on the 28th.

This ode, which gains much from being read aloud, as it was no doubt intended to be had anyone dared to do so, shows a perfect mastery of the traditional sizain in which he had been experimenting in various ways for the odes for Fanny Lecoulteux. Though the poem has a violent and, at times, a deliberately vulgar tone and impetuous movement which relates it to the *Ïambes*, it has also a certain majesty which comes of the perfect control of the medium. Only once (in the first two stanzas) does Chénier allow the stanzas to overflow one into the other, but though the rest are all end-stopped the movement is smooth and continuous throughout. With perfect art he turns from the heroine to the victim, then to the wider political significance of the action, ending with more universal generalizations. In spite of the elevated tone of the poem as a whole, there are signs of that enlarged poetical vocabulary which makes all Chénier's political poems so modern. Long before Hugo he put 'the red bonnet on the old dictionary' with expressions like 'fanges du Parnasse', 'impudent reptile', 'eunuques vils', 'Ces parricides, / de rapine, de sang, d'infamie engraissés'. It is truly surprising that Sainte-Beuve never mentioned this poem in his comparison of Chénier and Mathurin Régnier; for never since the sixteenth century had any French poet written with this destructive energy. But its venom is properly balanced against other poetic qualities: for instance Chénier yields to his constant temptation to situate current events (as he did in the *Ïambes*) against a wider, classical context, as in the fifth stanza:

> La Grèce, ô fille illustre, admirant ton courage,
> Épuiserait Paros, pour placer ton image
> Auprès d'Harmodius, auprès de son ami;
> Et des chœurs sur ta tombe, en une sainte ivresse
> Chanteraient Némésis, la tardive Déesse,
> Qui frappe le méchant sur son trône endormi.

Further, the poet's constant lyrical impulse comes to the surface in the beautiful lines in which he meditates on the mystery of how this outwardly mild young woman could have laid such a careful plan in secret: here he finds the imagery and harmony that were to be characteristic of French poetry some forty years later:

> Longtemps, sous les dehors d'une allégresse aimable,
> Dans ses détours profonds ton âme impénétrable

Avait tenu cachés les destins du pervers.
Ainsi, dans le secret amassant la tempête,
Rit un beau ciel d'azur, qui cependant s'apprête
A foudroyer les monts et soulever les mers.

In this poem we see Chénier's verse taking a new direction. The powers of a great journalist are now thrust back into poetry, widening its range, becoming at moments an *anti-poetry*. Already he is beginning to celebrate the three qualities—Justice, Truth, and Virtue—which were to dominate in the last *Ïambes* as an ironical reply to Liberty, Equality, and Fraternity, none of which was to be found in France at that time. Already it has that fusion of the pure lyrical impulse, the classical background, the robust irony, the extreme contrasts of vocabulary which were to mark the *Ïambes*. Here also was that implacable hatred which was rapidly becoming his dominant passion, and that reproach to the deity which was to reappear later in the *Ïambes*:

Un scélérat de moins rampe dans cette fange.
La vertu t'applaudit. De sa mâle louange
Entends, belle héroïne, entends l'auguste voix.
O Vertu, *le poignard, seul espoir de la terre*
Est ton arme sacrée, alors que le tonnerre
Laisse régner le crime, et te vend à ses lois.

By now Chénier had turned the corner into the same desperate nightmare of violence as his enemies. But he had already taken that step before writing this ode, for, in an unfinished ode celebrating the 14th of July 1793, he had written:

Se jeter sur le faible est aussi leur courage.
    Ils vivent aussi de carnage.
Voir du sang est leur seule volupté.

Mais n'osez pas flétrir de votre ignare estime
    Des mortels semblables aux Dieux.
Dans leurs mâles écrits quel foudre magnanime
    Tonne sur vous et le crime!
Ah! si le crime et vous pouviez baisser les yeux!

Though in failing health, Chénier was still working on his 'pure' poems, the *Bucoliques*. During this period he also tried his hand at some satirical comedies, but the fragments he left show little dramatic talent. It must have been about this time that he abandoned the idea of continuing his *Hermès*, saying farewell to it in that elegy or so-called epilogue beginning 'O mon fils, mon Hermès, ma plus belle espérance'. Though Dimoff suggests that this was written in 1789, Hartmann seems to be nearer the truth when he dates it 1792 or 1793.[1] He saw in the lines

> . . . le mensonge est puissant.
> Il règne. Dans ses mains luit un fer menaçant . . .

a reference not to the old régime but to the Jacobin terror. This is surely right. If there remained any doubt, it is dispelled by the last lines of the poem, in which Chénier questioned even the future of the French language:

> Perdu, n'existant plus qu'en un docte cerveau,
> Le français ne sera dans ce monde nouveau
> Qu'une écriture antique et non plus un langage.

This could even be a reference to Barère's proposal to 'democratize' the French language, which Chénier attacked in January 1794 (see below, pp. 308–9). In any case this was probably the last personal poem that Chénier left us, for after that he expressed himself only in some political odes and the *Ïambes*.

In almost all the work that followed the *Ode à Charlotte Corday*, it may be said that Chénier dedicated his art to a kind of chronicle of outstanding events in the Revolution during 1793 and 1794. For the most part the odes and *Ïambes* of this last phase are poetic journalism; a healthy outlet, no doubt, for Chénier's outraged feelings as well as a commentary on the evils of a time when every human and natural law was held in suspense. But it was a long time before these fundamentally anti-aesthetic works were to become works of art in their own right and achieve a life independent of the events which inspired them. It was only the last *Ïambes*, written in prison, which became works of art.

To return, for a moment, to the ode on the celebrations of the 14th of July 1793, we see that Chénier had not yet the idea of using, as his weapon of satire, the *ïambe* form which he had used the year before in attacking the fête for the Swiss mutineers. He was too busy experimenting with the ode. On this occasion David, as usual, was charged with the decorations and had to set up triumphal arches and sceneries in various parts of Paris. Chénier rightly attacked the foul taste with which the decorations were executed. His friend Arnault, who had married one of Mme de Bonneuil's daughters, commented on the event as follows:

La fête du 14 juillet 1793 semblait avoir été ordonnée par des cannibales.

[1] F50, and F34, t. i, p. 92.

L'arc, élevé au milieu d'une voie triomphale dont les colonnes occupaient le boulevard Italien, était orné de bas-reliefs peints, qui retraçaient les massacres du 6 octobre et du 10 août, et de trophées modelés en pâte de carton, où se groupaient les dépouilles des gardes du corps, surmontés des têtes de ces malheureux auxquelles on avait laissé leurs cadenettes ou leurs queues, de peur qu'on ne les reconnût pas. J'en parle pour l'avoir vu.[1]

It seems incredible that David should have lowered his art to glorify massacres, using victims' heads as decorations, but this is typical of the insensitiveness that reigned in France at that time. This is what Chénier made of it (though writing in a kind of shorthand, and often putting down only the initial letter of a word, or writing certain words in Greek):

> O gardes de Louis sous les voûtes royales
>   Par nos Ménades déchirés,
> Vos têtes sur un fer ont pour nos Bacchanales
>   Orné nos portes triomphales.
> A ces bronzes hideux, nos monuments sacrés,
>
> Tout ce peuple hébété que nul remords ne touche,
>   Cruel même dans son repos,
> Vient sourire au succès de sa rage farouche
>   Et, la soif encore à la bouche,
> Ruminer tout le sang dont il a bu les flots.
>
> Arts dignes de nos yeux! pompe et magnificence
>   Digne de notre liberté,
> Digne des vils tyrans qui dévastent la France,
> Du stupide D . . . . qu'autrefois j'ai chanté. . . .

It was Sainte-Beuve who suggested that the D . . . . in the last line should read *David*, but in view of the number of words given in Greek in the manuscript it could also read *Démos*. It is hard to see for whose satisfaction but his own Chénier was embarking on these political poems, but it is possible that he read them to his friends. This ode is a good illustration of how Chénier was shaking off the conventions of the eighteenth century and writing with a directness that belongs to fifty years later. The circumlocutions are few, and all that lingers is a tendency to use certain classical terms—'Ménades', 'Bacchanales'— with no attempt, as yet, to find their equivalents in French.

    It was probably in the autumn of 1793 that Chénier returned to the *ïambe* form which he had used the previous year for the *Hymne aux*

---

[1] F3, t. iii, p. 361.

Suisses de Châteauvieux. The second *ïambe* is usually taken to be a poem of dedication, in which he makes a kind of apology for his avenging Muse, pointing out that, unlike his model Archilocus, he had never written satire for his personal advantage, but only in the public cause:

> 'Sa langue est un fer chaud. Dans ses veines brûlées
>   Serpentent des fleuves de fiel.'
> J'ai douze ans en secret dans les doctes vallées
>   Cueilli le poétique miel.
> Je veux un jour ouvrir ma ruche tout entière;
>   Dans tous mes vers on pourra voir
> Si ma Muse naquit haineuse et meurtrière.
>   Frustré d'un amoureux espoir,
> Archiloque aux fureurs du belliqueux ïambe
>   Immole un beau-père menteur.
> Moi, ce n'est point au col d'un perfide Lycambe
>   Que j'apprête un lacet vengeur.
> Ma foudre n'a jamais tonné pour mes injures.
>   La patrie allume ma voix;
> La paix seule aguerrit mes pieuses morsures;
>   Et mes fureurs servent les lois.
> Comme les noirs Pythons et les hydres fangeuses
>   Le feu, le fer arment mes mains;
> Extirper sans pitié les bêtes venimeuses,
>   C'est donner la vie aux humains.

Assuming that Chénier regarded his serious work as a poet as beginning in about his twentieth year, the 'douze ans' would enable us to ascribe this *ïambe* to 1793. He had already mentioned Archilocus, whom he much admired, in several other manuscripts, including the *République des Lettres* in which he described how the modern Cyclops

> Et d'outrage, de fiel, de calomnie amère
> Forgent sous le marteau l'ïambe sanguinaire.

As for Archilocus, he was born on the island of Paros in the Cyclades and died young. After his betrothal to the daughter of Lycambes, his prospective father-in-law broke his word, upon which Archilocus wrote such a powerful satire against him that he hanged himself. Few of the works of Archilocus survive (there were only two fragments in Brunck's *Analecta*) but he was held in high esteem in Greece. The iambic, in Greek poetry, was associated with familiar mockery and its rhythm was close to that of prose, though it could have a slight musical accompaniment. Looking at the poem above we see that although

Chénier does not, at this stage, exploit all the possibilities of his medium (for instance through using enjambment, or breaking the line to obtain more varied rhythms), he is at times obedient to this tradition of skimming close to prose; when we put some of the lines together they read very straightforwardly, as common speech almost: 'Dans tous mes vers on pourra voir si ma Muse naquit haineuse et meurtrière.' The first two lines, which are probably a quotation from some Greek tribute to Archilocus, have not so far been traced.

As for the remaining *ïambes* it is most unlikely that, as some biographers take for granted, they were all written in prison. They would lose much of their point if that were the case, for many of them describe events which had occurred before his imprisonment in March 1794. They must be arranged in chronological order, according to the events they describe. Then it is possible, also, to appreciate the malicious joy with which, in secret, Chénier was writing mock-hymns that competed with and contradicted those of Marie-Joseph Chénier, Cubières, Audouin, and other poetasters of that time, whose fulsome praise of the same events or personalities—Marat, Barère, the massacres at Nantes and elsewhere, Robespierre, and the cult of the Supreme Being—is mercilessly caricatured.

Thus in November 1793 Chénier celebrated in a fierce *ïambe* the Convention's plan to remove Marat's body to the Panthéon. This is a poem of fifty-two lines, signed 'Par le citoyen Archiloque Mastigophore'. It was on the 14th of November that the Convention voted that Marat should be interred in the Panthéon, after David had made a violent but tearful speech on the proposal. Marie-Joseph was entrusted with drawing up a report on the matter, in which he had to look into the possibility of removing the remains of Mirabeau from the Panthéon and substituting those of Marat. To his credit, Marie-Joseph did not even mention Marat in his report, most of which dealt with Mirabeau. André Chénier's deliberately ugly poem, in which he exploits low vocabulary, has none the less the beauty of energy and conviction, for in spite of its lack of restraint the irony is handled with supreme intelligence, recalling T. S. Eliot's curious statement that great poetry may be made out of the negative emotions. It begins only at the level of sarcasm in its attack on David:

> Voûtes du Panthéon, quel mort illustre et rare
> S'ouvre vos dômes glorieux?
> Pourquoi vois-je David qui larmoie, et prépare
> Sa palette qui fait des Dieux?

The invective mounts as he describes the unclean soul of Marat rising
into the sky:

> Brissot, qui n'a jamais menti,
> Dit avoir vu dans l'air d'exhalaisons impures
> Un noir nuage tournoyer,
> Du sang, et de la fange, et toutes les ordures
> Dont se forme un épais bourbier;
> Et soutient que c'était la sale et vilaine âme
> Par qui Marat avait vécu.
> De ses jours florissants, par la main d'une femme,
> Ce lien aimable est rompu!
> Le Calvados en rit. Mais la potence pleure.

Chénier had learnt through his journalism every trick of irony, and
cunningly he ends here with those two sharp statements. The first,
'Le Calvados en rit', is not only a reference to the fact that Charlotte
Corday was from Normandy: there is a significant variant in the manuscript, 'l'aristocrate en rit', for Normandy was still a centre of opposition to the Jacobins. As for 'Mais la potence pleure', meaning that
the gallows had been robbed of its prey, this idea is taken up again later,
in a frightening prophecy of greater slaughter to come:

> Il était né droit vassal de la potence.
> Il était son plus cher trésor.
> Console-toi, gibet, tu sauveras la France.
> Pour tes bras la Montagne encor
> Nourrit bien des héros dans ses nobles repaires:
> Le Gendre, *élève de Caton*,
> Le grand Collot d'Herbois, fier patron des galères,
> Plus d'un Robespierre, et Danton,
> Thuriot, et Chabot; enfin toute la bande . . .

He went on to name Anacharsis Clootz, Cabanis, Grouvelle, Laclos,
Garat. Most of the men he named went to the scaffold sooner or later,
or came to a bad end.

Chénier probably wrote two or three other *ïambes* before he was
cast into prison, and copied them out, when he was there, on his little
slips of paper. One of them can be dated January or February 1794.
It is an attack on Barère, who had proposed to the Convention, in
a speech published on the 28th of January, that the French language
should be officially reformed to make it more democratic. Barère's
statement—which is one of great interest to philologists, for it is true
that the Academy, in its century and a half of existence, had atrophied

the official language, which was quite out of touch with French as it was really spoken or written by most people—reads as follows:

Il faut populariser la langue, il faut détruire cette aristocratie de langage *qui semble établir une nation polie au milieu d'une nation barbare.* Nous avons révolutionné le gouvernement, les lois, les usages, les mœurs, le costume, le commerce et la pensée même. Révolutionnons donc aussi la langue qui est l'instrument journalier.

He then went on to suggest that special teachers should be appointed in all the communes in order to spread a proper knowledge of the French language.[1] It is quite likely that Chénier would have approved of this enlightened idea if it had come from anyone but Barère and been accompanied by less revolutionary cant: the majority of the nation could not read or write, never mind speak properly, in any case. Barère's clumsy phrasing made him fair game for Chénier, who seized on the expressions 'nation polie' and 'nation barbare', for Barère's argument as he formulated it implied that the 'langue polie' would be abolished and a 'langue barbare' set in its place. Chénier's *ïambe* is an address to the Muses, whom he represents as being shocked by Barère's proposal to vulgarize French. The Muses, he argues, would be obliged to enlarge their vocabulary in order to call Barère 'pied-plat, gredin, cuistre, et d'autres maudissons'. At the same time he apologized for his own extension of the poetic vocabulary, which was unfit for the Muses:

> Ces gens n'ont point votre langage;
> N'apprenez point le leur. Un ignoble courroux
> Justifie un ignoble outrage.

Another *ïambe* which might have been written at this stage was a draft for a poem describing the guillotine at work, in which Chénier showed whole families spending a day's holiday watching executions:

> L'échafaud est pour eux une source féconde.
> Ils se travaillent à l'envi
> A lui trouver cent noms les plus gentils du monde . . .

L'un l'appelle la . . . l'autre la . . . . Il rentre de ce spectacle. Il y mène sa femme et ceux de ses enfants qui ont été sages; les autres au retour quittent leur tambour et leurs jeux pour venir entendre. Il leur conte, quelle mine il avait, etc. . . . Tous trépignent de joie; on bénit . . . Humanité héréditaire. Ceux qui l'ont vu sont l'objet de l'envie. Puis ils dorment contents. . . .

Chénier ironically hoped that their souls would pass at their death

[1] *Le Moniteur*, 28 Jan. 1794.

into the bodies of wolves and panthers. Noticing the readiness with
which in the *Iambes* Chénier compared his enemies with wolves,
tigers, panthers, hyenas, and other animals, one cannot help thinking
that he was remembering the theories of Lavater, whom he had met in
Switzerland, concerning the resemblance of men to animals.

Another *Iambe*, which is complete, is a description of the famous, or
rather infamous, 'Noyades de Nantes'. Though it is written out as if
it were prose, the words closely squeezed together, so that the version
which has survived was probably transcribed by Chénier when he was
in prison, it was probably written in February–March 1794. In December–January the Jacobin, Carrier, had been responsible for 'cleaning
up' the Loire area, and in the process some 8,000 people perished.
Large numbers of them were piled into specially-built boats or rafts,
from which the bung was pulled out and the victims, tied together,
were drowned. Carrier, proud of his exploit, wrote to the Convention:
'tous les brigands sur la rive droite de la Loire ont été enfin exterminés.
. . . Il n'existe plus d'armée catholique et royaliste dans cette partie de
la République. . . . Nous en avons tué environ six mille formant la
totalité de leur bande fugitive.'[1] He omitted to mention that a large
number of them were old men, women, and children. Carrier was
recalled to Paris in February 1794 in order to account for his activities,
and it is unlikely that Chénier would have waited till the summer
before writing his poem about this event. However, the transition from
a description of the Nantes massacres to an attack on Fouquier-Tinville
and his henchman suggests that if the poem was begun at liberty it was
completed in prison:

> Et ces porte-plumets, ces commis du carnage,
> Ces noirs accusateurs Fouquiers,
> Des Dumas, ces jurés, horrible aéropage
> De voleurs et de meurtriers . . .

He described them—as other contemporary witnesses say that they
were—drinking themselves stupid at the bar of the Conciergerie, crack-
ing jokes about their victims after the day's work, and profiting from
the behaviour of the wives of the accused, many of whom gave themselves in the hope of saving their husbands, and others for other
reasons, perhaps to save their own lives. Here Chénier strikes us as
unnecessarily cynical and failing to realize the motives from which
these women acted:

[1] 'Documents révolutionnaires', in BN, NAF 307.3094.

Car ce sexe ébloui de tout semblant de gloire,
Né l'héritage du plus fort,
Quel que soit le vainqueur, suit toujours la victoire.

The whole poem is so full of disgust with the human race that it is certainly influenced by his experience in Saint-Lazare. As yet, while he had chastised his enemies to his own satisfaction, it cannot be said that any of these *Ïambes* had become a valid work of art. It needed direct personal suffering, closer contact with the tribunal's victims, and perhaps an examination of his own conscience, to enable Chénier to transcend immediate circumstances and discover heroism.

During this winter Chénier had been toying with the idea of writing a satirical comedy, *Les Initiés*, of which a few fragments have survived. It includes the initiation of a new member of the Jacobin Club and the denunciation of a 'suspect', as well as a discussion between a terrorist and a moderate. All that is interesting in this draft is a short preface in which the poet described himself. Recalling that a Greek writer had once been put to death for writing a satirical work, he forecast that he, Chénier, would probably suffer the same fate for describing the 'sanglantes orgies' of the Jacobins. He went on:

Il est las de partager la honte de cette foule immense qui en secret abhorre autant que lui, mais qui approuve et encourage, au moins par son silence, des hommes atroces et des actions abominables. La vie ne vaut pas tant d'opprobre. Quand les trétaux, les tavernes, et les lieux de débauche vomissent par milliers des législateurs, des magistrats et des généraux d'armée qui sortent de la boue pour le bien de la patrie, il a, lui, une autre ambition; et il croit ne pas démériter de sa patrie en faisant dire un jour:

'Ce pays, qui produisit alors tant de prodiges d'imbécillité et de bassesse, produisit aussi un petit nombre d'hommes qui ne renoncèrent ni à leur raison, ni à leur conscience; témoins des triomphes du vice, ils restèrent amis de la vertu et ne rougirent point d'être gens de bien. Dans ces temps de violence, ils osèrent parler de justice; dans ces temps de démence, ils osèrent examiner; dans ces temps de la plus abjecte hypocrisie, ils ne feignirent point d'être des scélérats pour acheter leur repos aux dépens de l'innocence opprimée; ils ne cachèrent point leur haine à des bourreaux qui, pour payer leurs amis et punir leurs ennemis, n'épargnaient rien; car il ne leur en coûtait que des crimes. Et un nommé A.C. fut un des cinq ou six que ni la frénésie générale, ni l'avidité, ni la crainte, ne purent engager à ployer le genou devant des assassins couronnés, à toucher des mains souillées de meurtres, et à s'asseoir à la table où l'on boit le sang des hommes.'[1]

[1] D22, p. 581.

Such was the proud, unshakeable conviction, which sustained Chénier in the few months while he was waiting for death. It was this single-ness of purpose and purity of intention which led him, in the end, to pass beyond his own suffering to a plane of heroism worthy of a great poet.

13

SAINT-LAZARE

AFTER the setting up in March 1793 of the Revolutionary Tribunal which worked in close contact with the Committee for Public Safety, the police, the spies, the provincial committees of inquiry, the net of oppression spread tighter over France, and tighter still after the *Loi des Suspects* was passed in September and enforced in December 1793. Never was there a more zealous Public Prosecutor than Fouquier-Tinville, who, with the help of a number of henchmen who could not denounce his methods because it would then be their turn for 'the red Mass', and a number of jurors whom he chose himself and who held permanent appointments, was anxious to prove by statistics that the Revolution was far from being over. Mass trials such as those of the Girondins in October swept away the last scruples over legal procedure: there was no longer any defence; all the witnesses, if any, were provided by the prosecution, and it was almost enough for a prisoner's identity to be publicly established for him to be condemned and executed on the same day; for it was already a crime, in that Kafkaish court, to have been imprisoned in the first place. It is indeed remarkable that Chénier, who had been proscribed in August 1792, managed to keep out of harm's way for some nineteen months, especially after helping, however surreptitiously, in the defence of Louis XVI. It is quite possible that, by a usual irony, he was caught only because, his health improving, he began to be a little more adventurous, less cautious in his movements than before. But once taken as a suspect he must have known that there was little hope for him.

To use his own words, Chénier was not one to 'buy his own comfort at the expense of oppressed innocence', and it was like him to be arrested when he was active in helping others. In December the Lecoulteux were hauled away to prison. The net began to close round what remained of his circle of friends, but as they were rich and there were pickings to be had, he was in less danger than they. On the 4th of March a house which François de Pange had taken in the rue Basse, at Passy, was closed and sealed. On the same day a warrant was taken

out for the arrest of the marquis de Pastoret, who had taken a house
in the rue des Vignes near the Château de la Muette at Passy, where he
had installed his wife and mother-in-law, Madame Piscatory.[1] Pastoret
had been one of the leaders of the moderates during the Legislative Assembly. It emerged from the questions put to Chénier by the
police that he had known these people for at least five years, having
met them at the Trudaines'. It is possible that Chénier had heard about
the warrant against the Pastorets and had come to warn them. It is
also known that François de Pange, who was intending to emigrate,
had left 900 *louis d'or* to be buried in the Pastorets' courtyard and/or
garden, and it is thus possible, also, that he had either come for news
of de Pange or to act on his behalf.

On the evening of the 17th Ventôse (7 March 1794) Chénier was detained by the police while he was visiting Pastoret's house. François
de Pange, who was there, managed to escape. It so happened that
a certain Gennot or Guénot was on his way there with his assistant,
Duchesne. This same Guénot, acting on behalf of the Committee of
General Security, had recently completed some investigations in the
provinces, and in the process had visited the Château de Passy (Passy-
sur-Yonne) where the remaining members of the Montmorin family,
including Madame de Beaumont, were 'hiding' with the Sérillys in the
hope of passing unobserved, although they were well known in the
region. Guénot must have had a special mission to trace the whole
de Pange family—to whom, it will be remembered, the Sérillys were
related—as well as the Montmorins. Sérilly was imprisoned with his
wife and they were both condemned to death in May: however, Mme
de Sérilly managed to survive and actually produced her own death-
certificate, which had been made out in advance, when she appeared
as a witness at Fouquier-Tinville's trial.[2] Guénot also arrested
Mme de Montmorin and one of her daughters (Mme de La Luzerne)
but Mme de Beaumont was spared.[3]

Chénier was caught either in the Pastorets' house or on the point of
leaving. In the house were four ladies: Mme de Pastoret, Mme Piscatory, Mme Chalgrin (daughter of the painter Joseph Vernet), and
a Mlle d'Estat from Versailles. According to the police report drawn

---

[1] The Pastorets' house, demolished when the Avenue Mozart was built, stood at the
top of the rue des Vignes, in the present Chaussée de la Muette. The rue Basse (rue
Raynouard) was at the lower end of the rue des Vignes, so that François de Pange was
a close neighbour.   [2] F60, p. 345.

[3] F6(a), p. 208. Mme de La Luzerne died in Saint-Lazare in May 1794, the day before
she was to be executed.

up the next day, when Chénier was asked what he was doing there he did not offer a straight answer, but showed his identity-card, issued by the Brutus ward, and said he was returning to Paris.[1] He added that he was with a lady from Versailles[2] and was on his way to the coaching-station to find a carriage, and (in the policeman's picturesque spelling) 'qu'il étoit Bon citoyent et que cetoit la premiere foy qu'il venoit dans cette maison . . . il nous a fait cette déclaration à dix heure moins un quard du soir à la porte du bois de Boulogne en face du ci-devant chateaux de La muette'. After this first examination, says the document, as Chénier had not given a plain answer when asked what his business was, Guénot decided to keep him in custody until the warrant was carried out. The house was searched. Pastoret was not to be found. The next step was to question Chénier further and have him taken to Paris, 'pour y estre detenu par mesure de suretté gènèrale'. It is noticeable that the decision to take him to Paris was made before the second interrogation took place: it was no doubt this announcement, together with his anxiety over Mlle d'Estat, which made Chénier answer more sharply than was wise.

Much fun has been made by Chénier's admirers, from Sainte-Beuve onwards, of the stupidity and illiterate spelling of his guards; but, after all, the answers were taken down rapidly and in longhand, and probably not by Guénot himself. Guénot knew much about the circles in which the poet moved, and whatever his lack of education he managed to obtain the kind of information he wanted, and more than Chénier was really obliged to give.

Some useful information about Chénier came out of these questions. For instance, we learn that the Chéniers had been living in the rue de Cléry, near the Porte Saint-Denis, since 1792. When he was made a juror in February of that year his address was still rue du Sentier, so they must have moved after that. He said that he had been living on an allowance from his father since 1790, and this confirms that he never returned to London. He put the allowance at about 800 to 1,000 *livres* a year. The smallness of that amount raised Guénot's suspicions, so that he asked him 'quelle mannierre il prend son existence'. Chénier

[1] This document was first given by Sainte-Beuve as an appendix to 'A.C., Homme politique' in 1851 and may be seen in full in E2 and E3. As for the others who were present, see B. W. Jasinski's recent article 'L'Arrestation d'A.C.' in *MF*, oct. 1962. Madame Chalgrin's father had been a friend of Mme Chénier's.

[2] In view of note 1 above, it may now be assumed that the person was Mlle d'Estat, who lived at Versailles. Either she or her sister had been the mistress of Ocariz, the Spanish envoy, in whose plot Chénier was involved.

replied that he ate either with his father or his friends, or in restaurants. It was a mistake to answer in this way, for he was at once asked who those friends were. Chénier was then forced to refuse to give their names: the first real mark against him. Asked whether he had ever dined at the Pastorets' house, he answered that he had only dined with them in Paris:[1] we have to remember that Passy was then a village of less than 2,000 inhabitants, and only became part of Paris in 1856.

So far, the questions had been of a routine nature; but either there is something missing from the police report or else Guénot had some inside knowledge of his victim, for the next thrust was to ask him whether he had ever corresponded with enemies of the Republic. Chénier replied in the negative and was then asked 's'il n'a pas reçu des lettres d'anglaitaire depuis son retour dans la République?' Chénier confessed that he had received letters from Barthélemy, who was then Minister plenipotentiary in England, but that he had received no others.[2] Asked when he had received them, and to produce them, he could only answer that he no longer had them. Guénot, pressing the point, now wanted to know why he had destroyed them, and when. More and more irritated, Chénier said that the letters were only about trivial matters such as the dispatch of his 'effects' (*effets*). Guénot took the word 'effets' in its commercial sense and argued that the letters should have been kept, so as to enable him to claim his goods. To this the poet replied that it was not a commercial transaction. Now it was Guénot's turn to become annoyed, asking 'pourquoy il nous cherche des frase' (*phrases*)—in other words, accusing him of beating about the bush and trying to be clever.

Questioned about his relations with the Pastorets, Chénier now unwisely mentioned the Trudaines, at whose house he had met them. After further misunderstandings he was asked the question which, at that time, was put to every suspect: where had he been on the 10th of August, when the King was arrested? He said that he had been ill that day with nephritis. Guénot clung to his question, even asking the poet to produce a medical certificate for two years ago. In spite of his protests, Guénot accused Chénier of being a bad citizen, for even bedridden cripples had taken up arms on the 10th of August. He was then questioned, even, as to the whereabouts of his father's servant on that

---

[1] E2, pp. lii–lvi.

[2] See Dimoff's recent discovery (H3) of a letter from A.C. to Barthélemy sending copies of 'L'Avis au peuple français' to London on 8 Sept. 1790: one of these was for Restif de la Bretonne, to whom Chénier sent 'mes tendres amitiés'.

day. This was practically the end of the interrogation, and all that Guénot really had to go on, in formally arresting Chénier, was his failure to take part in the rising of the 10th of August. Or so, perhaps, Chénier thought: looking back over the report, such things stand out as the mention of Trudaine, whose name was known to all; the suspicious circumstances of going to Versailles so late at night; the fact that he had no employment, and that his allowance was too small for a man of his station; the fact that he had corresponded with Barthélemy; that he mentioned a brother who was in Spain; and, above all, that he had not concealed his annoyance when being questioned by an official. To make matters worse, when the report was read over to him, Chénier refused to sign it: it carries the signatures 'Gennot, Cramoisin, Boudgoust, Duchesne'. Guénot did his job thoroughly and in the proper form, since Cramoisin and Boudgoust were representatives of the revolutionary committee of Passy, on whose beat he had trespassed.

So, on the morning of the 18 Ventôse (8 March) Chénier was handed over to Duchesne, who led him off to the Luxembourg, which was then bursting at the seams with prisoners. There, the janitor refused to take him in, either because there was no room or, just as likely, because Chénier had been arrested without a proper warrant: all that existed was a warrant for the arrest of Pastoret, and at the most it could be said that Chénier had been questioned as a witness in that case. At the same time it has to be remembered that the Law against Suspects allowed anyone to be held on suspicion, and that the signatures of Guénot and Boudgoust should have been enough, at least to enable Chénier to be registered, even if he were then released.

Duchesne, who had no doubt attached himself to the poet's wrist, was at a loss what to do next, and took him to the headquarters of the Committee of General Security. There he found the indefatigable Guénot, who himself led the poet off to the prison of Saint-Lazare. It was only on the following day, 19 Ventôse, that his name was entered on the register, as follows:

André Chénier, âgé de trente et un ans, natif de Constantinople, citoyen, demeurant rue de Cléry, numéro 97;

Taille de cinq pieds deux pouces, cheveux et sourcils noirs, front large, yeux gris bleus, nez moyen, bouche moyenne, menton rond, visage carré;

Amené céans en vertu d'ordre du Comité révolutionnaire, commune de Passy-les-Paris, pour être détenu par mesure de sûreté générale.

Signé: Bouchot, Cramoisin, commissaires,
Guénot, porteur d'ordre du Comité de sûreté générale.

It will be noted that the only order or warrant that Guénot had concerned Pastoret, and that in a sense the poet was being confined under false pretences. At the same time no charge was preferred against him, and he could expect either to be left alone or to be released as suddenly as he had been arrested.

Saint-Lazare, formerly a convent of the religious order of that name, lay not far outside the Porte Saint-Denis, and in order to reach there Chénier must have passed within a few yards of his father's house. The prison was an old, ugly building, of which the last remaining wings have only recently been destroyed, and which is now used as a place of detention and hospital for prostitutes, who are rounded up at night and taken there for questioning.[1] It had, however, the advantage of having large windows which, in those days, commanded a splendid view of the countryside. It was requisitioned as a prison in December 1793 and the first batches of prisoners began to arrive in January. At first the prisoners were ill-lodged, for Roucher, who was transferred there from Sainte-Pélagie at the end of January, found hardly a stick of furniture in his room, which he had to share with two other men: 'Nous sommes arrivés à sept heures et demie; les chambres ici sont nues. Envoyez-moi un lit de sangle, 2 matelas, couvertures etc., une table, une chaise, un balai.'[2] Thus the prison gradually became furnished at the prisoners' expense. A few days later, Roucher was able to look at the brighter side of things, writing, 'L'air, ici, est aussi pur que celui des champs. Nous avons devant nous un immense horizon, et du côté de la salubrité résultant de l'espace et de l'air, point de comparaison avec Sainte-Pélagie.'[3] Things were so bad, at first, that they even lacked water, while the three of them were cramped into a space thirteen feet by nine. Roucher, who, it will be recalled, was the poet of *Les Saisons*, the translator of *The Wealth of Nations*, and one of Chénier's comrades in waging the anti-Jacobin battle in the *Journal de Paris*, was a man whose fine character is nowhere better revealed than in the pages he wrote while in prison. Kind, patient, thoughtful, he was not a man who would complain for nothing. On each floor there was a long corridor which could be divided into sections by a grill:

Parvenus au 3ᵉ étage, un long, large et lugubre corridor, bien éclairé, nouvellement blanchi, se présente à nous. . . . Point de verrous aux portes,

---

[1] Saint-Lazare, originally a leper hospital, was founded in the twelfth century; taken over by St. Vincent de Paul, 1632; pillaged in 1789; turned into a prison in 1793. It is now the Hôpital Lariboisière: almost nothing of the former buildings remains.

[2] F84, p. 248.   [3] Ibid., p. 253.

mais des serrures intérieures dont on a la libre disposition. Point d'heures fixes de retraite, mais la liberté de voisiner, toute la nuit, dans le même corridor; durant tout le jour, communication permise entre tous les étages, et, dans peu, jouissance d'une grande et vaste cour qu'on bat, en ce moment, et qu'on sable.[1]

Although Roucher, for a time, was allowed to have his young daughter with him in the prison, it was not long before he began to have forebodings. Saint-Lazare started off by being one of the least irksome of prisons, but the discipline was gradually tightened. On 13 February (1794) he noticed that some of the prisoners were making constant efforts to escape, particularly those who, lacking private means, had been cast into the ground floor to sleep on straw and who were consequently called the 'pailleux'. He did not know that, later, both he and Chénier were to be charged with taking part in the so-called 'conspiration des prisons' and that trumped-up charges would be based partly on what he now described:

25 *Pluviôse, an II.*

Cependant, au rez-de-chaussée, ces hommes qu'en terme de prison on appelle *pailleux*, parce que, selon une autre expression du même genre, on les *gerbe*, ces hommes travaillent des pieds, des mains, à percer les murs, à mettre le feu aux boiseries de la grande pièce où ils sont déposés. Ils s'ouvrent une issue, et quelques-uns parviennent à échapper de la barbe des sentinelles qu'ils trompent.[2]

Thus, while there was no truth in the Jacobin tale of a widespread 'prison conspiracy'—that is to say, involving all the prison communities in Paris, who on this pretext were to be mercilessly slaughtered—it was true that in Saint-Lazare some concerted attempts to escape had been made. Reaction set in, and on 27 February all communication with the outside world was cut off for a time. This was the beginning of the repressive measures which were to be further tightened in April and May.

By the time Chénier entered the prison in March, the number of prisoners had swollen to over six hundred. Over a hundred more were to be packed into the building in the next month or two. About a hundred of the detained were women. The prisoners ranged from soldiers and lawyers and 'ci-devant' aristocrats, down to grocers, butchers, artisans, labourers, adolescents who had been seized at the same time as their parents and went to the guillotine with them. Among

---

[1] F84, p. 267. [2] Ibid., p. xvii.

those who went to the scaffold with Chénier and Roucher were priests,
nuns, wives of *émigrés*, policemen, lackeys, schoolteachers, and Ameri-
cans. The time had gone when the Jacobins could pretend to be waging
a war against the aristocrats: anyone was a suspect so long as he dared
to open his mouth.

Chénier was housed on the second floor, below Roucher. There can
be no certainty as to the immediate effects of his imprisonment.
According to his nephew Gabriel, his father Louis came to inquire
at Saint-Lazare but was told by the concierge, 'Je n'ai pas ce nom-là
parmi ceux qu'on a amenés hier.'[1] The implication was that it was owing
to the father's indiscretion that Chénier was registered on the 19th.
According to Gabriel, the father then 'vole au Comité de Salut public
pour demander la liberté de son fils, arrêté par erreur sans doute, puisqu'il est détenu sans écrou'. This is most unlikely. In the first place,
André had been imprisoned by Guénot on behalf of the Comité de
Sûreté Générale, not the Comité de Salut Public. Moreover, it was not
until May that the committee took notice of the prisoner. The family
tradition—which seems to be wrong in almost all respects—tells that
he also went several times to plead with Barère for his son's release.
The fact is that no formal warrant was issued until 7 Prairial (26 May),
that is to say two and a half months after the arrest. But it was issued
not by the Committee of Public Safety but by the same body as
Guénot represented, that is to say the Committee of General Security,
in other words, the police:

> Le Comité de sûreté générale, instruit que le nommé André Chénier a été
> arrêté et traduit dans une maison d'arrêt de Paris par le comité révolution-
> naire de Passy, *sans mandat*, inscrit sur le registre du comité, arrête que ledit
> André Chénier, dont la renommée a publié depuis le commencement de la
> révolution la conduite incivique, restera en arrestation jusqu'à ce qu'il en
> soit autrement ordonné.
>
> Signé: Élie Lacoste, Vadier, Dubarran,
Louis du Bas-Rhin et Jagot.[1]

On the same day a formal warrant (at last) was sent to Saint-Lazare
from Passy, and Chénier's name was again entered into the register.
With a travesty of justice worthy of Kafka's *Trial*, a warrant of arrest
was thus issued long after the arrest had been accomplished, but still
with no specific charge.

It is almost impossible to decide, at this stage, whether his father's

---

[1] D7, t. i ,p. cix.   [2] E3, p. xvii.

intervention resulted in the concoction of these formal documents. However, on 13 March it had been announced that a special commission would be set up to look into the circumstances in which thousands of suspects had been thrown into jail. As this news came only a week after Chénier's arrest it is quite likely that Louis de Chénier, or the poet himself, thought that this was an opportunity for making an appeal. Though the appeal written by Louis has no date, it was this which, according to family tradition, resulted in the formal committal that we have given above.

This family tradition, doing its best to protect Marie-Joseph from the accusation of refusing to help his brother, unfortunately turned the evidence against the father. According to this, Marie-Joseph advised that inactivity was the wisest course, and that nothing should be done to attract attention to his brother. On whatever date he sent it (if he did) Louis de Chénier's appeal was a masterpiece of unwisdom. It drew attention to his son's activities in no uncertain way. He began by outlining the circumstances of the arrest and interrogation, mentioning that his son ought to have been handed over to his own Section (Brutus) for questioning, and that Chénier had refused to sign the document only after pointing out its numerous inaccuracies. ('Ces observations et ce refus firent éclater le citoyen Guénot en expressions de l'emportement le plus violent.') He then went on to say:

Le citoyen André Chénier est un patriote dont la vie fut toujours irréprochable. Il se fit connaître et s'attira des inimitiés honorables par la franchise et le courage avec lesquels il dénonça, comme des intrigants, Brissot, Pétion, Manuel, Danton, sur lesquels son opinion est devenue l'opinion générale.[1]

Yes, all those had since met their death; but it was foolish to draw attention to the political journalism of the most savage critic of the Jacobins, who were now at the height of their power. He went on to give other particulars which had better remained concealed, for they might have incriminated others:

Dans les deux dernières années sa vie a été encore plus retirée. Constamment soumis aux lois, étranger à toute intrigue, il allait quelquefois soigner sa santé dans la plus profonde solitude à Versailles, où plusieurs citoyens, ses voisins, rendront témoignage de la vie qu'il a menée. Il a été malade plusieurs mois; et c'est après sa convalescence que, de retour à Paris, le hasard l'a conduit en visite chez la citoyenne Pastoret.

[1] D7, t. i, pp. cxxvi–cxxviii.

When we consider that Chénier had denounced such powerful men as Barère and Collot, it is hard to understand how his father imagined that such a statement would effect his son's release. There is no doubt whatever that the document was his: it is to be seen in the library at Carcassonne and ends with the words:

Le soussigné âgé de 72 ans, père d'André Chénier, reconnu pour très bon citoyen de la section de Brutus, soumet ces observations à la Commission chargée de l'examen des détentions. Il espère que les Citoyens, membres de cette Commission, approuveront la représentation d'un Père irréprochable qui réclame un fils irréprochable, et privé depuis trois mois de sa liberté, qu'il n'a jamais mérité de perdre.[1]

The words *trois mois* bring us down to the end of May or early June; but if that were not enough, it is curious that biographers quoting this document have not noticed that it was dated *Prairial an 2*. Prairial was a month running from the 20th of May to the 18th of June. How far may we go in ascertaining whether this plea was responsible for his son's fate?

Chénier's formal committal on 7 Prairial (26 May) came when the government was beginning to concern itself with what was called the 'conspiration des prisons'. It was only on 3 Messidor (21 June), however, that Robespierre and the Committee of Public Safety set up new machinery to investigate these plots. Looking a little closer, we find that the decree to set up Commissions to investigate detentions, voted on 13 March, was very slow in taking effect, as the commissions came into being only on the 4th of May. Even then, it was only on 15 May (25 Floréal) that their duties were properly defined: 'Si elle découvre des Citoyens qui lui paraissent injustement arrêtés, elle en formera la liste et l'enverra au Comité de Salut Public et au Comité de Sûreté Générale, qui prononceront définitivement sur leur mise en liberté.' It appears most unlikely that Louis de Chénier's appeal could have been dealt with, first by the Commission, then by the two committees, between the 20th and the 26th of May, that is, the 1st and the 7th Prairial, when the warrant was issued. If, of course, Louis de Chénier went and presented the petition in person, insisting on prompt action, then he might have been responsible for having his son's arrest confirmed. At the same time, this would make nonsense of Marie-Joseph's argument that nothing should be done to draw attention to André. It is said that Marie-Joseph was able to have pressure brought to bear on

[1] BMC 11815/437/339/6.

PLATE 5

Within the engraving:

PEINT A S^T LAZARE
LE 29 MESSIDOR L'AN 2
PAR JB SUVÉE

Chénier in Saint-Lazare prison: an engraving of Suvée's portrait, by Jacquemin

Fouquier-Tinville to hold up the case of Louis-Sauveur, who was now imprisoned in the Conciergerie.[1] Why, then, could he not do the same for André? If his father had unwisely drawn attention to André, then surely the case had been brought into the open, and after the 7th Prairial action of some kind ought to have been taken?

During the five months of Chénier's imprisonment the conditions in Saint-Lazare gradually became worse. There was a period of a fortnight, shortly after his arrest, when all communication with the outside world was cut off. Those who had money could have all kinds of foodstuffs sent in, and even have great banquets cooked for them, but this became more difficult after a general dining-hall was opened. Parcels were now closely inspected, and even the collection of washing was organized so that it was undertaken by the prison authorities, who decided to 'blanchir les prisonniers'. This disposed of the legend that Chénier sent out his poems with his washing: all that is true about it is that he had to write his last *Iambes* on strips of the brownish paper in which washing was wrapped for collection. The private arrangements for meals came to an end when, in June, the prisoners were all forced to eat in the new dining-hall, and were loaned a few sous each day for this purpose. It was now forbidden to receive newspapers. As long ago as 15 April, according to Roucher, it had been forbidden for relatives to come into the courtyard:

> On vous laissait approcher dans la cour, jusque sous les fenêtres; ces approches ont été défendues. . . . Nous pouvions au moins écrire à nos amis, à nos parents, tout ce que nous sentions pour eux d'attachement, de tendresse, de reconnaissance; la reconnaissance est défendue, la tendresse est proscrite comme inutile.

What had happened was that the prison authorities, to stop the traffic in letters, had issued a *pro forma* on which the prisoners could enter their requests, in an impersonal way, to their families, 'des chiffons de papier, chargés uniquement de la demande et de l'envoi de nos demandes'. On the 6th of May the right to circulate from one corridor to another was suspended. The cells were searched and everything that could be used as an instrument for escape was confiscated, 'rasoirs, couteaux, ciseaux, canifs, compas, on s'en empare. Les montres, ainsi

---

[1] Stationed at Breteuil in September 1793, Louis-Sauveur defended Doby against the deputy, André Dumont. After further intrigues he issued a pamphlet against Dumont in March 1794, after which he was imprisoned at Beauvais and then in the Conciergerie in Paris. He was questioned on the 6th Prairial—significantly enough, the day before the warrant was issued against André. Is it possible that these events drew attention away from Louis-Sauveur to his brother? See F26.

que les bagues et les anneaux, l'argent et l'or monnayés sont pris'.[1]
This wholesale robbery was part of a plan to prevent bribery and to
reduce the prisoners all to the same level of dependence. They were
allowed to keep only 50 *livres* for their own use, and after 27 May they
were given a daily 'loan' of 50 *sous* per head. At the same time they
knew that there were a number of stool-pigeons living among them
and listening to everything: their names were Gagnant, Coquery,
Manini, Jaubert.

Apart from these general circumstances, which help us to form an
idea of the prison background, there is little reliable information about
Chénier's last days. If he was able to write to his father, either his letters
were not kept because they were compromising, or they were later
destroyed by his mother or by Marie-Joseph. Fellow prisoners who
survived sometimes mentioned his name but had little to say about
him: he obviously kept to himself. Even friends sometimes remained
aloof from each other in case of mutual incrimination. Maybe Chénier
was the irritating friend who, for a time, got on Roucher's nerves by
talking of nothing but politics. A paper in the Carcassonne library
relates that a M. Saint-Prix, a deputy who voted with the Girondins,
'raconta qu'ayant fait une pétition pour obtenir d'être mis en liberté
ou jugé, promptement, il conseilla à André de déchirer sa pétition et de
faire le mort'.[2] Loizerolles recorded in 1813 that 'André Chénier avait
dessiné sur le mur de sa chambre un arbre qui penchait sa tête languissante, dont les rameaux étaient abattus par le vent'.[3] Under this tree
were inscribed the words *Fructus matura tulissem*, meaning that it
would have borne fruit in its proper season. However, Boissy d'Anglas
related that it was the younger Trudaine who had written a poem on
the wall of his cell about a fading flower ('La fleur, laissant tomber sa tête
languissante / Semblait dire au Zéphyr: pourquoi m'éveilles-tu?. . .'),
which is on a similar theme.[4] De Chazet wrote in a book published in
1831 that one of Chénier's friends told the poet that if he jumped
over one of the courtyard walls, which was only twelve feet high, he
would be in open country and could hide before his escape was known.[5]
According to him, Chénier went to the spot that had been indicated
but did not jump for fear of breaking his leg. The so called *Souvenirs
de la marquise de Créquy* contains several anecdotes about Chénier in

    [1] F84, t. ii, p. 171.
    [2] BMC 11827/3. This suggests another possibility: that André himself drew up the
petition in his father's name, and that it was never sent.
    [3] F67.   [4] F14.
    [5] A. de Chazet, Mémoires, t. iii, p. 32.

prison.[1] While these memoirs were denounced as false by Sainte-Beuve and others, anyone familiar with such writings of the Revolutionary period knows that—for instance in the case of Garat and Suard—it was quite common for them to be rehandled, though not 'invented', by a second party. It is obvious that the writers who rehandled the Créquy memoirs based them on genuine papers, full of gossip, by the marquise de Créquy. There was no reason why she should bother to invent stories about Chénier. One of these stories is in keeping with the poet's character in his lighter moments. One of the poet's fellow prisoners being the ex-Jacobin, Clément, Chénier always addressed him ironically in verse. On one occasion, when Clément spoke about Louis XVI's death, Chénier is said to have replied:

> Oui, quand il serait vrai que l'absolu pouvoir
> Eût entraîné Louis par-delà son devoir,
> Qu'il en eût trop suivi l'amorce enchanteresse,
> (Quel homme est sans erreur, et quel roi sans faiblesse?)
> Est-ce à vous de prétendre au droit de le punir,
> Vous tous, nés ses sujets, vous, faits pour obéir?

Clément was overwhelmed, not knowing that the lines were from Voltaire. Another anecdote in the Créquy memoirs tells how Chénier helped his fellow prisoners:

> Cet excellent jeune homme allait panser tous les matins un vieux juif italien nommé Fioraventi, qui s'opiniâtrait à conserver deux vésicatoires derrière les oreilles et qui ne voulait jamais quitter son lit de sangles. Il apostrophait quelquefois rudement son jeune infirmier, qui n'en tenait compte et qui lui disait avec une patience admirable, 'Je fais de mon mieux. Si vous vous fâchez contre moi, qui est-ce qui viendra vous soigner?' Il partageait ses aliments et son argent avec les nécessiteux; il se dépouillait de ses vêtements pour couvrir les nus, et le plus beau de son affaire était de s'en cacher comme il aurait fait d'un vice ou d'un ridicule. Je n'ai jamais vu réunir un si tendre cœur à plus de fermeté de caractère, à plus de souplesse et d'originalité dans l'esprit.

Against those who dismissed these memoirs as wholly fictitious, we have the witness of a contemporary, Théodore de Lameth, who said of them, 'Il est évident, d'après les idées, le style, les expressions, les tournures, les prétentions, les détails vrais sur de petites choses, que

[1] F30, t. iv, p. 305: Chénier lends Gessner's idylls to Mme d'Hinnisdal; p. 349 makes fun of Clément; p. 351 takes care of an old man.

des notes d'une femme vivant il y a 60 ans et plus, dans la haute société, en ont été la base; et tout porte à croire qu'elles sont de Mme de Créquy.'[1]

What is certain is that Chénier continued studying and writing while he was in prison. His famous ode, *La Jeune Captive*, which more than any other single poem helped to build up a legend about him in the nineteenth century, was supposedly written for the comtesse Aimée de Coigny, duchesse de Fleury, and biographers and critics were not slow to imagine that it was based on a flirtation.

Whatever the hardships of prison life, they were to some extent softened by the presence of women and children, and at times the prisoners could have the feeling of being one great family. Among the womenfolk was the outstanding—and indeed notorious—beauty Aimée de Coigny, then only twenty-five. There were also the comtesse Desvieux, twenty-eight; the baroness Hinnisdal, thirty-five, and the duchesse de Saint-Aignan, who was then twenty-nine.

Aimée de Coigny came of the Franquetot family, who from being rich bourgeois in the seventeenth century had climbed high in the aristocracy. Her family had no difficulty in marrying her to the duc de Fleury when they were both only fifteen years of age. She was separated from him in 1793 after being the mistress of a number of nobles, including the duc de Lauzun and Lord Malmesbury. She had been living on her estate at Mareuil with the comte de Montrond, whom she had already known during her stay in England, when they were both arrested and brought to Saint-Lazare. This Montrond was a notorious rake, living on gambling and what he could extort from women, but he was a great wit, and his intelligence was appreciated by Talleyrand. He was now hoping to lay his hands on what remained of Aimée's fortune: after tricking her into marriage not long after their release from prison, he spent a good part of it before they were divorced. Aimée de Coigny, whose senses were unquenchable, then became the mistress of a further series of lovers, including the mediocre journalist and actor, Mailla-Garat; the duc de Boisgelin, whom she helped in his intrigues against Napoleon; the poet Lemercier, and perhaps Talleyrand. She died in 1820 at the age of fifty-one.

Chénier knew all about Aimée de Coigny and must have seen at once that she and Montrond were inseparable, so that the legend of a romance between her and the poet cannot have any foundation. The

[1] F62 ,p. 83.

famous ode was first printed through the good offices of a fellow prisoner, the abbé Millin: he passed it to Ginguené, who had long been a close friend of the poet Le Brun.[1] Ginguené had the poem printed in the *Décade philosophique* (20 Nivôse, An III) under the title *Ode pour une jeune captive*. Becq de Fouquières saw a manuscript of the poem nearly a century later, and said that this title was given on it; but the recently discovered manuscript at Nantes (which looks like a fair copy) bears that title in another hand.[2] There is no mention on it, or in Ginguené's notes, of Aimée de Coigny. The first mention of her is in a note on the poem written at that time, or later, by Marie-Joseph:

> *La Jeune Captive*, Ode, par André Chénier, massacré le 7 Thermidor avec le malheureux Roucher et vingt autres prisonniers de Saint-Lazare, convaincu, comme eux, d'être l'auteur ou complice de la conspiration des prisons. C'est, dit-on, Mademoiselle de Coigny, détenue dans cette même prison, qui a inspiré ce délicieux morceau de poésie. André Chénier n'avait que 30 ans. Il avait beaucoup étudié, beaucoup écrit et publié fort peu. La poésie, la philosophie et l'érudition antique ont fait en lui une perte irréparable.[3]

The poem was subsequently reprinted in the *Almanach des Muses* (1795–6) and in the *Magasin encyclopédique*, after which it was a common item in anthologies. The last-named reprinting was made by Millin. He did not state, as biographers have averred, that he received the manuscript from Aimée de Coigny, but wrote, 'Cette Ode a été composée pour Madame de M* * * par André Chénier pendant que nous étions ensemble dans la prison de Saint-Lazare, sous le règne de Robespierre. J'ai le manuscrit de sa main.' It has never been established that Millin ever had the original of the poem in his possession, and it is difficult to discover who, at that time, had it. Marie-Joseph's version is written out in his own hand. Sainte-Beuve asserted that Chateaubriand had the poem from Madame de Beaumont,[4] but she could have copied it from the *Décade philosophique*. There was certainly no dedication on the manuscript. Millin's statement 'J'ai le manuscrit de sa main' is ambiguous, for it could mean, either that he had received it from Mme de M[ontrond], or that he had the manuscript in the poet's handwriting. In any case, there was a difference between Marie-Joseph's statement that Aimée de Coigny 'inspired' the poem, and Millin's

---

[1] On Ginguené's share in the publication, see Walter, G101, pp. 345–6.

[2] G7, pp. 52–54.

[3] BN, NAF 6852, fo. 53.

[4] Sainte-Beuve: 'M. de Chateaubriand tenait cette pièce de Madame de Beaumont, sœur de M. de La Luzerne', in *Œuvres* (Pléiade), t. i, p. 823. Chateaubriand himself (F23, t. ii) said that Mme de Beaumont had a collection of the poet's manuscripts.

statement that he wrote it 'pour' Mme de M* * *'. From this it was an
easy matter to pass from the rumour 'On dit que . . .', as stated to
Marie-Joseph, and from that to Millin's hint, then on to Lemercier's
'C'est elle que chanta, dans sa jeunesse, le poète André Chénier dans
son ode intitulée *La Jeune Captive*',[1] and, finally, to the flirtation
described by Alfred de Vigny in *Stello*. Chénier himself added to the
mystery, writing at the end of the poem:

> Ces chants, de ma prison témoins harmonieux,
> Feront à quelque amant des loisirs studieux
> Chercher quelle fut cette belle.

As for Aimée de Coigny, at the age of fifteen she had inherited
a large estate at Mareuil and went to live there on her marriage in 1784.
This meant that she was the close neighbour of another 'county'
family, the de Panges, at a time when, as a young man, Chénier used
to spend long periods at Mareuil. So they must have known each other
long before they met in prison. She was, in all respects, a person who
might have interested the poet, had she not been already involved with
Montrond. She was extremely well-read, interested in politics, while
her notorious sensuality was fully matched by her intelligence, beauty,
and wit. Her obituary notice in the *Moniteur universel* said that she was
'également familière avec les belles-lettres françaises et latines, elle
avait tout l'acquis d'un homme. Sa conversation éclatait en traits
piquants, imprévus et originaux. Elle résumait toute l'éloquence de
Mme de Staël en quelques mots perçants.' But those who were not her
friends did not see her in the same light: Mme de Genlis described her,
with feminine malice, as 'légère, étourdie, avec des accès de gaieté qui
ressemblent un peu à la folie', and added that there was 'quelque chose
d'indécent' about her.[2] On the other hand, Mme Vigée-Lebrun said,
'Le goût et l'esprit de la duchesse de Fleury brillaient par-dessus tout.'[3]
Horace Walpole wrote of her in 1792, 'I have seen the Duchess of
Fleury, who is much the prettiest Frenchwoman I ever beheld. Though
little, and more than nut-brown, she is perfect of her size, with very
fine eyes and nose, and a most beautiful mouth and teeth, and natural
colour. She is but two and twenty, very lively and very sensible.'[4]
    There is a further and most interesting hypothesis to be considered,
which was first stated by Alfred de Vigny in his *Stello*, published in

---

[1] For this and other information on Mlle de Coigny, see F4.
[2] *Souvenirs de Félicie*, 1804, p. 180.
[3] *Souvenirs*, 1828.   [4] *Letters*, London, 1905.

1832.[1] Over a hundred pages of this work concern Chénier's imprisonment and death. In it, he suggested that Chénier was either in love with
or was loved by the duchesse de Beauvilliers de Saint-Aignan. Her
husband was executed on 6 Thermidor, the day before Chénier, but
she escaped from the guillotine on the grounds of being pregnant.
Saint-Aignan was only twenty-seven when he died, while she was
twenty-nine. One of the interesting things about Vigny's references
to *La Jeune Captive* is that he was distantly related to Aimée de Coigny
and perhaps better situated than most to know the truth. In *Stello* he
imagined the narrator sitting down in an enormous chair in Mme de
Saint-Aignan's cell, then seeing that the chair was carved all over with
names and various statements by prisoners. In the next chapter (xxvii)
he gave the four following lines which were inscribed on the chair:

> J'ai vu sur d'autres yeux, qu'Amour faisait sourire,
>   Ses doux regards s'attendrir et pleurer,
>   Et du miel le plus doux que sa bouche respire
>   Un autre s'enivrer.

These particular lines are usually regarded as belonging to the
Fanny Lecoulteux cycle—though in fact there is no evidence for that,
either.[2] Here they become a pretext for jealousy between Mme de
Saint-Aignan and Mme de Coigny. The narrator and Mme de Saint-
Aignan discuss Chénier as follows:

'N'effacez pas cette écriture-là,' dit-elle d'une voix douce et presque
musicale, en se penchant tout à fait sur mon épaule. 'Il était dans cette cellule;
on l'a transféré dans une autre chambre, dans une autre cour. M. de Chénier
est tout à fait de nos amis, et je suis bien aise de conserver ce souvenir de lui
pendant le temps qui me reste.'

Je me retournai, et je vis une sorte de sourire effleurer sa bouche sérieuse.

'Que pourraient vouloir dire ces deux derniers vers?' continua-t-elle.
'On ne sait vraiment pas quelle jalousie ils expriment.'

'Ne furent-ils pas écrits avant qu'on ne vous eût séparée de M. le duc de
Saint-Aignan?' lui dis-je avec indifférence.

Depuis un mois, en effet, son mari avait été transféré dans le corps de logis
le plus éloigné d'elle.

Elle sourit sans rougir.

---

[1] The text used here is the Pléiade edition.

[2] We have already quoted from this ode (p. 294 above) as though it belonged to the
'Fanny' cycle. In the manuscript collection (NAF 6852) it is numbered 174 and figures
among the poems written for Fanny, which are confused with others that were written
in prison. Latouche (1819), who saw the manuscripts in their original state, printed it as
Ode IV, followed by 'Aux premiers fruits de mon verger' which was certainly for Fanny
Lecoulteux.

'Ou bien,' poursuivis-je sans le remarquer, 'seraient-ils faits pour made-moiselle de Coigny?'

Elle rougit sans sourire, cette fois, et retira ses bras de mon épaule avec un peu de dépit. Elle fit un tour dans la chambre.

'Qui peut,' dit-elle, 'vous faire soupçonner cela? Il est vrai que cette petite est bien coquette; mais c'est une enfant. Et,' poursuivit-elle avec un air de fierté, 'je ne sais pas comment on peut penser qu'un homme d'esprit comme M. de Chénier soit occupé d'elle, à ce point-là.'

The duchess went on to open a box bound in mauve morocco, which contained a portrait of André Chénier, saying:

'Vous savez que M. de Saint-Aignan, à vingt-sept ans, est à peu près du même âge que M. de Chénier. Vous avez pu remarquer qu'ils ont beaucoup d'attachement l'un pour l'autre. M. de Chénier s'est fait peindre ici: il nous a fait promettre de conserver ce souvenir si nous lui survivons. C'est un quine à la loterie, mais enfin nous avons promis; et j'ai voulu garder moi-même ce portrait, qui certainement serait celui d'un grand homme si on connaissait les choses qu'il m'a lues.'

While thus hinting at a romance of some kind between the poet and the duchess, in the following chapter Vigny gave a short description of Mme de Coigny (whom he wrongly gave the age of sixteen or seventeen), saying, 'C'était bien la jeune captive qui ne veut point mourir encore.'

In this 'romanced' biography Vigny was suggesting, first, that if *La Jeune Captive* was written about Aimée de Coigny, there was a double love-affair underneath it. In modern terms he was 'debunking' the legend which his contemporaries accepted. Secondly, regardless of the feelings of the Chénier or Saint-Aignan families, he more than hinted at a romance between the poet and Mme de Saint-Aignan. He also took liberties with the poet's father, treating him disrespectfully as 'ce vieux bonhomme', and painted Marie-Joseph as a cowardly fool. Indeed, the whole episode is written with none of that delicacy which might be expected of Vigny. It is not surprising, therefore, that the poet's nephew Gabriel was angry and replied with *La Vérité sur la famille de Chénier* which appeared in 1844. But neither he nor anyone else was able to refute the suggestions about Mme de Saint-Aignan. That Vigny was perfectly sincere about this part of his story—and that is why we are giving attention to it—is shown, however, by a note in his *Journal d'un Poète* in 1832:

La duchesse de Saint-Aignan était en prison avec André Chénier. Ma mère l'a connue. Elle vient de me raconter qu'elle l'avait vue souvent depuis à

art—'Aux douces lois des vers je pliai les accents / de sa bouche aimable et naïve'—a temporary distraction from evil; and at the same time a farewell to poetry.

La Jeune Captive (unless the words 'ces chants', in the plural, meant that he wrote more than one poem of this kind, which have been lost to us) was the last poem in which Chénier wrote with such tenderness. Maybe the *diminuendo* at the end of it indicates that Chénier had what he thought to be other more important themes in mind. We have already examined six of the *Ïambes*. The seventh, *La Fête de l'Être Suprême*, is incomplete, if by that we mean that the long prose draft was not fully versified; but, as we have shown elsewhere, it contains two substantial verse fragments which, if joined together, make a satisfying and powerful poem. This *Ïambe* gives a wonderful demonstration of Chénier's strength and gives the lie to those critics who might take him for an effeminate poet. He achieves a powerful contrast, by clashing together two extremes of language, between concentrated beauty and a colloquial brutality which is in itself anti-poetic.

Someone ought to write a *History of the Supreme Being during the French Revolution*, for this idea played as active a part in it as Louis XVI or Robespierre. Nothing better illustrates the influence of the *Encyclopédie* and of Voltaire on this generation than its ambiguous attitude to the deity. While churches were destroyed and priests guillotined or turned into civil servants, and the God of Christianity mocked and defiled, they were conscious of a gap that they must fill, and brought their abstract, Cartesian, Supreme Being to their aid. He even slipped into the first 'Déclaration de l'homme et du citoyen', which was drawn up 'In the presence and under the auspices of the Supreme Being'. That was in 1789, and could be expected of the first wave of revolutionaries. La Fayette only brought the bare bones of it from America, but Virieu, a convinced Rousseau-ist, had no difficulty in persuading his contemporaries that the declaration had to carry 'the seal of God' for, whatever their upbringing, everyone, from Mirabeau to Sieyès, down to the man in the street, realized that this gave a certain seal of respectability to the whole affair. Only, of course, their Supreme Being was not the one worshipped in churches or in hearts, but an intellectual symbol. But in 1791, thanks to the Girondins, there was no further mention of the Supreme Being in the preamble to the new Constitution (September). He was only officially revived by the Jacobins, when Hérault de Seychelles, much to the satisfaction of Robespierre, who had charged the Girondins with atheism, restored him to the Declaration.

This does not mean that the Supreme Being was completely idle between 1791–3, for his name was frequently invoked, especially at public ceremonies. Those who had renounced the Christian God and had no use for the Supreme Being meanwhile found other linguistic solutions to their problem: for instance Madame Roland's last appeal was to the 'Dieu de la Justice'—a formula which might suggest that there are many gods, each useful in an emergency. Chénier himself was to fall into this trap. Others were not so humble: was not Pétion 'the Messiah of Paris'? It was, however, in the autumn of 1793 that the Jacobins began to show some perplexity over this question of republican theology, and this was to be their own undoing. The Christian calendar was neatly disposed of by Fabre d'Églantine, who imposed on France a pretty pastoral calendar which was to endure for some years, its only disadvantage being that no other country in Europe adopted or understood it. Dumont, at Abbeville, was one of the first to challenge Christian ritual by introducing one of his own, to celebrate 'Le Culte de la Raison': Laignelot turned the parish church at Rochefort into 'Le Temple de la Vérité'. The Hébertistes had hard going to persuade the French that nothing was needed to replace the old religion—nothing, that is, but the worship of the Revolution itself. Not only Reason but Nature also had been worshipped, in that year, before the high altar in Notre-Dame. Rousseau had made it plain that something had to be worshipped in order to keep citizens in order. Robespierre firmly believed that a rational religion, devoid of superstition, was possible, and as late as November 1792 he went so far as to say that the attack on Catholicism was an attack on 'popular morality': it was he who said that if there were no God we should be obliged to invent one.

The Supreme Being, then, began to make mischief for the Jacobins when on the 7th of May 1794 the Convention decreed that they would authorize a 'Fête de l'Être Suprême'. The Being was generously defined as including the Christian God, the philosophic Absolute, and the 'patron saint' of the Constitutions of 1791 and 1793. The immortality of the soul was recognized, and on every tenth day the citizens were to hold festivals celebrating the great events of the Revolution, the virtues of mankind, and the blessings of nature. However, showing a large degree of tolerance, the Assembly decreed that those who did not believe in the new religion would not be persecuted. What was made clear, however, was that the 'Culte de la Raison' was not enough: it was a heresy.[1]

[1] See Mathiez: *The Fall of Robespierre, and other essays*, London, 1927, ch. iv.

Chénier probably wrote his poem on 'La Fête de l'Etre Suprême' in May, for it was a whole month before the first official fête took place. The draft begins with an ironic fragment of verse:

> Grâce à notre Sénat, le ciel n'est donc pas vide!
>   De ses fonctions suspendu,
> Dieu . . .
>   Au siège éternel est rendu.
> Il va reprendre en main les rênes de la terre.

Maybe, said Chénier, God would behave a little better after having been suspended for a few months, and would now take the opportunity of punishing his new worshippers: 'Quoi! Dieu tout-puissant, tu souffres que de pareils personnages te louent et t'avouent; tu endures la dérision avec laquelle ils te bravent, et croient que tu existes quand ils vivent!'[1] Denouncing the Jacobins as murderers, and describing Couthon and Lequinio 'gnawing human bones', he wondered why God did not strike them down: 'Quoi, tu ne fais pas éclater ta foudre, lorsque des hommes entassés sont écrasés sous leur prison par l'explosion du canon!' In Collot's heart, God can surely see 'Bouillir dans sa poitrine un fétide mélange / De vol, de calomnie, et de merde et de fange'. Is nobody left, then, but the poet to denounce these creatures? 'Et tu ne tonnes pas et les cris de tant d'infortunés ne montent pas jusqu'à toi! et tu laisses un pauvre diable de poète se charger de la vengeance et tonner seul sur ces scélérats, et sur l'horrible tribunal et jury etc. . . .' Then the poem begins, consisting of two fragments which make a whole, once the order is reversed:[2]

LA FÊTE DE L'ÊTRE SUPRÊME

> Ils vivent cependant et de tant de victimes
>   Les cris ne montent point vers toi.
> C'est un pauvre poète, ô grand Dieu des armées,
>   Qui seul, captif, près de la mort,
> Attachant à ses vers les ailes enflammées
>   De ton tonnerre qui s'endort,
> De la vertu proscrite embrassant la défense,
>   Dénonce aux juges infernaux

---

[1] Followed by the four powerful lines (written out as though in prose) which ironically sum up eighteenth-century scepticism:

> Tu ne crains pas qu'au pied de ton superbe trône
>   Spinoza, te parlant tout bas,
> Vienne te dire encore: Entre nous, je soupçonne
>   Seigneur, que vous n'existez pas?

[2] This reconstruction of the text is explained in my *Poems of A.C.* (D25).

Ces juges, ces jurés qui frappent l'innocence,
    Hécatombe à leurs tribunaux.
Eh bien, fais-moi donc vivre, et cette horde impure
    Sentira quels traits sont les miens.
Ils croyaient se cacher dans leur bassesse obscure . . .
    Je les vois, j'accours, je les tiens.
Sur ses pieds inégaux l'épode vengeresse
    Saura les atteindre pourtant.
Diamant ceint d'azur, Paros, œil de la Grèce,
    De l'onde Égée astre éclatant,
Dans tes flancs où Nature est sans cesse à l'ouvrage,
    Pour le ciseau laborieux
Vit et blanchit le marbre illustre de l'image
    Et des grands hommes et des Dieux.
Mais pour graver aussi la honte ineffaçable,
    Paros de l'ïambe acéré
Aiguisa le burin brûlant, impérissable.
    Fils d'Archil[oque], fier A[ndré],
Ne détends point ton arc, fléau de l'imposture.
    Que les passants pleins de tes vers,
Les siècles, l'avenir, que toute la nature
    Crie à l'aspect de ces pervers:
Hou, les vils scélérats! les monstres! les infâmes!
    De vol, de massacres nourris,
Noirs ivrognes de sang, lâches bourreaux des femmes
    Qui n'égorgent point leurs maris;
Du fils tendre et pieux; et du malheureux père
    Pleurant son fils assassiné;
Du frère qui n'a point laissé dans la misère
    Périr son frère abandonné.
Vous n'avez qu'une vie . . . ô vampires . . .
    Et vous n'expierez qu'une fois
Tant de morts et de pleurs, de cendres, de décombres,
    Qui contre vous lèvent la voix!

This is one of the great *ïambes* of the last phase, to which those that have already been considered were a prelude. It could be the first to have been written entirely in prison. It is great poetry, rich in every element that makes for satire: the ironical antithesis between the poet's weakness and an indifferent God's strength, in the one line 'C'est un pauvre poète, ô grand Dieu des armées'; the learned pun which presents the iambic hopping along after his enemies ('Sur ses pieds inégaux'), followed by that sublime image of the Paros marble from which the

unbreakable stylus was hewn for Archilocus—a native of Paros—to
avenge himself. Against that highly complex image which reaches
towards the very essence of noble poetic diction, he then clashes vulgar
speech, with that *Hou*, a French word both vulgar and comic. At the
same time a personal note seems to enter into the last few lines, in the
reference to the 'malheureux père' and the brother who did not allow
his own brother to perish. These two bitter lines suggest that he might
have been referring to his own brother, Marie-Joseph. The word
'misère' does not mean misery, but extreme poverty, and poverty in
prison was then the surest bar to escape. Marie-Joseph, at that time,
also wrote a hymn to the Supreme Being, to which André's *ïambe*
might well have been a reply. At the same time, early in that year
Marie-Joseph wanted to stage his play *Timoléon*, which showed two
brothers at loggerheads over politics—it was to cause a scandal when
it was put on after André's death. It was banned by the Jacobins, and
Marie-Joseph was forced to burn his manuscript in the presence of
Barère, but it is evident that he must have kept a copy of it.[1]

   Chénier certainly felt himself abandoned in prison and it is likely
that he did not approve of Marie-Joseph's policy of doing nothing. At
the same time he probably did not understand that Marie-Joseph was
falling out of favour: in the previous year he had introduced a priest
into his play, *Fénelon*: it was criticized because it 'énervait l'énergie
républicaine', and withdrawn. However, in another of his *Ïambes*,
Chénier complained bitterly:

> Que pouvaient mes amis? Oui, de leur main chérie
>   Un mot à travers ces barreaux
> Eût versé quelque baume en mon âme flétrie,
>   De l'or peut-être à mes bourreaux.

As Aimée de Coigny and Montrond were saved from the guillotine
by paying—or rather, promising to pay—100 *louis d'or* to have their
names taken off the list, while Joly escaped for the price of a bottle of
brandy, it does seem surprising that the Chéniers or his friends could
not do the same for him. However, such rich and powerful people as
the comte de Vergennes (Louis de Chénier's former superior in Constantinople, guillotined at the age of 71) were unable to save themselves,
either. As for Chénier's friends at that time, Mme de Bonneuil was

---

[1] Marie-Joseph had already been in trouble over his play *Caius Gracchus*, which contained the words 'Des lois, et non du sang!' But the choice of the Timoleon theme,
intended to placate the Jacobins, was a subconscious attempt to dissociate himself from
his brother.

imprisoned in Sainte-Pélagie, where she had been since 11 Septembe
1793; the Trudaines joined Chénier in Saint-Lazare in June and wer
put to death the day after him; Thomas de Pange was dead; Françoi
and Abel de Pange had a price on their head and had fled to Metz
de Brazais had fled the country in 1791 to serve in the rebel army
against France, then after a breakdown in health was later to spend two
years in a monastery; the poet Le Brun was too poor to help him
Fanny Lecoulteux who had gone to Dieppe was too ill. Chénier's
friends, then, were in no position to intervene.

What, then, of Marie-Joseph? To be fair to him, we have to recall that his own power with the Jacobins was not what it had been.
His biographer, Labitte, perhaps went too far in saying that after the
suspension of *Timoléon* he was a 'suspect', for Marie-Joseph was never
on the list of suspects. But he pointed out that even those of his works
which had been regarded as famous revolutionary plays were now
banned from the stage, 'dès lors un véto absolu lui interdit le théâtre.
On prohiba *Charles IX* comme royaliste, *Gracchus* comme aristocrate,
Fénelon comme favorisant le fanatisme.'[1] With his brothers Louis-
Sauveur arrested at Beauvais and cast into the Conciergerie and André
in Saint-Lazare, 'Marie-Joseph sentait qu'en frappant sa famille on
arrivait à lui'. In this period Marie-Joseph not only wrote his famous
Chant du Départ 'dans l'espoir de désarmer le Comité de Salut public';
he also wrote an ode against the Terror.

Unfortunately, Chénier wrote an ode about his brother Marie-Joseph
which left little doubt about his feelings. This poem is classified in the
third collection of manuscripts in the Bibliothèque Nationale alongside those which are definitely known to have been written in prison:
it is on folio 180, while the others are on folios 188, 189, and 190. It
is hardly likely that this classification was an accident, for Chénier's
father would presumably put together these last poems in the order
in which he received them: however, it is still open to doubt whether
the *Ode à son Frère* was written before or after André went to prison.
Here is the unfinished poem, as it stands:

> Mon frère, que jamais la tristesse importune
> Ne trouble ses prospérités.
> Qu'il remplisse à la fois la scène et la tribune.
> Que les grandeurs et la fortune
> Le comblent de leurs biens qu'il a tant souhaités.

[1] F56, p. lxiii.

Que les Muses, les Arts, toujours d'un nouveau lustre
    Embellissent tous ses travaux,
Et que cédant à peine à son vingtième lustre
    De son tombeau la pierre illustre
S'élève radieuse entre tous les tombeaux.

Mais . . . . . .
    Infortune, honnêtes douleurs,
Souffrance, des vertus superbe et chaste fille,
    Salut. Mes frères, ma famille,
Sont tous les opprimés, ceux qui versent des pleurs,

Ceux que livre à la hache un féroce caprice;
    Ceux qui brûlent un noble encens
Aux pieds de la vertu que l'on traîne au supplice,
    Et bravent le sceptre du vice,
Ses caresses, ses dons, ses regards menaçants,

Ceux qui devant le crime, idole ensanglantée
    N'ont jamais fléchi les genoux,
Et soudain à sa vue impie et détestée
    Sentent leur poitrine agitée
Et leur front s'enflammer d'un généreux courroux.

The ode is 'finished' but for one line. At first sight there is nothing in it which could be interpreted as directly attacking Marie-Joseph. However, in the last stanza the line 'N'ont jamais fléchi les genoux' could refer to Marie-Joseph's vote for the death of Louis XVI. The first two stanzas could well represent an ardent desire on Chénier's part to praise and in a sense pray for his brother. What is disquieting, however, is the sharp contrast between those fine sentiments and the finer ones which follow, in which the poet adopts as brother and family all those who are oppressed—by whom, if not the Jacobins, of whom Marie-Joseph was one? This contrast between his brother's prosperity and his own revolt and solitude is so ironical in its historical context that it was natural for many critics to see the ode as a terrible indictment of Marie-Joseph. Labitte, though he wrote impartially, and indeed sympathetically, about Marie-Joseph in his introduction to his works in 1844, wrote in the same year, in the *Revue des Deux Mondes*, 'La fin de l'ode tournait à l'ironie, à une ironie blessante'. The poet's nephew Gabriel was indignant at this interpretation and took the opposite view, while giving us some further information in the process: he wrote in 1874:

Aujourd'hui, on ne se méprendra plus sur le sens de ce cette ode, qui est empreinte, non d'ironie, comme l'a pensé M. Labitte, mais d'une triste et douloureuse résignation. André connaissait l'arrestation de son frère Louis-Sauveur, la mise en suspicion de Marie-Joseph; il le savait sans aucun crédit auprès du gouvernement révolutionnaire. Il était informé du plan adopté par Marie-Joseph et par son collègue Isoré pour sauver les prisonniers, et il appréciait les dangers que courait toute sa famille; c'est dans cette triste préoccupation qu'il composa cette Ode, qui ne porte aucun titre.[1]

It is not unimportant to notice that Gabriel, who as a very young man saw the manuscripts (in 1819) before their order had been disturbed, took it for granted that this was one of the poems written in prison. Chénier's mother must have had a different impression from Gabriel's, however, for she tried to forge—there is no other word for it—a false copy of this poem. There is a manuscript in her hand (at Carcassonne) in which she copied out only the first ten lines and wrote '*Fin, ainsi est l'original*'.[2] Unfortunately she forgot to destroy the original manuscript. H. de Latouche (the pressure on whom by Louis-Sauveur and his son Gabriel is well known) tried to camouflage the poem, in his turn, not only by printing only the first ten lines but by putting them into the second person and changing the fifth line to read 'Te comblant de leurs biens, au talent mérités'. Gabriel tried to explain this away by saying that Latouche 'pensait qu'en 1819, où l'on était au plus fort de

[1] D7, t. iii, p. 357.
[2] BMC 11816. In Mme Chénier's hand it is headed 'La Muse byzantine à son frère':

Mon frère!
Que jamais la tristesse importune
ne trouble tes prospérités
qu'il remplisse à la foi [*sic*] la scène et la tribune
que les grandeurs et la fortune
le comblent de leurs biens qu'il a tant mérités
que les muses les arts toujours d'un nouveau lustre
embellissent tous ses travaux
et que cédant à peine à son vingtième lustre
de son tombeau la pierre illustre
s'élève radieux entre tous les tombeaux.

This is followed by the words '*Fin, ainsi est l'original*', then by another version, also in her hand, as follows:

'Mon frère, que ton nom avec gloire retentisse au théâtre ainsi qu'à la tribune, que les Muses toujours fidèles ne cessent jamais de te prodiguer leurs trésors, puisse-tu n'avoir jamais d'autre peine que celle que ton bon cœur te fera ressentir pour le malheur des autres, qu'une santé parfaite et les honneurs et les grandeurs et les richesses accompagne [*sic*] votre vie jusque passe vingt lustre [*sic*], et qu'alors doucement et sans douleur vous arriviez au repos qui ne fini [*sic*] plus, et que la pierre illustre de votre tombeau s'élève radieuse entre tous les tombeaux.'

This second version might be based on a prose draft of the first two stanzas, which has not survived.

réaction du parti royaliste, il n'y avait point d'explications à donner, et surtout point à revenir sur les faits de la Révolution'.[1] This is obviously nonsense, for, on the contrary, it was the last part of the ode, not the first, that would have been most calculated to please the royalist party, while Latouche had not hesitated to give part of the *Ïambes*. It was this kind of cheating on the part of Madame de Chénier, Latouche, and Gabriel de Chénier that added fuel to the legend of the two brothers' disharmony at the end of André's life. The worst element of all is that the poem itself is ambiguous. It does not necessarily, from internal evidence, suggest 'a wounding irony'—that irony arises in the mind of the reader who knows the works and lives of the two brothers, and is conscious of the contrast between false contemporary glory, on the one hand, and heroism and posthumous fame on the other. If the poem had been written in 1793 and not in 1794, its interpretation might be different: but internal evidence does suggest that it was written during the Terror. Our own interpretation is that André Chénier obviously set out with the generous intention of reconciling himself with his brother—and yet the fact that he did so in the third person chills the heart—and after the tenth line was carried away by a feeling of isolation, hatred for his oppressors, and compassion for the persecuted. The two parts hardly make a satisfactory poem, by any standards.

At this stage, in defence of Marie-Joseph, we might consider the witness of a man who knew him well and who did not like him. This was Barère himself, to whom Louis de Chénier in vain went on his knees in the hope of saving his son's life. Barère wrote in his memoirs, about Marie-Joseph:

Il était vain et bilieux. Après avoir été très lié avec moi jusqu'à la fin de 1794, il se tourna contre moi quand je ne fus que malheureux et accusé, et il se plaça au premier rang au nombre de mes accusateurs et de ceux qui, le 12 Germinal, au milieu d'une émeute, demandaient ma mort. Cependant, comme j'aime par-dessus tout à rendre justice, même à mes plus cruels ennemis, je dois cet hommage à la vérité et au cœur de Chénier, qu'il pleura amèrement la mort de son frère (je l'ai vu); que loin, comme on le dit méchamment dans les salons de Paris, d'avoir contribué à la mort de son frère qui n'était pas de la même opinion que lui, il a, au contraire, fait des démarches personnelles pour le dérober au supplice. *Devant moi, il a imploré l'intérêt actif et vrai que notre collègue Dupin mettait à ces sortes d'affaires malheureuses, d'aller au Comité de Sûreté générale et tâcher de sauver son frère.* Les hommes se doivent la vérité, et je la dis même en faveur de mon accusateur.[2]

---

[1] See p. 342, note 1, above.   [2] F8, t. ii, p. 263.

There is another important witness, Arnault, who married one of
Mme de Bonneuil's daughters and knew André Chénier well, and whose
testimony has been neglected. According to Arnault, Marie-Joseph
wrote *Le Chant du Départ* in order to save his brother:

> C'est surtout pour désarmer les accusateurs, les juges, les bourreaux de son
> malheureux frère, de ce pauvre André Chénier, que Marie-Joseph l'a im-
> provisé; c'est pour fléchir le comité de salut public, insensible jusqu'à
> présent à ses supplications qu'il multiplie sous toutes les formes.[1]

As Arnault had this information from Méhul himself, who wrote the
music for the *Chant du Départ*, there is no reason for doubting it. Moreover, Arnault, who disliked Marie-Joseph intensely, actually met him
more than once at Méhul's:

> Comme Méhul me parlait encore de ces faits, Chénier entra. L'expression
> de sa figure me fit pitié; elle me disait tout ce que sa fierté me taisait, elle me
> disait que cet homme qu'on croyait si puissant n'avait que l'existence d'un
> suppliant . . . elle me disait que son cœur, tourmenté par d'éternelles terreurs,
> était aussi torturé par le désespoir. Tant que dura cette longue angoisse . . .
> Chénier revenait tous les jours rendre compte à Méhul de ses inutiles dé-
> marches . . . . J'intervins souvent dans ces tête-à-tête. . . . Chénier me cachait
> ses larmes, mais je voyais au fond de ses yeux celles que refoulait ma présence
> et qui n'attendaient que mon départ pour s'échapper.

Many biographers have related how, on hearing of André's death—
for his trial and execution appear to have come about so swiftly that
the family did not know about it until afterwards—Marie-Joseph
bitterly reproached his father for having interfered. If we are to believe
Jacob and others, the father had written his petition without consult-
ing Marie-Joseph. It is possible that the father's actions cut across the
efforts which, according to Barère and Arnault, Marie-Joseph was
making behind the scenes. The rest of his life was made a misery
by those—Suard, Lacretelle, Sevrin, Léger, Dupont de Nemours,
Michaud, Rivarol, Millot, Fonvielle, Dumont, and so many others—
who held him responsible for his brother's death. He did not improve
matters by being the most ill-tempered and unhelpful member of the
Institut and the Académie. The formula 'Caïn, qu'as-tu fait de ton
frère?' which appeared in *La Quotidienne*, was given such variants as
'Où est ton frère Abel?' Roederer, who disliked Marie-Joseph, wrote
in a letter, 'Il n'a point commis de crime, mais il a professé tous les
mauvais principes qui les font commettre; il n'a point été l'assassin de

[1] F3, t. ii, pp. 78 ff.

son frère, mais l'ami de ses assassins.'[1] Looking at the matter as ob-
jectively as possible, we must conclude that perhaps Marie-Joseph was
maligned by his contemporaries. He certainly did nothing to hasten his
brother's death, and did something, though not enough, to prevent it.
His policy of doing nothing was one which he tried to impose on his
father alone; but he does not seem to have followed it himself.

[1] Roederer, *Œuvres*, t. iv, pp. 157–62.

14

THERMIDOR

MEANWHILE, as the end approached, André Chénier must have withdrawn more and more into himself. One sad consolation was that the Trudaines came to join him in June: they could at least talk about old times, and discuss political events. But the remaining *Iambes* show a bitter sense of isolation. In one of them he compares the prisoners with sheep awaiting the slaughter, and mocks them, also, for playing games, like children, living much the same futile life as they did in the decadent society of the old régime:

> Beaux poulets sont écrits; maris, amants, sont dupes;
> Caquetage, intrigues de sots.
> On y chante, on y joue, on y lève des jupes;
> On y fait chansons et bons mots . . .

Yet he never turned his eyes away from the doom that was awaiting them and felt the threat of death in the midst of all this pathetic amusement:

> Et sur les gonds de fer soudain les portes crient.
> Des juges tigres nos seigneurs
> Le pourvoyeur paraît. Quelle sera ta proie
> Que la hache appelle aujourd'hui?
> Chacun frissonne, écoute; et chacun avec joie
> Voit que ce n'est pas encor lui:
> Ce sera toi demain, insensible imbécile.

This harsh poem was only a rehearsal for the last and most eloquent of the *Iambes*. Before it came another, addressed to his friends. It begins with the same mocking irony, before he opens his heart. Here the image of the sheepfold is handled with the wit of La Fontaine:

> Les enfants qui suivaient ses ébats dans la plaine,
> Les vierges aux belles couleurs
> Qui le baisaient en foule et sur sa blanche laine
> Entrelaçaient rubans et fleurs,
> Sans plus penser à lui le mangent s'il est tendre . . .

More than any of the preceding *Iambes* it becomes a deeply personal poem. The poet exhorts himself to grow used to the idea of neglect and oblivion, reproaching his friends for his fate in the lines 'Que pouvaient mes amis? . . .' which we have already quoted above (p. 339). But, while not achieving the noble heroism of the last *Ïambe*, there are signs that Chénier was trying to reconcile himself with everyone and to stifle unworthy feelings. If he could write 'A mon tour aujourd'hui mon malheur importune' we have to see the line in its context:

> Mais tout est précipice. Ils ont le droit de vivre.
> Vivez, amis, vivez contents.
> En dépit de [Fouquier] soyez lents à me suivre.
> Peut-être en de plus heureux temps
> J'ai moi-même, à l'aspect des pleurs de l'infortune
> Détourné mes regards distraits.
> A mon tour aujourd'hui mon malheur importune.
> Vivez, amis; vivez en paix.

The terrible days of Thermidor were now approaching. So far, only an occasional victim had left Saint-Lazare in the tumbril, never to return to civilization. But the days were not far off when they would be piled into tumbrils by the score; trundled through the streets of Paris like cattle, with their hands tied behind their back; tried in batches at the Conciergerie; carted off to the guillotine, executed and thrown into pits, and covered with quick-lime.

If Chénier's family appeared inactive, his enemies showed no such weakness. There is no room here for going into all the documents in the case, for there are over thirty of them. On 3 Messidor (21 June) Herman, who had been appointed President of a commission of inquiry into the so-called prison plot, addressed a memorandum to the Convention which was approved and signed by Robespierre, Billaud-Varenne, and Barère. The other commissions (see above, p. 322), with their more generous mandate, were now conveniently forgotten, and it is possible to understand how Louis de Chénier's petition, addressed to a benevolent commission, became a damning document when it fell into the hands of a malevolent one: this, I believe, is the real key to what happened, for it is also unlikely that either Louis or Marie-Joseph Chénier ever had wind of this secret statement drawn up by Herman. It contains such virulent paragraphs as

. . . Il serait possible de connaître ceux qui, dans chaque prison, servaient et devaient servir les diverses factions, les diverses conjurations; qui, dans ce moment même, ne peuvent contenir leur rage ni s'empêcher de se prononcer tout ce qu'ils sont. Il faudrait peut-être purger en un instant les prisons et déblayer le sol de la liberté de ces immondices, de ces rebuts de l'humanité. Justice serait faite et il serait plus facile d'établir l'ordre dans les prisons.[1]

Four days later Robespierre, Barère, Collot, and others signed a decree (*arrêté*) approving Herman's report. Meanwhile the spies were at their work in Saint-Lazare, listening at doors, peeping through key-holes, taking notes. On 23 Messidor (11 July) Manini and Faro drew up a report after questioning a number of people in Saint-Lazare. Isnard, Allain (a teacher), Scelle, Gautier were alleged to be planning to escape and were given away by Coquery and Manini. Allain, when he was asked his opinion about Robespierre, had the courage to reply, ironically, that he had no opinion about Robespierre, 'et que d'ailleurs on n'a point d'opinion en prison'. As for the Jacobins, 'A répondu qu'il n'a jamais été aux Jacobins, et quant à leurs opinions cela les re-gardait'. This long report, with its supporting documents, was sent to the Comité de Sûreté générale on the following day, 12 July.[2] No doubt similar reports were sent in about other prisoners, but the docu-ments have not survived. Meanwhile two Belgian spies, Jaubert and Robinet, after consultation with the others drew up a list of thirty-eight suspects, 'Noms des détenus que nous croyons en notre âme et conscience être ennemis du peuple et ne pas aimer le gouvernement actuel de la République française'. This bears no date. Among those on the list were the baron Trenck, the baronne d'Hinnisdal, and 'Fleuri, ex-marquise, accusée d'aristocratie puante'; Vergennes; Loyserolle [*sic*]; his son who was accused of writing a poem in honour of Durosoy, and both the Saint-Aignans. Chénier's name was not on this list. Jaubert admitted that there was no proof of conspiracy:

Nous croyons que les individus, dont nous venons de transcrire les noms, sont des ennemis du peuple, du gouvernement républicain et révolutionnaire; nous n'avons pas de preuves matérielles qui établissent cette conviction, elle est acquise par des remarques [i.e. observations] que nous avons faites.

The next step was for Herman himself to come and inspect the prison, making a formal round, looking at the register and individual dossiers, questioning the staff and spies. He is probably the sinister person mentioned in one of the unfinished *Ïambes*:

Mais quel est ce grand brun (décrit en 4, 6 ou au plus 8 v.)? Ne l'ai-je pas connu jadis, le dos couvert de longs cheveux dont il poudrait les fauteuils de damas, et ricanant, et ne disant rien, et ambitionnant le nom d'homme d'esprit, etc.? Et vraiment, c'est *H*, c'est lui-même.

---

[1] Given in E2, p. lx.   [2] Ibid., pp. lxiv–lxxii.

Réputé Cicéron chez toute la basoche
Et bel esprit chez les catins.

Oh! qu'il se rend bien justice, quand il se met au dernier rang des valets,
etc.

Tu te croyais trop vil pour avoir rien à craindre,
Et que je ne te verrais pas.
Et peut-être en effet il eût mieux valu feindre
Et ne point descendre si bas.

Collot d'Herbois and Hérault de Seychelles have been named as
possible candidates for this *ïambe*; but neither of them, being leaders
of the Jacobins, could be described as lackeys (valets), whereas Herman, a lawyer and an old crony of Robespierre's, could be called so
for accepting the job of spying in prisons. The last lines suggest
that Chénier, instead of ignoring him, must have returned Herman's
salute, then regretted it.

To the forty names on Jaubert's list, Herman himself added a further
twenty-six, 'dans la chambre du concierge Semé'. Among them were
'Rouché [*sic*] auteur du poème des mois'; three priests; the count
Créquy-Montmorency; the marquis de Montalembert, and the two
Trudaine brothers. The third on this list was André Chénier, *the only
one with a formal charge after his name*: 'avait recélé les papiers de
l'ambassadeur d'Espagne et [les avait] soustraits aux recherches du Comité de Sûreté générale depuis qu'il était à la maison Lazare.' This
means that Chénier must have been questioned, and no doubt by
Herman himself.

Lanne, Ridon, and other officials came regularly to the prison, and
gradually the list lengthened. A number of prisoners including Montrond, the duchesse de Fleury, and the abbé Millin managed to have
their names taken off the list, by bribery. Dusaulchoy was shown a list,
by Robinet, containing eighty-two names.[1] This was subsequently re-
discovered by Becq de Fouquières.[2] It contains the names of Roucher
and Chénier; the Saint-Aignans, Mme de Fleury, and the two Trudaines. This list was sent on to the Comité de Sûreté générale, which
must have passed it on to the president of the Tribunal, Fouquier-
Tinville. Fouquier went through it, cutting out three names and
adding another, so that there remained eighty accused. Against the
names he made one, two, or three strokes, according to the batch or
'fournée' in which they were to be tried: Roucher and Chénier had

[1] Dusaulchoy: *L'Agonie de Saint-Lazare sous la tyrannie de Robespierre*, s.d., p. 37.
[2] E2, pp. lxxx–lxxxii.

two strokes against their names. Fouquier then sent this list to Trin-
chard, head of the 'popular commission', for advice and further
information.

Fouquier's next task, growing more urgent as the Jacobins and
especially Robespierre were demanding severe action, was to prepare
a general act of accusation which would be applied to all the eighty
culprits, while individual dossiers were being completed. Without the
slightest concern for truth or even plausibility, Fouquier lumped together a number of 'conspirators' who had perished in recent months
—Dillon, Chaumette, Ronsin, and Hébert—and asserted that these
eighty prisoners had been their accomplices:

Conspiration de prison

Antoine-Quentin Fouquier, accusateur public du tribunal Révolutionnaire, expose qu'en vertu d'arrêté du Comité de salut public publié de la
Convention nationale,

Charles-Michel Alain etc. etc. . . . ont tous été traduits au tribunal révolutionnaire comme prévenus de s'être déclarés les ennemis du peuple par des
complots, trames et manœuvres contre-révolutionnaires:

Qu'examen fait des pièces adressées à l'accusateur public il en résulte que
Dillon, Ronsin, Chaumette et Hébert avaient des agents et des complices de
leurs conspirations perfides dans toutes les maisons d'arrêt pour y suivre
leurs trames et en préparer l'exécution. Depuis que le glaive de la loi a frappé
ces grands coupables, leurs agents, devenus chefs à leur tour, ont tout tenté
pour parvenir à leurs fins et exécuter leurs trames liberticides . . . .

According to the evil fairy-tale which Robespierre, Barère, Collot, and
the others had begun to spin, when they drew up and signed the
decree of 7 Messidor and urged Herman and Fouquier to hurry up
and empty the prisons, these eighty people, as well as hundreds in the
other prisons, were all plotting together—for what?—to

s'évader et dissoudre, par le meurtre et l'assassinat des représentants du
peuple, et notamment des Comités de salut public et de sûreté générale, le
gouvernement républicain et de rétablir la royauté.

Of course, looking at it from poor, overworked Fouquier's point of
view, it would be mere quibbling to make too much fuss against
a general accusation of this sort. The government had made it plain
that there was a plot, so a plot there must be. And in time of war, too.
If you have eighty people to deal with at once, in batches of between
twenty and thirty, you have to have a general statement so as to bring
them from prison to the bar. The main point is to have a look at them.

The forms are observed, after all—separate statements are drawn up for each group, and each prisoner is given, the night before, a copy of the charge against him, so that he can think it over. What a lot of work! Of course, once in court, much time will be taken in establishing each prisoner's identity. They—or at least some of them—will be given a chance to speak. There will be real witnesses—for the prosecution, of course. Anyway, by comparison with trying dozens of Girondins and people like Danton, these are only small fry.

The first that the prisoners knew about all this was on 23 July (5 Thermidor), at about four o'clock on a hot afternoon, when two enormous tumbrils jolted into the prison courtyard. The heat was so great that they were all resting. The governor of the prison was handed a warrant for the transfer to the Conciergerie of the first batch to be tried; twenty-five of them. The warders spread through the prison in groups of three, assembling the prisoners, then the names on this list were called out. Dusaulchoy relates how they all stood in ranks, watching them go past, 'some as pale as death, others full of calm and courage'. While they all knew that this was to happen sooner or later, after the tumbrils rolled away there could be no sleep for anyone— who would be called the next day, and the day after? Would any of those who had gone, return to Saint-Lazare? The only one to be spared was the duchesse de Saint-Aignan, who returned to Saint-Lazare on the following day, just as Chénier was leaving.

It is not hard to imagine what a night Chénier passed, between the 5th and 6th Thermidor. With the intuition of his own fate, it was the night when he wrote his last *Ïambe*, a finely integrated work of eighty-eight lines, half elegy, half satire, one of the most noble poems ever written in French. But first he would gather together his books, in a coffer, and destroy a few papers after looking through his wallet. He would roll his few clothes together, for his father would have the right to collect his belongings a few days later.[1] Less than half a mile

---

[1] A list of these (which was probably made on 14 Thermidor when his effects were examined) is as follows: 3 habits, un fourré, un vert et un noir; 1 manteau écarlate; 1 robe de chambre; 2 pantalons ou grandes culottes; 4 culottes noires; 3 vestes noires; 14 gilets de différentes couleurs; 1 chapeau à plumes; 1 brosse à cheveux; 1 compas pour rouler les cheveux; 1 drap de lit; 2 vestes de Basin; 15 chemises; 16 caleçons; 6 paires de bas de coton; 7 p. de bas de soie; 2 peignoirs; 1 serviette; 2 cravates noires; 2 cravates blanches de soie; 8 mouchoirs de cou, blancs; 1 p. de manchettes de deuil; 1 petit paquet enveloppé de papier; 2 pistolets de poche dans la caisse aux livres, 1 canne, 1 portemanteau avec le cadenas; 1 p. de bottes, 1 tire-bottes; 1 écritoire; 1 petit tableau vitré; 1 sac-de-nuit; 1 sac doublé de peau, 1 paquet enveloppé d'une serviette; 1 drap de lit. [BMC 11815/437/339, No. 8.]

away was his father's house, and yet there was no means of letting him know what was going on. André Chénier did not know that on the 4th of Thermidor, that is, only yesterday, his father had come to visit him but had been turned away. Marie-Joseph had hinted to him that Robespierre's days of power were numbered, and that he and Isoré were involved in the plot against him. On the same day Louis went to see Barère and threw himself at his feet, asking him to intervene personally to save his son. Barère, a calculating man with a cold manner, whose heart was not completely dead but who put power and his own survival first, replied with only six words—'Votre fils sortira dans trois jours'—and showed the old man to the door.[1] What was the real meaning of Barère's words? Barère was president of the Comité de Salut public and must have known that André's name was on the second *fournée*, for the names had to be approved by the Committee. Could he be so cruel as to mean that André had but three days to live? Or, knowing that Robespierre was in for trouble, and himself standing on the touch-line watching which way to jump, did he mean that he, Barère, would release André Chénier as soon as Robespierre fell? What is known is that Marie-Joseph wept with rage when he knew that his father had been to see Barère. He was aware that Barère had refused to help him, Marie-Joseph, and had referred him to Dupin, whose influence was slight. Barère wanted to keep out of it. And perhaps André would have wept, also, if he had known that the man he most despised had been asked to intercede for him—it was as humiliating as if his father had asked Collot. All this helps to explain why, under the Directory, Marie-Joseph came into the open as an enemy of Barère. But although the Chénier family, right down to Gabriel, maintained that Barère's six words were meant in the most evil sense, this seems to us impossible to believe. There was, of course, an absence of good faith: if Barère wanted to help at all, he could have told Louis or Marie-Joseph that André Chénier was to be committed for trial in that very week. The opinion of the Chénier family, that Barère's words were 'une sanguinaire hypocrisie', is too simple. Chamfort, in his *Pensées et Maximes*, summed up Barère in the words 'C'est un brave homme que ce Barère: *il vient toujours au secours du plus fort*'. Why, at this stage, would any man in his senses take sides with a Marie-Joseph Chénier, against a Robespierre? But he must have seen that the chances of André Chénier's survival were fifty-fifty: his six words

[1] This story was first related by Latouche in 1819 (D1), when Barère (1755–1841) was still alive to refute it: he never did.

to the poet's father were a concession that survival was possible, and that a decision was not far off. Where the Chéniers went wrong was in relaxing their efforts and inquiries at this stage.

André Chénier, as he sat down to write his last poem, could know nothing of all this. All that he knew was that he had seen the two tumbrils roll away, with Madame de Saint-Aignan and other friends in them. The first thirty lines reflect the chill that had seized him when he saw the prisoners bound and led away, and imagined himself in the same predicament. Writing in the night, in minute writing on a tiny slip of brown paper used for wrapping washing in, a slip no wider than a ruler, and with the finest of pens and the help of a magnifying-glass, he heard in the silence the loud tick of the clock, and the rhythmic beat of the warder's steps up and down the corridor, and brought all this into his poem. The first movement is slow, tortuous, trying to convey suspense and activity at the same time:

> Comme un dernier rayon, comme un dernier zéphyre
> Animent la fin d'un beau jour,
> Au pied de l'échafaud j'essaye encor ma lyre.
> Peut-être est-ce bientôt mon tour.
> Peut-être avant que l'heure en cercle promenée
> Ait posé sur l'émail brillant
> Dans les soixante pas où sa route est bornée,
> Son pied sonore et vigilant,
> Le sommeil du tombeau pressera ma paupière.

The poet knew full well that he would not be put to death in an hour: but, as the poem shows at a later stage, what was in his mind was the idea of suicide—suicide within an hour, after writing a poem. But a poem, for its writer, is in the first place a catalyst: he might set out with the notion of expressing his thoughts or feelings, but in the process discovers what they really are, not what he thought they were. Now Chénier lived in advance the horror that had to be faced:

> Avant que de ses deux moitiés
> Ce vers que je commence ait atteint la dernière,
> Peut-être en ces murs effrayés
> Le messager de mort, noir recruteur des ombres,
> Escorté d'infâmes soldats,
> Ébranlant de mon nom ces longs corridors sombres,
> Où seul dans la foule à grands pas
> J'erre, aiguisant ces dards persécuteurs du crime,

> Du juste trop faibles soutiens,
> Sur mes lèvres soudain va suspendre la rime;
> Et chargeant mes bras de liens,
> Me traîner, amassant en foule à mon passage
> Mes tristes compagnons reclus,
> Qui me connaissaient tous avant l'affreux message,
> Mais qui ne me connaissent plus . . .

Though Chénier had already shown himself to be a master of narrative in his *Bucoliques*, he had never written in this way before, in such tortuous syntax in which qualifying circumstances are piled one on to the other, a delaying device which serves to put off the final vision as well as to accumulate horror. But this is no more than the setting: the poet now has to face the notion of death itself, and his first impulse, out of disgust, is to welcome it:

> Eh bien! j'ai trop vécu. Quelle franchise auguste,
> De mâle constance et d'honneur
> Quels exemples sacrés, doux à l'âme du juste,
> Pour lui quelle ombre de bonheur,
> Quelle Thémis terrible aux têtes criminelles,
> Quels pleurs d'une noble pitié,
> Des antiques bienfaits quels souvenirs fidèles,
> Quels beaux échanges d'amitié,
> Font digne de regrets l'habitacle des hommes?
> La peur fugitive est leur Dieu;
> La bassesse, la feinte. Ah! lâches que nous sommes
> Tous, oui, tous. Adieu, terre, adieu.
> Vienne, vienne la mort! — Que la mort me délivre!

It is not from self-pity but from frustrated idealism that the poet welcomes death: it is curious to notice, also, how in these few lines, the whole vocabulary is selected from that which the eighteenth century reserved for its conception of the hero—*l'honnête homme*. And it is not surprising that a few lines later the poet actually pronounces those words, after a sudden and vigorous expression of the will to live:

> Ainsi donc mon cœur abattu
> Cède au poids de mes maux? Non, non. Puissé-je vivre!
> Ma vie importe à la vertu.
> Car l'honnête homme enfin, victime de l'outrage,
> Dans les cachots, près du cercueil,
> Relève plus altiers son front et son langage,
> Brillants d'un généreux orgueil.

We have already seen, in Chénier's elegies; in what he wrote in Hood's Tavern in 1789; in his refusal to draw his salary for doing nothing; in his political journalism; in his replies to Guénot when he was arrested, and in his letters to his father and in the previous *Ïambes*, that one of his dominating characteristics, perhaps indeed the strongest, was pride. It was this pride, this self-respect, that dominated his last hours of life, though perhaps in using the words 'généreux orgueil' he was not fully conscious of how far they were self-revelatory. The poem is too long for us to comment on it in its entirety, but one conviction that Chénier had always had was that he had a special mission of some kind to fulfil. Never did a man more firmly believe in his own genius, his compelling destiny. In the remarkable lines which follow, and which are an address to his pen, he formulated this commitment, this dedication, as never before:

> S'il est écrit aux cieux que jamais une épée
> N'étincellera dans mes mains,
> Dans l'encre et l'amertume une autre arme trempée
> Peut encor servir les humains.

He appeals to truth and justice (not to God) to save him so that he might take vengeance on the 'hideous blackguards', 'slimy hangmen', 'maggots devouring France'; moving with incredible ease from lofty poetic diction to, once more, the grossest idiom that he can find. The heroism of his last hours may well be measured by the difference between his present outlook and that which he had when he was in London only a few years earlier: then it was 'Je vis, je souffre encore'; but now, 'Je souffre, mais je vis'.

Everything around him, he went on—the persecution of his friends, the success of climbers and tyrants, the death and ruin of honest men—

> Tout eût tari ma vie; ou contre ma poitrine
> Dirigé mon poignard . . .

Suicide was a temptation, the temptation to which Condorcet and Roland had succumbed. But Chénier, arriving at last to the level of true heroism, which is self-forgetfulness, dedication against all the odds, transcended himself in his last lines, in which we see him at last not only as a great poet but a great man, compassionate and courageous:

> Mais quoi!
> Nul ne resterait donc pour attendrir l'histoire
> Sur tant de justes massacrés?
> Pour consoler leurs fils, leurs veuves, leur mémoire,
> Pour que des brigans abhorrés

Frémissent aux portraits noirs de leur ressemblance,
    Pour descendre jusqu'aux enfers
Nouer le triple fouet, le fouet de la vengeance
    Déjà levé sur ces pervers?
Pour cracher sur leurs noms, pour chanter leur supplice?
    Allons, étouffe tes clameurs;
Souffre, ô cœur gros de haine, affamé de justice.
    Toi, Vertu, pleure si je meurs.

Such, then, was the farewell to the world and to poetry of this fine
spirit, as rich in heart as in intellect, at the mention of whose name so
many people in France, ignorant of the real nature of his work or the
message that it contains, lift their eyebrows in amused surprise that
anyone, especially a foreigner, should spend time on reading anything
but *L'Aveugle* and *La Jeune Tarentine*. But, like Stendhal, he has his
happy few.

On the 6th Thermidor (Thursday, 24th of July), at about half past
three in the afternoon, the tumbrils once more lumbered into the courtyard of Saint-Lazare and stood waiting for three hours. The governor
again received a warrant, this time for 'Roucher et 26 autres', signed by
the prosecutor's substitute, Gribauval. Chénier was second on the list.
After a quick farewell to the Trudaines (to whom he no doubt passed
some manuscripts) his hands were tied behind his back and he mounted
into the tumbril, next to Roucher. Parisians with nothing better to do
jeered at them as they passed southwards to the Conciergerie. Again
Chénier passed within a few yards of his father's house, and the poet's
memory must have again been stirred as he passed through the quarter
of the Marais, where he had spent part of his boyhood.

At the Conciergerie there would be the usual bunch of idlers waiting
to enjoy themselves. Beugnot, describing his own arrival there, said
that the Palace steps were full of women, sitting as in the theatre stalls,
waiting for their favourite show. They rose to their feet as he got down,
shrieking and laughing like cannibals. During the few steps through
the courtyard he was covered with filth from head to foot as they
aimed at him, making him dread the moment when he would have to
come out again.[1] Prisoners were then taken through a kind of gallery,
into a room on the left which was used as the prison registry. This
registry was part of a large hall, cut in half: in the other section were
kept those prisoners who had already been tried and were waiting to
have their hair shorn off.

[1] F11, p. 159.

Chénier must have spent the last night of his life in a terrible dilemma. After being handed over by their guard, Château, to the concierge, Richard, and formally registered, the prisoners were each handed a charge-sheet which provided some food for thought. Chénier at once saw from his sheet that he had been confused with his brother, Louis-Sauveur, who was somewhere in the same building. It is unlikely that the two brothers were allowed to see or speak to each other. On looking at the document in his hand, André read the following description of himself, which bore the date 6 Thermidor and Fouquier's signature:

André Chénier, âgé de 31 ans, né à Constantinople, homme de lettres, *exadjudant-général chef de brigade sous Dumouriez*, demeurant rue de Cléry.[1]

Chénier must have laughed outright at Fouquier's stupidity before reading the rest of the accusation with increasing anger. First came the general charge, which they all received:

Ont été traduits au tribunal révolutionnaire comme prévenus de s'être rendus ennemis du peuple, par des complots, trames et manœuvres contrerévolutionnaires . . . .

In the personal charge, Fouquier named Roucher and Chénier together:

En effet, Roucher et Chénier n'ont-ils pas été les écrivains stipendiés du tyran, pour égarer et corrompre l'esprit public, et préparer tous les crimes du despotisme et de la tyrannie? N'étaient-ils pas, en 1791 et 1792, les salariés de la liste civile et les mercenaires du comité autrichien, pour provoquer, en les diffamant, en les calomniant, la dissolution des sociétés populaires et la proscription de tous les patriotes qui en étaient membres? N'étaient-ils pas eux qui, émules des Royou, des Fontenay, des Durosoy, rédigeaient le supplément du *Journal de Paris*, où, sous l'apparence de soutenir de prétendus principes constitutionnels, on préparait la contre-révolution?

These were almost all general charges, which would have taken a long time to be proved. It could not be proved that they received money either from the Court, or the so-called 'Comité autrichien', or from the civil list. It could be proved that they had attacked the Jacobins (sociétés populaires) but there was no law against that. It could be proved that they had written in the *Journal de Paris* (which was not a crime, either); and that they had supported the principles of the constitution, but that was no legal offence. These were all vague charges, but on the next day it became evident that Fouquier had wisely kept some ammunition in reserve.

[1] For the complete document see E2, pp. xci–xciii.

Chénier must already have felt uneasy at the mistake in his identity, but his indignation must have increased as he read on:

Depuis, Chénier, ayant cherché comme bien d'autres traîtres à se soustraire à la surveillance des autorités publiques, s'est confondu parmi ses défenseurs, où il a eu le grade d'adjudant-général, chef de brigade de l'armée du Nord; il paraît qu'il a secondé le plus adroitement qu'il a pu les trahisons de l'infâme Dumouriez, avec lequel il a eu des liaisons les plus intimes; mais après la défection du traître Dumouriez, il s'est occupé de laisser ignorer la part qu'il y avait prise . . . .

So it went on to describe how Louis-Sauveur had written a memorandum against Dumont, and to attribute all this to the poet. In the document that has come down to us, this paragraph is struck out, but the first paragraph describing him both as 'homme de lettres' and 'ex-adjudant-général chef de brigade' was left unchanged. But the poet received the entire document, and must have spent a sleepless night over his dilemma: whether to draw attention to this enormous inaccuracy, or not. To protest would result in drawing attention to Louis-Sauveur, whose case until now, thanks to a little bribery, had been quietly tucked away. Chénier's biographers have, naturally enough, invented what seemed to them a plausible account of what happened, though none of the prisoners survived and none of the others present ever recorded the complete proceedings. Thus Gabriel de Chénier asserts that, at the trial, 'André fit observer qu'il n'avait jamais été adjudant-général.' Becq de Fouquières wrote that it was on receiving his charge-sheet that Chénier made that observation. Lacroix, more cautiously, wrote, 'André protesta sans doute . . . .' G. Walter says that the chairman of the court, Coffinhal, who for some reason replaced Fouquier-Tinville on the 7th Thermidor, did not allow prisoners to say much, but 'Il a dû faire cependant une exception pour André Chénier afin de lui permettre de signaler l'erreur commise dans l'acte d'accusation à son égard. Liendon ne s'en montra nullement embarrassé. Il prit sa plume et d'un trait biffa les trente et une lignes relatives à Louis-Sauveur. Et la séance suivit son cours.'[1] Whereas both Walter and Gabriel de Chénier say that it was Liendon who struck out the lines, according to Becq it was Fouquier. Who knows? The proceedings of the trial were written out in advance (further evidence of what goes on in so-called 'People's Courts'), so that all this is conjecture.

[1] References are to G. de Chénier (D7, t. i, p. cxxxv); Becq de Fouquières (E2, p. xci); Jacob (E1, p. vi); Walter (F101, p. 319).

But knowing what we do of André Chénier's character, it is hard to believe that he would draw attention to this matter and thus denounce his brother. It is just as likely that Coffinhal or Liendon, or one of the three judges, pointed out the error.

At 9 a.m. on the morning of the 7th Thermidor (25 July 1794) the accused men and women were led into the court-room, which was, ironically, named Liberty Hall (Salle de la Liberté). Coffinhal presided, with, on the table in front of him, the whole of the proceedings, as well as the sentence, written out in advance by the indefatigable Fouquier. If anyone were acquitted, all he had to do was to cross out the name. The case for the prosecution, also written out in advance (so that none of the accused's replies are given), was led by Liendon, before three judges and nine permanent jurors. As he looked round Liberty Hall, Chénier would see the bust of Brutus, as well as the effigies of the two assassinated 'martyrs' of the Revolution, Lepelletier and Marat. Behind a barrier stood the gaping public, come to gloat and comment on the proceedings. After the accused took their places on the benches, which rose in tiers facing the window, Liendon read through the collective accusation, interrupting his performance now and then to fire a question at one of the accused, some of whom were described in detail, others not at all, the only proofs required against them being their name, age, and address. The witnesses were two stool-pigeons, Manini and Coquery, five employees from Saint-Lazare, including the concierge, and a certain Pépin-Desgrouettes who was later accused of being a stool-pigeon but who maintained (at the trial of Fouquier-Tinville not long afterwards) that he had been chosen as an impartial representative of his fellow prisoners at Saint-Lazare. As there was no court of appeal, and as nobody ever appeared twice before this efficient court, the deposition of the witnesses was not taken down. After the three witnesses had been heard, each accused was, or was supposed to be, asked whether he had any reply to make, and the chairman, prosecutor, judges, and jurors were free to intervene with further remarks or questions. Then Liendon gave his summing-up, which was commented on by the chairman, Coffinhal, 'l'ayant réduite à ses points les plus simples et fait remarquer aux jurés les faits et preuves propres à fixer son attention tant pour que contre l'accusé'.[1] All that is missing from the official account is the intervention of the 'people', who by applauding or booing expressed their judgement on the accused.

---

[1] Moland, E3, p. lxii.

One of the accused, Constant, was at once released, probably because he had acted as an informer. Then Liendon handed the Jury all the documents in the case, 'excepté les déclarations écrites des témoins', after which the accused were led out of the hall. The suppression of the witnesses' written statements is significant: they had not been allowed to give all their evidence, and had been silenced by Coffinhal.

Before going into Liberty Hall, Chénier must have felt that he had a good case, if he were allowed to defend himself. There was no proof that he had been on the civil list; if he had attacked the Jacobin Club he had also attacked the Girondins, who had now vanished from the earth. If he had defended the Constitution, the Jacobins had maintained until 10 August 1792 that they did, also. He knew that he had nothing to do with the prison conspiracy. Nothing had been mentioned—not a single thing—about his examination by Guénot on that night at Passy—nothing about Pastoret, nothing about his income, nothing about his correspondence with Barthélemy or Ocariz. Being confused with his brother was, of course, a problem; if it was raised, it could help to condemn his brother—at the same time, being related to a general who had been a friend of Dumouriez and who had attacked Dumont was hardly a recommendation. Here, he was trapped. Indeed, when the matter was discussed, it is more than likely that Liendon would seize happily on the mistake, pointing to André Chénier and denouncing him as the brother of a suspect, as well as being one himself.

As we have already mentioned, Coffinhal or Fouquier had reserved some ammunition against Roucher and Chénier. It did not figure in the 'acte d'accusation' they had received, but either Liendon or Coffinhal must have looked through Chénier's dossier, which had been passed down from the Comité de Salut Public (was it by Barère?) to the court. Maybe the points that follow were discussed in some sharp exchanges between Chénier and Liendon; maybe they were produced at the last minute, but in any case they are damning. The questions put to the Jury about them were as follows:

Jean-Antoine Roucher, 48 ans etc.
André Chénier, 31 ans etc.

Sont-ils convaincus de s'être déclarés les ennemis du peuple en participant à tous les crimes commis par le tyran, sa femme et sa famille, dans les journées du 28 février 1791, du 20 juin et 10 août, en insultant les patriotes, en approuvant le massacre du Champ de Mars et les tyrannies exercées sur les patriotes qui avaient échappé au massacre; en écrivant contre la fête de Château-

vieux, contre la liberté et en faveur de la tyrannie; en entretenant des correspondances avec les ennemis intérieurs et extérieurs de la République; en
discréditant les assignats; enfin en conspirant dans la maison d'arrêt de
Saint-Lazare, à l'effet de s'évader et de dissoudre, par le meurtre et l'assassinat des représentants du peuple, notamment des membres des Comités de
salut public et de sûreté générale, le gouvernement républicain et rétablir
la royauté en France?

COFFINHAL

Here there was no further mention of being paid from the civil list,
or of attacking the 'sociétés populaires'. Chénier or Roucher must
have been able to give satisfactory answers to those accusations. Nor
is there any more mention of their constitutional position. Guénot's
question about corresponding with Barthélemy, and Herman's accusation of concealing letters from Ocariz, must have been brought up
again: indeed the phrase 'en entretenant des correspondances', &c.,
with the mention 'ennemis *intérieurs*', suggests that the Committee
must have got wind of Chénier's letter to the Minister of Justice. The
general accusation of writing in the *Journal de Paris* has now been
cleverly pointed to specific events on which they had taken a stand:
the reference to the '28 février 1791' points to Chénier's condemnation
of the 'Journée des Poignards' in his 'Réflexions sur l'esprit de Parti'
when the mob had marched on Vincennes while the nobles took up
arms at the Tuileries, with the result that La Fayette arrested 64 rioters
and 8 royalists. But if Coffinhal had looked closely at Chénier's article he would have seen that the poet had come down heavily on the
aristocrats' behaviour on that day, 'impudents et misérables parasites, qui
en osant se nommer les défenseurs du roi, ont pris le seul moyen qu'ils
pussent avoir de lui faire tort'. But, of course, Chénier was defending
the King. The reference to the '20 juin' (see above, p. 277) is to Chénier's article of that title, describing the invasion of the Louvre by the
mob, the cowardice of Pétion, and the dignity of the King. This could
certainly be held against him. As for the next date mentioned, '10 août',
this refers to Guénot's cross-questioning at Passy, when the poet offered the pretext of illness to explain why he had not taken part in the
mass rising and deposition of the monarchy. Finally, there remains the
reference to the 'fête des Suisses de Châteauvieux', against which both
Roucher and Chénier had waged a prolonged campaign and in the
process attacked both the municipality and the Jacobins. The evidence
was so overwhelming that (even if the verdict had not been given
against twenty-five victims at once) it is not surprising that the jury

pronounced them guilty. The only one exonerated by the jury was Auphant. Coffinhal now wrote:

> La déclaration du juré est affirmative, sur tous les accusés, à l'exception de François Auphant, envers lequel elle est négative.
> A Paris, le 7 thermidor, an I de la République française une et indivisible.
>   NEIROT, greffier. COFFINHAL

All else that is known about the conduct of the trial is what came out in evidence during the subsequent trial of Fouquier-Tinville, who defended himself fiercely before going to the guillotine.[1] Manini, aged 47, who described himself as an 'homme de lettres', had been one of the principal witnesses and was, indeed, a witness at the three trials on 6, 7, and 8 Thermidor. Questioned about his part in the trials that took place on those days, he said that he had never known Fouquier-Tinville. He had spent four months as a 'prisoner' in the Madelonettes; five to six months in Saint-Lazare; several weeks in Plessis; several in the Luxembourg, several in the 'Port-Libre où il est actuellement'. In other words he was a hired spy. According to him it was Coquery who had told him about the prison-plot while he was in Saint-Lazare. He had heard Isnard, Scelle, and Alain offer between 20,000 and 100,000 *livres* to Coquery in exchange for steel files for sawing the bars away, 'pour s'évader et aller avec leurs amis extérieurs tuer, massacrer la Convention'. They had paid 25 *livres* to have an uncensored letter sent out of the prison. He admitted having denounced the conspirators to the Comité de Sûreté générale. As for the trial,

> Il observa que plusieurs des accusés sur les interpellations qui leur étaient faites par les juges, accusateur ou jurés, prenaient quelquefois jusqu'à cinq ou six fois la parole pour leur défense, et qu'ils ont parlé aussi longuement qu'ils ont voulu sans qu'ils fussent interrompus, excepté un des accusés que le déclarant croit avoir été mis hors des débats parce qu'il se défendait par des sarcasmes et des injures contre ceux qui siégeaient. . . .[1]

Knowing Chénier's impetuousness and his sharp tongue, it might well be supposed that it was he who attacked the court: the only way of silencing him and putting him 'en dehors des débats' would be to take him outside. Fouquier replied to Manini's evidence about the prison conspiracy, 'Je n'ai pas reçu les lettres dont parle le témoin. Je n'ai pas été à Saint-Lazare. Je n'ai eu nulle correspondance avec Coquery et Maligny [*sic*], ni avec Pépin. Les listes m'ont été envoyées par le

---

[1] For what follows about this trial, see Lenôtre, *Le Tribunal révolutionnaire*, ch. viii, and Moland, op. cit., pp. lxviii–lxxv.

gouvernement, signées des membres du Comité. Les noms des témoins m'ont été transmis par la même voie.' From this it is clear that Barère knew, or ought to have known, that Chénier's name was down for trial.

As for Manini, he stated that, informed by Coquery ('il était dans la misère, il partageait mes haricots') about the plot, 'Je me mis aux écoutes à la porte d'une chambre, et j'entendis moi-même le complot.' Accordingly he at once informed the police, and subsequently drew up a list of names. He pointed out that the prisoners were not all tried for conspiracy, 'mais pour des délits particuliers'. Pépin Desgrouettes was the most interesting of these witnesses: he was a lawyer and had presided over a people's court in 1792: by an odd coincidence he lived at 25 rue du Sentier, near where Chénier had lived. He had been taken away from Saint-Lazare and questioned at 7 o'clock on the morning of 6 Thermidor, and replied that he knew nothing of any plot, and that while he did not know most of the accused 'il en défendit cinq avec chaleur'. As for Coffinhal's handling of the trial,

... il fut profondément indigné de la conduite tenue par Coffinhal, président ce jour-là, qui défendit aux témoins de parler à la décharge des accusés et qui apostropha personnellement lui déclarant en lui disant: 'Tu n'es pas ici défenseur, tu n'as rien à dire à leur décharge. . . .'

The prisoners were supposed, according to the law, to be led back into Liberty Hall to hear the sentence, but, instead, it was announced to them outside, no doubt in order to avoid any scenes or violence. The public prosecutor lost no time in informing the military commandant of the Paris region of the steps to be taken:

AU NOM DE LA RÉPUBLIQUE. L'accusateur public près du tribunal révolutionnaire, établi à Paris par la loi du 10 mars 1793, en exécution du tribunal de ce jourd'hui, requiert le citoyen commandant général de la force armée parisienne de prêter main-forte et mettre sur pied la force publique nécessaire à l'exécution du dit jugement, rendu contre Roucher, Chénier et autres au nombre de vingt-cinq, et qui les condamne à la peine de mort, laquelle exécution aura lieu ce jourd'hui à quatre heures de relevée sur la place publique de la barrière de Vincennes de cette ville. Le citoyen commandant général est requis d'envoyer ladite force publique, cour du Palais, le dit jour à trois heures précises de relevée.

When the sentence was read out, towards noon, it is said that Chénier's reaction was to exclaim, 'Les misérables assassins!' Roucher replied, 'Allons, Chénier, mon ami, du calme! Ils sont plus à plaindre que nous.' Other stories, about Chénier putting his hand to his brow and saying 'Et pourtant, j'avais quelque chose là', or of him and Roucher reciting Racine to each other as the tumbril passed across Paris, or of a 'faithful friend' walking all the way beside them, have not been authenticated. The two Trudaines went to the scaffold on the next day. As for the survivors from Saint-Lazare who were saved by Robespierre's downfall on 9 Thermidor, they were more anxious to forget their experience than to dwell on it in their memoirs.

Chénier's life ended shortly after four o'clock on Friday the 25th of July 1794, on the scaffold at the Barrière de Vincennes. Formerly called the Place du Trône, it is now known as the Place de la Nation. In the evening the bodies were carted to an improvised cemetery in a field behind the Picpus convent, hardly a quarter of a mile away. Here they were stripped and thrown into a common grave. It contains the remains of eleven hundred and nine men and a hundred and ninety-seven women, all of whom perished between the 14th of June and the 27th of July 1793, without a voice being raised in their defence.[1] It is evident that Chénier died as proudly as he had lived; he wrote an epitaph, which later his mother copied out and left with his papers, which reads:

> Tu dors, ô mon génie! Un Dieu t'appelle; accours,
> Éveille-toi. La vie échappe, et de nos jours
> Il ne reste après nous que les heures sublimes
> Où, dans la sainte ardeur de nos chants magnanimes,
> D'un invincible acier notre cœur revêtu
> A terrassé le crime et vengé la vertu.

[1] For a complete list of the victims buried at Picpus, see Lenôtre, *Le Jardin de Picpus*, Perrin, 1928. He breaks down the figures as follows: men, 579 gens du peuple, 178 gens d'épée, 136 gens de robe, 108 gens d'église, 108 ex-nobles; women, 123 femmes du peuple, 51 ex-nobles, 23 religieuses.

CONCLUSION

THE best way of defending Chénier's memory is, obviously, not by taking sides in the political struggle to which he gave the last part of his short life. At times, like all his critics and biographers, we have yielded to the temptation to do so, while knowing that the reader might hold different views or be better informed. After showing what part he played at a time when French politics were in a state of flux and confusion, we are then obliged to recall that many of Chénier's enemies were worthy of his pen, for they also had elements of greatness in them. Unlike them, who were not only engaged in elaborating or defending political theories, Chénier was not involved in the ways and means by which ideas are applied to daily life. He was as outspoken and as arrogant as his enemies, but a certain rigid idealism prevented him from compromising with the bad against the worse. For this he has been criticized, but for some of his admirers this intellectual purity appears to be one of his finest qualities. His enemies, on the other hand, were unused to power, and could only rule and save France in the midst of a war by abusing it. They were apprentices in the art of government, just as much as Chénier was. But when all that is said, at all times there are men who serve to keep alive some idea of what the public conscience ought to be, and the poet was one of those. The Republican leaders never managed at any time to understand the basic principles of democracy; but Chénier did. Many of them came to neglect and even to mock the very fundamentals of humanity, but Chénier did not. If the choice is to be made between the 'greatness' of a Robespierre and that of Chénier—perhaps it is a foolish one to propose— it is almost inevitable that the literary critic will prefer the poet, while the historian (G. Walter, for example) will prefer the Jacobin.

If so much attention has been given to Chénier's political activities, in this book, it is not only because they affected his work and brought about his death, but because they have, ever since, done much to determine his place in literature. Throughout the nineteenth century the struggle in France between monarchists of various kinds, and republicans, conservatives and liberals, naturally coloured the attitude of critics, historians, and literary historians towards Chénier as a poet. Because his name was associated with the trial of Louis XVI, and with both anti-Girondism and anti-Jacobinism, he was wrongly regarded as a reactionary royalist. This was far from the truth; but in our own time he has suffered from the patronage of writers of the extreme right wing, such as Maurras and Brasillach, with whom he had little in common. Situated in his own time, his political outlook was more English than French, and he could almost be described as a Whig. But the whole fallacy underlying his journalism is that, while believing in a monarchical constitution and a representative House, he imagined that it was possible to govern without a party system. It was the same fallacy that undermined the Jacobins, who, though they also had many admirable ideas (as can be seen from their draft Constitutions), could tolerate the existence of no party but their own.

What is a lesson for our own time is to watch a poet evolving from a conception of poetry as pure intellectual activity into a poetry of commitment which, breaking down an old aesthetic, includes the germs of an anti-poetry. He can be seen as a bridge between Racine and Hugo. The last phase of his life appears, also, as a kind of heroic experiment, the experiment of trying to be, in practice, the incarnation of the *imago* of the 'honnête homme' which was one of the obsessions of the eighteenth century. Even those who are not attracted to his politics, or even his poetry, must respect that ascent, in his journalism and his last *Ïambe*, from self-centredness to a passionate regard for others.

Chénier's work took some time to impose itself in France, because of his untimely death, his father's death a few months afterwards, and the moral weakness and physical ill-health of his brother Marie-Joseph, who died at the age of forty-seven. When his work appeared for the first time, twenty-five years after his death, rapidly going into new editions over a period of fifty years, it was his legend and personality, as much as his verse, which imposed itself on the Romantics. He became, for them, a symbol of the Poet as Hero—to use Carlyle's words—rather than one whose work was to be closely studied and imitated. He and his friends Alfieri and Niemcewicz were in the fore-front of that great tide which, with Chateaubriand, Byron, Lamartine, Hugo, and so many others, brought poetry and action together.

But however much we like or dislike that legend, real satisfaction is better found in the work itself: in the pure poetry of the *Bucoliques*, the sensibility of the best elegies and odes, the vitality of the *Ïambes* in which conflicting gifts come together. In spite of the claims of Voltaire to that position, Chénier is the poet of the eighteenth century, and represents that century at its best. That is the most modest claim that can be made for him. Sainte-Beuve made a larger one, in relating him to Racine. His subsequent adoration by the Parnassians and the École Romane is nothing, compared to the distinction of being a necessary link in the great French tradition; for he had his roots not only in the thought and literature of the Ancients but in Montaigne, Racine, and La Fontaine. Without being entirely modern in his manner or outlook, he holds a central place in which such terms as classical, romantic, and modern hardly need to be discussed. Above that, he has a strong claim to be considered as a vital element in the European tradition itself. If his work shows a very serious attempt to keep the past alive and to reconcile it to the present, to listen sensitively to the voices of another age and preserve their echoes, at the same time his short but varied life, his thought, his engagement in public affairs, his singular heroism, all point to an easily recognizable pattern of what we expect a good European to be. His life, his work, and his legend cannot be forgotten, though it may be neglected, in considering France's history or that of Europe. But the only answer to critics and historians who disagree so strongly about his merit is to open his unfinished book and enjoy its great variety of enchantments, from its 'extases choisies' to its last and unforgettable appeal to the conscience.

APPENDIX A

BOISSY D'ANGLAS ON CHÉNIER

(Les Études littéraires et poétiques d'un vieillard, 1825)

... On a imprimé longtemps après les funestes événements que je rappelle, un recueil des poésies d'André Chénier qui ne l'avaient pas été de son vivant, et qui, dans leur imperfection même, auraient fait espérer pour l'auteur, un talent et des succès distingués. On voit qu'il était né poète, et qu'il ne lui manquait que de l'application et du travail, pour obtenir un rang honorable dans la république des lettres.

Son recueil renferme beaucoup d'élégies; plusieurs sont pleins de sentiments, et quelquefois d'idées profondes: le caractère de ce poète était, avec celui de sa personne, dans une parfaite harmonie; il était naturellement mélancolique et accablé, si je peux parler ainsi, sous le poids d'une sensibilité dominatrice; il n'était pas né pour être heureux, et la terrible catastrophe qui termina sa carrière, avant même qu'elle ne fût commencée, ne fut peut-être douloureuse que pour ses amis, et funeste pour sa patrie, qu'il eût honorée en la servant. Mais ce qu'on ne peut trop regretter en lui, c'est la profondeur de sa raison, c'est la fermeté de ses principes et la droiture de ses vues. Il aimait avec passion la liberté, mais il l'aimait pour elle-même, et non pour aucun motif étranger aux avantages qu'elle procure; mais il la voulait pure et sans tache; mais il la voulait pour le bonheur du monde. Oh! qu'il était loin de s'en servir, ainsi que tant d'autres, comme un marche-pied pour arriver à la domination ou pour cacher sous son manteau les insignes de la tyrannie! Il frémissait d'indignation quand on attaquait cette liberté son idole, par d'insidieux raisonnements, ou quand on cherchait à la détruire par des excès commis en son nom; il combattait avec la même plume, le même zèle, le même courage, et j'ajouterai le même talent, les déclamations et les sophismes de l'anglais Burke, les rétractions de l'abbé Raynal, et les actions bien plus funestes à sa noble cause, des révolutionnaires jacobins.

(T. ii, pp. 98–99)

... Il n'est pas exact de dire qu'André Chénier fut le rédacteur d'une lettre de Louis XVI à la Convention, pour interjecter, après sa condamnation, un appel à la nation elle-même, et que cette lettre fut signé dans la nuit du 17 ou 18 janvier. Je ne sais pas si elle fut signée, mais, hélas! ce que je sais trop bien, c'est que les trois défenseurs de cet infortuné prince, vinrent à la vérité lire de sa part une note dans cette intention, et qu'elle n'avait rien de commun avec la prétendue lettre attribuée à André Chénier, et imprimée à la fin de ses œuvres; la noble brièveté de cette note la rendait bien plus convenable que la lettre dont il s'agit, quelque pathétique et quelque éloquente qu'elle puisse paraître à ses lecteurs.

(Ibid., p. 100)

... Marie-Joseph ... était hautain, irascible, violent, plein d'amour-propre, tandis que son aimable et malheureux frère était le plus doux, le plus posé, et le plus modeste des hommes.

(Ibid., p. 101)

APPENDIX B

LINES WRITTEN IN HOOD'S TAVERN

London, Covent-Garden, Hood's Tavern.
Vendredi, 3 avril 1789, à 7 heures du soir

COMME je m'ennuie fort ici, après y avoir assez mal dîné, et que je ne sais
où aller attendre l'heure de se présenter dans quelque société, je vais tâcher
de laisser fuir une heure et demie sans m'en apercevoir, en barbouillant un
papier que j'ai demandé. Je ne sais absolument point ce que je vais écrire, je
m'en inquiète peu. Quelque absurde et vide et insignifiant que cela puisse
être (et cela ne saurait guère l'être autant que la conversation de deux Anglais
qui mangent à une table à côté de moi, et qui écorchent de temps en temps
quelques mots de français, afin de me faire voir qu'ils savent ou plutôt qu'ils
ne savent pas ma langue), je reverrai peut-être un jour cette rapsodie, et je
ne me rappellerai pas sans plaisir (car il y en a à se rappeler le passé) la triste
circonstance qui m'a fait dîner ici tout seul.

Ceux qui ne sont pas heureux aiment et cherchent la solitude. Elle est pour
eux un grand mal encore plus qu'un grand plaisir: alors le sujet de leur
chagrin se présente sans cesse à leur imagination, seul, sans mélange, sans
distraction; ils repassent dans leur mémoire, avec larmes, ce qu'ils y ont
déjà repassé cent fois avec larmes; ils ruminent du fiel; ils souffrent des
souffrances passées et présentes; ils souffrent même de l'avenir; car, quoique
un peu d'espérance se mêle toujours au milieu de tout, cependant l'espérance
rend méfiant, et cette inquiétude est un état pénible. On s'accoutume à tout,
même à souffrir. — Oui, vous avez raison, cela est bien vrai. — Si cela n'était
pas vrai, je ne vivrais pas, et vous qui parlez, vous seriez peut-être mort aussi;
mais cette funeste habitude vient d'une cause bien sinistre: elle vient de ce
que la souffrance a fatigué la tête et a flétri l'âme. Cette habitude n'est qu'un
total affaiblissement: l'esprit n'a plus assez de force pour peser chaque chose
et l'examiner sous son juste point de vue, pour en appeler à la sainte nature
primitive, et attaquer de front les dures et injustes institutions humaines;
l'âme n'a plus assez de force pour s'indigner contre l'inégalité factice établie
entre les pauvres humains, pour se révolter à l'idée de l'injustice, pour
repousser le poids qui l'accable. Elle est dégradée, descendue, prosternée;
elle s'accoutume à souffrir, comme les morts s'accoutument à supporter la
pierre du tombeau; car ils ne peuvent pas la soulever. Voilà ce que c'est que
s'accoutumer à tout, même à souffrir. Dieu préserve mes amis de cette triste
habitude! Les petits chagrins rendent tendre; les grands rendent dur et
farouche. Les uns cherchent la société, les distractions, la conversation des

amis; les autres fuient tout cela: car ils savent que tout cela n'a aucun pouvoir à les consoler, et ils trouvent injuste d'attrister les autres, surtout inutilement pour soi-même. Peut-être aussi ont-ils quelque pudeur de laisser voir à l'amitié qu'elle-même et son doux langage, et son regard caressant et des serrements de main, ne peuvent pas guérir toutes les plaies; et cependant la vue et les soins de mes amis m'ont toujours fait du bien, même s'ils ne m'ont pas entièrement guéri.

Mais ici je suis seul, livré à moi-même, soumis à ma pesante fortune, et je n'ai personne sur qui m'appuyer. Que l'indépendance est bonne! Heureux celui que le désir d'être utile à ses vieux parents et à toute sa famille ne force pas à renoncer à son honnête et indépendante pauvreté! Peut-être un jour je serai riche: puisse alors le fruit de mes peines, de mes chagrins, de mon ennui, épargner à mes proches le même ennui, les mêmes chagrins, les mêmes peines! Puissent-ils me devoir d'échapper à l'humiliation! Oui, sans doute, l'humiliation. Je sais bien qu'il ne m'arrive rien dont mon honneur puisse être blessé, je sais bien aussi que rien de pareil ne m'arrivera jamais, car cette assurance-là ne dépend que de moi seul. Mais il est dur de se voir négligé, de n'être point admis dans telle société qui se croit au-dessus de vous; il est dur de recevoir, sinon des dédains, au moins des politesses hautaines; il est dur de sentir . . . — Quoi? qu'on est au-dessous de quelqu'un? — Non; mais il y a quelqu'un qui s'imagine que vous êtes au-dessous de lui. Ces grands, même les meilleurs, vous font si bien remarquer en toute occasion cette haute opinion qu'ils ont d'eux-mêmes! Ils affectent si fréquemment de croire que la supériorité de la fortune tient à celle de leur mérite! Ils sont bons si durement! Ils mettent tant de prix à leurs sensations et à celles de leurs pareils, et si peu à celles de leurs prétendus inférieurs! Si quelque petit chagrin a effleuré la vanité d'un de ceux qu'ils appellent leurs égaux, ils sont si chauds, si véhéments, si compatissants! Si une cuisante amertume a déchiré le cœur de tel qu'ils appellent leur inférieur, ils sont si froids, si secs! Ils le plaignent d'une manière si indifférente et si distraite! comme les enfants qui n'ont point de peine à voir mourir une fourmi, parce qu'elle n'a point de rapport avec leur espèce.

Je ne puis m'empêcher de rire intérieurement, lorsque dans ces belles sociétés je vois de fréquents exemples de cette sensibilité distinctive, et qui ne s'attendrit qu'après avoir demandé le nom. Les femmes surtout sont admirables pour cela: dès qu'un prince qu'elles ont rencontré au bal, dès qu'un grand, qui est leur intime ami, car elles ont dîné avec lui deux fois, est malade ou affligé pour avoir perdu une place ou un cheval, elles y prennent tant de part! elles déplorent son malheur de si bonne foi! elles se récrient si pathétiquement! et véritablement elles croient être au désespoir; car, presque toutes étant dépourvues de la sensibilité franche et vraie, et naïve, elles croient que ces singeries et ces vaines simagrées sont en effet ce que l'on entend par ce nom.

Allons, voilà une heure et demie de tuée; je m'en vais. Je ne sais plus ce que j'ai écrit, mais je ne l'ai écrit que pour moi : il n'y a ni apprêt, ni élégance. Cela ne sera vu que de moi; et je suis sûr que j'aurai un jour quelque plaisir à relire ce morceau de ma triste et pensive jeunesse. Puisse un jour tout lecteur en avoir autant à lire ce que j'aurai écrit pour tous les lecteurs!

APPENDIX C

DÉCLARATION DES AMIS DE LA CONSTITUTION CI-DEVANT RÉUNIS AUX FEUILLANTS

Paris ce janvier 1792

LES citoyens soussignés rassemblés pour former une société d'instruction sur les divers objets qui réclament plus que jamais le zèle et la sollicitude des fidèles amis de la constitution, croyent devoir consigner dans une déclaration souscrite par chacun d'eux, les sentiments qui les animent, les principes qui les dirigent, le but qu'ils se proposent.

Ils déclarent qu'ils regardent les associations de Citoyens comme très favorables aux progrès de la raison publique, au développement des vertus sociales, mais ils pensent qu'à l'époque où une grande révolution a produit une constitution solennellement jurée par tous les citoyens de l'Empire, ces sociétés doivent prendre de sévères précautions, pour ne pas encourir le reproche de s'interposer comme un parti puissant, entre la nation et ses représentants, dans le dessein d'influer sur la délibération des lois; entre la nation et ses agents, dans le dessein d'en entraver l'exécution; elles ne doivent prétendre à aucune autre influence qu'à celle qui appartient à la discussion des bons esprits, au zèle des bons citoyens.

Se dévouer sans réserve au maintien de la constitution, ne chercher qu'en elle seule les moyens de la servir, lui obtenir ce dernier triomphe de n'avoir plus besoin pour se soutenir que du jeu régulier de ses propres institutions; tel est le sentiment convenu; tel est le but que se proposent les membres de cette société.

Ils déclarent qu'ils croyent qu'une société composée d'une partie considérable de membres de l'assemblée nationale, et d'un grand nombre de citoyens dont le patriotisme s'est fait connaître par leurs services pendant le cours de la révolution, n'a pas besoin pour se concilier l'estime publique de faire d'avance sa profession de foi politique.

L'exposition de leurs principes est toute entière dans la devise simple et précise qu'ils ont choisie, et dont ils font leur règle unique; ils ne prétendent pas se la réserver, mais la rendre commune à tous les Français. Cette devise est *la Constitution, toute la Constitution, rien que la Constitution.*

Devant cette éclatante et formelle déclaration, doivent tomber toutes ces accusations méprisables qui se renouvellent et se varient sous toutes les formes.

Pour se garantir à elle-même la pureté de sa composition, la société a adopté le moyen le plus efficace; un scrutin épuratoire lui permettra d'écarter de son sein, les membres dont les principes ne s'accorderaient pas avec ceux qu'elle professe uniquement, ou dont la réputation pourrait nuire à la considération publique, seule force dont la société veuille s'environner.

La société ne formera donc pas un parti, ou plutôt elle est dès ce moment confondue avec le seul qui doive exister, celui de la constitution; ceux-là seront ses amis et ses alliés qui voudront vivre et mourir pour la liberté et l'égalité; pour la liberté, premier droit de l'homme, dont la loi étend et perfectionne l'exercice; pour l'égalité, première et continuelle jouissance de celui qui sait s'honorer dans ses semblables.

Ceux-là seront ses amis qui ne reconnaissent de limites dans l'exercice des droits naturels et politiques, que celles posées par la loi elle-même; ne reconnaissent de distinctions que celles des fonctions publiques qui protègent l'égalité, et des vertus et des talents dont l'égalité est la source la plus pure et la plus féconde, maintiendront et défendront avec elle, l'inaliénable souveraineté du peuple; la libre action des pouvoirs séparés, dont il a délégué l'exercice, et le respect dû aux autorités constituées.

La Société tient pour ses ennemis, tous les ennemis de la Constitution, sous quelque bannière qu'ils se rangent, sous quelque forme qu'ils se cachent; et les parricides armés contre leur patrie, dont ils ont méconnu la voix, et ceux qui la déchirent avec les armes qu'elle leur a confiées pour la défendre.

La Société, après avoir entendu la lecture de la présente déclaration, l'a adoptée unanimement, a arrêté qu'elle serait inscrite à la tête du catalogue de ses membres, souscrite individuellement par chacun d'eux, présentée à toutes les personnes qui auront sollicité leur admission dans son sein, pour être pareillement signée par elles, et qu'elle sera publiée par la voie de l'impression.

Suit un grand nombre de signatures.

Paris, le 6 janvier 1792

BIBLIOGRAPHY

All printed works are published in Paris, unless otherwise stated.

A. BIBLIOGRAPHIES

A1   BECQ DE FOUQUIÈRES (see D6).
A2   DIMOFF (see F34).
A3   FABRE (see F36).
A4   GLACHANT (see G34).
A5   TALVART et PLACE, *Bibl. des Auteurs modernes de langue française*, t. iii, 1931.
A6   THIEME, *Bibl. de la litt. fr. de 1800 à 1930.* 1933 (2nd ed. 1953).
A7   WALTER (see D22).

B. ICONOGRAPHY

B1   SARRAUTE, G., *Essai d'Iconographie d'A.C.* (Appendix to F96.)

C. MANUSCRIPTS OF ANDRÉ CHÉNIER

C1   Bibliothèque Nationale (BN), collections NAF 6848–51; also 6852 (M.-J. Chénier); 23687 (divers docs.); 22181 (MSS. E. Le Brun).
C2   Bibliothèque municipale de Carcassonne (BMC), dossiers 11786–839 (in process of reclassification).
C3   General: see D6, D12, D13, D25, G6, G7, and H. Clergue, 'A.C., his manuscripts and his editors', in *The Nineteenth Century*, 1926, pp. 271–85.
C4   Reproductions of manuscripts: see D7, D12, D23, D24, H1.

D. POETICAL AND COLLECTED WORKS

D1   1819, H. DE LATOUCHE, *Œuvres complètes* [sic] *d'A.C.*
D2   1820, 1822, idem.
D3   Idem, augm. 1833, 1839, 1841, 1847, &c.
D4   1824, *Œuvres complètes* [sic] *de M.-J. et A. Chénier*, 8 vols.
D5   1826, D. ROBERT, *Œuvres d'A.C.*, 2 vols.
D6   1862, BECQ DE FOUQUIÈRES, *Poésies d'André Chénier*, Charpentier. Repr. 1872 (augm.), 1884, 1888, &c.
D7   1874, GABRIEL DE CHÉNIER, *Œuvres poétiques d'André de Chénier*, Lemerre, 3 vols.
D8   1878, L. MOLAND, *Œuvres poétiques*, Garnier, 2 vols.
D9   1883, L. JOUBERT, *Poésies*, Firmin-Didot.
D10   1884, E. MANUEL, *Œuvres poétiques*, Libr. des Bibliophiles.
D11   1888, A. REBELLIAU, *Choix de poésies*, Hachette.
D12   1906, 1907, HEREDIA, *Les Bucoliques*, Rombaldi.
D13   1908, DIMOFF, *Œuvres complètes*, vol. i, Delagrave. Vols. ii, iii followed in 1910 and 1912. The 3 vols. often repr. *s.d.* after 1919.

D14 1912, *Choix de poésies*, Renaissance du Livre.
D15 1913, F. ROZ, *Textes choisis*, Plon.
D16 1919, G. PLACE, *Poésies* (choix), Lardanchet, Lyon.
D17 1923, *Bucoliques* (choix), édns de la Sirène.
D18 1923, L. BARTHOU, *Œuvres poétiques*, édns Ami des Livres.
D19 1924, A. BELLESSORT, *Œuvres poétiques*, Garnier, repr. 1932, &c.
D20 1927, L. CLOUARD, *Œuvres* (choix), édns de La Cité des Livres.
D21 1928, B. CRÉMIEUX, *Poésies* (choix), Firmin-Didot.
D22 1950, G. WALTER, *Œuvres complètes*, édns de la Pléiade, Gallimard (the only complete ed. in 1 vol.).
D23 1957, R. BRASILLACH, *Poésies* (choix), Club du Libraire.
D24 1958, J.-M. GERBAULT, *Choix de textes*, Seghers (with a record by J. Bolo).
D25 1961, F. SCARFE, *Poems of A.C.* (selection), Blackwell, Oxford.

E. PROSE WORKS

E1 1840, JACOB, *Œuvres en prose*, Gosselin.
E2 1862, BECQ DE FOUQUIÈRES, *Œuvres en prose*, Charpentier: revised 1872.
E3 1879, L. MOLAND, *Œuvres en prose*, Garnier.
E4 1914, A. LEFRANC, *Œuvres inédites*, Champion.
E5 1945, *Les Autels de la peur*, Les Trois Anneaux [Geneva].

[See also, above, D1, D2, D3, D5, D15, D22, D24.]

F. BIOGRAPHY

F1 *Almanach des Muses*, 1792.
F2 ALFIERI, *Mémoires* (1810); *Memoirs*, revised by E. Vincent, O.U.P., 1961.
F3 ARNAULT, *Souvenirs d'un Sexagénaire*. 4 vols., 1833.
F4 ARRIGON, *La Jeune Captive: Aimée de Coigny et son temps*, 1921.
F5 ATALONE (J. de Pange), *A.C. et les frères de Pange*, Metz, 1908.
F6 AZAÏS, J., *Les Attaches méridionales d'A.C.*, 1925.
F6(a) BARDOUX, A., *La Comtesse Pauline de Beaumont*, Calmann-Lévy, 1884.
F7 BAREILLES, B., 'Les Origines d'A.C.', in *MF*, 1 avril 1924.
F8 BARÈRE, *Mémoires*, 4 vols., 1842.
F9 BARTHÉLEMY, F., *Mémoires historiques* (ed. Soulavie), s.d.
F10 —— *Papiers*, 5 vols., 1856.
F11 BEUGNOT, *Mémoires, 1783–1815*, 2 vols., 1866.
F12 BOIGNE, Ctesse de (née Osmond), *Mémoires*, 2 vols., 1921.
F13 BOISSY D'ANGLAS, *Essai sur la Vie etc. de M. de Malesherbes*, 3 vols., 1819.
F14 —— *Études litt. et poétiques d'un vieillard*, 6 vols., 1825.
F15 BONNIÈRES, R. DE, 'La Vie de Mme de Chénier' (introd. to her *Lettres*, 1879).
F16 BORN, S., *A.C., ein Dichterleben aus der Zeit der Fr. Rev.*, Basel, 1878.
F17 BOURGEOIS, E., *L'Opinion contemporaine sur les deux Chénier*, 1908.
F18 BRENTHEL, F., *A.C., als Dichter und Politiker*, 1882.
F19 BRISSOT, *Mémoires*, 4 vols., 1830.
F20 BURGADA, G., *Vittorio Alfieri e Andrea Chénier*, 1897.
F21 CHALLAMEL, A., *Les Clubs contre-révolutionnaires*, 2 vols., 1895.
F22 CHAMFORT, N., *Pensées, Maximes etc.*, 1860.

F23 CHATEAUBRIAND, *Le Génie du Christianisme*, 1802.
F24 —— *Mémoires d'Outre-tombe* (ed. Levaillant), 2 vols., Flammarion, 1949.
F25 CHÉNIER, G. DE, 'Notice biographique sur A.C.', in D7.
F26 —— *La Vérité sur la famille Chénier*, 1844.
F27 CHÉRON, F., *Mémoires et récits*, 1882.
F28 COIGNY, AIMÉE DE, *Mémoires* (1820), ed. 1902.
F29 COURTIER, L., 'Abel de Malartic, ami d'A.C.', *Rev. de Gascogne*, 1881.
F30 CRÉQUY, MARQUISE DE, *Mémoires* (ed. Cousin), 7 vols., 1834–5.
F31 DAUNOU, preface to *Œuvres posthumes de M.-J. Chénier*, 1824.
F32 DELSAUX, H., *Condorcet journaliste*, Champion, 1931.
F33 DESNOIRESTERRES, G. *de la Reynière et son groupe*, 1877.
F34 DIMOFF, P., *La Vie et l'œuvre d'A.C. jusqu'à la Révolution*, Droz, 2 vols., 1936.
F35 DUSAULCHOY, *L'Agonie de Saint-Lazare sous la tyrannie de Robespierre*, s.d.
F36 FABRE, J., A.C., *l'Homme et l'œuvre*, Hatier-Boivin, 1955.
F37 Fabre d'Églantine (MSS.), BN, NAF 24347, 24348.
F38 Feuillants: Beaulieu, *Journal du Jour*, 13 sept. 1791.
F39 —— *Déclaration des*, BN, Lb. 40, 804.
F40 —— *Grand détail de ce qui s'est passé aux Feuillants*, BN, Lb. 39, 5628.
F41 —— List of members. BN, Lb. 40, 805 and Lb. 40, 3284.
F42 —— Michon, *Essai sur l'Histoire des Feuillants* (doctoral thesis), 1924.
F43 GALZY, J., *Vie intime d'A.C.*, ENF, 1947 (romanced biography, unreliable).
F44 GARAT, *Mémoires sur la Révolution*, An III de la République.
F45 —— *Mémoires historiques sur le XVIIIᵉ siècle et sur M. Suard*, 1821.
F46 GENLIS, MME DE, *Souvenirs de Félicie*, 1804.
F47 GERBAULT, see D24.
F48 GINGUENÉ, 'Notice biographique', in *Œuvres de Le Brun*, t. i, 1811.
F49 GOWER, EARL, *Despatches, 1790–92*, Cambridge, 1885.
F50 HARTMANN, K., *Chénier-studien*, Leipzig, 1894.
F51 HERBILLON, E., *André Chénier*, Tallandier, 1949.
F52 HENRIOT, E., 'Un Ami de Chénier: François de Pange', *Le Temps*, 21 avril 1925.
F53 JACOB (known as 'le Bibliophile') (Lacroix), 'Notice historique sur le procès d'A.C.', in E1.
F54 JOUBERT, *Pensées*, &c. (includes letters to Mme de Beaumont), 2nd ed., 1850.
F55 La Bédoyère (collection), MSS. sur la Révolution, BN, NAF 307–12.
F56 LABITTE, C., 'M.-J. Chénier', in RDM, t. 5, 1844.
F57 LACRETELLE, C. DE, *Dix Années d'épreuves sous la Révolution*, 1842.
F58 —— *Testament philosophique et littéraire*.
F59 LENÔTRE, G., *Le Jardin de Picpus*, Perrin, 1928.
F60 —— *Le Tribunal révolutionnaire*, Perrin, 1932.
F61 LAMETH, TH. DE, 'Papiers' (MSS.), BN, NAF 1387–9.
F62 —— *Notes et souvenirs*, 1914.
F63 LATOUCHE, H. DE, 'Notice sur la vie d'A.C.', in D1.
F64 —— *La Vallée aux Loups*, 1833.
F65 LEE, H., 'The Place of A.C. in Revolutionary Politics', in *Queen's Quarterly*, 1914, pp. 279–94.

F66   LEGROS, 'A.C. en Angleterre', in *MLR*, 1924.
F67   LOIZEROLLES, F. (fils), *La Mort de Loizerolles*, 1813 and 1828.
F68   MALLET DU PAN, *Mémoires et Correspondance*, 2 vols., 1851.
F69   MALO, H., *Le Beau Montrond*, Émile-Paul, 1926.
F70   MALOUET, *Mémoires*, 2 vols., Plon, 1872.
F71   MORELLET, ABBÉ, *Mémoires sur le XVIIIe siècle*, 1822.
F72   MONTLOSIER, *Souvenirs d'un émigré, 1789–1798*, Hachette, 1851.
F73   MORIOLLES, *Mémoires sur l'émigration, 1789–1833*, 1902.
F74   'Nancy, l'affaire de', BMN 852/382 and 1324/902.
F75   PALEWSKI, *Mme Pourrat, ses filles et ses amis*, Versailles, 1934.
F76   PANGE, F. DE, *Œuvres*, éd. Becq de Fouquières, Charpentier, 1872.
F77   PERROUD, C., 'A.C. après le 10 août 1792', in *Rev. du XVIIIe siècle*, 1913.
F78   —— 'A.C. à Versailles en 1793', *RF*, 326–51, 1913.
F79   —— 'Fanny, l'amie d'A.C.', *RF*, 324–35, 1917.
F80   REUMONT, *Die Gräfin von Albany*, Berlin, 1860.
F81   RIVAROL, *Petit Dictionnaire des grands hommes de la Révolution*, 1790.
F82   —— *Mémoires*, 1824. (Repr., Galic, 1962.)
F83   ROEDERER, *Journal et chronique des cent jours*, s.d.
F84   ROUCHER, *Consolations de ma captivité*, 2 vols., 1797.
F85   ROUQUET, *Les Chénier*, 1891.
F86   SAINTE-BEUVE, 'A.C., homme politique' (see G68).
F87   SCARFE, F., 'Un Hommage à A.C. — des vers inédits de Le Brun', in *Le Bayou*, no. 75, 1958.
F88   —— 'A Letter from the Ministry of Justice to A.C.', in *Essays Presented to C. M. Girdlestone*, Newcastle upon Tyne, 1960.
F89   —— 'Introduction' to D25.
F90   SUARD, *Mémoires et correspondance inédite, 1726–1816*, 1858.
F91   —— Lettres (MSS.) in BN, NAF 23640.
F92   SUARD (MME), *Essais de Mémoires sur M. Suard*, 1881.
F93   TALMA, *Correspondance avec Mme de Staël*, 1928.
F94   —— *Mémoires*, 4 vols., 1849–50.
F95   VALLÉE, O. DE, *A.C. et les Jacobins*, 1881.
F96   VENZAC, G., *La Jeunesse d'A.C.*, Gallimard, 1957.
F97   —— 'Retour à l'ascendance grecque d'A.C.', *RHLF*, lvii. 2.
F98   VIGÉE-LEBRUN, MME, *Souvenirs*, 1828.
F99   VIGNY, A. DE, *Stello* (in *Œuvres compl.*, Pléiade t. i), 1948.
F100 —— *Journal d'un poète*, ibid., t. ii.
F101 WALTER, G., *A.C., son milieu, son temps*, Laffont, 1947.
F102 —— *Histoire des Jacobins*, Somogy, 1946.
F103 WELSCHINGER, 'A.C. sous-lieutenant à Strasbourg', *REH*, 1929.
F104 WILLIAMSON, E., *Richard Cosway, his wife and pupils*, London, 1896.

G. CRITICAL STUDIES, ETC.

G1   ALFIERI, V., *Del Principe e delle lettere libri tre*, 1795, and (transl.) *Du Prince et des Lettres*, Paris, 1818.
G2   BADOLLE, M., *J.-J. Barthélemy et l'hellénisme en France dans la 2e moitié du XVIIIe siècle*, P.U.F., 1926.

G3 BALDENSPERGER, F., 'Gessner en France', *RHLF*, 1903.

G4 BERTRAND, L., *La Fin du classicisme et le retour à l'antiquité dans la 2ᵉ moitié du XVIIIᵉ siècle en France*, 1897.

G5 BARBEY D'AUREVILLY, 'Les poètes du 19e siècle — A.C.', in *Les Œuvres et les hommes*, Lemerre, 1889.

G6 BECQ DE FOUQUIÈRES, *Documents nouveaux sur A.C.*, Charpentier, 1875.

G7 —— *Lettres critiques sur la vie, les œuvres etc. d'A.C.*, Charavay, 1881.

G8 BORN, S., 'A.C.' (repr. lecture), *Revue des cours publics*, 1878.

G9 BRASILLACH, R., *André Chénier*, Les Sept Couleurs, 1947; repr. in D23.

G10 BRUNETIÈRE, F., *L'Évolution des genres dans l'histoire de la littérature*, t. i, Hachette, 1890.

G11 —— *L'Évolution de la poésie lyrique en France au XIXᵉ siècle*, t. i, Hachette, 1894.

G12 CANAT, R., *La Renaissance de la Grèce antique, 1820–1850*, Hachette, 1911.

G13 —— *L'Hellénisme des Romantiques*, t. i, Didier, 1951.

G14 CHATEAUBRIAND, *Le Génie du Christianisme*, 2ᵉ partie, livre III, ch. vi, 1802.

G15 CHESPACK, C., 'The structure of A.C.'s *L'Invention*', *PMLA*, lxxii. 1.

G16 DESCHAMPS, 'André Chénier' (review of 1819 ed.), *La Muse Française*, 1823.

G17 DIMOFF, P. (see F34).

G18 EGGER, E., *L'Hellénisme en France*, t. ii, Didier, 1869.

G19 ÉTIEMBLE, 'D'André Chénier à Paul Nizan', in *Les Temps Modernes*, oct. 1947: see also *Hist. des Littératures*, Pléiade, t. iii, 1958.

G20 FABRE, J. (see F36).

G21 FAGUET, É., *André Chénier*, Hachette, 1916.

G22 —— *Le XVIIIᵉ siècle — Études littéraires*, pp. 519–55, 1890.

G23 —— *Histoire de la poésie française*, t. x, 1936.

G24 FAYOLLES, 'Vers inédits d'A.C.', *Mélanges littéraires*, 1816.

G25 FOLKIERSKI, W., 'A.C.', in *PIFMLL*, VIᵉ congrès.

G26 —— *Entre le Classicisme et le Romantisme: études sur l'esthétique et les esthéticiens du XVIIIᵉ siècle*, Cracow and Paris, Champion, 1925.

G27 FRANCE, ANATOLE, *La Vie littéraire*, 2ᵉ série, Calmann-Lévy, 1890.

G28 FRÉMY, A., 'A.C. et les poètes grecs', *Rev. Indépendante*, 1844. (Answered by Sainte-Beuve, 'Un Factum contre A.C.'—see G68.)

G29 FUSIL, C., *La Poésie scientifique de 1750 à nos jours*, 1917.

G30 GAIFFE, F., *Les 'Bucoliques'*, Cours de Sorbonne, 1937.

G31 GAUTIER, TH., 'Les Progrès de la poésie depuis 1830', in *Histoire du Romantisme*, Charpentier, 1874, 1882.

G32 GERUZEZ, E., *Histoire de la litt. fr. pendant la Révolution*, Charpentier, 1859.

G33 GIRARDIN, S., *Cours de litt. dramatique*, t. iv, ch. liv, 1843.

G34 GLACHANT, P., *A.C. critique et critiqué*, Lemerre, 1902.

G35 GRAMMONT, M., *Le Vers français*, Champion, 1913.

G36 HARASZTI, J., *La Poésie d'A.C.*, Hachette, 1892.

G37 HENRIOT, E., 'Les MSS. d'A.C.', *Le Temps*, 26 août 1919.

G38 HEREDIA, 'Les MSS. des *Bucoliques*', *RDM*, nov. 1905.

G39 HOUSSAYE, A., *Le 41ᵉ Fauteuil de l'Académie française*, 1845.

G40 HUGO, V., 'Sur André Chénier', 1819: repr. in *Littérature et philosophie mêlées*. Also, 'Sur un poète apparu en 1820' (Lamartine), in *Le Conservateur littéraire*, 1820.

G41 KRAMER, C., *A.C. et la poésie parnassienne*, 1925.

G42 —— 'A.C. et Pascal', in *Neophilologus*, xx, 1934.

G43 LE HIR, YVES, 'L'Expression du sentiment religieux dans l'œuvre d'A.C.', *LR*, avril 1954.

G44 —— 'La Qualification dans les *Bucoliques* d'A.C.', in *FM*, 1954.

G45 —— 'La Versification d'A.C. dans les *Bucoliques*', in *Information littéraire*, 1954.

G46 —— 'L'Expression du sentiment amoureux dans l'œuvre d'A.C.', in *Les Lettres Romanes*, 1955.

G47 LABITTE, C., *Études littéraires*, 2 vols., 1846.

G48 LAMARTINE, A. DE, *Cours de littérature*, 1856-67.

G49 LECONTE DE LISLE, 'A.C. et la poésie lyrique à la fin du siècle', *Variété*, avril 1840, mars 1841.

G50 LEMERCIER, N., 'A.C.' (review), in *Revue Encyclopédique*, oct. 1819.

G51 LOYSON, C., 'A.C.' (four articles), in *Le Lycée Français*, ii, 1819.

G52 MARON, *Hist. litt. de la Révolution*, 2 vols., 1856.

G53 MASSON, P. M., 'L'Influence d'A.C. sur A. de Vigny', *RHLF*, 1909.

G54 MAURRAS, 'A.C.', in *Poésie et Vérité*, Lyon, 1944.

G55 —— 'A.C.', in *Tableau de la litt. fr. aux XVIIe et XVIIIe siècles*, Gallimard, 1939.

G56 MAUZI, R., *L'Idée du bonheur au XVIIIe siècle*, Colin, 1960.

G57 MILLEVOYE, 'Discours sur l'Élégie', in his *Œuvres* (ed. Sainte-Beuve), 1874.

G58 MOREAU, P., 'Les trois *Hylas*', in *Mélanges offerts à J. Vianey*, 1934.

G59 MORILLOT, P., *André Chénier*, Lecène et Oudin, 1894.

G60 NISARD, *Histoire de la litt. fr.*, t. iv, ch. iv, 1844.

G61 NODIER, 'A.C.', in *Annales de 1823*, t. x.

G62 PALISSOT, 'Notice sur A.C.', *Œuvres*, t. iii, 1788.

G63 PAUPHILET, A., 'Romantisme et antiquité dans la poésie d'A.C.', in *Rev. de l'Univ. de Lyon*, 1946.

G64 PICON, GAËTAN, 'La Fin du 18e siècle — A.C.', in *Hist. des Littératures*, Pléiade, t. iii, 1958.

G65 PLANCHE, GUSTAVE, *Portraits littéraires*, 2 vols., and 'A.C.', in *RDM*, 15 juin 1838.

G66 POTEZ, H., *L'Élégie en France avant le Romantisme*, Calmann-Lévy, 1897.

G67 RAYNOUARD, 'Œuvres complètes d'A.C.' (review), in *Journal des Savants*, 1819.

G68 SAINTE-BEUVE:
'Mathurin Régnier et A.C.', 1829; 'Sur A.C.', 1834; 'Quelques docs. inédits sur A.C.', 1839; Un Factum contre A.C.', 1844; 'Poésies d'A.C.' (These articles are collected in *Les Grands Écrivains Français* (*18e siècle*, *Auteurs dramatiques et poètes*), ed. M. Allem, Garnier, 1930.)

G69 —— *Vie, poésie et pensées de Joseph Delorme*, 1829.

G70 TOGNOZZI, O., *Vittorio Alfieri e André Chénier*, Pistoia, 1906.

G71 VILLEMAIN, *Tableau de la litt. fr. au XVIIIe siècle*, tt. ii, iv, 1840.

G72 VENZAC, G., 'A.C., "athée avec délices"', in *CAIEF*, 10, 1958.

G73 ZYROMSKI, E., 'L'Humanisme de Chénier et son poème sur l'Invention', in *Rev. des Lettres françaises et étrangères*, juillet 1899.

G74 VIANEY, 'Les Poésies antiques de Chénier et l'épopée contemporaine', in *Rev. des Lettres françaises et étrangères*, oct. 1899.

G75 VAN TIEGHEM, P., *Le Préromantisme*, 2 vols., Rieder et Alcan, 1924 and 1930.

G76 VIATTE, A., *Les Sources occultes du romantisme*, t. i, *Le Préromantisme*, Champion, 1928.

H. ADDENDA

H1 BALAYÉ, S., *André Chénier* (Catalogue of the B.N. exhibition of A.C.'s work), 1962.

H2 ENGEL, C. E., 'Le Voyage en Suisse d'A.C.', in *RDM*, 1er mai 1962.

H3 DIMOFF, P., 'Une Lettre inédite d'A.C. à François Barthélemy', in *RHLF*, avril–juin 1963.

H4 SHIELDS, H., 'Un Manuscrit d'A.C. retrouvé' (MS. of *Aux premiers fruits de mon verger*), *RHLF*, avril–juin 1963.

INDEX

PRINTED IN GREAT BRITAIN
AT THE UNIVERSITY PRESS, OXFORD
BY VIVIAN RIDLER
PRINTER TO THE UNIVERSITY